A Troubled Peace

A Troubled Peace

U.S. Policy and the Two Koreas

CHAE-JIN LEE

The Johns Hopkins University Press
Baltimore

2 4 6 8 9 7 5 3 1

The Johns Hopkins University Press
2715 North Charles Street
Baltimore, Maryland 21218-4363
www.press.jhu.edu

Library of Congress Cataloging-in-Publication Data
Lee, Chae-Jin, 1936–
A troubled peace: U.S. policy and the two Koreas / Chae-Jin Lee.
p.   cm.
Includes bibliographical references and index.
ISBN 0-8018-8330-X (hardcover : alk. paper)—ISBN 0-8018-8331-8 (pbk. : alk. paper)
1. United States—Foreign relations—Korea. 2. Korea—Foreign relations—United
States. 3. United States—Foreign relations—Korea (North). 4. Korea (North)—
Foreign relations—United States. 5. United States—Foreign relations—Korea
(South). 6. Korea (South)—Foreign relations—United States. I. Title.
E183.8.K6L38 2006
327.730519—dc22   2005021650

A catalog record for this book is available from the British Library.

To Jack L. Stark and Yoo Chong Ha

Contents

Acknowledgments

There is an old saying in Asia suggesting that when we drink water from a well, we should think of those who dug it long ago. As I reflect upon my forty years in academia, I cannot help but remember those who dug the well of knowledge from which I gained enormous benefits. As a student at Seoul National University, I was fortunate to have been educated by two towering pioneers: Min Byung Tae, an eminent scholar of political philosophy, and Lee Yong Hee, a doyen of contemporary international studies in Korea. They inspired me to pursue graduate work in the United States. At the University of California at Los Angeles, H. Arthur Steiner, an outstanding specialist of international relations and comparative governments, taught me how to sustain rigor, discipline, and reason in academic life. Other mentors—William P. Gerberding and Hans Baerwald—trained me in the fields of U.S. foreign policy and Asian politics, respectively. I remain deeply indebted to them. As a product of two very different educational systems and cultural traditions, I have aspired to be an intellectual and professional bridge between the United States and Korea. My longstanding aspiration is reflected in this book.

Over the years I have relied upon a large number of government officials, college professors, military officers, policy analysts, and personal friends both in the United States and in Korea. I would like to express my appreciation to Michael Armacost, Raymond Burghardt, Robert Carlin, Richard Christensen, Robert Gallucci, the late William Gleysteen Jr., Ronald Hays, Thomas Hubbard, Arnold Kanter, Charles Kartman, Anthony Lake, David Lambertson, Ronald Lehman, James Lilley, William Perry, C. Kenneth Quinones, Stanley Roth, Susan Shirk, and the late Richard Walker for sharing their experiences and thoughts with me. I cherish the friendship and support of the late George Beckmann, Victor D. Cha, Donald Clark, Bruce Cumings, John Duncan, Carter J. Eckert, Richard Ellings, Ward Elliott, G. Cameron Hurst III, Young Whan Kihl, Hong Nack Kim, Ilpyong Kim, Samuel S. Kim, Young C. Kim, Byung Chul Koh, Chong-Sik Lee, Hong Yung Lee, Kwang Soo Lee, Manwoo Lee, Norman Levin, Patrick Morgan, Michael Munk, Marcus Noland, James Palais, Han Shik

Park, Kyung Ae Park, Arthur Rosenbaum, Robert A. Scalapino, Scott Snyder, David Steinberg, and Dae-Sook Suh. They all enriched my professional growth and broadened my intellectual horizons. In particular, I owe a special debt of gratitude to Han-Kyo Kim for reading this entire manuscript and for giving me thoughtful comments and suggestions and to Martin Schneider for copyediting the manuscript with extreme care and appropriate suggestions.

In South Korea, I wish to thank Choi Ho Jung, Chung Chong Wook, Han Seung Soo, Han Sung Joo, Jeong Se Hyun, Kang Young Hoon, Kim Kyung Won, Lee Hong Koo, Lee Jong Sok, Lee Sang Ock, Lee Tae Sik, Lim Dong Won, Oh Jae Hee, Park Jae Kyu, Park Kun, Park Tong Jin, Ro Jai Bong, SaKong Il, Wi Sung Lak, and Yang Sung Chul for talking to me about their experiences in the development of U.S.–South Korean relations. Among those scholars who were particularly helpful to my research in Seoul are the late Baek Kwang Il, Chang Daljoong, Choi Dae Seok, Choi Sang Yong, Gong Sung Jin, Ha Yong Chool, Hahn Bae Ho, Lee Daewoo, Lew Young Ick, Kim Dalchoong, Ohn Chang Il, Park Doo Bok, and Rhee Sang Woo. It was useful to talk to a number of North Korean officials, including Chun Gum Chol, Chung Jun Gi, Han Song Ryol, the late Ho Jong Suk, Hwang Chang Yop, Kim Jong Su, and Pak Yong Su. In addition, I was enlightened by discussions with distinguished individuals from Japan (Kato Takatoshi, Kuriyama Takakazu, Okonogi Masao, the late Sato Hideo, and Sunobe Ryozo), China (the late Han Xu, Huang Hua, Ji Chaozhu, Tao Bingwei, and Wang Jisi), and Russia (Oleg A. Grinevsky and Alexander Panov).

I am grateful to Mary Anderson and Carol Reed for able administrative service; Therese Mahoney for meticulous editorial assistance; Kay Mead for typing documents well; Adriana Andrews, Michael Albertson, Thomas J. Devine, Susan Freese, Kathy Gumbleton, Stephanie Hsieh, Margaret Kaiser, Annie Lee, Julia Rindlaub, Jimmy Shang, and Karen Takishita for dedicated research assistance; Mija Kang, Chae Deuk Lee, Chae Ju Lee, Natalie C. Lee, and Theodore J. Lee for continuing moral support.

I acknowledge with appreciation financial assistance from the U.S. Education Department's Fulbright-Hays Faculty Research Fellowship Program, the Korea Foundation, and the Keck Center for International and Strategic Studies and the Office of President Pamela Gann at Claremont McKenna College. My affiliation with the Center for International Studies at Seoul National University during the fall semester of 2002 was very helpful, as was the Institute of Foreign Affairs and National Security and the National Institute of Korean History in Seoul. The Office of Information Programs and Services, U.S. Department of State, was cooperative in releasing confidential diplomatic documents to me under the Freedom of Information Act.

This book is dedicated to Jack L. Stark, who has generously supported my professional and administrative activities at Claremont McKenna College, and to Yoo Chong Ha, who has encouraged my scholarly pursuits over the course of our remarkably close and devoted friendship of five decades.

I must make it clear that none of the persons or organizations mentioned here should be held responsible for any part of my interpretations and judgment or for any omissions I may have made.

Abbreviations

APEC	Asia-Pacific Economic Cooperation
ARF	ASEAN Regional Forum
ASEAN	Association of Southeast Asian Nations
AWACS	airborne warning and control system
CFC	Combined Forces Command
CIA	Central Intelligence Agency
CINCUNC	commander-in-chief, United Nations Command
CPV	Chinese People's Volunteers
CSCE	Conference on Security and Cooperation in Europe
CVID	complete, verifiable, and irreversible dismantlement
DJP	Democratic Justice Party
DMZ	demilitarized zone
DPRK	Democratic People's Republic of Korea
ECA	Economic Cooperation Administration
EM-9	Emergency Measure 9
FMS	Foreign Military Sales
FOIA	Freedom of Information Act
FOTA	Future of the ROK-US Alliance Policy Initiative
G-7	Group of Seven
G-8	Group of Eight
GATT	General Agreement on Tariffs and Trade
GNP	gross national product
HEU	highly enriched uranium
IAEA	International Atomic Energy Agency
IMF	International Monetary Fund
INF	intermediate-range nuclear force
JCS	Joint Chiefs of Staff
JSA	Joint Security Area

KAL	Korean Air Lines
KCIA	Korean Central Intelligence Agency
KEDO	Korean Peninsula Energy Development Organization
KPG	Korean Provisional Government
LWR	light-water reactor
MAC	Military Armistice Commission
MDP	Millennium Democratic Party
MFN	most-favored nation
MOA	memorandum of agreement
MOU	memorandum of understanding
MTCR	Missile Technology Control Regime
MW	megawatt
MW(e)	megawatt (electric)
NATO	North Atlantic Treaty Organization
NPT	Nuclear Nonproliferation Treaty
NSC	National Security Council
OECD	Organization for Economic Cooperation and Development
OSS	Office of Special Services
POW	prisoner of war
PRC	People's Republic of China
PRM	Presidential Review Memorandum
PSI	Proliferation Security Initiative
ROK	Republic of Korea
SALT	Strategic Arms Limitation Treaty
SCNR	Supreme Council for National Reconstruction
SOFA	Status of (U.S.) Forces Agreement
START	Strategic Arms Reduction Treaty
TCOG	Trilateral Control and Oversight Group
UNC	United Nations Command
UNCOK	United Nations Commission on Korea
UNCURK	United Nations Commission for the Unification and Rehabilitation of Korea
UNICEF	United Nations Children's Fund
UNTCOK	United Nations Temporary Commission on Korea
USFK	United States Forces Korea
USSR	Union of Soviet Socialist Republics
WMD	weapon of mass destruction
WTO	World Trade Organization

Note on Korean, Chinese, and Japanese Terms

For all Korean, Chinese, and Japanese personal names, I follow the custom of putting the family name first except for Syngman Rhee and other names that have traditionally appeared in English with the family names last.

I generally use the McCune-Reischauer system for the romanization of Korean materials cited in the notes and for Korean names from the narrative sections preceding 1945, but without diacritical marks.

With some exceptions I spell contemporary Korean names as they are commonly used in South Korea and North Korea, respectively.

The Wade-Giles system is used for Chinese names cited prior to 1945, but the *pinyin* system is used for Chinese names and materials since the establishment of the People's Republic of China.

For Japanese names and materials I adopt the Hepburn system but without diacritical marks.

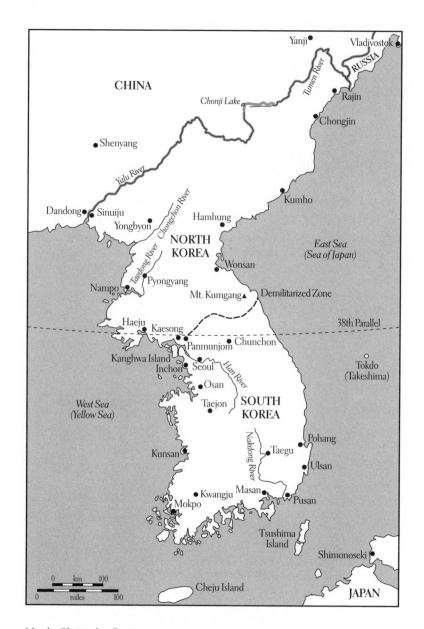

Map by Christopher Brest

A Troubled Peace

CHAPTER ONE

Introduction

Ever since the end of World War II, the United States has played a key role in the management of Korean affairs. With the defeat of Japan in 1945, the United States terminated Japan's thirty-five years of colonial rule over Korea and, together with the Soviet Union, divided the peninsula along the 38th Parallel, occupying South Korea and North Korea, respectively. After prolonged negotiations failed to impose a multinational trusteeship in Korea, mainly because of emerging global conflicts between the United States and the Soviet Union and the irreconcilable cleavages among the diverse Korean groups, the United States referred the Korean question to the United Nations and sponsored the establishment of the Republic of Korea (South Korea) under President Syngman Rhee in August 1948. Soon thereafter, the Soviet Union supported a rival regime, the Democratic People's Republic of Korea (North Korea), under Premier Kim Il Sung. Not unexpectedly, the two opposing Korean governments developed a hostile relationship that mirrored the animosity between their respective superpower patrons.

During the Korean War (1950–53), the United States led the U.N.-mandated efforts to rescue South Korea after North Korea launched a civil war and in so doing engaged the People's Republic of China in a bloody and costly military confrontation. After the armistice agreement in 1953 left Korea again fractured across the demilitarized zone (DMZ), the United States promptly embraced South Korea as one of its client states in the Asia-Pacific region, concluded a mutual defense treaty with South Korea as an essential link in its regional containment system, and continued to play a vital role in guaranteeing peace and stability on the Korean Peninsula. At the same time the

United States also pursued military containment, diplomatic isolation, and economic sanctions toward North Korea.

As South Korea recovered from its earlier war-torn and poverty-stricken circumstances, achieved rapid economic growth, and assumed an assertive diplomatic posture toward the end of the 1960s under President Park Chung Hee's authoritarian rule, President Richard M. Nixon, a classical realist, promulgated the Guam Doctrine, initiated a process for structural changes in the U.S.–South Korean relationship, and decided to withdraw one of the two U.S. infantry divisions from South Korea. When Nixon began to pursue a policy of détente toward China and the Soviet Union, however, the unfolding inter-bloc accommodation generated tensions and disagreements in intra-bloc relations. The evolving relations between the United States and South Korea were no exception to this general trend. So President Park Chung Hee's overwhelming sense of abandonment and suspicion toward the United States led him to implement several countermeasures—to increase self-reliant military power, to seek inter-Korean dialogue and cooperation, and to strengthen his domestic power base. President Park's response was understandable in view of the close relationship between the United States and South Korea. In discussing the misperceptions and paranoia that can arise in an intimate and friendly bilateral alliance, Richard E. Neustadt in *Alliance Politics* aptly observes, "Misperceptions evidently make for crisis in proportion to the intimacy of relations. Hazards are proportionate to the degree of friendship. Indifference and hostility may not breed paranoia; friendship does. . . . Close acquaintance was more burdensome than beneficial, more conducive to misreading than accurate perception."[1] After an uncertain interlude under President Gerald Ford, the Carter administration continued to adopt the basic framework of Nixon's Guam Doctrine and sought a further readjustment in the U.S.–South Korean military relationship. Guided by his liberal orientation, however, President Jimmy Carter attached a high priority to human rights and political democracy in foreign affairs, and he became very uneasy when confronted with the increasingly repressive domestic policies of Presidents Park and Chun Doo Hwan. Mutual distrust, acrimonious communications, and an erosion of confidence plagued U.S.–South Korean relations in what would prove the most difficult period in the history of U.S.–South Korean relations. Despite the asymmetrical nature of the aggregate structural power between the United States and South Korea and the indispensability of the U.S. commitment for South Korea's national security, the junior alliance partner (South Korea) defiantly assumed a nationalistic posture, at times even resisting its senior partner's advice and pressure. Examining the dynamics of such asymmetrical interactions, I. William Zartman suggests that "the aggregate power position of a state cannot be directly translated into relevant and available power in any particular situation. Powerful states may turn out to be weak in a given confrontation with seemingly weaker states."[2] Indeed, South Korea adroitly manipulated the "weakness" of the United States to maximize its own national interests. Moreover, in his seminal work, *After Hegemony*, Robert O. Keohane points out: "Cooperation takes place only in situations in which actors perceive that their policies are actually or potentially in conflict, not where there is harmony. Cooperation should not be viewed as the absence of conflict, but rather as a reaction to conflict or potential conflict. Without the specter of conflict, there is no need to cooperate."[3] These general suggestions by Zartman and Keohane shed light on the complex and seemingly contradictory mix of cooperation and conflict found in the relations between the United States and South Korea, especially during the Nixon and Carter presidencies.

However, President Ronald Reagan, an unabashed anti-Communist warrior, changed Carter's liberal foreign policy, accepted the legitimacy of President Chun's authoritarian regime, and strengthened the military alliance and diplomatic cooperation with South Korea, mainly for the sake of the U.S.-led containment system. He tended to deemphasize the importance of human rights and political liberalization in his foreign policy but nevertheless played a positive role in saving the life of the leading political dissident (and future president) Kim Dae Jung in 1981 and in encouraging a peaceful transfer of power in South Korea in 1987 and 1988. Reagan presided over the unmistakable transformation of the U.S.–South Korean relationship from a hierarchical and unequal alliance into the interdependent partnership that emerged toward the end of the 1980s.

This transformation was most pronounced in their changing economic relationship: while the United States suffered from an appreciable decline in economic performance relative to Japan and the European Economic Community, South Korea registered phenomenal economic growth and foreign trade in the 1980s, thanks in part to the accessible U.S. market. The South Koreans not only graduated from U.S. economic assistance programs, they also increased their gross national product (GNP) at an average annual rate of 10% from the early 1960s through the 1980s, and per capita GNP grew from $88 in 1961 to $4,040 in 1988. The United States now even had more trade with South Korea than with many of its traditional European trading partners: South Korea became the seventh-largest trading partner for the United States and the second-largest market for U.S. agricultural products. The volume of annual trade between the United States and South Korea rose to $34 billion by the end of the Reagan presidency.

In view of the passing of the global cold war, President George H. W. Bush, a moderate pragmatist, recognized the distinct possibility of peaceful Korean unification on the German model. He also supported President Roh Tae Woo's ambitious northern diplomacy toward the Soviet Union, China, and East European countries and endorsed the peaceful purpose of dialogue between the two Korean governments, as demonstrated by the Agreement on Reconciliation, Nonaggression, Exchanges and Cooperation and by the Joint Declaration on the Denuclearization of the Korean Peninsula, which came into effect in February 1992. The relaxation of regional and global conflicts brightened the prospects for inter-Korean accommodation. In an attempt to improve its relations with North Korea, the Bush administration cautiously experimented with bilateral negotiations at the Beijing Talks.

In addition to continuing Bush's conciliatory approach toward North Korea, President William J. Clinton initiated a number of liberal measures to modify America's traditional policy of military containment, diplomatic isolation, and economic sanctions toward North Korea. He sought constructive engagement between Washington and Pyongyang despite South Korean President Kim Young Sam's lingering cold war ambivalence and zero-sum mentality. Unlike his predecessors, who had primarily dealt with a bilateral relationship between Washington and Seoul, Clinton faced the hitherto uncharted challenge of managing a complicated triangular relationship with South Korea and North Korea along with concomitant cooperation with other major powers—China, Japan, and Russia. While sustaining the time-honored framework of close military, diplomatic, and economic linkages with South Korea, the Clinton administration at the same time commenced a difficult but important new diplomatic dialogue with North Korea to discuss such issues as nuclear proliferation, confidence-building measures, and a peace mechanism on the Korean Peninsula. Marginalized by the rapid progress of bilateral negotiations between the United States and North Korea, the strong-willed and independent-minded South Korean president Kim Young Sam voiced his displeasure with Clinton's North Korea policy but eventually acceded to its functional utility. A number of Republican hardliners in the U.S. Congress, however, accused Clinton of engaging in a policy of "appeasement" toward Pyongyang and of succumbing to North Korean "blackmail" and "extortions."

As graphically illustrated by the Geneva Agreed Framework on nuclear issues signed in October 1994, the Four-Party Talks for Korean peace (1997–99), and the U.S.-DPRK Joint Communiqué issued in October 2000, the Clinton administration was committed to exploring the possibility of reducing mutual hostilities with North Korea and of normalizing diplomatic and economic relations. In addition, the United States enthusiastically applauded President Kim Dae Jung's celebrated "sunshine policy" toward North Korea and welcomed the inter-Korean summit meeting in Pyongyang in June 2000. Mutual trust, personal rapport, and close policy cooperation

between Clinton and Kim ushered in the best period in U.S.–South Korean relations. On Kim's recommendation, President Clinton, too, planned to hold a summit
meeting with Chairman Kim Jong Il and dispatched Secretary of State Madeleine K.
Albright to Pyongyang to make arrangements. A combination of unforeseeable circumstances both internal and external, however, forced him to abandon this plan
toward the end of his presidency. Influenced by the Kantian school of liberalism,
Clinton heralded the concept of democratic peace as one of the principal guidelines of his foreign policy, but there was no evidence that he applied it consistently
in his administration's dealings with North Korea.

The George W. Bush administration attempted to change President Clinton's
liberal engagement policy toward North Korea, adopting a hegemonic posture toward Kim Jong Il and articulating a set of new concepts—such as the "axis of evil"
and the doctrine of preemptive attack—to confront the irresponsible and aggressive
behavior of "rogue states," especially after the terrorist attacks on September 11, 2001.
With Reagan as a precursor, Bush took the Wilsonian notion of American moral exceptionalism one step further, assuming the self-righteous mission of imposing its
universal application by force, if necessary. He declared that "America has unique
power and unmatched influence, and we will use them in the service of democracy,
spreading peace across the world and across the years." One of his critics, Joseph S.
Nye Jr., warns in *The Paradox of American Power*, however, that "the danger posed
by the outright champions of hegemony is that their foreign policy is all accelerator
and no brakes. Their focus on unipolarity and hegemony exaggerates the degree to
which the United States is able to get the outcomes it wants in a changing world."[4]
This sober warning is reminiscent of Jean-Jacques Rousseau's dictum: "The strongest
is never strong enough to be always the master, unless he transforms strength into
right, and obedience into duty."[5]

Although President Bush still recognized the political necessity for official contacts and negotiations with North Korea, he was morally indignant when it came to
Kim Jong Il's dictatorial and inhumane rule and became profoundly skeptical of
the wisdom of President Kim Dae Jung's sunshine policy toward North Korea. In
a highly personalized fashion, Bush despised Kim Jong Il—much as he did with
Saddam Hussein—and distrusted Kim Dae Jung in any case. Reacting to the Bush
administration's hardline neoconservative policy, North Korea vigorously confronted
the United States in 2002 and 2003: it expelled the International Atomic Energy
Agency (IAEA) inspectors from the nuclear facilities at Yongbyon, nullified the
Geneva Agreed Framework, withdrew from the Nuclear Nonproliferation Treaty
(NPT), and started to reprocess spent nuclear fuel rods for the extraction of weapons-
grade plutonium. The United States in turn terminated delivery of heavy fuel oil to

North Korea and suspended the multinational project for constructing light-water nuclear reactors in North Korea. It was incongruous that President Bush emphasized a multilateral approach for dealing with North Korea—he stressed the importance of focusing on the Six-Party Talks to resolve Kim Jong Il's nuclear programs by diplomatic means—but against Saddam Hussein he adopted a unilateralist approach. In view of deteriorating U.S.–North Korean relations, South Korea, together with China, attempted to mediate between Washington and Pyongyang—but the outcome was not always satisfactory.

The Bush administration struggled with cognitive dissonance and policy cleavages when dealing with the liberal, populist, and nationalistic president Roh Moo Hyun as the two governments conferred on relations with North Korea and other important issues, such as the reduction and realignment of U.S. forces in South Korea, the growth of anti-American sentiment among young South Koreans, and the participation of South Korean troops in postwar reconstruction efforts in Iraq. President Bush managed to patch together a semblance of alliance cohesion with South Korea in regard to multilateral talks: the Three-Party Talks (April) and the Six-Party Talks (August) on North Korean nuclear issues in 2003 and the subsequent rounds of the Six-Party Talks (February and June) in 2004. The United States utilized the Trilateral Coordination and Oversight Group (TCOG) to harmonize its positions on North Korea with those of South Korea and Japan, solicited active assistance from China and Russia in achieving North Korea's nuclear disarmament, and took advantage of several international and regional organizations, including the United Nations, the IAEA, the ASEAN Regional Forum (ARF), the Missile Technology Control Regime (MTCR), and the Proliferation Security Initiative (PSI), a new multinational forum to stop North Korea's illegal proliferation activities. Meanwhile, the relationship between the United States and North Korea, rife with mutual misperceptions, deteriorated into open hostility. The Iraq War and the disputes over North Korea's clandestine program for highly enriched uranium were major sources of tension between Washington and Pyongyang. More important, the United States faced very serious strains in its alliance system with South Korea. There emerged the possibility that the United States might unwisely alienate South Korea while simultaneously antagonizing North Korea. The future of U.S. policy toward the Korean Peninsula was, to put it mildly, in a state of flux.

In order to elucidate the changing nature of U.S.–Korean relations, this study examines the manner in which the United States has historically formulated its goals for Korea, publicly and privately articulated those goals, and selected the methods and instruments with which to implement them. In so doing, the study lays bare the historical patterns of continuity and change in U.S.–Korean relations and seeks to illuminate the underlying philosophical approaches driving those patterns. In his book *What Is Political Philosophy?* Leo Strauss explored the motivations for political continuity and change: "All political action aims at either preservation or change. When desiring to preserve, we wish to prevent a change to the worse; when desiring to change, we wish to bring about something better. All political action is then guided by some thought of better or worse. But thought of better or worse implies thought of the good."[6] Even though it is not my intention to offer a normative judgment about the history of U.S. foreign policy in general, I will discuss whether the United States has maintained a judicious balance between continuity and change in its actions with respect to the Korean Peninsula and how U.S. actions have made its relations with Korea better or worse than before. Other important questions include: What factors have influenced change in U.S. policy toward Korea over six decades? How has the United States been able to narrow the gap between the goals and means of its policy toward Korea? How have the United States, South Korea, and North Korea perceived each other? How have they sought to present themselves to each other? What issues have continued to be salient over time? What issues have faded from view? How have the United States as the superpower and the two smaller Korean states managed or mismanaged their asymmetrical relations? What lessons should we learn from the successes and failures of U.S. policy? What scenarios can we envision for a better U.S. policy toward Korea?

In an effort to examine these and other relevant questions, I focus especially on (1) changing domestic conditions in the United States, South Korea, and North Korea with emphasis on political leadership, theoretical orientations, decision-making processes, and state capabilities; (2) the shifting balance and relationship between South Korea and North Korea; (3) the effects of the hexagonal linkages among the United States, the Soviet Union (Russia), China, Japan, South Korea, and North Korea; and (4) the transformation of regional and global systems, with emphasis on bipolarity, multipolarity, and hegemony. Throughout this study I draw on a few organizing concepts and ideas such as liberalism, realism, containment, deterrence, engagement, preemption, isolation, appeasement, and misperception. This study focuses primarily on diplomatic and military relations, but other factors such as economic interactions and cultural milieu are also addressed.

In this study, I refer often to contrasting styles of presidential leadership—such as those of Theodore Roosevelt and Woodrow Wilson, Jimmy Carter and Ronald Reagan, Bill Clinton and George W. Bush, Kim Young Sam and Kim Dae Jung—and competing theoretical paradigms—such as realism and liberalism, national interests and moral prescriptions, unilateralism and multilateralism. I do not, however, propose absolute and rigid dichotomies, but rather suggest appreciable differences of degree, tendency, and priority. As Henry Kissinger suggested, excessive realism produces stagnation; excessive idealism leads to crusades and eventual disillusionment.[7]

As a general guideline, I do not entertain any ideologically inspired or preconceived notions about the successes or failures of U.S. policy toward Korea. Nor do I have any particular personal or political hidden agenda in this study. My credo is to be reasonable, eclectic, and evenhanded. Yet I am fully cognizant of Harold J. Laski's wise admonition that "we are all so much the prisoners of our experience that we are, usually unconsciously, coerced by it into identifying our personal insights with inescapable truth."[8] I consciously attempt to minimize whatever personal emotions I may have and to avoid the unsubstantiated view, the flimsy argument, the idle tangent. This study emphasizes the importance of primary documents and empirical evidence as the main basis of analytical interpretations and substantive judgments. Even though a majority of the documents and materials used in this study are from U.S. sources—including declassified archival documents—I make every effort to examine and draw upon South Korean and North Korean documents in an attempt to discern *Korean* points of view and to offer balanced and objective narrative and interpretations, as far as possible. For this purpose I have read a variety of memoirs and other recollections written in Korean by South Korean policymakers, and I have interviewed a large number of past and present South Korean leaders (prime ministers; ministers of foreign affairs, national defense, national unification, and finance; ambassadors to the United States and the United Nations; senior secretaries to the president for foreign affairs and national security; members of the National Assembly; and military officers). I have also spoken to a few North Korean officials, including cabinet ministers, party secretaries, ambassadors to the United Nations, and other diplomats despite the obvious obstacles to candid discussions. In addition, I have interviewed a wide range of U.S. officials (cabinet secretaries, national security advisers, ambassadors, military commanders, members of the Departments of State and Defense, and members of the U.S. Congress) and a limited number of Japanese, Chinese, and Russian leaders. I hope that this study will present a new and comprehensive perspective on the dynamic transformation of U.S. policy toward the Korean Peninsula during the past six decades, especially since Korea may dominate the headlines over the next few years.

CHAPTER TWO

The United States Faces Korea

Geographically and culturally worlds apart, the United States and the Korean Peninsula in the early nineteenth century had little in common. Yet they were about to enter a turbulent period of conflict and cooperation that would last for more than a century and a half. As early as the 1830s, the United States government believed that one of the advantages of opening Japan to the West would be the possibility of trade with Korea. The Korean ruling elite during the Choson Dynasty (1392–1910), however, was ill prepared to deal with the West. They were unable to foresee the emerging collision between their Sino-centric worldview, with its hierarchical and insular East Asian traditions, and the Western concept of equal, independent, and competitive nation states. Not until the outbreak of the Opium War (1840–42) did they begin to recognize the impact that the influx of European and American influences would have on their familiar international order.[1] Even after they received a belated and vague report about the war from Korean tributary missions to China, they failed to comprehend the ominous implications of China's loss in the war and of the Treaty of Nanking (1842), in which China agreed to cede Hong Kong to England and to open five ports to British trade. Nor were the Koreans fully aware of Commodore Matthew C. Perry's visit to Japan in 1853 and of the Treaty of Kanagawa that Perry signed with Japan in 1854. Moreover, they did not fully understand the causes and consequences of the Anglo-French War with China (1856–60), except for the shocking news that foreign forces had occupied Peking and that the Chinese Emperor had fled to Jehol north of the Great Wall.

Meanwhile, a small number of Korean scholars and officials began to piece together a general introduction to Europe and America from books imported from

China in the middle of the nineteenth century. These sources painted a benign picture of America: they said that the United States had fought for political independence from autocratic British rule, had become a rich but just country, and refrained from bullying small states. From 1853 to 1866 shipwrecked foreigners, among them American sailors and fishermen, washed up in the coastal areas of Korea. Startled local Korean leaders referred to them as strange "barbarians" but nonetheless kindly provided them with food, clothing, and shelter and safely returned them, mostly via China. In particular, Koreans rescued the crew of an American whaling ship, the *Two Brothers*, in July 1855 and an American schooner, the *Surprise*, in June 1866 and handed them over to the Chinese authorities. This was a time when U.S. maritime activities intensified in the Asia-Pacific region. As Hahm Pyong Choon suggests, Koreans routinely responded to these isolated incidents of foreigners in distress with humanitarian assistance.[2]

FIRST ENCOUNTERS

However, the first major confrontation between the United States and Korea was violent and tragic for both countries. The ambitious Taewongun (grand prince, 1821–98), who governed the Choson Dynasty as a regent for his young son, King Kojong (r. 1864–1907), enforced a rigid policy of seclusion from Western powers and Catholic influence. An American merchant ship, the *General Sherman*, challenged that policy by sailing down the Taedong River toward Pyongyang in 1866.[3] The marauding crewmen—Americans, English, Chinese, and Malays—not only killed, wounded, and kidnapped Koreans, they also demanded grain, gold, silver, and ginseng as conditions for their withdrawal. Furious Korean soldiers and residents set fire to their ship and killed all twenty-four crewmen on board. Koreans suffered thirteen casualties.[4] This incident was followed by violent and destructive "disturbances" on the Han River near Seoul and at Kangwha Island near Inchon inflicted by the French Navy.

Hearing the news about the *General Sherman*, the American legation in Peking sent an urgent diplomatic inquiry through the Chinese *Tsungli Yamen* (Office for General Management), which was in charge of foreign affairs. The Choson government replied that "a strange British [sic] ship illegally approached Pyongyang, engaged in arrogant activities, ran aground, and perished by fire." Because an Anglican missionary, Robert J. Thomas, who served as an interpreter and guide for the *General Sherman*, had presented himself as British, the Choson government identified the ship as British too. To further the investigations, the United States dispatched the warship *Wachusett*, under Commander Robert W. Shufeldt, to the mouth of the Taedong River in January 1867 and another warship, *Shenandoah*, commanded by Captain John C. Febiger in April 1868. The two missions did not produce conclusive results but did demonstrate the power of the American navy along the west coast of Korea.

Three years later, in 1871, President Ulysses S. Grant, a Civil War hero, ordered a detachment of five U.S. warships to Kanghwa Island to learn the fate of the *General Sherman*, to seek a shipwreck convention with Korea, and to force Korea to open its ports for trade. After haphazard attempts at communications and negotiations failed, armed clashes that lasted for forty-eight hours inflicted heavy casualties on both American marines and Korean defenders. The U.S. warships retreated to a station in Chinese waters.[5] The angry king declared his opposition to "making peace with the likes of dogs and sheep," and the Taewongun erected stone monuments in Seoul and elsewhere in Korea with the stern admonition: "Western barbarians invade our land. If we do not fight, we must then appease them. To urge appeasement is to betray our nation."[6] His strict anti-Western guidelines were clearly and widely distributed. As the Taewongun's ten-year rule on behalf of his young son drew to a close in 1873, however, the Choson government began to reconsider its extreme isolationist and exclusionist policy.

In spite of the two unfortunate skirmishes in 1866 and 1871, King Kojong was eventually persuaded by a moderate and cosmopolitan reformist, Kim Hong-jip, and other like-minded officials to accept the United States as a basically benevolent and friendly nation and to use it as an effective counterweight against other countries with imperialist designs on Korea. The Korean court accepted the recommendations included in "A Treatise on Korea Policy," which Chinese Counselor Huang Tsun-hsien wrote for Kim Hong-jip during the latter's visit to Tokyo in 1880.[7] Influenced by the vision of Li Hung-chang, the powerful viceroy of Chihli (a northern Chinese province), Huang argued that in order to counteract Russia's aggressive intentions, Korea should "be intimate with China, unite with Japan, and ally with the United States." Among other things, he explained that the United States was a strong, prosperous, just, and generous Christian country with no territorial ambitions abroad and that an alliance with the United States would help Korea avert calamities.

As a result of the initial negotiations that Li Hung-chang conducted with Commodore Robert W. Shufeldt in Tientsin on the basis of a draft prepared by China, Shufeldt and two Korean commissioners plenipotentiary (Sin Hon and Kim Hong-jip) signed a "Treaty of Peace, Amity, Commerce and Navigation between Corea and the United States" at Chemulpo (now Inchon) on May 22, 1882. Article One stated: "There shall be perpetual peace and friendship between the President of the United States and the King of Chosen and the citizens and subjects of their respective

Governments. If other Powers deal unjustly or oppressively with either Govern-ment, the other will exert good offices, on being informed of the case, to bring about an amicable arrangement, thus showing their friendly feelings."[8]

The Korean king had unrealistically high hopes about the "good offices" that the United States would assume on his behalf. The treaty specified exchanging diplomatic and consular representatives, opening ports for American residence and commerce, administering tariff issues, protecting merchants and merchant vessels, assisting wrecked ships, and dealing with criminal justice procedures. Most impor-tant, it granted extraterritorial privileges to U.S. citizens "either on shore or in any merchant vessel." Aside from the unequal Treaty of Kanghwa concluded between Korea and Japan in February 1876, the United States became the first Western coun-try to establish a formal diplomatic and commercial relationship with Korea. This treaty served as a model for subsequent treaties Korea would sign with other West-ern powers: Britain and Germany in 1883, Italy and Russia in 1884, France in 1886, and Austria-Hungary in 1889.[9]

King Kojong sent a royal envoy, Min Yong-ik, to the United States in 1883; he was the first Korean visitor to America. His eight-man delegation met President Chester A. Arthur in New York and toured a number of American cities.[10] On his return home after a ten-month journey in 1884, Min told the first U.S. minister to Korea, Lucius H. Foote, who had arrived in Seoul in May 1883: "I was born in the dark, I went out into the light, and now I have returned into the dark again; I cannot yet see my way clearly but I hope to soon."[11] He submitted a glowing report on the United States to King Kojong. Impressed by the goodwill of the United States, the king sought to appoint Americans as directors of foreign affairs, directors of the customs service, heads of the palace guards, military trainers, and, of course, English teach-ers. He came to befriend Americans as sympathetic and reliable advisers and assis-tants. He hoped that the United States would play an assertive role in protecting Ko-rean interests when power struggles arose among Japan, China, Russia, and Britain. Yet he grossly overestimated the extent of America's willingness and ability to pro-vide its "good offices" in the name of counterbalancing the other major powers. The succeeding American administrations had neither the military capability nor the po-litical will to render such assistance to Korea. In a telegram to the American chargé d'affaires in Seoul on August 19, 1885, for example, Secretary of State Thomas F. Bayard cautioned that "the United States can take no action which might even in appearance seem to favor or oppose the policy of either China or Japan, without impairing the position of friendly impartiality towards all which it is the duty and pleasure of this nation to maintain."[12] The first Korean minister to the United States, Pak Chong-yang, arrived in Washington to open the Korean legation in 1888.

On the eve of the Sino-Japanese War (1894–95), the U.S. minister in Seoul joined his British, French, and Russian counterparts in proposing that Chinese and Japanese troops simultaneously withdraw from Korea. The United States also offered its "good offices" toward Japan in stating that "the President will be painfully disappointed should Japan visit upon her feeble and defenceless neighbor the horrors of an unjust war."[13] Once the war over the Korean question began, however, the United States cautiously assumed a neutral position and scrupulously adhered to its policy of noninterference in Korea's internal affairs. It was in no position to counter the Japanese victory over China or the ascendancy of Japanese influence in Korea. The war led to a sudden increase in reports on Korea in U.S. media; according to John Chay, the New York Times Index listed 235 articles on Korea in 1894 and 195 in 1895. U.S. media reports were colored by a pro-Japanese and anti-Chinese perspective and portrayed Korea as uncivilized, weak, and poor.[14] The Treaty of Peace signed by Chinese Viceroy Li Hung-chang and Japanese Prime Minister Ito Hirobumi at Shimonoseki on April 17, 1895, stipulated: "China recognizes indefinitely the full and complete independence and autonomy of Corea, and in consequence, the payment of tribute and the performance of ceremonies and formalities by Corea to China in derogation of such independence and autonomy, shall wholly cease for the future."[15] The treaty in effect terminated China's traditional suzerainty over Korea, and the recognition of Korea's independent status provided the legal door for Japan's growing influence. Yet Russia promptly maneuvered to replace China as a rival to Japan over Korea.

After witnessing the sad state of affairs in Korea in the 1890s, Isabella Bird Bishop, a British author, reported in *Korea and Her Neighbours*: "This feeblest of independent kingdoms, rudely shaken out of her sleep of centuries, half frightened and wholly dazed, finds herself confronted with an array of powerful, ambitious, aggressive, and not always overscrupulous powers, bent, it may be, on overreaching her and each other, forcing her into new paths, ringing with rude hands the knell of time-honored custom, clamoring for concessions, and bewildering her with reforms, suggestions, and panaceas, of which she sees neither the meaning nor the necessity."[16]

When the U.S. minister to Korea took steps sympathetic to the Korean king after the murder of the queen by Japanese soldiers in 1895, Secretary of State Richard Olney reprimanded him, saying that "intervention in political concerns of Korea is not among your functions" and ordering him to confine himself strictly to the protection of American citizens and interests.[17] At that time only a small number of American citizens were engaged in commercial, missionary, medical, and educational activities in Korea. With the assistance of the U.S. legation in Seoul in 1895, an American businessman obtained from the Korean government timber and mining rights in Pyongan Province. In subsequent years, U.S. businesses were successful in securing a variety of concessions—pearl-fishing rights and contracts to construct the Inchon-Seoul railroad, streetcar lines, an electric plant, and the waterworks in Seoul.[18]

As the conflicts between Japan and Russia over Korea escalated in the late 1890s and early 1900s, the Choson government continued to appeal for assistance and protection from the United States. In a message to Minister Horace N. Allen in November 1897, Secretary of State John Sherman instructed: "It behooves the United States and their representatives, as absolutely neutral parties, to say or do nothing that can in any way be construed as taking sides with or against any of the interested powers. Any such partiality would not only be in itself improper, but might have the undesirable and unfortunate effect of leading the Koreans themselves to regard the United States as their natural and only ally for any and all such purposes of domestic policy as Korea's rulers may adopt."[19] Hence the United States rejected the Korean government's request that it take initiatives to organize an international agreement guaranteeing the independence, integrity, and neutrality of Korea. At this time the U.S. leaders faithfully observed George Washington's admonition that the great rule of diplomatic conduct was to extend commercial relations but to have few political entanglements abroad.

The United States did not remain completely inactive in the rest of Asia, however. As an extension of its war against Spain over Cuba, U.S. naval units directed by Assistant Secretary of the Navy Theodore Roosevelt defeated the Spanish fleet near Manila in 1898 and colonized the Philippines. In his assertive Open Door notes issued to the major international powers in 1899 and 1900, Secretary of State John Hay demanded and secured an equal opportunity for American trade with China. The United States also joined Japan, Britain, Russia, Germany, France, Italy, and Austria-Hungary in a joint expedition to rescue diplomatic and missionary establishments from the antiforeign Boxer rebels in Peking, Tientsin, and other northern Chinese cities in 1900 and received a large portion of the indemnity funds from the Chinese government.[20] To provide labor for its sugar plantations in Hawaii, the United States began to allow a small number of Korean workers to immigrate in January 1903; the number of Korean immigrants in Hawaii was to reach about 7,500 by 1905, when the door was closed after the Japanese protectorate was established over Korea. And the United States continued to enjoy the benefits of the Pax Britannica globally and to abide by the Monroe Doctrine in the Western Hemisphere.

The first twenty-three years of diplomatic relations between the United States and Korea (1882–1905) were fraught with asymmetrical interests, mutual misperceptions, and eventually profound disillusionment on the part of the Koreans. Disoriented by the sudden collapse of the Sino-centric international order, King Kojong, a weak and vulnerable ruler, sought protection in vain, first from Japan and then from Russia before he at last accepted the United States as the only country he could admire and trust. At this time, however, the United States was reluctant to become entangled in the intractable power struggles over Korea because it had no vital military and diplomatic interests there at that time. Even in the fields of economics and commerce, Korea was not as important to America's overall objectives as China and Japan were. The United States, harboring no territorial or imperialist ambitions in Korea, offered friendly support to the Korean government, but only as long as it involved no unnecessary risks or sacrifices.

With its emphasis on diplomatic passivity and military abstinence, the early U.S. approach toward Korea amounted to a minimalist policy. This was a pragmatic choice in view of Washington's reluctance to commit its limited resources in defense of Korea. Although the United States had surpassed Britain as the largest manufacturing nation in the world by 1900, its military and naval power remained weak and underdeveloped. Guided by the realist perspective of President Theodore Roosevelt, the United States, acting in its own national interests, did not fulfill misplaced Korean expectations but instead accommodated the growing power of the Japanese Empire. Unlike their Japanese and Chinese counterparts, such as Ito Hirobumi and Li Hung-chang, the inexperienced, inept, and factious leaders in Korea were ill-equipped to discern the true intentions and limited capabilities of the United States and to adjust their policies to the changing international reality in a timely and appropriate manner. They felt spurned and abandoned by Washington and had an even greater sense of impotence and victimization by power politics than ever.

JAPANESE ASCENDANCY IN KOREA

On the eve of the Russo-Japanese War (1904–5), the United States modified its position of strict neutrality with regard to the Korean question, clearly favoring Japan over Russia. In January 1904, Minister Horace N. Allen, a close confidant of Kojong, reported to Secretary of State John Hay that "we will make a real mistake if we allow sentimental reasons to induce us to attempt to bolster up this [Korean] 'Empire' in its independence. . . . Let Japan have Korea outright if she can get it," he argued, "for the good of the people and the suppression of oppressive officials, the establishment of order and the development of commerce."[21] This report reflected Allen's disappointment with the deteriorating situation in Korea and his conviction that Koreans could not govern themselves. He expressed the hope that Japan would remove the corrupt and incompetent bureaucrats and guarantee order and commerce in Korea. Sharing this unfavorable assessment and bolstered by his long-time friend George Kennan, who wrote a series of critical articles on Korea, President Theodore Roosevelt told Secretary Hay in January 1905 that the United States should not interfere in the Russo-Japanese War for the Koreans against Japan, stating that "Japan ought to have a protectorate over Korea (which has shown its utter inability to stand by itself) . . . while I should hope to see Manchuria restored to China." He admired Japan as a "great civilized nation" and recognized its formidable industrial and military power.[22] Moreover, Roosevelt assured the Japanese minister in Washington that the United States had no objection if Japan were to provide "protection, supervision, and guidance" for Korea.[23]

As formulated in a confidential memorandum between U.S. Secretary of War William Howard Taft and Japanese Prime Minister Katsura Taro on July 27, 1905, in Tokyo, President Roosevelt accepted Japan's preeminent influence over Korea in return for Japan's recognition of America's similar influence over the Philippines.[24] As a realist, Roosevelt ascribed to Darwin's theory of the survival of the fittest, accepted the concept of spheres of influence, and practiced a balance-of-power policy.[25] He intended to use Japan to counterbalance Russia in East Asia. Under Roosevelt's auspices, Japan and Russia signed the Treaty of Peace in Portsmouth, New Hampshire, on September 5, 1905; Russia acknowledged Japan's "paramount political, military and economic interests" in Korea and promised not to interfere with Japan's "measures of guidance, protection and control which the Imperial Government of Japan may find it necessary to take in Corea."[26] For his role in sponsoring the Russo-Japanese negotiations, Roosevelt became the first American recipient of the Nobel Peace Prize. After Ito Hirobumi coerced the reluctant and divided Korean cabinet to accept the Treaty of Protectorate with Japan on November 17, 1905, and took over the latter's diplomatic responsibilities, the U.S. legation promptly withdrew from Seoul, as did the Korean legation from Washington. In a last-ditch plea to the U.S. government, King Kojong dispatched his personal adviser, Homer B. Hulbert, an American missionary teacher, to Washington, charging that duress had been used in concluding the Treaty of Protectorate. He invoked the "good offices" clause in the 1882 Treaty of Peace, Amity, Commerce and Navigation, but Secretary of State Elihu Root told Hulbert clearly that the U.S. government could not help Korea. With financial support from an American company in Korea, Kojong secretly sent a three-member Korean delegation and Hulbert to the Hague Peace Conference in 1907. They were unable to attend the conference in the absence of proper diplomatic credentials. The Japanese used this incident to force Kojong to abdicate his throne in favor of his son Sunjong. For all practical purposes, the Kingdom of Korea ceased to be an independent and sovereign state. As the first Japanese resident-general, Ito Hirobumi managed Korea's domestic and foreign affairs.

Upholding the principle of noninterference in Korean domestic affairs, the United States under President William Howard Taft condoned the Japanese annexation of Korea on August 29, 1910. The 1882 Treaty of Peace, Amity, Commerce and Navigation between the United States and Korea was terminated, but the Japanese government assured the United States that Americans could still engage in their commercial activities, enjoy property rights and mining concessions, and conduct missionary and educational operations in Korea. No extraterritorial privileges would be allowed, however. Recognizing Korea as a colony of the Japanese Empire, the United States set up a consulate general in Seoul. Even though in 1919 President Woodrow Wilson's idealist principles of national self-determination inspired the Samil (March 1st) independence movement in Korea, in the era of isolationism the United States remained silent while Korea suffered under Japanese colonization. The Department of State sent explicit instructions to the U.S. embassy in Tokyo on April 18, 1919: "The Consulate [at Seoul] should be extremely careful not to encourage any belief that the United States will assist the Korean nationalists in carrying out their plans and it should not do anything which may cause Japanese authorities to suspect [the] American Government sympathizes with Korean nationalist movement."[27] The U.S. government refused to recognize the Korean Provisional Government (KPG) in exile set up at Shanghai with Syngman Rhee, a U.S.-educated nationalist leader, as its president or to accept the credentials of the Korean Commission in Washington, also chaired by Rhee.[28] The United States ignored Rhee's persistent public admonitions that the United States should use force against Japan while the latter was in no position to win a war against America.[29]

Overwhelmed by Japan's colonial dominance, the American interests in mining and other industrial operations in Korea were eventually transferred to Japanese ownership. America's commercial activities in Korea, too, decreased appreciably. In 1911, 7.9% of Korean imports came from the United States, but the number dwindled to 1.7% (about $7.7 million) in 1939. Korean exports to the United States dropped from 5.1% to 0.4% (about $1.2 million) during the same period. In 1939, the Japanese monopoly on Korean trade was almost complete.[30] The number of American visitors to Korea tapered off in the 1930s, and the small number of remaining American missionaries and educators were generally sympathetic with Koreans. Yet the strict imposition of Shintoist rituals forced the American missionaries to reduce or terminate their operations in Korea.[31] By 1940, about 400 Americans, most of them missionaries, had already left Korea. As of June 1941, there were only 126 Caucasian Americans in Korea, of which 109 were missionaries and their dependents.[32] On the day of the Japanese attack on Pearl Harbor, Japanese police arrested, interrogated, and interned a number of American missionaries and educators in Korea and placed others under house arrest. The Japanese government finally expelled all remaining Americans from Korea as well as from Japan in the summer of 1942.[33]

NATIONAL DIVISION

Japan's surprise attack on Pearl Harbor in December 1941 compelled President Franklin D. Roosevelt to respond forcibly and led to the emergence of the United States as a preeminent power in the Asia-Pacific region. In a series of interagency planning sessions and international meetings during World War II, the United States began to assume a direct leadership role in shaping Asia's new regional order. At the Cairo Conference (November 22–26, 1943), Roosevelt joined Prime Minister Winston Churchill and Generalissimo Chiang Kai-shek in expressing their joint resolve to "restrain and punish the aggression of Japan," to expel Japan from all territories it had taken "by violence and greed," and to procure the unconditional surrender of Japan. They declared: "The aforesaid three great powers, mindful of the enslavement of the people of Korea, are determined that in due course Korea shall become free and independent."[34] The Cairo Declaration released on December 1, 1943, did not specify the length of time implied by the ambiguous phrase "in due course." Yet the participants in the summit meetings in Teheran (November 28–December 1, 1943) and Yalta (February 4–11, 1945) patronizingly assumed that Korea would not be ready for independent governance immediately following Japanese defeat and that a period of multipower trusteeship over Korea would be desirable. In particular, Roosevelt strongly believed that Korea, like the Philippines, needed a long-term apprenticeship to compensate for its limited experience in self-government and representative democracy. At Teheran, Roosevelt and Joseph Stalin apparently agreed that Korea should be placed under a forty-year tutelage.[35] In a private conversation at Yalta on February 8, Roosevelt told Stalin that he favored a three-power trusteeship consisting of Soviet, American, and Chinese representatives in Korea for a period of twenty to thirty years, and Stalin replied that the period should be as short as possible. Roosevelt observed that it was not necessary to have British participation in the trusteeship, but Stalin mentioned that the British might be offended and should be invited.[36] During the Potsdam Conference (July 17–August 2, 1945) held by President Harry S. Truman, Churchill (later by a new prime minister, Clement Attlee), and Stalin, the United States, Britain, and the Republic of China issued the Potsdam Proclamation on July 26, which reconfirmed the terms of the Cairo Declaration.[37] When the Soviet Union declared war on Japan on August 9, it endorsed the Potsdam Proclamation.

In the last months of the Pacific War, the United States rejected Generalissimo Chiang Kai-shek's diplomatic maneuvering for American recognition of the Korean Provisional Government led by Kim Ku (since 1941) in Chungking but did allow the Office of Strategic Services (OSS) to train about seventy members of the Korean Restoration Army, a military wing of the KPG, at Xian and Kunming, China, for the purpose of sending them into Korea for espionage and sabotage against Japan.[38] Nor did the United States embrace Syngman Rhee, who had continued to campaign for Korean independence in the United States. In his letters to President Roosevelt and Secretary of State Cordell Hull, Rhee warned that the Soviet Union might create a Communist state in Korea and asked them to recognize the Korean Provisional Government.[39] The Truman administration denied the KPG's request to represent Korea at the San Francisco Conference, in which the organizational structure of the United Nations in April 1945 was set up. On June 8, 1945, Acting Secretary of State Joseph Grew explained that the Korean Provisional Government had never exercised administrative authority over any part of Korea and that the United States did not want to "compromise the right of the Korean people to choose the ultimate form and personnel of the government which they may wish to establish."[40] In addition, Grew believed that the KPG was under Chiang Kai-shek's control and that if the United States recognized the KPG, it might complicate the future of the U.S.-Soviet relationship. The United States urged China not to recognize the KPG and sought a degree of flexibility in dealing with the Korean situation after the war.

After the United States dropped an atomic bomb on Hiroshima on August 6, 1945, the Soviet Union entered the war against Japan and moved Russian military forces into Manchuria and Korea. In response, the Truman administration hastily proposed to draw the 38th Parallel as a temporary line where responsibilities between Soviet Union and the United States for receiving the surrender of Japanese forces on the Korean Peninsula would be divided. The United States hoped to prevent the Soviet Union from sweeping across the entire peninsula in a few days and to protect U.S. interests in Korea and Japan. Lieutenant Colonel Charles H. Bonesteel III and Major Dean Rusk, who served on the State-War-Navy Coordinating Committee (SWNCC) and recommended the 38th Parallel to Truman, understood that this line would block Soviet access to Seoul, the capital city, and Kaesong, an ancient dynastic capital.[41] In their view, U.S. control over these two cities had definite political and symbolic significance, especially after the Soviet troops had won a geopolitical and psychological advantage by capturing Berlin ahead of U.S. forces. On August 11, Secretary of the Navy James Forrestal suggested that the 39th Parallel should be proposed as the dividing line so that the United States could occupy Dairen in Manchuria, but all assumed that the Soviet Union would not accept this suggestion.[42]

When Truman communicated to Stalin the text of General Order No. 1, including the division of Korea along the 38th Parallel (which General Douglas MacArthur, as supreme commander for the Allied Powers, was obliged to announce to the Japanese government), Stalin, in his reply on August 16, acquiesced to the proposal for the 38th Parallel but questioned the portion of the order that asked Japanese forces in the southernmost Kurile Islands to surrender to the commander-in-chief of the U.S. Armed Forces in the Pacific. Stalin also proposed that Japanese forces in the northern half of Hokkaido surrender to the commander-in-chief of the Soviet forces in the Far East.[43] In fact, Truman was pleased by Stalin's prompt and unconditional acceptance of the U.S. proposal concerning Korea. It is conceivable that by accommodating U.S. interests in Korea, Stalin expected that Truman would agree to share the postwar administration of Japan or at least to allow the Soviet Union to control all or the northern half of Hokkaido. Stalin was aware that prior to the Russo-Japanese War, the czarist government had proposed to the Japanese government that a neutral zone north of the 39th Parallel should be created in Korea and that neither Russia nor Japan would introduce troops into that zone.[44] He was satisfied with the creation of a buffer zone in the northern half of the Korean Peninsula that would safeguard Soviet control over Manchuria. From Stalin's perspective, the division and occupation of Korea by the Soviet Union and the United States was preferable to the four-way zonal split of Germany. If the United States had insisted on a three- or four-way division of Korea by including China and/or Britain, the situation would have been more unfavorable to the Soviet Union. Almost a month after Soviet troops entered North Korea, the U.S. 24th Army Corps under Lieutenant-General John R. Hodge's command arrived at Inchon from Okinawa.[45] On September 9, Hodge signed an instrument of surrender with Japanese military officers and the Japanese governor general in Seoul. As a result of the de facto division of the Korean Peninsula into two zones of foreign military occupation, the prospects for Korean unification and independence became inevitably conjoined with the subsequent unfolding of U.S.-Soviet relations.

If the United States had been a reluctant and timid participant in the development of Korean affairs before 1905, emphasizing neutrality and noninterference, it now returned to Korea as a confident and determined hegemon after a forty-year hiatus. The United States was the only nuclear power and enjoyed 35–40% of the global GNP. The United States came up with the Bretton Woods system for postwar financial and economic order. With its renewed commitment to the Wilsonian ideal of collective security, the United States was instrumental in setting up the United Nations and was eager to assume unchallenged leadership in the new world organization. It was therefore taken for granted that the United States, fresh from a decisive victory over the Japanese Empire, had a legitimate role in undoing thirty-five years of Japanese colonial rule in Korea.

Unlike General Douglas MacArthur and his occupation forces in Japan, how-ever, General Hodge (commanding general, United States Forces Korea) and his men, whose number had reached about 78,000 by the end of October 1945, lacked any real appreciation of the history, culture, and aspirations of the country to which they had been so suddenly assigned.[46] In contrast to the comprehensive "United States Initial Post-Surrender Policy for Japan," which carefully and systematically guided MacArthur's disarmament, democratization, and social and economic re-forms in Japan, the comparable "Basic Initial Directive," which Hodge only received in piecemeal fashion, was ambiguous and contradictory.[47] While respecting "the rights of assembly and public discussion," the directive instructed Hodge to "im-mediately place under control all existing political parties, organizations, and soci-eties" and to abolish those whose activities were inconsistent with the requirements of the military occupation. Unlike MacArthur, Hodge received no clear blueprint for political democratization and social and economic reforms in Korea. His largely improvised approach, replete with misperceptions of the Korean reality, was often met with frustration. While scholarly controversies persist as to whether the United States military government in South Korea simply committed policy "blunders" or instead implemented "conscious planning for counter-revolution," there is little disagreement that Hodge felt that he had a mandate to suppress any political groups or activities associated with the Communists and to promote and strengthen the rightist forces.[48]

General Hodge denied the legitimacy of the Korean People's Republic (led by Lyuh Woon Hyung, Ho Hon, and Pak Hon Yong) and the People's Commit-tees, which leftist and centrist political forces had organized prior to his arrival, be-cause he viewed them as controlled by the Communists.[49] On the other hand, he also distrusted the officials of the Korean Provisional Government and the Korean Restoration Army, who had returned from exile in China. In a callous move that ignored the bitter Korean experience of suffering under brutal Japanese police tac-tics, he temporarily used Japanese police and colonial officials to maintain law and order. He also relied on support from conservative nationalists, local landlords, and U.S.-educated intellectuals. Unlike the method of indirect occupation administra-tion in Japan, the United States set up its own military government in South Korea and appointed Major General Archibald V. Arnold (commander, Seventh Army Division) as its first military governor. It turned out to be more difficult for Hodge and Arnold to create a viable political system in a liberated but divided nation than it was for MacArthur to govern a thoroughly defeated and demoralized nation. The two military officers in Korea never ceased to be bewildered by the seemingly endemic cycle of violent demonstrations, labor strikes, political assassinations, and armed insurrections.

In late 1945, the U.S. military government started to organize and train a modest defense constabulary to help stabilize internal order in South Korea and to secure the border. This constabulary attracted many Koreans who had served in rival military organizations, especially the Japanese Imperial Army and the Korean Restoration Army. More important, U.S. economic assistance programs specializing in relief and rehabilitation were indispensable for South Korea's postwar survival. From September 1946 to June 1949, the United States provided $356 million in aid to South Korea under the Government and Relief in Occupied Areas (GARIOA) program; included among U.S. supplies were food, fertilizer, cotton, coal, petroleum, and other essential goods and materials.[50] In view of the anticipated military withdrawal from South Korea, President Truman transferred authority over the aid program from the Department of the Army to the Economic Cooperation Administration (ECA).

On December 27, 1945, the United States, the Soviet Union, and Britain issued a joint communiqué in Moscow in which they agreed to set up a provisional Korean democratic government, to hold a U.S.-Soviet Joint Commission meeting, and to constitute a four-power trusteeship (consisting of the United States, the Soviet Union, Britain, and China) over Korea for a period of up to five years.[51] The Republic of China also decided to accept the communiqué. General Arnold and Colonel General T. F. Shtikov started the Joint Commission in Seoul on March 20, 1946. It held almost thirty sessions but failed to carry out the Moscow agreement throughout 1946 and 1947. The failure was indicative of the increasing conflict between the two global powers in Asia and Europe and the intense rivalries among diverse Korean political forces. Efforts for compromise between Korea's Communist and nationalist leaders across the 38th Parallel were effectively thwarted. Syngman Rhee, who had returned from his prolonged exile in the United States, emerged as a champion of the anti-Communist forces and vigorously led the popular campaign against the imposition of trusteeship over Korea. Hodge and Arnold did not particularly like Rhee, largely because of his intellectual arrogance and stubborn independent-mindedness, but eventually accommodated his preeminent political leadership in South Korea.

Faced with its growing cold war confrontation with the Soviet Union and the widespread rejection of trusteeship by Korean leaders (except for the Communists and their sympathizers), the United States decided to abandon the Moscow agreement on trusteeship altogether to explore a two-Korea solution and to use Korea as an important buffer zone in Northeast Asia. When the Soviet Union refused to discuss the U.S. proposal that called for holding free elections in the two zones under

U.N. observation, establishing a national provisional legislature in accordance with the two-to-one ratio of populations in South and North Korea and letting this legislature set up a "provisional government for a united Korea" in the fall of 1947, the United States removed the Korean question from the Joint Commission and referred it to the United Nations General Assembly where it could count on support by a majority of member states. In a resolution on November 14, 1947, the United Nations called for free elections throughout the Korean Peninsula under the supervision of the new nine-nation United Nations Temporary Commission on Korea (UNTCOK), but Stalin did not allow UNTCOK to enter North Korea, dismissing it as a compliant tool of U.S. policy and rejecting the concept of free elections in North Korea.

After the UNTCOK-supervised elections were held only in the U.S.-occupied zone on May 10, 1948, the Republic of Korea (ROK) under President Syngman Rhee was proclaimed on August 15, 1948, and the legal basis for the U.S. military government in South Korea ceased to exist. In the Soviet-controlled zone, the Democratic People's Republic of Korea (DPRK) under Premier Kim Il Sung, a leader of the anti-Japanese guerrilla forces in Manchuria, was established on September 9.[52] The weekly train between Seoul and Pyongyang ceased operation, and the 38th Parallel was completely closed. Although the United States and the Soviet Union legally terminated their three-year Korean occupation, the coexistence of their respective client states along the 38th Parallel ensured the continuation of the U.S.-Soviet conflict over the peninsula.

The Korean Peninsula had all the prerequisites, such as clear national boundaries and ethnic, linguistic, and cultural homogeneity, for becoming a unified nation state. And economically, North Korea, with its industrial development, hydroelectric power, and mineral resources, complemented South Korea, with its predominantly agricultural resources. While the North had the larger area (about 48,300 square miles) but only a third the population, the South encompassed about 37,000 square miles and over 20 million inhabitants.[53] This artificial national division came about for political reasons: it was a product of irreconcilable ideological and political cleavages not only between the United States and the Soviet Union but also among the indigenous Korean forces represented by Rhee and Kim. It marked the demise of Roosevelt's vision for imposing a long-term multinational trusteeship over Korea and for replacing Japan with an independent and unified China as a pillar of balance in East Asia. The Truman administration now felt compelled to view Korea as a buffer to protect the security and integrity of Japan in the larger context of America's regional and global policies.

The United States, along with other Western countries, promptly recognized the ROK government. President Truman appointed John J. Muccio, a career diplomat born in Italy who had served in Shanghai, Panama, and Germany, as the first American ambassador to South Korea. The United States also cosponsored a resolution adopted by the United Nations General Assembly in Paris on December, 12, 1948, which stated: "There has been established a lawful government having effective control and jurisdiction over that part of Korea where the Temporary Commission was able to observe and consult and in which the great majority of the people of all Korea resided; that this Government is based on elections which were a valid expression of the free will of the electorate of that part of Korea which were observed by the Temporary Commission; and that this is the only such government in Korea."[54] The resolution accorded a degree of international legitimacy to the Republic of Korea, recommended the withdrawal of occupying forces from Korea as soon as possible, and reorganized UNTCOK into a seven-nation United Nations Commission on Korea (UNCOK), whose primary responsibility was to promote the peaceful unification of Korea. The presence of UNCOK in South Korea intensified the political and diplomatic friction between the two Korean governments. After heading the South Korean delegation to the Paris meeting, Chang Myon (John M. Chang, a lay Catholic leader) opened a five-member embassy in Washington in January 1949.[55] This was the first Korean diplomatic presence in the United States since the Korean legation had been withdrawn forty-four years earlier.

Despite the Truman Doctrine, declared on March 12, 1947, "to support free peoples who are resisting attempted subjugation by armed minorities or by outside pressures" and despite George F. Kennan's advocacy of a containment strategy, the Joint Chiefs of Staff (JCS), led by General Dwight Eisenhower, concluded on September 26, 1947, that "from the standpoint of military security, the United States has little strategic interest in maintaining the present troops and bases in Korea."[56] They considered South Korea undefendable and thus a military liability for the United States. This recommendation was in sharp contrast with the principal theme of the memorandum known as NSC 68 (April 1950), which argued for a strong response to the military challenges presented by the Soviet Union and its allies. In a paper on "The Position of the United States with respect to Korea" (NSC 8), which was adopted on April 2, 1948, the National Security Council assessed three possible courses of action: (1) to abandon South Korea; (2) to support a South Korean government as a means of liquidating the U.S. commitment with minimum bad effect; or (3) to guarantee South Korea's independence and territorial integrity by force of arms if necessary. The NSC chose the second option.[57] For this purpose it decided that "every effort should be made to create conditions for the withdrawal of occupation forces by 31 December 1948."

Even though President Rhee, in a letter to President Truman on November 19, 1948, pleaded that it was imperative for the United States to maintain its occupation forces for the time being and to establish a military and naval mission as "a deterrent to aggression and consequent civil war," the Truman administration nonetheless completed the withdrawal of U.S. troops from South Korea by the end of June 1949, with the exception of the 495-man Korean Military Advisory Group (KMAG).[58] However, in order to prevent control of Korea by Soviet or Soviet-dominated forces, which would constitute "an extremely serious political and military threat to Japan," the United States agreed to use KMAG in training the South Korean Army (which grew from 65,000 in March 1949 to 98,000 in June 1950), to transfer U.S. military equipment (worth $56 million) to South Korea, and to provide military assistance ($20 million). The South Korean government also had a police force (45,000 men) and a coast guard (4,000 men). In addition, it purchased from the United States ten AT-6 aircraft for training purposes, but the U.S. government was reluctant to offer assistance in training and maintenance. President Rhee continued to request additional military assistance from the United States, citing the danger of a North Korean attack "in the immediate future," but President Truman was less than forthcoming.[59]

At this time, the United States assigned a relatively low priority to Korea in its global and regional strategic plans and feared that Rhee might use additional American military supplies to invade North Korea. It also suffered from the depletion of its military stockpiles following the end of World War II. In his speech before the National Press Club on January 12, 1950, Secretary of State Dean Acheson excluded South Korea and Taiwan from the U.S. "defensive perimeter," which ran from the Aleutians to Japan and the Ryukyu Islands and then to the Philippines.[60] While explaining that a U.S. guarantee for the security of such Pacific countries as South Korea and Taiwan was "hardly sensible or necessary within the realm of practical relationship," he hoped that in the event of military attack, those areas would rely initially upon their own defensive efforts and then upon "the commitments of the entire civilized world under the Charter of the United Nations." Whereas the Truman administration had reconfirmed its security commitment for Japan and the Philippines, it in effect disavowed direct or automatic responsibility for defending South Korea and Taiwan. This policy of selective military disengagement was to have disastrous consequences in Asia.

THE KOREAN WAR

Meanwhile, encouraged by recent developments—the withdrawal of U.S. troops from South Korea, the public announcement of Acheson's hands-off policy, the victory of the Chinese Communist Party over the Kuomintang, the Soviet Union's successful detonation of atomic bombs, and the conclusion of the Sino-Soviet Treaty of

Friendship, Alliance and Mutual Assistance—in the spring of 1950 Kim Il Sung set in motion his plan to unify Korea by military means. He was also concerned about the effective suppression of pro-Pyongyang insurrections and guerrilla activities in South Korea. Accompanied by his vice premier and minister of foreign affairs, Pak Hon Yong, Kim secretly traveled to Moscow in March and April and obtained Stalin's endorsement of his plan for armed unification, contingent on Mao Zedong's agreement. At that time Mao had already transferred to North Korea two Chinese divisions (the 164th and the 166th) and other military units comprised of ethnic Koreans. On May 13, Kim and Pak met with Mao and Premier Zhou Enlai in Beijing and informed them that Stalin had approved Kim's invasion plan but had also suggested a discussion between China and North Korea. Not fully convinced by Kim's message, Zhou asked Soviet Ambassador to China N. V. Roshchin to ascertain Stalin's personal clarifications directly. In his telegram addressed to Mao on the following day, Stalin confirmed the accuracy of Kim's message "in light of the changed international situation" and said that if the Chinese comrades had a disagreement with Kim's plan, it should be postponed until a new discussion could be held.[61]

On May 15 Mao questioned the overall soundness of Kim's plan. Kim explained that he had devised a three-stage plan that would (1) strengthen North Korean military preparedness; (2) offer a proposal for peaceful unification to South Korea; and (3) start military action as soon as South Korea rejected the peace proposal. In response to Mao's specific question, Kim confidently predicted that the United States would not intervene to defend South Korea, adding that even if the United States did so, it would be too late to block North Korea's blitzkrieg. After just having waged a successful revolutionary war against the Kuomintang with Kim's assistance, Mao was in no position to deny Kim the same opportunity. Mao apparently promised Kim that if the United States intervened, China would send its forces to assist North Korea.

With Stalin's and Mao's explicit blessings, on June 25 Kim Il Sung launched a surprise attack against South Korea along the entire 38th Parallel. So began the Korean War. The unprepared, outnumbered, and ill-equipped South Korean forces were unable to stop North Korea's rapid southward military advance. Contrary to Kim's predictions, the United States, after receiving Rhee's urgent appeal, swiftly responded to the North Korean attack. The quick response came about because Truman instinctively assumed that this was not merely a civil war but rather an integral part of a Stalin-led international Communist conspiracy to test U.S. resolve; as Truman saw it, if the United States did not stand up against the North Korean invasion, a devastating chain reaction might occur, particularly in Europe. This unexpected crisis had come on the heels of the Soviet blockade of Berlin, the Communist coup

in Czechoslovakia, and Mao's victory in China's civil war. Gone was Acheson's earlier reference to a limited U.S. "defensive perimeter" in the Pacific region. He now
believed that the war was "an open, undisguised challenge to our internationally-
accepted position as the protector of South Korea, an area of great importance to the
security of American-captured Japan."[62]

On June 25 South Korean Ambassador Chang Myon, who received instructions
by telephone from President Rhee, went to the Department of State and requested
military assistance from the United States. At the same time the Truman administration requested an emergency meeting of the U.N. Security Council, which passed
a resolution calling for the immediate cessation of hostilities and the withdrawal of
North Korean forces to the 38th Parallel. The U.N. Commission on Korea was asked
to monitor North Korea's compliance with this resolution and to keep the Security
Council informed on developments in Korea. The veto-wielding Soviet delegates
were conspicuously absent at the Security Council because they had walked out in
January 1950 to protest the Republic of China's representation. On the same day,
Truman held a top-level policy session at Blair House and authorized General
MacArthur to provide air cover for the evacuation of U.S. citizens from South Korea
and to supply South Korea with arms and other equipment. In fact, MacArthur was
told that in order to assist the evacuation, he could use, if necessary, the U.S. Air
Force and Navy to prevent the Inchon-Kimpo-Seoul corridor from falling into North
Korean hands. He also ordered the Seventh Fleet to the Taiwan Straits to neutralize the area. On the afternoon of June 26 Ambassador Chang met with President
Truman and Secretary of State Acheson and requested America's immediate assistance in providing artillery, tanks, and aircraft for South Korea. In a message to the
Department of State, Rhee wrote: "We again thank you for your indispensable aid
in liberating us and in establishing our Republic. As we face this national crisis,
putting up brave fight, we appeal for your increasing support and ask that you at the
same time extend effective and timely aid in order to prevent this act of destruction of world peace."[63] Truman told Chang that he had already ordered General
MacArthur to supply all items of ammunition and equipment for the South Korean
armed forces. He said that help was on the way and that the South Koreans must
develop the steadfast leadership to carry them through this crisis.[64]

On June 27 the Security Council adopted another resolution recommending
that "members of the United Nations furnish such assistance to the Republic of
Korea as may be necessary to repel the armed attack and to restore international
peace and security in the area." The resolution helped legitimize the U.S. military
involvement in the Korean War, but even without the U.N. authorization, the Truman administration was determined to commit U.S. forces for South Korea's defense.

As the North Korean forces fought their way toward Seoul on June 27, Rhee, along with Ambassador Muccio, fled the capital. Truman ordered that a regimental combat team and then two army divisions be redeployed from Japan to South Korea and appointed General MacArthur as commander-in-chief of the United Nations Command (CINCUNC). He was put in charge of all forces contributed by U.N. member states. On July 14, Rhee agreed to delegate "command authority over all land, sea and air forces of the Republic of Korea during the period of the continuation of the present state of hostilities" to MacArthur.[65] For a while, General MacArthur and Ambassador Muccio made all of the important wartime decisions for South Korea. In particular, Muccio established an informal line of communications with Rhee's wife (Francesca Rhee, a native Austrian) so as to influence the South Korean president's decisions and actions. Muccio remembered: "She quite frequently telephoned just to tip me off that he [President Rhee] was about to do something that she thought I should know about. There was a very helpful attitude on her part. I'd just drop in on the old man and if I sat there long enough whatever he had in mind would eventually come out."[66]

The commitment of combat troops by the United States and other U.N. member states failed to contain the North Korean onslaught that overran the entire peninsula in early August, except for a narrow southeastern strip stretching from Taegu to Pusan. Only MacArthur's daring amphibious landing at Inchon in September turned the tide of the war. The U.N. forces soon recaptured Seoul, reinstalled Rhee's government in the capital, and pursued the retreating North Korean troops north toward the 38th Parallel. There was serious debate in the Department of State whether U.N. forces should be allowed to cross the parallel. While George F. Kennan (counselor of the Department of State and director of the Policy Planning Staff), an architect of the containment policy, argued against crossing the parallel on the grounds that it might provoke a larger war, Dean Rusk (assistant secretary of state for Far Eastern affairs), who had recommended the parallel in 1945, argued in favor of crossing it.[67] It was Rusk's view that the parallel in 1945 had been a "temporary military expediency" and that the reunification of Korea was a United Nations objective. If the U.N. forces did not pursue and destroy the North Korean troops across the parallel, Rusk argued, they would regroup for further military action. Given this new situation, President Truman suddenly changed the objectives of his Korea policy from the repulsion of the North Korean aggressors to total military victory and territorial unification in Korea. Once the first operative phase of the U.N. Security Council Resolution of June 27, 1950—"to repel the armed attack"—was achieved, the second phase—"to restore international peace and security in the area"—was cited to justify the march into North Korea.

The desperate Kim Il Sung cabled a special appeal to Stalin on September 29, stating that "when the enemy crosses the 38th Parallel, it will be absolutely necessary for the Soviet armed forces to directly participate" in the war. If the Soviet Union were unable to do so, Kim went on, Stalin should at least "organize and send the international volunteer armies of China and other democratic countries to help our struggles." On receiving the North Korean appeal, Stalin promptly instructed Russian Ambassador to China N. V. Roshchin to tell Mao Zedong or Zhou Enlai that the Korean situation was very critical and that five to six divisions of Chinese volunteers should be sent to North Korea as soon as possible.[68] In fact, Mao, too, had also received an appeal from Kim. The North Korean leader said: "If the enemy capitalizes on our grave crisis, gives no respite to us, and continues to advance to the north of the 38th Parallel, it is impossible to overcome this crisis by our own capabilities. Hence we have no choice but to ask for your special assistance: if the enemy attacks the north of the 38th Parallel, we urgently request that you directly dispatch the Chinese People's Liberation Army to assist our military operations."[69]

On October 1, the South Korean armed forces, under explicit orders from President Rhee and with approval by General Walton H. Walker (commander, Eighth Army), crossed the 38th Parallel for the first time and marched northward. The following day General MacArthur issued an order for the U.N. forces to also do so soon.[70] In a futile attempt to deter the U.N. forces from crossing the 38th Parallel, Zhou Enlai met with Indian Ambassador to China K. M. Panikkar in the early morning of October 3 to transmit a message to the United States.[71] If the U.N. forces crossed the parallel, Zhou said, China would have no option but to send its troops across the Yalu River to defend North Korea. Although there was considerable debate in the U.S. bureaucracies about the seriousness of Zhou's warning, Dean Acheson did not take it as "an authoritative statement of policy." On October 7, the U.N. General Assembly adopted the U.S.-approved resolution to bring about "the establishment of a unified, independent and democratic government of all Korea." The following day the Truman administration allowed the First Cavalry Division to cross the parallel, dismissing the Chinese warning. President Rhee was elated at the imminent prospect of finally realizing his dream to unify Korea under his control. On October 12, he was able to visit Wonsan, where he presented special awards to all members of the South Korean First Army for their military successes. Rhee intended to extend his civil administrative control over North Korea quickly and decisively by installing the provincial governors in North Korea who had been appointed two years earlier. This policy, however, conflicted with General MacArthur's decision to appoint a military mayor of Pyongyang and military governors to administer the North Korean provinces as they were "liberated."

On October 15, President Truman met General MacArthur at Wake Island. MacArthur confidently predicted that the war would be over by Thanksgiving and that the U.S. Eighth Army would return to Japan by Christmas. Asked by Truman about the possibility of Chinese intervention in Korea, MacArthur responded that there was very little chance of such a possibility and that "if the Chinese tried to get down to Pyongyang there would be the greatest slaughter."[72] He explained that although the Russians had an air force in Siberia and excellent pilots, they did not have any ground troops readily available for the Korean War. In response to the president's further inquiry, MacArthur dismissed the possibility of coordinated action in Korea by Chinese ground forces and the Russian air force. Truman and MacArthur then went on to discuss how to deal with such post-victory issues as occupation, administration, rehabilitation, and elections in North Korea.

The combined forces of the United States and South Korea captured Pyongyang on October 19 and precipitously moved toward the Yalu and Tumen Rivers. MacArthur, overplaying his hand, even allowed President Rhee to deliver a triumphant speech to a large crowd at the City Hall in Pyongyang on October 30. MacArthur and Rhee held all Chinese troops—both Nationalist and Communist—in contempt and stubbornly refused to believe that the Chinese forces assembled in Manchuria intended to enter Korea. A day before the Wake Island meeting, the Far East Command's daily intelligence summary had reported that "a total of 24 [Chinese] divisions are disposed along the Yalu River at crossing points" but dismissed the threat, assuming that China's recent warnings "are probably in a category of diplomatic blackmail." The summary also concluded that the Soviet Union and China "have decided against further expensive investment in support of a lost cause," meaning Korea. The Central Intelligence Agency, too, reported that despite Zhou's threats and the troop movements in Manchuria, "there are no convincing indications of an actual Chinese Communist intention to resort to full-scale intervention in Korea." The Truman administration shared this ill-advised consensus assessment, tragically miscalculating Mao's real intentions and capabilities.

A massive force of Chinese People's Volunteers (CPV) crossed the Yalu River in late October and early November. On November 7 the Far East Command estimated that there were only 44,500 Chinese troops in Korea. Two days later it raised the Chinese military presence to 76,800, but this calculation included only about one-fifth of the actual Chinese forces (380,000) already deployed in Korea at that time. MacArthur declared that "with my air power . . . I can deny reinforcements coming across the Yalu."[73] U.S. airplanes launched large-scale bombing attacks against bridges, roads, and military facilities along the Yalu River. After fierce confrontations with the CPV throughout North Korea, MacArthur finally admitted to the Joint Chiefs of Staff on November 28: "The Chinese military forces are committed in North Korea in great and every increasing strength. No pretext of minor support under the guise of volunteerism or other subterfuge now has the slightest validity. We face an entirely new war."[74] The CPV commanders were surprised when the U.S. Eighth Army suddenly abandoned Pyongyang without a fight on December 5 and retreated south of the 38th Parallel on December 16. They captured Seoul without much resistance on January 4, 1951, and continued to press southward. MacArthur had failed to make good on his promise of victory by Thanksgiving. And Rhee's plan to rule a unified Korea was shattered.

In view of the CPV's overwhelming forces, Acheson and Secretary of Defense George Marshall agreed that the Chinese military intervention in Korea was evidence of a Stalinist conspiracy to pin down U.S. forces in Asia so that the Soviets could have a free hand in Europe. To them, Korea was not a vital arena—Europe was their primary concern. Acheson concluded that the United States was fighting "the wrong nation" and "the second team" and that the real enemy was the Soviet Union. In this context General J. Lawton Collins (army chief of staff) argued that "Korea was not worth a nickel" and went so far as to declare that the only chance to save the United States in Korea was to threaten to use atomic bombs. It was agreed that a ceasefire would be highly desirable and abandoning Korea and evacuating South Korean forces to Japan should be considered. The Joint Chiefs of Staff told MacArthur on December 29 that "Korea is not the place to fight a major war" and instructed him to inflict costly damage on the Chinese forces but to prepare for an orderly evacuation to Japan.[75] President Truman resisted MacArthur's recommendation to extend the war into China and to use atomic bombs. Nor did he permit U.S. aircraft to pursue Chinese MiGs into Manchuria lest China invoke the Sino-Soviet mutual defense treaty.

After U.N. forces launched successful counterattacks in the spring of 1951, crossed the Han River on March 7, and recaptured Seoul on March 15, a stalemate came about along a line near the 38th Parallel, and the positions of the U.N. and South Korean forces improved. Furious with MacArthur's political maneuvering, which had undermined Washington's policy for a limited war, Truman, on the unanimous recommendations from the Joint Chiefs of Staff as well as Secretary of State Acheson and Secretary of Defense Marshall, finally dismissed him both as the supreme commander for the Allied Powers in Japan and as CINCUNC in Korea. This decision was unpopular in the United States and in South Korea. Rhee and his South Korean associates regarded MacArthur as their savior, hero, and patron and admired his belief that there was no substitute for victory in war.

At this critical juncture Truman abruptly changed his objective yet again, from seeking a total military victory to entering into ceasefire negotiations. Without consulting with Rhee, on May 17, 1951, the Truman administration adopted an important document (NSC 48/5) specifying that the "ultimate objective" was "to seek by political, as distinguished from military means, a solution of the Korean problem."[76] The document confirmed the U.S. policy of not extending hostilities into China or into a general war with the Soviet Union while at the same time insisting that a political settlement should not "jeopardize the United States position with respect to the USSR, to Formosa, and to seating Communist China in the UN." On the following day the U.N. General Assembly adopted a resolution imposing an embargo on the export of arms, ammunition, and other strategically relevant materials to China and North Korea.

On the request of Secretary of State Acheson, George F. Kennan, who was on a leave of absence from the Department of State, secretly met Soviet Ambassador to the United Nations Yakov Malik on several occasions to explore whether Stalin, Mao, and Kim Il Sung would be interested in a negotiated settlement of the war.[77] About this time General Matthew B. Ridgway and Ambassador Muccio met President Rhee in one of the Quonset huts at Kimpo Airport and informed him that the United States had decided to talk to the Communists and explained why the U.S. had changed its strategy. Devastated by this news, Rhee grasped Ridgway's arm and said, "General, you're a very persuasive talker, but you have not convinced me that you cannot go to the Yalu if you wanted to." As soon as Rhee left, Ridgway told Muccio that he would "have to do a little more homework and come back in four or five days and take another shot at selling him the idea." Rhee, however, remained staunchly opposed to a ceasefire agreement. He was convinced that since Communism was cholera, no appeasement with such a deadly epidemic was permissible. The South Korean government took the rigid position that the United Nations Command (UNC) should not even talk to the Communists until they had been driven from Korea.[78] After Stalin, Mao, and Kim consulted, Malik publicly proposed negotiations for a ceasefire arrangement, which began at Kaesong on July 10, 1951, and continued at a truce village, Panmunjom. The five-member UNC delegation headed by Vice Admiral C. Turner Joy included only one South Korean general, but the Communist delegation led by North Korean general Nam Il had two other North Korean military officers as well as two Chinese generals. The Chinese made all the important decisions at Kaesong and Panmunjom but behaved as though they were Kim Il Sung's "guests" in Korea. For their part, the United States continued to disregard Rhee's importance not only in the substantive aspects of negotiations but also in terms of procedural form.

It took two years for both sides to iron out the terms of a ceasefire agreement, particularly over the status of prisoners of war (POWs), determination of the demilitarized zone (DMZ), and the composition and functions of the Neutral Nations Supervisory Commission (NNSC). Even though the Geneva Convention (1947) mandated the compulsory repatriation of all prisoners of war without delay after the cessation of active hostilities, President Truman strongly believed in the concept of voluntary repatriation. Among other things, he knew that some of the POWs automatically repatriated to the Soviet Union and other socialist states at the end of World War II had been mistreated. The United States insisted on the actual line of ground contact rather than the 38th Parallel as the basis for the DMZ. It felt that the parallel was a symbol of political division in Korea and that its restoration could be seen as a "reward" for North Korean and Chinese aggression. The domestic critics of Truman's Korea policy, including Senators Robert A. Taft and Richard M. Nixon, argued that a truce at the 38th Parallel would represent "appeasement." The U.S. military leaders assumed that the actual battle line—north of the parallel on the east and south of the parallel on the west—presented a more defendable position than did the parallel. Moreover, the Truman administration was sensitive to Rhee's outspoken opposition to the reinstatement of the 38th Parallel.

The United States found it especially difficult to persuade the adamant Rhee to accept a negotiated armistice agreement because he continued to insist that the truce was an appeasement far short of the ultimate goal of Korean unification. He demanded a mutual security treaty with the United States, refused to endorse the outline of the Korean Armistice Agreement, and finally, on May 15, 1953, withdrew South Korean delegates from Panmunjom altogether. Massive demonstrations with many high school and college students were organized in Seoul and other major South Korean cities to oppose the ceasefire. This mobilized "popular" and "democratic" sentiment served as an instrument to influence the United States.

In the early morning of June 18, 1953, Rhee unilaterally released about 27,000 anti-Communist North Korean POWs and about fifty Chinese POWs. This unexpected decision dramatized his opposition to an armistice, as did his refusal to turn them over to a neutral foreign committee led by Indian troops (Rhee suspected India of harboring a pro-Communist attitude). The freed POWs were temporarily given shelter and food in private homes but were subsequently unable to obtain appropriate civilian jobs. A large number of them eventually volunteered to join the South Korean armed forces, the only opportunity readily available to them. Angered and embarrassed by Rhee's "bombshell," President Dwight D. Eisenhower, who had made a campaign promise to end the Korean War, complained at the NSC meeting on June 18 that the United States had acquired another enemy instead of a friend. If Rhee did not behave himself, the president fumed, "we might have to move out."[79] Eisenhower feared that the Communist side might break off the ceasefire negotiations. However, Secretary of State John Foster Dulles suggested that the disaster was not irreparable and that the Communists were so anxious for an armistice that they would overlook Rhee's action. In a confidential letter to President Rhee, Eisenhower accused the South Korean president of violating the UNC's command authority and of reneging on his repeated promise not to take unilateral action without prior consultations with the United States. The letter declared: "Unless you are prepared immediately and unequivocally to accept the authority of the UN Command to conduct the present hostilities and to bring them to a close, it will be necessary to effect another arrangement. Accordingly, the UN Commander-in-Chief has now been authorized to take such steps as may become necessary in the light of your determination."[80]

At this time General Mark W. Clark (CINCUNC) and U.S. Ambassador to South Korea Ellis O. Briggs even seriously considered the possibility of invoking a secret contingency plan, code-named "Operation Everready," to remove Rhee from power by military means, thereby eliminating a major stumbling bloc to an armistice once and for all. Originally conceived as an attempt to get Rhee out of the temporary capital of Pusan and to place him "in protective custody incommunicado" in connection with a domestic political crisis in July 1952, this extraordinary top-secret plan subsequently envisaged a program "to take Rhee into custody, to proclaim martial law, to have ROK Army authorities enforce martial law, to place dissident civil and military commanders under custody of those who are loyal to the Commanding General of the Eighth Army, and . . . to establish military government under the U.N."[81] General Clark understood that General Paek Sun Yop, South Korean Army chief of staff, had tacitly indicated his willingness to cooperate with this plan, if necessary. Yet the United States refused to support a group of anti-Rhee political and military leaders led by Chough Pyong Ok, former minister of home affairs, who planned a coup d'état in the spring and summer of 1952.[82] Rhee and his advisers had long suspected that the United States might attempt to depose him either by declaring UNC martial law or by mobilizing South Korean generals and politicians, but they had no specific knowledge of the Everready plan.[83] In the end, however, the Eisenhower administration decided not to implement the contingency plan, in part because it was risky and in part because there was no viable alternative to Rhee, and instead proceeded to negotiate a mutual security treaty and to offer economic and military assistance programs to Rhee so that he would comply with the truce arrangement.

In a letter to Rhee on June 22, 1953, Secretary of State Dulles emphasized the principles of unity and interdependence between the United States and South Korea and pleaded with the South Korean president to accept the ceasefire arrangement.

Dulles told Rhee that "your Republic can share with us a mutual security pact and would enjoy a program of economic aid which of itself will set up a powerful attraction upon the North Koreans."[84] In addition, Dulles pledged to support the long-term goal of Korean unification and to cooperate with South Korea at a postwar international conference on the Korean question. For further discussions with President Rhee at the end of June 1953, Dulles dispatched to Seoul Assistant Secretary of State for Far Eastern Affairs Walter S. Robertson as Eisenhower's special envoy. Even though the Eisenhower administration vehemently denied its involvement in Rhee's earlier decision to free the prisoners and gave assurances that a similar situation would not arise, the CPV commanders assailed U.S. complicity in the "Syngman Rhee clique's criminal act" and demanded the return of the released prisoners. They launched the largest offensive against South Korean forces since the beginning of the negotiations. It was intended to punish Rhee and to show what might happen were he to violate the ceasefire agreement. The Communist side, however, did not use Rhee's action as an excuse to scrap the compromises already struck at Panmunjom.

The complex personality and undercutting maneuvers of President Rhee confused and frustrated his American interlocutors. A politician who understood the dynamics and limits of U.S. domestic politics and foreign policies, Rhee's adroit tactics of brinkmanship and unpredictability, combined with his personal charm and fluent English, allowed him to exploit his apparent weaknesses as the leader of the war-torn and poverty-stricken state so as to extract maximum concessions and promises from one of the superpowers. It is conceivable that his repeated public threats to march northward even without external military and logistic support were a carefully calculated negotiating ploy aimed at the United States as well as a patriotic appeal to South Koreans. After a contentious meeting with the South Korean president, Assistant Secretary of State Robertson submitted a scathing report to the Department of State on July 1, 1953: "Rhee in addition to being [a] shrewd, resourceful trader is also a highly emotional, irrational, illogical fanatic fully capable of attempting to lead his country into national suicide. . . . His cooperation is still possible but he must be led, as well as pushed."[85] Some Americans characterized him as unreasonable, stubborn, recalcitrant, childish, senile, dangerous, cantankerous, vain, and susceptible to flattery, while others recognized his high degree of knowledge and ability. While General Maxwell D. Taylor (commander, Eighth Army) colorfully described Rhee as "a curious mixture of an Old Testament prophet . . . and a shrewd Oriental politician," Ambassador Muccio recalled that Rhee was "a very determined willful person" but a very intelligent individual with "an excellent historical perspective."[86] Muccio added that Rhee was a "man who thought well and worked well under stress." After prolonged resistance, protests, and opposition, Rhee at last accepted the inevitability of an armistice, but only after he had wrung many military and economic promises from the United States.

The Korean Armistice Agreement signed on July 27, 1953, by General Mark W. Clark (CINCUNC), Peng Dehuai (commander, Chinese People's Volunteers), and Kim Il Sung (supreme commander, Korean People's Army) basically restored the status quo ante bellum in Korea and averted a larger international conflict in the region.[87] The United States had resisted the temptation to attack China or to use atomic bombs. It did not achieve its revised goal of unifying Korea by military means, but it did manage to repel the North Korean aggression. In the process, the United States preserved South Korea's territorial integrity and punished North Korea and China. Having suffered more than 142,000 casualties, including about 34,000 dead and about 106,000 wounded, the United States developed a strong vested interest in protecting South Korea's viability. As a continuation of its wartime policy, the United States pursued military containment, diplomatic isolation, and economic sanctions against North Korea and China. The North Koreans, who had been on the verge of total military victory, regarded China as their savior and the United States as their mortal enemy. They celebrated the war as a "victory" against the most powerful nation on the earth but suffered enormously from the death, destruction, and dislocation of its citizens. As a result of the three-year war, hostility and mistrust between North Korea and South Korea intensified, creating a potent obstacle to any future inter-Korean dialogue and reconciliation. Yet for all of its tragic and devastating elements, in a way the war served as an effective deterrent to another major armed conflict in Korea.

The South Koreans were grateful to the United States and the other allies for the tremendous sacrifices made throughout the war but were disappointed that the war did not unify the country under their control. The war inflicted significant damage on South Korea's economy. Physical losses amounted to almost $2 billion by September 1951—a figure greater than South Korea's gross national product (GNP) for 1949. In Seoul, over 80% of industry, public utilities, and transport; three quarters of the offices; and more than half of the dwellings were in ruins.[88] The human cost was horrendous. A large number of South Korean leaders had been "liquidated" by North Korea for political reasons. According to the U.N. report, South Korean military casualties were calculated at 47,000 killed, 183,000 wounded, and 70,000 missing soldiers and prisoners of war. Estimates put civilian casualties at over a million.[89] Over five million were left homeless, and an even greater number suffered from family tragedy, refugee status, and other wartime hardships. The sudden influx of about two million North Korean refugees put an additional burden on South Korea's war-torn economy. And President Rhee's political leadership in domestic politics was challenged.

THE CONTAINMENT SYSTEM

The three-year Korean War solidified South Korea as a U.S. client state par excellence in a wide range of military, diplomatic, and economic affairs. As a sponsor of the birth of the Republic of Korea in 1948, the United States had defended it from armed conquest by North Korea and then by China. From the beginning, the United States had assumed all responsibilities vital to South Korea's national security—strategic decisions, operational control, combat duties, military training, and the supply of war materiel. The South Korean armed forces, whose numbers fluctuated widely from 98,000 at the outbreak of the war to half that number in August 1950 and then up to 250,000 by 1952, depended almost completely upon U.S. leadership and support. The United States also helped organize the Korean Military Academy. It was only natural that the United States developed a strong vested interest in South Korea's security and welfare.

In retrospect, it is clear that the United States decided to conclude the Mutual Defense Treaty with South Korea not only as a device to obtain the recalcitrant Rhee's acceptance of the armistice arrangement but also as an essential link in its regional anti-Communist containment system. The first step in putting together the treaty came on May 30, 1953, when the Joint Chiefs of Staff under President Eisenhower's authorization explicitly informed General Clark and Ambassador Briggs that the United States was willing to undertake immediate formal negotiations for a mutual defense treaty with South Korea, subject to assurances from President Rhee that his government would refrain from opposing or agitating against an armistice, cooperate in its implementation, and leave South Korean armed forces under the operational control of the CINCUNC.[90] In a letter to President Rhee on June 6, 1953, President Eisenhower promised to negotiate with South Korea "a mutual-defense treaty along the lines of the treaties heretofore made between the United States and the Philippines, and the United States and Australia and New Zealand" in return for South Korea's acceptance of an armistice.[91] Mandated by the National Security Council to prepare a report on "U.S. Policy Toward Communist China in the Event of a Korean Armistice," the NSC Planning Board developed a statement of policy (NSC 154) on June 15, 1953, which proposed that, on the assumption that South Korea would cooperate satisfactorily with the United Nations in carrying out the terms of the armistice, the United States should "conclude a treaty with the Republic of Korea guaranteeing its political independence and territorial integrity."[92] The Joint Chiefs of Staff expressed reservations about the sweeping commitment for guaranteeing South Korea's "political independence and territorial integrity," instead favoring a more narrow focus on the defense of South Korea's national security.

In response to the draft treaty prepared by the United States along the lines of the JCS position and the U.S.-Philippine Mutual Defense Treaty (signed August 30, 1951), Rhee proposed on July 9, 1953, that the treaty should also state that the lawful jurisdiction of South Korea extends "throughout the traditional area of Korea and specifically northward to [the] Yalu and Tumen Rivers." Furthermore, the treaty would stay effective indefinitely and would allow the United States to "station its land, sea, or air forces in or about Korea," as in the case of the U.S.-Japan Security Treaty.[93] To demonstrate the continuity of friendly relations between the two countries, the South Korean draft treaty noted "with deep satisfaction" that "earliest formal relations between our two nations commenced with [the] Amity Treaty of 1882." Rhee also insisted, as did the NATO provision, that the treaty should require the United States to take immediate military action to defend South Korea in the event of an external attack. In a meeting with Secretary of State Dulles on August 5, 1953, President Rhee stated that "our whole life and hope depend" on the treaty.[94] There was no question about the vital importance of the treaty to Rhee's political viability and to South Korea's national security.

Although the United States did not agree to Rhee's demands to spell out an expanded South Korean territorial boundary and to give the treaty an indefinite duration, Secretary of State Dulles and South Korean Foreign Minister Pyun Yong Tae initialed the Mutual Defense Treaty on August 8 in Seoul and signed it on October 1 in Washington. Article 3 declared: "Each party recognizes that an armed attack in the Pacific area on either of the Parties in territories now under their respective administrative control, or hereafter recognized by one of the Parties as lawfully brought under the administrative control of the other, would be dangerous to its own peace and safety and declares that it would act to meet the common danger in accordance with its constitutional processes."[95] Dulles refused to accept Rhee's proposals to insert "effectively" in front of "meet" and to strike out the conditional requirement of "in accordance with its constitutional processes" in Article Three. On Rhee's request, in Article Four the United States accepted the right to dispose its land, air, and sea forces in and about the territory of South Korea "as determined by mutual agreement." Article Six specified that the treaty would remain in force indefinitely, but either party could terminate it one year after notice had been given to the other party. The treaty did not include a legally binding provision for immediate and automatic military action by the United States, but Dulles assured President Rhee in a confidential letter on July 24, 1953, that "If in violation of the armistice the Republic of Korea is subjected to unprovoked attack you may of course count upon our immediate and automatic military action. Such an attack would not only be an attack upon the Republic of Korea but an attack upon the United Nations Command and U.S. forces within that Command."[96] Even though this letter was only written to obtain Rhee's adherence to the Korean Armistice Agreement, its unconditional and categorical commitment was bound to haunt the subsequent U.S. administrations.

The U.S. commander in South Korea, in his capacity as commander-in-chief of the United Nations Command, was to retain his operational command authority over South Korean armed forces even after the cessation of hostilities. Rhee preferred to nullify this wartime agreement, but the United States regarded it as indispensable for preventing South Korea from violating the ceasefire system. This in effect was a system of dual containment—against the possibilities of North Korea's invasion and against provocation by South Korea. In the event that the UNC's operational control over South Korean forces was weakened or challenged, the commander of the U.S. Eighth Army in Seoul was instructed to invoke the top-secret Everready Plan, as revised on October 28, 1953.[97] If the South Korean government and military took "an independent course of action" or became overtly hostile toward the United States, he was authorized to undertake a number of drastic measures, including relieving disloyal South Korean commanders, bombing South Korean ammunition supply points, securing custody of dissident military and civilian leaders, and securing control of transportation and electric power facilities in South Korea. In addition, the plan mentioned other possible steps—withdraw recognition of the Rhee government, reduce military and economic aid, establish a naval blockade, initiate an anti-Rhee publicity campaign, or proclaim martial law. Even though it was only a contingency plan, the United States was nonetheless prepared to intervene directly in changing the South Korean political leadership. However, in a meeting with Vice President Richard Nixon in Seoul in mid-November 1953 and in an exchange of confidential letters with President Eisenhower, President Rhee explicitly disavowed any intention to take unilateral military action without full prior consultation with the United States. He told Nixon that "I pledge to you that before I take any unilateral action I shall inform President Eisenhower." This commitment made it easier for the Eisenhower administration to ask the U.S. Congress to ratify the U.S.–South Korean Mutual Defense Treaty and to provide economic assistance for South Korea.[98]

On November 20, 1953, the Eisenhower administration adopted a top secret report (NSC 170/1) entitled "U.S. Objectives and Courses of Action in Korea" to outline its postwar policy toward Korea. It stated: "The long-range objective with respect to the Korean problem is to bring about the unification of Korea with a self-supporting economy and under a free, independent and representative government, friendly toward the United States, with its political and territorial integrity assured by international agreement and with armed forces sufficient for internal security and capable of defending Korean territory short of an attack by a major power."[99] In order to carry out this long-term goal, the United States decided to accept the division of Korea on the DMZ and to maintain a "position of strength" in Korea in support of the U.N. commitment to oppose aggression. This would prevent the area from coming under Communist domination and would also tie South Korea into the U.S. security system. Like the revised Everready Plan, this report also stipulated a set of measures to take against Rhee if he unilaterally initiated military operations against Chinese or North Korean forces. The basic framework of this report was to remain in effect for several decades to come.

As specified in the Korean Armistice Agreement, an international conference on the peaceful unification of Korea was convened at Geneva in April 1954, but it turned out to be an exercise in futility. Mistrust and hostilities between the pro-Seoul and pro-Pyongyang delegations were too serious to be mended. While the United States and its allies endorsed the South Korean proposal for Korean unification through U.N.-supervised elections, the Soviet Union and China did not deviate from the North Korean insistence on what it called the principle of national self-determination. A declaration by the sixteen nations that had taken part in the Security Council's collective security actions in Korea referred the Korean question back to the United Nations.[100] Since neither South Korea nor North Korea were members of the United Nations, the United States and the Soviet Union continued to represent and protect the diplomatic interests of their respective Korean clients at the annual debates over the Korean question. While the United States upheld the importance of U.N. resolutions on the question of Korean unification, the Soviet Union denounced the legality of the United Nations Command and the activities of the seven-member United Nations Commission for the Unification and Rehabilitation of Korea (UNCURK), which had replaced UNCOK in October 1950 for the purpose of "bringing about the establishment of a unified, independent and democratic government of all Korea."

The failure of the Geneva Conference did not prevent President Rhee from exploring other options for achieving Korean unification with his American counterparts. At a summit meeting with President Eisenhower at the White House on July 27, 1954—the first anniversary of the Korean Armistice Agreement—Rhee passionately argued that the peaceful policy pursued by the United States would let the Communists conquer the democratic and free nations and that "Korea could not hang for an indefinite period of time through years of talking." Asked about U.S. policy toward Korea, Eisenhower categorically declared that "any deliberate resort to war is completely barred in our calculations." He added: "There is no disposition in America at any time to belittle the Republic of Korea but when you say that we should deliberately plunge into war, let me tell you that if war comes, it will be horrible. Atomic war will destroy civilization. It will destroy our cities. There will be millions of people dead. War today is unthinkable with the weapons which we have at our command. If the Kremlin and Washington ever lock up in a war, the results are too horrible to contemplate. I can't even imagine them. But we must keep strong. We must try to repulse aggression by united action."[101] The U.S. government was so concerned about the possibility that Rhee might criticize Eisenhower's policy publicly that it provided no audio coverage for a joint appearance of the two presidents at the White House; only photographs were allowed. The Eisenhower administration was particularly annoyed by Rhee's address before a joint session of the U.S. Congress on July 28 in which he denounced the "unwise armistice" and obliquely criticized U.S. softness on Communism. In the Agreed Minute of the Summit Meeting, however, Rhee grudgingly agreed to continue diplomatic efforts for Korea's unification within the United Nations. In turn, the Eisenhower administration promised to continue its program of helping to strengthen South Korea politically, economically, and militarily.[102]

After the conclusion of the war, the United States reduced the number of its troops stationed in South Korea from 302,483 in July 1953 to 102,865 in December 1954 and 59,910 in December 1955. In addition to preventing another Korean War, the continuing U.S. military presence in South Korea was intended to serve other objectives—to bolster U.S. political influence in South Korea, to protect South Korea's diplomatic and economic activities, to provide a training ground for U.S. troops, and to stabilize the balance of power in the Asia-Pacific region. In particular, the United States regarded its military position in the Korean Peninsula as an effective shield for protecting Japan's security interests. For this reason, the United States sustained the two sets of defense treaties with South Korea and Japan and encouraged diplomatic normalization between South Korea and Japan.

As promised to Rhee, the United States delivered massive economic aid for the relief and reconstruction of its Korean ally. With this economic patronage, the United States intended to bolster South Korea's political stability and to underwrite its substantial defense expenditures. For the 1953–61 period, for example, America's total direct assistance to South Korea exceeded $4 billion—$2.6 billion in economic aid and $1.8 billion in military aid. The United States allocated an almost equal amount of economic assistance to Japan from 1945 through 1961, but a considerable portion of the economic aid to South Korea was used indirectly for military purposes. Almost all U.S. funds to South Korea were given in the form of grants-in-aid because the recipient's economic ability was too limited to bear the burden of loan repayment. As measured by the per capita amount of aid, South Korea ranked as one of the top recipients of U.S. economic and military assistance in the world throughout the 1950s and early 1960s. The binational Combined Economic Board was entrusted with the responsibility of administering U.S. aid programs to South Korea, but the United States Operations Mission (USOM) exercised a virtual veto power in the event of policy conflicts between both sides. The USOM ensured that South Korea adhered to a "buy-America" policy and maintained close links with the U.S.-dominated international economic and financial order. At times Rhee resisted the USOM's excessive power but to no avail. The United States fully utilized its economic dominance over its weaker ally as a crucial instrument to influence South Korea's domestic politics and foreign affairs and to solidify the U.S. anti-Communist containment system in the Asia-Pacific region.

In addition to its primary efforts to strengthen South Korea's military preparedness and economic development, the United States encouraged the process of political democratization and respect for human rights in South Korea as much as it could. When the 85-year-old Syngman Rhee, along with his vice presidential running mate Lee Ki Pung, speaker of the National Assembly, emerged victorious in the presidential elections on March 15, 1960, there were serious allegations of massive electoral irregularities. The sudden death of Chough Pyong Ok, the presidential candidate of the opposition Democratic Party, at Walter Reed Hospital in Washington in February, assured Rhee's relatively easy electoral victory, but Lee Ki Pung faced a tough challenge from Vice President Chang Myon, who had defeated him in the election for vice presidency in 1956. In spite of his earlier service as Rhee's first ambassador to the United States and prime minister, Chang had become a symbol of the prodemocracy struggles in South Korea. Violent anti-Rhee riots began to spread from the southern coastal city of Masan to Seoul and other major cities, threatening political stability in South Korea. General Carter Magruder (CINCUNC) permitted the South Korean government to use its troops to restore order, but this decision was not publicized.[103] On May 16, Secretary of State Christian Herter called in South Korean Ambassador Yang Yu Chan and expressed his concern about election abuses and South Korea's intransigent attitude toward Japan. Among other things, Herter stated that electoral pressures in South Korea exceeded "the norms of democratic practices and processes" and that the events might adversely affect the U.S. aid program to South Korea.[104]

The Rhee government blamed the surging prodemocracy demonstrations on Communist-inspired plots, but CIA Director Allen Dulles reported to the National

Security Council on March 17 that "the elections were marked by violence, intimidation and fraudulent counting."[105] It was taken for granted by U.S. officials, from Secretary of State Herter to Ambassador Walter P. McConaughy, that the United States had the right as well as the responsibility to assume a direct role in the management of domestic political affairs in South Korea. In his confidential telegram to the Department of State on April 2, McConaughy candidly asserted that "our blood, money, reputation and security are heavily invested in Korea. We have perhaps less reason to be passive observers here than anywhere else and the times call for a more vigorous effort to convey a clearer understanding of our viewpoint."[106] He added that the South Koreans should understand that their line of credit in the United States was becoming depleted and that their international standing was fading.

The opportunity for McConaughy to make a more vigorous effort arose quickly on April 19, 1960, when a large number of college and high school students and other concerned citizens held rallies in front of the National Assembly and the Central Government Building in Seoul and demanded a new presidential election. As the demonstrators marched toward the Presidential Palace, apprehensive security guards fired indiscriminately at them. A day of death, destruction, and chaos ensued until President Rhee declared martial law and obtained permission from the UNC commander-in-chief to use the 15th Army Division to restore order and impose an early curfew. This student uprising, however, quickly spread to Pusan, Taegu, Kwangju, and other major cities. It was estimated that at least 115 persons died and 730 injured.

Faced with this crisis, Ambassador McConaughy immediately issued, on his own authority, a statement deploring any resort to violence and urging both demonstrators and authorities to settle "justifiable grievances."[107] In a telephone conversation with Herter, President Eisenhower made it clear that the United States should be tough with Rhee and tell him "that we fought for the freedom of South Korea and that unless Rhee permits free elections and the people are given the right to vote, there is just no sense in our being in Korea."[108] On the evening of April 19, McConaughy made an urgent request to see President Rhee. The ambassador found Rhee "tired, somewhat nervous and shocked by crisis" and felt that he was "substantially out of touch with realities of present situation and wrong in his assessment of causes, nature and probable consequences of uprisings."[109] McConaughy attempted to explain to Rhee the seriousness of electoral fraud and the depth of the political crisis. Rhee condemned his political rival, Vice President Chang Myon, for fomenting the demonstrations, and his ministers of national defense and home affairs claimed that the demonstrators were under Communist direction. In the end, McConaughy recommended that Rhee set aside the election of March 15 and call for a new presidential election. In effect, McConaughy supported the principal demands of the student demonstrators. A similar message was included in a very tough aide-mémoire that Secretary Herter gave South Korean Ambassador Yang on April 19 in Washington. As someone who had been imprisoned for over five years because of his participation in the antigovernment demonstrations almost six decades earlier, Rhee probably had mixed feelings—both anger and empathy—about the student demonstrators; he visited hospitals to console the students who had been wounded.

On April 21, Ambassador McConaughy met with President Rhee.[110] The president again blamed Vice President Chang and the Catholic Church for inciting riots, refuted the main thrust of the American aide-mémoire, and dismissed Secretary Herter as a "newcomer" to diplomatic matters and "too pro-Japanese." The ambassador characterized this meeting as "unsatisfactory" and noted that Rhee was "dangerously uninformed and misinformed." He added that Rhee was "receptive to flattery and to statements which play upon his well-known prejudices but critical statements only prompt him to suspect the motives of the speaker rather than to ponder the content of the criticism." Frustrated by Rhee's defiant and defensive positions in his meeting with McConaughy, Secretary of State Herter, in a telegram to the ambassador on April 23, assailed Rhee's repressive and dictatorial rule and explored the idea of isolating Rhee and his extremist supporters and bringing about a broad-based administration that would uphold democratic principles, enjoy popular support, and be able to rule effectively.[111] This idea was reminiscent of the abortive "Everready Plan" intended to remove Rhee from power toward the end of the Korean War. In addition, Herter alerted the ambassador to the possibility that in an effort to divert public attention, Rhee might make some drastic move like attacking North Korea or moving on Japan (e.g., Tsushima Island). Herter's distrust of President Rhee was fundamental and pervasive.

Confronted with yet another wave of demonstrations, President Rhee finally relented. In his four-point announcement on April 26, Rhee (1) indicated his willingness to resign from the presidential office; (2) suggested that another presidential election be held; (3) requested the resignation of Lee Ki Pung from all political positions; and (4) called for a constitutional amendment to create a new cabinet system. In a meeting with Rhee on the same day, McConaughy began by praising Rhee and hailing him as Korea's George Washington but then stated in the strongest possible terms that the best option for him was to resign promptly for the protection of South Korean as well as American interests.[112] At the same time the National Assembly unanimously adopted a resolution calling for the immediate resignation of President Rhee and invalidating the March 15 election. It also stipulated that the constitution should be amended to provide a new system of cabinet government and that new elections for the National Assembly should be held immediately after the constitutional amendment was enacted. The following day Rhee resigned and returned to his private residence in Seoul. Abandoned by the president and turned away from the secure military compound, Lee Ki Pung, his wife, and their two sons, one of whom had been formally adopted by Rhee, all committed suicide. After the resignation of Vice President Chang Myon, Minister of Foreign Affairs Huh Chung, who had served as acting prime minister and mayor of Seoul, became acting president in charge of the interim government.

It has been suggested that this historic development, commonly referred to as the "April Uprising" or "April Revolution," was achieved half by the student demonstrations and half by the U.S. embassy. Even though this view underestimated the courage, sacrifice, and contribution on the part of the student demonstrators, who paid little attention to the statements and activities of the U.S. embassy, the United States did play an important role in presenting accurate and objective information to President Rhee and in persuading him to resign from his presidential office for the sake of his country. So did Huh Chung and Minister of National Defense Kim Chung Yul, whom Rhee trusted. His sense of indebtedness toward the United States and his conception of popular sovereignty allowed Rhee to heed the well-meant advice from the American and South Korean officials. At a press conference on April 27, President Eisenhower categorically stated that "no interference of any kind was ever undertaken by the United States" in South Korea. This statement was diplomatically appropriate but not quite accurate. At the request of Mrs. Francesca Rhee and with Acting President Huh's cooperation, the United States extended an invitation and visa privileges to the Rhees so that they could leave Kimpo Airport for Honolulu, which they did on May 29. Since for sensitive political reasons Ambassador McConaughy refused to provide U.S. military air transportation, the Rhees flew in a chartered aircraft arranged by their supporters in Hawaii.[113]

On June 19, President Eisenhower arrived in Seoul. After his planned trip to Tokyo had been cancelled due to anti-U.S. demonstrations, he was impressed by a crowd of about one million flag-waving citizens who welcomed him to South Korea. He held a summit meeting with Huh Chung, addressed the National Assembly, and issued a joint communiqué with Huh on June 20.[114] The two leaders recognized the vital importance of preserving their bilateral alliance and agreed to "foster economic independence, assist social progress, and provide a strong foundation for democratic institutions." The "April Uprising" was not mentioned in the joint communiqué or in the Eisenhower-Huh meeting, but it was not difficult to imagine how satisfied Eisenhower was to see one of his policy goals, political democratization, being realized in South Korea.

In the relatively free and democratic legislative elections held on July 29, the op-position Democratic Party captured a commanding majority with 177 seats in the 233-member House of Representatives and a majority of 31 seats in the 58-member House of Councillors. A joint session of both houses elected Yun Po Sun to the cer-emonial position of president. After Yun's nomination, the House of Representatives elected Chang Myon to the political position of prime minister on August 19. Since the Democratic Party was split between old and new factions, the Chang govern-ment included members from both factions. Aside from the burden of interfactional struggles, the Chang government faced a number of very difficult economic, social, and diplomatic issues.[115] The United States still hoped that the Chang government would be able to take care of the unsettled situation in South Korea through peace-ful means.

This hope was dashed in the early morning of May 16, 1961, when a small group of young army and marine officers led by an obscure general, Major General Park Chung Hee (deputy commander, Second Army), staged a coup d'état. Even though the U.S. embassy in Seoul and the Central Intelligence Agency had heard rumors of political unrest in the South Korean armed forces—including a plot by Park Chung Hee—as early as April 21, the new Kennedy administration's contingency plan had not yet been formulated, and the United States was forced to improvise in response to the domestic crisis in Korea.[116] The coup forces swiftly occupied all ma-jor government and military facilities and the radio station in Seoul, dissolved the National Assembly, and arrested radical student leaders, politicians suspected of corruption, and leading businessmen. They met with little organized resistance, and the coup was nearly bloodless. Upon hearing this news in the early morning of May 16, Prime Minister Chang, accompanied by his wife, fled their suite in the Bando Hotel near the Seoul City Hall, attempted to enter the residence of the U.S. ambassador without success, and finally took refuge in the Carmelite Convent in Seoul. They remained in hiding for two full days. Many of his cabinet ministers dis-appeared too. General Chang Do Yong, South Korean Army chief of staff, called General Magruder and requested the use of U.S. troops to put the coup down. The UNC commander-in-chief rejected this request, insisting that he was only respon-sible for protecting South Korea against external attack. Seizing this fortuitous op-portunity, General Chang promptly changed his mind, joined the coup forces, and agreed to become chairman of the new Military Revolutionary Committee. This committee announced a six-point program—the new government would (1) be strictly anti-Communist; (2) root out corruption; (3) observe the U.N. Charter and all international agreements and cooperation with the United States and all other free nations; (4) endeavor to stabilize the national economy; (5) unify Korea as an anti-Communist nation; and (6) turn over the reins of government to honest and competent political leaders.[117]

In the absence of explicit instructions from Washington, General Magruder released a statement on May 16 in which he called on all military personnel in his command to support the deposed Chang government and called on the chiefs of the South Korean armed forces to return military control to the lawful government authorities. Endorsing the Magruder statement, Chargé d'Affaires Marshall Green made it clear that the United States supported "the constitutional government of the Republic of Korea as elected by the people of the Republic last July and as constituted last August with the election of a Prime Minister." The two U.S. leaders in Seoul, however, were baffled by the sudden disappearance of Prime Minister Chang and his cabinet ministers during this national crisis. To their dismay, they also noticed that there was no tangible sign of popular opposition to the coup. In a telephone call to Green, Chang, without divulging his whereabouts, expressed his appreciation for the statements issued by Magruder and Green and urged the two leaders to take care of the situation.[118]

In a hastily arranged meeting with President Yun at the Presidential Palace, Green and Magruder registered their opposition to the coup and expressed their support for the lawful government under Prime Minister Chang. Yun responded that South Korea needed a strong government, but Prime Minister Chang had proven incapable of providing such leadership.[119] He explained that popular disillusionment with the Chang government was widespread and that corruption was extensive, extending to the top levels of government. When Magruder, with Green's concurrence, asked for Yun's permission to use 40,000 troops from the First Army under General Lee Han Lim for the purpose of surrounding about 3,600 insurgents and returning them to their home units, President Yun responded that as the commander-in-chief of the South Korean armed forces, he opposed it because bloodshed among military units would be disastrous with a hostile external military force amassed just beyond the DMZ.[120] In Magruder's assessment, President Yun appeared to consider the coup as an acceptable method of getting rid of his political rival, Prime Minister Chang. If Prime Minister Chang had courageously resurfaced and ordered General Lee Han Lim of the First Army to suppress the insurgents, Magruder would have been prepared to support him. He was reluctant to do so on his own authority, however. Soon thereafter, the coup forces arrested General Lee Han Lim.

In a telegram to Green on May 16, Acting Secretary of State Chester Bowles harshly denounced the military clique's reckless challenge against the lawful government under Prime Minister Chang but advocated a "cautious attitude of wait-and-see."[121] Unless the Chang government indicated its ability and willingness to save itself, he instructed, "we will refrain from additional public identification of U.S. with fate of what may be a lost cabinet." In spite of the information about General Park's past pro-Communist activities, Bowles concluded that the coup was not Communist-inspired. The Kennedy administration was not prepared to accept the urgent appeal from South Korean Ambassador Chang Lee Wook and Minister-Counselor Koh Kwang Lim in Washington that the United States should intervene to rescue their government in Seoul.[122]

While the coup forces continued to consolidate their power in Seoul and throughout the nation, the Department of State changed its "wait-and-see" policy to an interim position of working with the Military Revolutionary Committee. In a new instruction to the U.S. embassy in Seoul on May 17, Green was asked to accomplish two objectives—"to encourage early emergence of broadly based, responsible nonpartisan government of national unity and of predominantly civilian composition with which we can work constructively and cooperatively in atmosphere of mutual trust" and "to confer on successor government to maximum attainable extent an aura of legality, continuity and legitimate constitutional succession."[123] Whereas the Military Revolutionary Committee made a long-term commitment for accommodating the first objective, it satisfied the second objective by persuading President Yun not to resign from his presidency. Hence the semblance of constitutional continuity was maintained. On May 18 Prime Minister Chang came out of hiding and returned to his office to tender his resignation. His cabinet followed suit. The Military Revolutionary Committee set up a Supreme Council for National Reconstruction (SCNR) with a wide range of legislative and executive powers and enacted a complete reorganization of the government by appointing military officers as cabinet ministers. The sweeping militarization of the South Korean political system was all too apparent. As Green reported to the Department of State, "democratic institutions have suffered a serious setback, some recovery from which can only come as a result of measures as soon as possible to reinstitute government by and of the Korean people."[124] The Kennedy administration assumed that the tough, nationalistic, authoritarian, and determined coup leaders would be less receptive to U.S. guidance and would assert their independence in military, economic, and political affairs.[125]

In his first meeting with General Park on June 9, Green said that the United States accepted the SCNR "as an established government with which it is prepared to work in good faith on [a] friendly and cooperative basis."[126] The normalization of official relations between the U.S. government and the SCNR meant that in less than a month following the coup, the Kennedy administration had no more viable option than to recognize the changing political reality in South Korea. So long as the new military leadership in South Korea upheld a staunch anti-Communist posture, the United States felt that its containment system was protected. For the Kennedy administration, stability was more important than democracy at this moment: the United States had just suffered the Bay of Pigs fiasco; tension with the Soviet Union over Berlin, Laos, Vietnam, and the Congo was growing; and conditions in the Middle East, especially Iran, were becoming unstable. And the U.S. embassy in Seoul was assured that General Park, who replaced General Chang as chairman of the SCNR in July, would carry out his reform agenda and improve relations with Japan.

On November 14 and 15, 1961, General Park Chung Hee, SCNR chairman, had a summit meeting with President John F. Kennedy at the White House.[127] At the outset Kennedy reviewed the current world crises and promised to give Park "the maximum support as possible" in economic assistance. Invited to offer ideas on Vietnam, Park said that "as a firm anti-Communist nation, Korea would do its best to contribute to the security of the Far East" and proposed to send South Korean troops to Vietnam or to recruit volunteers if regular troops were not desired. Saying that there were limits on what an Occidental country could do in Vietnam, Kennedy expressed "deep appreciation" and suggested that Secretary of Defense Robert McNamara and General Lyman L. Lemnitzer, chairman of the Joint Chiefs of Staff, pursue detailed discussions with Chairman Park. It is conceivable that Park's proposal on Vietnam was based on his genuine commitment for regional containment against Communist forces. In view of lingering suspicions about his past record as a pro-Communist military officer, he may have wanted to remove whatever reservations the Kennedy administration might have had about his ideological stand.[128] Moreover, his proposal may have been designed to obtain additional economic assistance from the United States.

At Kennedy's request, Park explained that daily food consumption and civilian living standards in North Korea were low, but also that its basic industries and mineral resources were superior to those of South Korea. He added that the North Korean and South Korean ground forces and navy were about evenly matched—but in air power North Korea was four times as strong. He also emphasized his twin goals: to maintain the present strength of South Korean armed forces and to implement economic reforms and rejuvenation. For this purpose, Park asked for special foreign aid assistance during 1962, but Kennedy responded that such a request would not be reviewed for six months. Park was unable to achieve his objective of receiving a $100 million loan as a special stabilization fund, $70 million from the Development Loan Fund (DLF), and $8 million in technical assistance.[129] In their joint communiqué issued on November 15, the two leaders recognized their common interests as "bulwarks of the free world against Communist expansion." The Kennedy administration embraced General Park's rule to protect the overriding imperative for an anti-Communist containment system, but with the understanding that Park would fulfill his promise to bring about a democratically elected civilian government by the summer of 1963. A month thereafter, U.S. Ambassador Samuel Berger reported to Secretary of State Dean Rusk that the friendly reception of Park Chung Hee during his visit to the United States was perhaps decisive in stabilizing the situation in South Korea. And he made a positive and optimistic report on Park as "a forceful, fair and intelligent leader" who could be trusted to keep the revolution "on the path of decency and moderation."[130] It was indeed extraordinary that the U.S. view on Park underwent such a dramatic transformation in only seven months.

Meanwhile, the North Koreans took the initiative to formalize and strengthen their military ties with the Soviet Union and China in 1961, mainly because they were worried about the new Kennedy administration's aggressive anti-Communist foreign policy as exemplified by the abortive Bay of Pigs invasion and also because they were worried about the adverse spillover effects of the disputes between the Soviet Union and China. Although the Soviet Union had sponsored the DPRK's establishment and sustenance, China had become Kim Il Sung's savior during the Korean War. The Chinese had completed the last phase of the CPV's withdrawal from North Korea in October 1958 but still retained a strong security interest in the Korean Peninsula. The Soviet Union and China continued to assist North Korea in military, economic, and diplomatic affairs. Alarmed by the unmistakable signs of a Sino-Soviet conflict, Kim Il Sung was able to conclude almost identical bilateral defense treaties with the Soviet Union and China in 1961. The two treaties, which went into effect on the same day in September, contained the following provision: "Should either of the Contracting Parties suffer armed attack by any state or coalition of states and thus find itself in a state of war, the other Contracting Party shall immediately extend military and other assistance with all the means at its disposal."[131]

This article, a more direct and categorical commitment than any in the U.S.–South Korean Mutual Defense Treaty, was a carbon copy of Article One of the Sino-Soviet Treaty of Friendship, Alliance and Mutual Assistance. There were a few notable differences, however, between the two treaties signed by Kim Il Sung. Whereas the Soviet–North Korean Treaty referred to the goals and principles of the United Nations, that reference was conspicuously absent in the Sino–North Korean Treaty. Both China and North Korea had fought against the United Nations Command and had been excluded from the world organization. Moreover, the U.N. General Assembly had branded both China and North Korea as aggressors during the Korean War. In contrast to the Soviet–North Korean accord, the Sino–North Korean Treaty emphasized the importance of Marxism-Leninism, proletarian internationalism, and brotherly relations. Compared with their Soviet counterparts, the Chinese espoused a greater sense of stability in their military relations with North Korea. The Soviet–North Korean Treaty stipulated that either party could abrogate the treaty after the initial ten-year period (by giving the other party one year of advance notice every five years), but neither China nor North Korea were allowed to amend or terminate their treaty without mutual consent. The two Korean governments were now fully integrated with the opposing cold war alliance systems. Any attempt for inter-Korean negotiations on security matters was unthinkable. And neither Korean side enjoyed a significant degree of policy autonomy with respect to its powerful external patrons.

In an attempt to consolidate its containment system in the Asia-Pacific region, the United States took every opportunity to achieve the goal of diplomatic and economic normalization between its two Asian allies, South Korea and Japan. It was not necessary for the United States to practice the classic tactic of "divide and rule" for the purpose of controlling both Asian countries, as their respective dependency on American hegemony was unquestionable. On the contrary, the United States strongly believed that the absence of cooperative relations between Seoul and Tokyo was harmful not only to their own national interests but also to Washington's strategic considerations. The U.S. efforts to encourage reconciliation between its two Asian allies had been unsuccessful, however. When Secretary of State Dulles came to Seoul to finalize and initial the U.S.–South Korea Mutual Defense Treaty in August 1953, he told President Rhee that it was necessary for the safety of the western Pacific to have a close and cooperative relationship between South Korea and Japan.[132]

However, Rhee continued to resist the U.S. pressure for improving relations with Japan. As a guest of General Mark Clark, Rhee had met with Japanese Prime Minister Yoshida Shigeru in Tokyo in January 1953. Prodded by General Clark and U.S. Ambassador Robert D. Murphy, Rhee and Yoshida agreed to adopt good-neighborly relations and to resume the bilateral talks that had been suspended for over eight months.[133] Rhee explained to Dulles that the South Koreans were worried more about Japan than the Soviet Union because Japan still clung to its old colonial ideas. In his view, the Japanese were extremely clever in handling Western psychology and would persuade the Americans that Japan needed Korea back, which would build up sympathy in America for Japan. He urged Dulles to force Japan to abandon the idea of reoccupying Korea and to stop building up Japan militarily and economically. Rhee criticized the U.S. policy of using Economic Cooperation Administration (ECA) funds to buy Japanese goods for South Korea's use. As a lifelong champion of the Korean liberation from Japanese colonial rule, he was afraid that if Japan regained its prewar economic capabilities, it might be tempted to control the Korean Peninsula again.

Dulles assured Rhee that "the United States does not want Japan again to become a dominant power any more than the Koreans do" and that the U.S.–South Korean Mutual Defense Treaty would protect South Korea from Japan as well as from the Soviet Union. Dulles emphasized the strategic importance of the anti-Communist arc in the Far East from Korea and Japan to Taiwan, the Philippines, and Indochina. "If that arc can be held and sufficient pressures developed against the Communists," Dulles stated, "it might be possible eventually to overthrow Communist control of the mainland."[134] He said: "However, if any part of that strategic position is lost, the whole position will go under. Since the United States must be concerned with the whole position, it must give its attention to Japan in order for Japan to have a chance to live and not turn to the USSR." The secretary of state suggested to Rhee that he should recognize that keeping the Japanese economy viable and strong was a necessity for South Korean national security. "Otherwise," he warned, "Japan might become Communist, for it would starve without trade with the free world." In essence, Dulles developed logical arguments based on the U.S. anti-Communist strategy in an attempt to prompt cooperation between South Korea and Japan.

Under the auspices of the United States, South Korea and Japan resumed talks for their diplomatic normalization in October 1953. The intermittent negotiations, however, failed to produce any tangible results because of deep-seated mutual mistrust and irreconcilable policy cleavages, especially in the area of financial settlements. The resignation of President Rhee in April 1960 finally enabled the South Korean government, first under Prime Minister Chang Myon and then under General Park Chung Hee, to accelerate its negotiations with Japan. Unlike Rhee, General Park, who had graduated from the Manchurian Military Academy as well as the Japanese Military Academy and had served in the Manchukuo Army, had no intrinsic anti-Japanese sentiments. As an enthusiastic admirer of the Meiji oligarchs' modernization model and a witness of the rapid industrialization in Manchukuo, a Japanese puppet state, Park believed that normal diplomatic and economic relations with Japan would not only assist his ambitious first five-year economic plan but would also strengthen anti-Communist solidarity in East Asia. The Kennedy administration seized upon this new opportunity to mediate the differences between Seoul and Tokyo. In a meeting with Japanese Prime Minister Ikeda Hayato on June 20, 1961, Kennedy suggested that it would be most helpful to bring about diplomatic agreement between Japan and South Korea and that Japanese assistance, particularly for electric power development in South Korea, would be very useful.[135] Ikeda complained that it was difficult to deal with the South Koreans because they were "exclusive and self-willed" but admitted that Japan had "a very vital stake" in Korea. He expressed his willingness to accept the South Korean military government because it was anti-Communist. In his meetings with Ikeda on November 2 and with Park on November 5, Secretary of State Rusk emphasized the importance of Tokyo-Seoul cooperation. On his way to the United States on November 12, Park met with Ikeda in Tokyo and agreed on a general framework for diplomatic and economic normalization between the two countries. They shared a view that the issues of property claims between them should be regarded as a form of economic cooperation rather than as a settlement of longstanding colonial grievances. Park had a separate meeting with Japan's senior conservative leaders Kishi Nobusuke (former prime minister) and Ishii Mitsujiro (speaker of the House of Representatives). And Yasuoka Masahiro, an eminent Confucian scholar and a spiritual leader of Japanese conservative forces, endorsed diplomatic normalization between Japan and South Korea in the interest of anti-Communist solidarity.[136]

Nevertheless, the resumed negotiations between Seoul and Tokyo were less than productive due in part to the domestic political opposition faced by Ikeda and Park. The United States, eager to render assistance to both, became impatient. In National Security Action Memorandum No. 151 (April 24, 1962), President Kennedy stated: "I am concerned over the apparent impasse which has again developed between Japan and South Korea over the issues which they have been discussing for so long. Since these negotiations have been progressing fitfully for over a decade, I believe that we must make every effort to bring them to a prompt and successful conclusion." "While recognizing the need for tactical flexibility as to timing," he continued, "I hope that we can try to keep up momentum toward a settlement, using US good offices to the extent required."[137] In response to this memorandum, the Department of State developed a paper on "Korean-Japanese Relations" on May 17, 1962.[138] The paper argued that it was in the U.S. interest to promote an early settlement of differences between South Korea and Japan for four reasons: (1) rapid South Korean economic development, crucially necessary for stability, would be materially accelerated by Japanese economic aid added to continued U.S. aid; (2) South Korea would gain greater access to Japanese markets for its exports; (3) a significant impediment to Free World unity and strength in Asia would be removed; and (4) South Korean prestige would be bolstered in the increasingly serious competition with North Korea. The paper hoped to persuade both South Korea and Japan that it was in their interest to settle their differences through a realistic and forthcoming attitude and that delay would be contrary to their own interests. The United States intended to help narrow the huge gap between the South Korean request for $700 million in economic assistance and the Japanese offer of $70 million. Calling the Japanese amount unrealistically low, Secretary Rusk reported to President Kennedy that U.S. influence toward a settlement should be exerted more on the Japanese than on the Koreans.[139]

The U.S. pressure paid off in November 1962 when Kim Jong Pil, director of the Korean Central Intelligence Agency and the second most powerful man in South Korea, struck a compromise with Japanese Foreign Minister Ohira Masayoshi in Tokyo. The Kim-Ohira memorandum, dated November 12, 1962, stipulated a ten-year package of Japanese financial commitments—$300 million in grants-in-aid, $200 million in long-term low-interest government loans, and more than $100 million in commercial loans.[140] When Secretary of State Rusk inquired about the highly emotional and sensitive territorial dispute over Tokdo (in Korean) or Takeshima (in Japanese) Island between the two countries, Kim Jong Pil replied that it was only a "place for sea gull droppings." He even suggested to the Japanese that it should be blown up so that this bone of contention could be removed once and for all.[141] Even after this major breakthrough, however, it took two more years for South Korea and Japan to reach a final agreement on all of the other issues on which they disagreed. A number of U.S. officials were instrumental in moving that process forward. Since the South Koreans were suspicious that the United States might reduce its aid to them following diplomatic normalization with Japan, Secretary of State Rusk declared that "the basic policy of the United States military and economic assistance to the Republic of Korea would not be affected by normalization of relations between Korea and Japan."[142] Assistant Secretary of State for Far Eastern Affairs William Bundy recalled that "after I became Assistant Secretary in March of 1964, I did play an active role in mediating between the two nations at the time when they were trying to work out normalization."[143] He took a discreet but purposeful position to encourage reasonable communication between the parties and to convince them that normalization would be constructive if it could be achieved on a mutually agreeable basis. At the same time, he stressed the strategic importance of a Seoul-Tokyo rapprochement in the larger context of U.S. regional and global policy.

After fourteen years of extremely difficult negotiations, the governments of South Korea and Japan on June 22, 1965, signed the seven-article Treaty on Basic Relations and other agreements, protocols, and notes on property claims and economic cooperation, fisheries, cultural assets, and the legal status of Korean residents in Japan.[144] The two sides professed their adherence to the principles of "good neighborliness" and "mutual respect for sovereignty" and agreed to establish diplomatic and consular relations. The disagreement over Tokdo or Takeshima Island remained unresolved, but both sides promised to seek a peaceful settlement. Needless to say, the United States was pleased with the successful consummation of its patient, friendly, and cooperative efforts in cementing the pivotal link of the anti-Communist strategic arc in East Asia.[145]

As an extension of South Korea's participation in the U.S.-led regional containment system, President Park Chung Hee decided to dispatch his armed forces to
South Vietnam in support of the American war effort. The United States sought to
have more non-Communist nations involved in Vietnam, and South Korea was expected to contribute. From its modest beginnings as a group of noncombat troops
for engineering and medical operations in 1964–65, the number of South Korean
marines and other military personnel rose to about 48,000 by the end of 1969.[146] At
a farewell rally for South Korean troops bound for Vietnam in February 1965, Park
defended his decision as "part of our moral responsibility in furtherance of Asia's
collective security."[147] Behind Park's lofty anti-Communist rhetoric, however, was
a rather pragmatic pursuit of South Korea's own security and economic interests.
Park, who had already offered South Korean troops in support of U.S. policy in Vietnam at his meeting with President Kennedy in November 1961, believed that if he
did not send South Korean troops to Vietnam, the United States would transfer at
least one of its two combat divisions from South Korea to Vietnam. The grateful
Johnson administration gladly agreed to underwrite all expenses for South Korea's
military activities in Vietnam and to offer a substantial quantity of military equipment to South Korea. In addition, it decided to procure South Korean supplies and
services for the United States and South Vietnam as much as possible and to increase the loans for South Korean economic programs from the U.S. Agency for
International Development (AID). This commitment reversed a steady decline in
the amount of U.S. economic and military assistance to South Korea in recent years.
Moreover, U.S. leaders reaffirmed their defense obligations for South Korea and
promised not to reduce the number of U.S. troops stationed in South Korea without
prior consultation.

In his visit to Seoul in February 1966, Vice President Hubert H. Humphrey unequivocally stated that "as long as there is one American soldier on . . . the demarcation line, the whole and entire power of the United States of America is committed
to the defense of Korea."[148] After their summit meeting held at Seoul in November
1966, President Lyndon B. Johnson assured President Park that the United States was
determined to render prompt and effective assistance to defeat any North Korean
armed attack against South Korea and that he had no plan to reduce the level of U.S.
forces in Korea.[149] The two presidents agreed to continue their joint military efforts
against the Communist aggression in Vietnam.

At a meeting with President Park in Canberra in December 1967, President
Johnson, who was facing the worsening situation in Vietnam, hoped for a full additional division from South Korea. Citing the National Assembly's filibustering on

the budget, Park said that it would be easier for him to obtain the National Assembly's consent for more troops to Vietnam if the United States made a firm financial commitment. Johnson was prepared to accommodate Park's requests for military and economic assistance and for the timely delivery of a staple of the Korean diet, kimchi, to the troops. Johnson quipped that "the bureaucracy in Washington gave him more hell about the kimchi than it did about the war in Vietnam," but Johnson did manage to get it. In response, Park said that the kimchi would certainly lift the morale of the South Korean troops in Vietnam. Assistant Secretary of State for Far Eastern Affairs William Bundy added that "the problem of canning the kimchi had delayed arrival. It was being sent as fast as possible and the VC [Vietcong] would never be able to hold the Koreans once it arrived."[150] A week after the Canberra meeting, National Security Adviser Walt W. Rostow agreed to support a package of South Korean requests: two destroyers, three helicopter companies, counter-infiltration and counterguerrilla equipment, equipment for eight additional battalions, self-propelled eight-inch Howitzers, a 5,000-man civilian logistics corps in Vietnam (at high pay scales), and a light division of 11,000 men in Vietnam.[151] He did not, however, accept the requests for one F-4 air squadron and heavy equipment for the construction of the Seoul-Pusan superhighway.

Critics in the South Korean National Assembly and in the U.S. Congress contended that Park had agreed to supply and sacrifice South Korean troops solely for economic benefit. In February 1970, Senator J. William Fulbright (D-AK), chairman of the Senate Committee on Foreign Relations, denounced Park's decision as a "good business deal at our request and urging."[152] Others argued that by participating in the anti-Communist crusade in a foreign country, South Korea had gained a reputation as a cold war "mercenary" and increased its isolation in the third world. The North Koreans, together with the Soviets and the Chinese, vigorously attacked Park's decision to commit South Korean troops to Vietnam.

The United States greatly appreciated and generously rewarded South Korea's assistance in Vietnam, but this did not resolve its serious policy disagreement with South Korea in regard to North Korea's renewed militancy in the late 1960s. Not long after President Park requested counter-infiltration equipment from the United States on December 21, 1967, and presided over a highly publicized emergency conference on internal security in Wonju on January 6, 1968, North Korea sent a 31-member commando team to attack the Blue House (President Park's official residence) in Seoul on January 21, 1968. The attack failed to materialize. The United Nations Command hastily called for a meeting of the Military Armistice Commission at Panmunjom. Only two days after the Blue House raid, North Korea seized the USS *Pueblo* in international waters in the East Sea (Sea of Japan) and towed it to Wonsan Harbor. One American sailor died, and Commander Lloyd Bucher decided to surrender without firing a single shot, the first time the U.S. navy had ever done so in its entire history. The North Koreans charged the United States with spying and aggression in violation of their twelve-mile territorial waters. The *Pueblo*'s intelligence-gathering operations along the North Korean coast had been so secret that even U. S. Ambassador to South Korea William Porter had not been informed. Even if the United States had wanted to rescue the *Pueblo*, all twelve U.S. F-4 jet fighters in South Korea were equipped with nuclear payloads. At that time it required at least two hours to replace the nuclear payloads with conventional bombs, but it took only half an hour for the *Pueblo* to be spirited inside North Korean territorial waters. The U.S. aircraft in Japan were too far away.

On January 23, the Johnson administration instructed U.S. Ambassador William Porter to advise the South Korean government "in strongest terms against any attempt at action against North Korea in retaliation for [the] Seoul raid," particularly in light of the added tensions arising from the *Pueblo* seizure.[153] Porter immediately conveyed this message to South Korean Prime Minister Chung Il Kwon. In a meeting with Porter on January 24, President Park complained that while the United States asked North Korea for an apology and the immediate return of the *Pueblo*, it did not demand that North Korea never again undertake raids of any kind into South Korean territory.[154] The angry president urged the United States to launch air strikes on North Korean naval ships along the east coast after first neutralizing the North's air power, expressing his willingness to cooperate in such a venture. He also said that he would like to strike and eliminate the six centers of North Korean commandos. However, he promised not to undertake unilateral reprisals against North Korea — yet.

In the UNC's assessment of the two incidents, North Korea had the original objectives of diverting efforts from Vietnam, harassing South Korean economic development, encouraging South Korean revolutionaries, and achieving unification on their terms. The UNC agreed with the Park government that North Korea had intended to foment a split between the two allies.[155] The Johnson administration weighed the lessons learned from the Cuban Missile Crisis and carefully considered a wide range of options for retaliatory action against North Korea. The options included launching air and naval strikes against selected targets, seizing or sinking North Korean ships at sea, mining Wonsan Harbor or other North Korean harbors, blocking all coastal ocean-going traffic, destroying a North Korean outpost along the DMZ and capturing the garrison, asking Japan to impose economic sanctions against North Korea, urging the South Koreans to seize a Soviet hydrologic ship as a counterhostage, and letting the South Koreans take offensive action across the DMZ.

When asked for advice, former president Dwight Eisenhower proposed to bomb the bridges over the Yalu River and to consider dropping atomic bombs on North Korea. He did not see much danger of a nuclear war arising over this crisis.[156]

In the end, however, President Johnson overruled President Park's request for reprisals against North Korea and decided not to escalate the tensions in Korea, mainly because he could not afford a second military front in Asia. He also feared that retaliatory action would make it more difficult to secure the release of the *Pueblo* and the crew. Secretary of State Dean Rusk felt that, in response to U.S. military retaliation, the North Koreans might execute the crew of the *Pueblo*.[157] The Department of State was sensitive to the mutual defense treaties that North Korea had signed with the Soviet Union and China because it assumed that the seizure of the *Pueblo* was undertaken with the consent of both of its Communist allies. This assessment completely ignored that the incident coincided with the worst period of the Pyongyang-Beijing relationship (1967–68) and that China was at the height of its chaotic Cultural Revolution. While the CIA disputed China's role in the *Pueblo* case, it did recognize the possibility of collusion between North Korea and the Soviet Union to divert U.S. attention and forces from Vietnam.

On January 26, President Johnson stated that "we shall continue to use every means available to find a prompt and peaceful solution to the problem."[158] The United States called about fifteen thousand reservists to active service, sent its nuclear-powered aircraft carrier (USS *Enterprise*) with its 90 planes toward Korea, and brought F-105s to Osan Air Base in South Korea. At an emergency session of the U.N. Security Council, U.S. Ambassador Arthur Goldberg assailed the forcible seizure of the *Pueblo* as a "knowing and willful aggressive act" in violation of the Korean Armistice Agreement, the United Nations Charter, and international law, but expressed the U.S. intention to settle the matter peacefully by diplomatic means.[159] The United States did not introduce a resolution to condemn the North Korean actions at the U.N. Security Council because of the anticipated Soviet veto. The Security Council adopted a mild Canadian proposal to recommend a private discussion among members, but no important outcome was made. Much to Park's chagrin, the United States sought to gain the release of the crew and the ship through direct bilateral negotiations at the Military Armistice Commission, which started on February 1 in Panmunjom. The United States considered whether it should refer the case to the International Court of Justice, but decided against it because North Korea was expected to reject it. President Johnson also asked for assistance from the Soviet Union, U.N. Secretary General U Thant, and the Neutral Nations Supervisory Commission in Korea and requested the International Red Cross to intercede on behalf of the captured crew.

There emerged a sharp divergence in perceptions and priorities between the United States and South Korea. Whereas the Johnson administration was preoccupied with the status of the *Pueblo* crew and feared a potentially explosive crisis in the event of retaliation against North Korea, the South Koreans were more concerned about the commando raid aimed at the Blue House, after all a national symbol, and at President Park himself and were confident that North Korea was not prepared to counter any U.S. or South Korean punitive action. They also felt marginalized because they were excluded from the Panmunjom negotiations. They were not reassured by Secretary of State Rusk's statement that "North Korea will make a grave error if it interprets our restraint as a lack of determination or deludes itself into thinking that the American commitment to defend the Republic of Korea has weakened in the slightest."[160] In the aftermath of the Tet offensive, in which North Vietnamese and Vietcong forces entered Saigon and seized Hue (an ancient capital) toward the end of January, the Johnson administration was unwilling and unable to escalate the crisis in Korea.

In order to counteract Park's extreme frustration and suspicions about America's reliability as a security guarantor, Johnson told the South Korean president in a letter dated February 3, 1968, that he would give his "personal attention" to new ways in which North Korean infiltration could be met.[161] In his response, Park argued that "the Communists should be taught a lesson that any aggressive action cannot escape due punitive action."[162] This stern lecture, of course, did not impress President Johnson. Nor was he prepared to teach a lesson to North Korea through military means. Even though Secretary of State Rusk understood the South Koreans to be "an especially sensitive people," he was frustrated with their continuing suspicions about America's basic motives and purposes. In a telegram to the U.S. embassy in Seoul in February 1968, he stated: "We have invested over 33,000 battle deaths, 20,000 non-battle deaths, and over 100,000 wounded in the security of an independent Republic of Korea. We have maintained large forces in that country for 17 years. We have invested over six billion dollars (almost half the total Marshall Plan) in economic and military assistance. . . . You should find ways to make it clear that Korean suspicion against this record is simply incomprehensible to the American people. The danger is that it will be deeply resented back here with potentially disastrous results for both countries."[163]

For further discussions with Park, President Johnson sent former deputy secretary of defense Cyrus R. Vance, a methodical lawyer, as his special envoy to Seoul on February 11 through 15. In his two meetings with Park, which lasted about seven hours, Vance made it clear that the United States attached as much importance to the Blue House raid as to the *Pueblo* seizure and that it was impossible to have a

South Korean presence in the private meetings over the *Pueblo* issue between the United States and North Korea because of the latter's absolute objection.[164] More important, he confidentially explained to Park that the immediate release of the *Pueblo* and the crew was "a very serious matter" on the American domestic political scene. The South Korean president was in effect being asked to cooperate with U.S. negotiations with North Korea because the early resolution of the *Pueblo* matter would help Johnson's reelection, which Park favored. Park promised not to undertake unilateral retaliatory actions against North Korea at this time, but he warned Vance that he might be compelled to punish North Korea in the event of another armed provocation. When Prime Minister Chung Il Kwon mentioned that the National Assembly might force his government to withdraw South Korean troops from Vietnam, Vance told him flatly that "we would reciprocate by withdrawing our troops from Korea."[165] The Vance mission confirmed an additional $100 million aid package for South Korea, which augmented $400 million already committed for annual military and economic assistance. F-4 fighter planes would be provided to counter North Korea's MiG-21s, and Vance also promised to supply small arms, including M-16 rifles, for South Korea's National Reserve Forces. The two sides agreed to initiate annual meetings between the U.S. secretary of defense and the South Korean minister of national defense to discuss and consult on defense and security matters of mutual interest and common concern.

In a memorandum submitted to President Johnson on February 20, Vance reported that President Park partially blamed the United States for the Blue House raid because North Korean commandos had infiltrated the DMZ area, which was defended by U.S. forces. He added: "Highly emotional, volatile, frustrated and introspective, Park wanted to obtain from me a pledge for the United States to join his Government in instant, punitive, and retaliatory actions against North Korea in the event of another Blue House raid or comparable attack on some other important South Korean economic, governmental, or military facility. He wanted my assurance of an "automatic" U.S. response in the event of another serious raid against the ROK. I refused to give any such assurances." This description of Park's personality and policy was remarkably similar to Robertson's characterization of President Rhee fifteen years earlier. Vance refused to modify the Mutual Defense Treaty and accept a long shopping list of expensive military equipment worth $1.5 billion from South Korea. He also emphasized the provocative nature of recent South Korean armed infiltrations across the DMZ into North Korea—about twice per month in 1967. In this sense, the report observed that in both Koreas there were few "doves" or "hawks"— most appeared to be "tigers." It concluded: "President Park personally assured me that he would not withdraw any ROK forces [from Vietnam]. I in turn reassured the

[South] Koreans that the obligation of the United States under the Mutual Security Treaty would be met."[166]

The Vance-Park agreement was reconfirmed at the summit meeting between Presidents Johnson and Park in Honolulu on April 17.[167] However, Park opposed Johnson's decision to halt bombing in North Vietnam and to seek a negotiated settlement of the Vietnam War with Hanoi. Since he had developed a good and trustworthy working relationship with Johnson, Park was upset about Johnson's sudden announcement not to seek reelection mainly due to the further deterioration of his positions both in Vietnam and at home. Aside from South Korea's exclusion from the secret negotiations between the United States and North Korea in regard to the *Pueblo* issue, Park was concerned that in the negotiations at Panmunjom, the United States might become too soft on North Korea, recognize the legitimacy of the North Korean regime, and go too far in the direction of making an apology to North Korea. He explained to Johnson that contrary to his earlier commitment made in Canberra, it would now be difficult for him to obtain the National Assembly's consent to send a light division of 11,000 persons to Vietnam, despite the initial implementation of additional U.S. military assistance. The circumstances in the Korean Peninsula had changed after the Blue House raid and the *Pueblo* seizure. Now Park was convinced that North Korea wanted to create a second Vietnam in South Korea and that the South Korean army should strengthen its defense in rear areas. Unlike the earlier Johnson-Park joint communiqué (1966), the text of the Johnson-Park joint communiqué issued on April 17, 1968, did not include the U.S. promise not to reduce the number of its troops stationed in South Korea. Moreover, the United States rejected a number of demands made by Park: (1) to strike out the provision "in accordance with its constitutional process" in Article Three of the U.S.–South Korean Mutual Defense Treaty so that the United States can commit "immediate and automatic intervention" for South Korea's defense in the event of external armed attack; (2) to include guerrilla infiltrations such as the Blue House raid in the term "external armed attack"; and (3) to transfer the U.S. command authority over the South Korean troops deployed near the DMZ to the South Korean government.[168]

After twenty-eight long, acrimonious, and tortuous meetings with his North Korean counterpart at Panmunjom over eleven months, General Gilbert H. Woodward at last agreed to accept the document prepared by the North Koreans in December 1968. In the document, the United States admitted that the *Pueblo* had illegally intruded into North Korean territorial waters, apologized for the "grave acts of espionage" committed by the *Pueblo* against North Korea, gave firm assurances that no U.S. ships would again intrude into North Korean territorial waters, and asked for North Korea's lenient treatment of the *Pueblo* crew.[169] This amounted to total capitulation to the North Korean demands. On December 23, General Woodward wrote on the document an acknowledgment of the receipt of the *Pueblo* crew. Exactly eleven months after their surrender and just before Christmas, eighty-two *Pueblo* crew members headed by Commander Bucher, carrying one dead body, crossed the Bridge of No Return in Panmunjom. The *Pueblo* itself was not returned. As soon as the crew was released, the United States resorted to a clever ploy to disavow the document by insisting that all General Woodward had done was acknowledge the receipt of the crew, not the contents of the document. The admission of guilt as well as the apology by Woodward were publicly disavowed.

The United States had earlier considered a number of methods, including intercepting North Korean fishing vessels being constructed in Rotterdam, to secure the return of the *Pueblo,* but no action was taken. It decided to decommission *Pueblo*-type ships that could not defend themselves in international waters and to assign intelligence-gathering missions to destroyers and other vessels equipped with self-defense capabilities. The whole *Pueblo* saga was a painful, disgraceful, and ominous experience for the United States that the incoming Nixon administration could not help but notice. In fact, Nixon, during his presidential campaign, criticized the *Pueblo* incident as an example of the Johnson administration's failure in foreign affairs. While the North Koreans celebrated their "victory" against the most powerful nation in the world in seizing the *Pueblo* with impunity, the South Koreans were dismayed that the United States failed to counter North Korea's illegal activities and shrewd manipulations and that North Korea was not punished for the Blue House raid.

On the day the *Pueblo* crew members were freed, the Senior Interdepartmental Group (SIG) chaired by Undersecretary of State Nicholas Katzenbach submitted a status report on "Review of United States Policy Toward Korea" to President Johnson.[170] It succinctly identified the objectives of U.S. policy toward Korea: to keep South Korea out of hostile hands; to reduce the probability of large-scale North-South hostilities; to maintain a stable compromise among the great powers with interests in Korea; to increase South Korea's ability to defend itself; to promote South Korean economic and political development; and to encourage a greater Japanese contribution to South Korean security and prosperity. It stated: "There must be no question about the strength and importance of our commitment to the security of South Korea in the face of an aggressive adversary. But as time goes by, it *is* appropriate to reconsider the question of whether our present posture decided many years ago is still an optimal one for meeting our commitment." More specifically, the status report raised a number of questions, including: Was the U.S. combat presence (50,000 troops), fifteen years after the Korean War, an irreplaceable element of deterrence against North Korean attack? How much of a South Korean defense was needed to replace U.S. forces, and what would it cost? What would be the effect of a U.S. troop withdrawal from South Korea on the American position in Asia? To what extent was a "trade-off" between U.S. and South Korean forces compatible with American objectives for South Korean political stability and development? These questions were left for the new Nixon administration to answer. Of course, there was no way for the South Koreans to foresee that the Katzenbach report, along with National Security Action Memorandum No. 298 (May 5, 1964), which had explored the possible redeployment of one of the two U.S. divisions from South Korea, would sow the seeds of a drastic structural change in U.S.–South Korean military relations in the 1970s.[171]

CHAPTER THREE

The Dynamics of Structural Adjustment

From Nixon to Carter

The structure of relations between the United States and South Korea shifted dramatically in the period from the beginning of the Nixon administration (January 1969) to the end of the Carter presidency (January 1981) and required a significant change in each country's policy toward the other. As a result of its costly and ill-fated entanglement in the Vietnam War, the United States began to reassess the conceptual foundations and policy prescriptions of its traditional containment system in the Asia-Pacific region. The momentum for this reassessment was accelerated under President Richard M. Nixon, who sought an honorable exit from the Vietnam quagmire and pursued a policy of détente toward China and, to a lesser extent, toward the Soviet Union. According to Henry Kissinger, Nixon did not accept the Wilsonian assumptions about the essential goodness of man but divided the world between friends and antagonists. "In Nixon's perception," Kissinger explained, "peace and harmony were not the natural order of things but temporary oases in a perilous world where stability could only be preserved by vigilant effort."[1] Like Theodore Roosevelt, he counted on a balance of power for international stability and recognized the realistic requirements for U.S. security policy in the world.

For this purpose Nixon developed a new strategic idea known as the Guam Doctrine and used it to call for the reduction of the U.S. military presence on South Korea. In response, the South Korean government under President Park Chung Hee attempted to preserve the integrity of its alliance system with the United States as much as possible while attempting to increase its self-reliant military capabilities and adapt its foreign policy to the rapidly changing international situation. Drawing on South Korea's advantageous position due to its growing economic and technological strength, Park initiated a lessening of tensions with North Korea. He also re-sorted to the controversial step of suspending elements of the constitution in a ref-erendum that solidified and extended his domestic power, despite opposition from Washington.

After an uncertain and unstable two-year interregnum under President Gerald R. Ford, President Jimmy Carter, coming to power in a post-Vietnam era, inherited the basic framework of the Guam Doctrine. His idealistic perspective, with its para-mount emphasis on championing human rights, led to diplomatic friction with many countries that had formerly enjoyed military ties or friendly relations with the United States. The Korean Peninsula was no exception to Carter's policy. The Park government vigorously resisted the triple challenges from the Carter administra-tion—(1) the planned withdrawal of U.S. forces from Korea; (2) the wide-ranging investigations of the Koreagate scandals; and (3) the intensifying external pressure to correct the violations of human rights and institute free and democratic norms. In the end, the friction between the United States and South Korea formed a backdrop for the assassination of President Park in 1979. The ensuing political turmoil in South Korea presented to the United States a host of new problems, ranging from the coup d'état and the ascendancy of General Chun Doo Hwan to the violent up-rising at Kwangju and the persecution of a leading dissident, Kim Dae Jung. Hence alliance cohesion and diplomatic cooperation between the United States and South Korea were severely tested.

THE GUAM DOCTRINE

In his inaugural address on January 20, 1969, Richard M. Nixon declared: "The greatest honor history can bestow is the title of peacemaker. This honor now beck-ons America—the chance to help lead the world at last out of the valley of turmoil and onto that high ground of peace that man has dreamed of since the dawn of civ-ilization."[2] Like Dwight D. Eisenhower with the Korean War, Nixon was determined to fulfill his campaign promise for achieving "peace with honor" in the Vietnam War. Even before his new administrative staff was fully constituted, however, Nixon's search for the title of peacemaker faced an imminent and formidable obstacle—not from Vietnam but from Korea. On April 14, 1969, two North Korean MiG aircraft shot down an unarmed four-engine propeller-driven reconnaissance airplane (EC-121) with thirty-one crew members about ninety miles southeast of Chongjin, far beyond North Korea's claimed airspace. The airplane's main mission was to gather intelli-gence about troop movements and dispositions in North Korea and to issue an alert in the event of a surprise attack. The new Nixon administration found this major international crisis a little too reminiscent of the Bay of Pigs fiasco at the beginning of the Kennedy presidency for comfort. In view of Nixon's well-publicized earlier anti-Communist crusades, the South Koreans fully expected that Nixon would respond much more forcefully to the North Korean provocation than his predecessor had done during the *Pueblo* crisis a year earlier.

In response to the EC-121 disaster, the U.S. Department of Defense immediately suspended all reconnaissance flights over the Soviet Union, China, Cuba, and the Mediterranean Sea. Suddenly the United States faced a dilemma: Retaliation against North Korea could lead to a second war, at a time when Nixon was hoping to seek a negotiated settlement of the Vietnam War. If, however, Nixon did not retaliate at all, it could send the wrong message to Pyongyang, Hanoi, and other adversaries and raise questions about his political will and diplomatic skills. He weighed a number of options—a verbal protest at Panmunjom, air strikes on North Korean military installations, mining Wonsan Harbor, torpedoing a North Korean naval vessel, and seizing a North Korean merchant ship at sea. Inclined toward the latter, he quickly discovered that at that moment there were no North Korean merchant ships at sea. On the consensus recommendations of Secretary of State William P. Rogers, Secretary of Defense Melvin Laird, and CIA Director Richard Helms, Nixon chose not to take any military action at all against North Korea. His earlier criticisms of Johnson's ineptitude during the *Pueblo* incident would come back to haunt him.

He instructed the Department of Defense to resume reconnaissance flights and to escort them with fighter aircraft and sent two aircraft carriers to the East Sea (Sea of Japan). In a display of toughness and resolve, Nixon also ordered intense bombing of North Vietnamese sanctuaries in Cambodia. At the Military Armistice Commission meeting in Panmunjom on April 17, the United States characterized North Korea's destruction of the EC-121 as an "unprovoked attack" and a "calculated act of aggression" and asked North Korea to take "appropriate measures" to prevent similar incidents in the future.[3] The United States, however, did not even demand an apology or compensation from North Korea and refrained from threatening inevitable retaliation in the event of another "calculated act of aggression." Henry A. Kissinger, assistant to the president for national security affairs, who had favored punitive action against North Korea, complained that Nixon had "no stomach for retaliation" and that America's "weak, indecisive, and disorganized" reaction emboldened adversaries and demoralized friends.[4] The North Koreans had tested and exposed the weakness of Nixon's foreign policy with impunity, and South Koreans were dismayed by what they perceived as America's timidity and cautious policy of self-restraint, which had continued unabated since the Johnson era. They felt that Nixon's inaction would only further encourage North Korean militancy, and they seriously questioned whether the United States, bogged down in the Vietnam War and facing a growing erosion of its global influence, would be willing and able to defend South Korea in the event of an external armed attack.

In the aftermath of the EC-121 tragedy, Nixon issued National Security Study Memorandum 53 on April 26, 1969, in which he directed that "a full range of military contingency plans be prepared in the event of future provocations by North Korea." He instructed that Secretary of Defense Laird submit such plans to him within two weeks and that the NSC Interagency Korean Coordinating Committee meet to consider a range of political and military options.[5] The specific options adopted by the Interagency Korean Coordinating Committee under the direction of Kissinger remain confidential, but the Nixon administration was presumably better prepared to meet another military crisis with North Korea.

Once the furor over the EC-121 incident died down, Nixon articulated his vision of the strategic requirements in the Asia-Pacific region. On his way to Southeast Asia, he stopped over in Guam, and at a press conference on July 25, 1969, he stated that the threat to peace in Asia was presented by the growing power of China and the belligerence of North Korea and North Vietnam, but that Japan, South Korea, Taiwan, Thailand, Singapore, and Malaysia had achieved a high rate of economic growth.[6] The United States would keep its treaty commitments, he promised, but as far as the problem of internal security and military defense was concerned (except for the threat of a major power involving nuclear weapons), "the United States is going to expect that this problem will be increasingly handled by, and the responsibility for it taken by, the Asian nations themselves." He did not wish to be "dragged into conflicts such as the one that we have in Vietnam." In five to ten years, he envisioned a system of collective security for "free Asian nations." Nixon's successful presidential campaign was due in large part to his instinctive understanding that the American people had wearied of their military overreach in Asia, and his long experience in Asian affairs led him to surmise correctly that the ideal of self-defense would strike a chord with Asia's proud nationalistic leaders. The doctrine enunciated at Guam became a cornerstone of Nixon's policy toward Korea and the rest of Asia.

At his summit meetings with Nixon in San Francisco on August 21 and 22, 1969, President Park publicly expressed support for the Guam Doctrine, especially Nixon's emphasis on "Asia for Asians" and on the spirit of self-determination and self-reliance. In welcoming Park, Nixon stated that "the Republic of Korea maintains armed forces that are strong enough to assume the major share of the responsibility for defending Korea against the threat from the North." Park responded that "superior strength" was the only way to restore peace in Korea and advocated the "principle of responsive actions" in dealing with the Communists.[7] This was an indirect criticism of Nixon's handling of the EC-121 incident. When Nixon, embarrassed by a group of demonstrators with placards protesting Park's visit and the Vietnam War, assured Park that they did not represent the "silent majority" in the United States, Park responded that he did not know English and had assumed that the demonstrators had come out to welcome him.[8] It is important to note that Park had not treated Nixon well in September 1966 during his visit to Seoul as a private citizen; Park had refused to host dinner or lunch for Nixon but had briefly received him at the Blue House over tea.[9]

The joint statement signed by Nixon and Park on August 21 made it clear that South Korean forces and U.S. troops stationed in Korea must remain strong and alert and that they reaffirmed the determination of their governments to meet any armed attack against South Korea in accordance with the Mutual Defense Treaty.[10] The joint statement, however, failed to mention earlier U.S. commitments—prompt and effective assistance in defending South Korea and no reduction in the number of U.S. forces stationed in Korea. However, Park left San Francisco with the belief that Nixon, despite his plan for Vietnamization, would not withdraw U.S. troops from South Korea so long as South Korean troops remained in Vietnam and that if he eventually decided to do so, it would only take place after full consultation with South Korea in advance. Park was also confident that the summit meeting had mustered support for his plan to amend the South Korean constitution so that he would be allowed to run for the four-year term of the presidency more than twice.[11]

President Park's positive impressions of the summit meeting turned out to be short-lived, for his misperception of Nixon's intentions soon became apparent.[12] In December 1969 the Nixon administration suddenly informed South Korean Ambassador Kim Dong Jo that plans for a phased reduction of U.S. forces in South Korea were in the works. When he heard this disquieting information, President Park set up a special committee to address this urgent issue.[13] The committee, which met in February 1970, included the prime minister, the ministers of national defense and foreign affairs, the chairman of the Joint Chiefs of Staff, and the director of the Korean Central Intelligence Agency. On March 20, 1970, Henry Kissinger transmitted Nixon's top-secret National Security Decision Memorandum 48 to the secretaries of State and Defense, the chairman of the Joint Chiefs of Staff, and other relevant persons.[14] This document spelled out Nixon's decision to reduce the U.S. military presence in South Korea by 20,000 personnel by the end of fiscal year 1971 and to relocate the remaining forces away from the DMZ, and it directed that consultation be undertaken with President Park to inform him of U.S. intentions and to explore the timing and conditions of withdrawal. Nixon planned to provide U.S. military assistance to South Korea over a five-year period at a level of $200 million per year on average and to increase U.S. economic assistance to South Korea. The Department of Defense was directed to develop a five-year plan to evaluate the feasibility and timing of even further reductions in the U.S. military presence in South Korea.

When the United States formally notified the South Korean government of Nixon's decision on the following day, Park felt betrayed and abandoned because he assumed all along that South Korea had cemented "special relations" with the United States by participating in the Vietnam War and because he had repeatedly been promised a U.S. commitment for mutual military cooperation. Even though Park was not entirely taken by surprise by Nixon's decision, he was particularly outraged because Nixon had come to this decision unilaterally and then had conveyed it to South Korea as a fait accompli. The timing was especially unfavorable for Park, who expected to face a tough challenge from one of the three young, energetic, and popular opposition leaders (Kim Dae Jung, Kim Young Sam, and Lee Chul Sung) in the forthcoming presidential election in 1971. Meeting with U.S. Ambassador William Porter, Park argued that the United States had no right to withdraw its troops from South Korea because Article Four of the Mutual Defense Treaty required their "mutual agreement" before determining the disposition of U.S. forces in South Korea.[15]

The South Korean government launched an all-out campaign to reverse or at least postpone Nixon's decision. High-level South Korean officials painted an alarming scenario. Prime Minister Chung Il Kwon warned that the entire South Korean cabinet could resign in protest and that South Korean troops would not be able to fill the gap left by the departing U.S. forces in the DMZ. While South Korean Ambassador Kim Dong Jo even hinted at an early withdrawal of South Korean troops from Vietnam, the South Korean National Assembly unanimously adopted a resolution urging Nixon to reconsider his decision. Minister of National Defense Jung Nae Hyok went so far as to place a large advertisement in the September 25, 1970, edition of the *Washington Post* arguing against the withdrawal of U.S. troops. The South Koreans contended that since North Korea enjoyed military superiority over South Korea, the withdrawal of U.S. troops would substantially increase the North Korean threat against South Korea. They suggested that if the United States waited to withdraw its troops from South Korea until after the completion of its third five-year economic development plan in 1976, South Korea would be in a better position to defend itself. As a compromise, they even proposed that the United States withdraw two brigades from one division and one brigade from the other rather than an entire infantry division from South Korea so that South Korean troops could replace them under U.S. command.[16]

South Korea's negative reaction to Nixon's announcement placed the U.S. government in a very uncomfortable position and undermined the foundation of their mutual confidence as well as the very integrity of their alliance system. In response the United States argued that South Korea already possessed sufficient self-defense capabilities and that the combined strength of South Korean forces and the remaining American troops would provide an effective deterrent against North Korean military incursions. Once the South Koreans were convinced that Nixon would not alter his decision, they took up another agenda—to extract significant U.S. assistance (about $4 billion) for their military modernization program and to prevent further U.S. troop reductions. After a series of acrimonious negotiations and high-level exchanges of leaders between Washington and Seoul, the United States and South Korea agreed on a framework for withdrawal on February 6, 1971.[17] The United States was scheduled to withdraw the Seventh Infantry Division (20,000 troops) from South Korea by June 1971 and to reposition the Second Infantry Division and other U.S. troops away from the DMZ. The tripwire effect of the U.S. military presence in South Korea was to be greatly diminished. In return, the United States agreed to provide a package of $1.5 billion in military aid to South Korea over a five-year period. The Nixon administration promptly withdrew the Seventh Infantry Division, but it took seven years for the United States to complete the delivery of its $1.5 billion of aid. In August 1971, Secretary of Defense Laird issued a Program Decision Memorandum to reduce the Second Infantry Division to one brigade by the end of fiscal year 1974; a year later, the target date was extended to the end of 1975.[18] Yet this plan ended up being cancelled because of opposition by Henry Kissinger, pro-Seoul legislators, and U.S. military officials. Stung by Nixon's substantive policy reversals and procedural insensitivities, Park turned to lessening South Korea's dependency on its unreliable U.S. defense commitment. He determined more firmly than ever to accelerate his military modernization plans and to initiate a new program for missile and nuclear development. Even though the United States made it clear that the continued presence of South Korean forces in Vietnam was not linked to possible U.S. redeployments from South Korea, Park began to withdraw South Korean troops from Vietnam in 1972, completing their withdrawal in 1973; South Korean casualties numbered just short of 16,000, including 4,960 dead and 10,962 wounded.[19]

NIXON'S CHINA POLICY

While carrying out plans to withdraw U.S. troops from both South Korea and South Vietnam in the spring of 1971, Nixon was also fashioning a grandiose archi-

tecture for changing the regional and global balance of power. When Nixon triumphantly announced on July 15, 1971, that Kissinger had secretly met with Chinese Premier Zhou Enlai in Beijing and that Nixon had accepted Zhou's invitation to visit China "at an appropriate date before May 1972," Park Chung Hee was
undoubtedly stunned by the dramatic transformation of the U.S. containment policy in the Asia-Pacific region. The U.S. opening of China was predicated on Nixon
and Kissinger's underlying assumption that the United States needed to adjust its
policy to the Chinese reality and, in so doing, to restructure the international order. They explained that the isolation of one-fourth of the human race did not reflect the emerging multipolar world and tended to reinforce China's own sense of
insecurity.[20] "There could be no stable world order if one of the major powers remained outside it and antagonistic toward it," Nixon insisted. In fact, Nixon
planned to cultivate and support China as a strategic counterweight to the Soviet
Union. It was a classic realist ploy to play one power off against another. He believed that China's understanding and cooperation would help his efforts to end
the Vietnam War, to apply the Guam Doctrine to Korea, and to moderate Japan's
increasingly uncooperative economic policy toward the United States. It seems
likely that Nixon viewed his China initiative as a major foreign policy achievement
during his presidency that he could tout as an outstanding accomplishment during
his reelection campaign.

On the same day that Nixon made his announcement, Zhou Enlai secretly traveled to Pyongyang to brief Kim Il Sung on the Kissinger visit and returned to Beijing
late in the evening.[21] He had already visited Hanoi two days earlier. Yet Kim could
not resist the temptation to characterize Nixon as visiting China carrying a "white
flag," implying the defeat of U.S. policy toward Asia. Once the initial shock of Nixon's
announcement wore off, a new pattern of political realism emerged in South Korea.
Briefed by a Kissinger aide, the South Korean Ministry of Foreign Affairs officially
praised Nixon's China visit and suggested that as a result of U.S.-Chinese accommodation, China would now constrain North Korea's aggressive intentions. Hence
South Korea conspicuously refrained from its customary denunciation of China's
"aggressiveness."[22] In his testimony before the National Assembly, Foreign Minister
Kim Yong Shik asserted that the United States would not discuss the Korean question with China without advance consultation with Seoul.

On September 21, Foreign Minister Kim met Secretary of State William Rogers
in Washington.[23] Anticipating China's vigorous promotion of North Korean interests and positions, Kim urged that Nixon should neither discuss any questions directly relevant to South Korea's sovereignty and security nor diminish the importance of the U.S.–South Korean military alliance in his meetings with Chinese

leaders. Rogers agreed to Kim's suggestions. In response to similar concerns voiced by President Park, Nixon made the following clarification on November 29:

> You can be sure, Mr. President, that in taking steps toward the goal of a peaceful Asia, the United States will not overlook the interest of its allies and friends nor seek any accommodations at their expense. My talks in Peking will not deal with issues primarily involving third countries, but rather will be concerned with bilateral issues between the United States and the People's Republic of China. Should issues affecting Korea be raised by the People's Republic of China, I will of course affirm our strong ties with the Republic of Korea. . . . The United States will continue to consult closely with your Government on issues which affect the security of the Korean Peninsula.[24]

In addition, Nixon assured Park that "the United States does not now have plans for the withdrawal of additional troops stationed in your country" and that "before deciding on additional force reductions in the Republic of Korea, we will consult fully with you and will undertake with you a joint assessment of any threat to your country's security." Secretary of State Rogers instructed U.S. Ambassador Philip Habib to deliver Nixon's letter to Park in person. Habib was to use this letter to assuage Park's "sensibilities" because Nixon was unable to accept Park's proposal for a summit meeting prior to his China visit. Rogers said that as a way for Park to save face, however, he could publicize the receipt of the personal letter of assurances from Nixon.[25] This took place at the time when Park invoked emergency measures (on October 15 and December 6) to suppress growing opposition to his leadership and to strengthen his domestic power base in dealing with the rapidly changing external environment.

At their summit meetings in February 1972, Nixon and Zhou had "extensive, earnest, and frank discussions" on a wide range of international issues and agreed that "neither should seek hegemony in the Asia-Pacific region and each is opposed to efforts by any country or group of countries to establish such hegemony." In the joint communiqué issued with Nixon in Shanghai on February 27, 1972, Zhou endorsed North Korean proposals for achieving peaceful Korean reunification and for abolishing the United Nations Commission for the Unification and Rehabilitation of Korea (UNCURK).[26] The status of the United Nations Command in South Korea, which North Korea vociferously opposed, was not even mentioned. Nixon made it clear, however, that the United States would maintain close ties with South Korea and support South Korea's efforts "to seek a relaxation of tension and increased communication in the Korean Peninsula." According to Kissinger's report, Mao and Zhou specifically disavowed any Chinese threat against Japan and South Korea and did not ask Nixon to withdraw U.S. forces from South Korea.[27] Nixon and Mao agreed in principle that China would do nothing to exacerbate the situation in Indochina or Korea and that neither China nor the United States should allow the Soviet Union to dominate Asia. Kissinger called this emerging relationship a "de facto alliance."[28]

The Chinese had been more tactful toward their allies (North Korea and North Vietnam) than the United States had been toward South Korea and Japan. While Zhou Enlai himself, after his one-day trip to Hanoi, visited Pyongyang to hold discussions with Kim Il Sung for three days, Nixon only sent the much lower-ranking Marshall Green (assistant secretary of state for East Asian and Pacific affairs) and John Holdridge (one of Kissinger's aides) to Seoul to brief Foreign Minister Kim.[29] Even though Green had not even attended any important bilateral meetings during Nixon's China visit, he assured the South Koreans that in his discussions with Zhou Enlai, Nixon had firmly supported South Korea's positions and that they had reached no agreement or understanding harmful to South Korea's national interests. Afterwards, the South Korean Ministry of Foreign Affairs released a press statement expressing satisfaction with Green's report.[30] On Kim's recommendation, President Park reluctantly agreed to see Green, who was less than welcome because he had opposed the coup d'état in May 1961.

The rapid unfolding of Sino-American rapprochement had an unsettling effect on both Park Chung Hee and Kim Il Sung. Although they had been enemies for years, they felt compelled to take the unprecedented step of opening a dialogue between Seoul and Pyongyang. They were both equally suspicious of the dynamics of big-power diplomacy, which they felt might undermine their vital national interests. Each leader recognized a need to reorganize his political system and to reorient his policies in accordance with the new external environments. Just a month after Kissinger's secret visit to China, Choi Tu Sun, president of the South Korean Red Cross, proposed to his North Korean counterpart that they begin negotiating to reunite the estimated ten million family members separated since the end of the Korean War. He was surprised by North Korea's immediate acceptance. Representatives from each side held meetings in Seoul and Pyongyang, but negotiations became deadlocked. In the aftermath of Nixon's China visit, however, the two Korean governments secretly sent their top leaders (Lee Hu Rak, director of the South Korean Central Intelligence Agency, and Pak Song Chol, North Korea's second vice premier) to each other's capital and announced a joint communiqué on July 4, 1972. The South Korean government had notified the U.S. embassy in Seoul of the communiqué a few days earlier.

The two sides agreed to seek a peaceful and independent unification of Korea "without being subject to external imposition and interference" and to realize national unity by transcending "differences in ideas, ideologies, and systems."[31] They also pledged to end armed provocations, to promote various exchange programs, and to set up a hotline between Seoul and Pyongyang. A promise was made to ensure the early success of the Red Cross talks. The new North-South Coordinating Committee was entrusted with the implementation of these agreements and related matters. This historic breakthrough in inter-Korean relations was widely acclaimed both at home and abroad. The United States welcomed the joint communiqué as a contribution to peace and stability in Asia. Yet it was also somewhat apprehensive about the possibility that both Koreas might strike a secret deal potentially detrimental to Washington's interests.

The new principle of peaceful unification without foreign interference was open to conflicting interpretations and led to intense political maneuvering by Seoul and Pyongyang. Whereas North Korea tried to use the principle as a tool to dislodge the U.S. military presence from the Korean Peninsula, South Korea invoked it to limit an unproductive debate over the Korean question at the U.N. General Assembly. In September 1972, the United Nations imposed a moratorium on a Sino-Soviet maneuver that could have required the withdrawal of U.S. troops from South Korea and the dissolution of UNCURK. The following year the United States and China cooperated to seek a compromise between the two rival draft resolutions on the Korean question and to adopt a consensus statement at the U.N. General Assembly. The Chinese persuaded North Korea to abandon a pro-Pyongyang draft resolution that would have required the abolition of the United Nations Command and the withdrawal of U.S. forces from Korea. The consensus statement adopted on November 18, 1973, noted that "a joint communiqué was issued by the North and the South of Korea on 4 July 1972" and hoped that "the South and the North of Korea will be urged to continue their dialogue and widen their many-sided exchanges and cooperation in the above spirit so as to expedite the independent peaceful reunification of the country." The statement called for the immediate dissolution of UNCURK, but made no such demand on the United Nations Command. At his meeting with Chinese Vice Premier Deng Xiaoping in New York on April 14, 1974, Secretary of State Kissinger said: "We appreciate your acts with respect to the United Nations Command last year very, very much, and particularly appreciate the meticulous way in which you carried out our understanding."[32] Diplomatic cooperation between the United States and China did indeed have a positive effect on the Korean Peninsula.

Closely associated with the inter-Korean accommodation and the compromise at the United Nations were efforts by Seoul and Pyongyang to solidify their respective political structures, for both sides felt that a strong internal position would be useful for handling external events. On October 17, 1972, Park proclaimed martial law and suspended elements of the constitution on the grounds that South Korea needed sweeping structural reform to carry on the dialogue with North Korea and to cope with the rapidly changing international situation.[33] No doubt he was referring to Nixon's overtures of détente with China and withdrawal of the Seventh Infantry Division from South Korea and to the diplomatic normalization between China and Japan in September 1972. The subsequent referendum on a constitutional amendment in South Korea passed, allowing Park to extend his presidency indefinitely and to institute a highly authoritarian and repressive system (*yushin*) in South Korea. The Nixon administration publicly distanced itself from Park's undemocratic action and pointed out that it had held no prior consultation with him. However, declassified diplomatic documents clearly show that the United States had privately expressed "grave reservations" about the course of action contemplated by Park.[34] It had demanded that U.S. foreign policy should not be cited as a rationale for Park's *yushin* pronouncements. When South Korean Foreign Minister Kim Yong Shik asked U.S. Ambassador Habib to issue a statement in support of Park's decisions, the United States refused and eventually adopted a policy of noninterference in South Korea's domestic affairs. The diplomatic relationship between Washington and Seoul remained less than cordial for the rest of Nixon's presidency.

On the other hand, the constitutional revision in North Korea, which among other things upgraded Kim Il Sung's formal status from premier to president, a title comparable to Park's, may actually have been precipitated by external events. In view of South Korea's heightened political regimentation and economic prosperity, Kim lost interest in promoting inter-Korean reconciliation and cooperation. Guided by the *chuche* (self-reliance) ideology, Kim asserted a degree of autonomy in foreign affairs and attempted to turn the Sino-Soviet competition to his own advantage. As part of its foreign policy adaptation, moreover, North Korea began to cultivate informal contacts with Seoul's two principal allies — the United States and Japan. Kim initiated his "people's diplomacy" toward the United States in the early 1970s and expressed his willingness to establish diplomatic relations with Japan without an abrogation of the Japan–South Korea treaty for diplomatic normalization. At that time, however, neither the United States nor Japan was prepared to respond favorably to his peaceful overtures.

FORD'S INTERREGNUM

In an attempt to improve the strained relationship between Washington and Seoul and to dispel Park's fear of further U.S. military reductions in South Korea,

President Gerald R. Ford, who succeeded Nixon in August 1974, decided to pay a two-day visit to Seoul on his way to Vladivostok in November 1974. As a first-term Republican congressman from Michigan, Ford had supported President Truman's policy toward the Korean War and had regarded North Korea as the evil regime. In his meeting with Park, Ford stressed that "the United States, as a Pacific power, is vitally interested in Asia and the Pacific and will continue its best efforts to ensure the peace and security of the region."[35] Specifically, he reaffirmed "the determination of the United States to render prompt and effective assistance to repel armed attack against the Republic of Korea in accordance with the Mutual Security Treaty" and categorically stated that the United States had "no plan to reduce the present level of United States forces in Korea." Ford promised to assist South Korea in its military modernization program and in the development of its indigenous defense industries. As he recalled later at the National Security Council meeting, Ford had a "forthright" discussion with Park about "his oppressive domestic tactics," but he added that "it doesn't hurt to have a strong leader in that part of the country, with all the problems there."[36] The South Koreans were especially pleased with the renewed U.S. pledge of "prompt and effective assistance." Furthermore, the application of the Guam Doctrine to South Korea was suspended for a while.

In Indochina, however, the Guam Doctrine ultimately led to a different outcome. In early 1975 the United States refused to recommit its armed forces for the purpose of saving South Vietnam from Hanoi's outright military takeover and thus suffered a major setback in its sustained efforts to contain the spread of Communist influence in Asia. As a direct participant in the Vietnam War, South Korea was not only disheartened by the U.S. failure in Indochina but also concerned about its adverse repercussions on the Korean Peninsula. In the aftermath of the Vietnam debacle, the Ford administration articulated a clear distinction between Vietnam and Korea and offered a number of public statements to guarantee South Korea's national security. Asked about U.S. policy toward Korea in the post-Vietnam era, Secretary of State Kissinger answered in May 1975: "In South Korea there can be no ambiguity about our commitment because we have a defense treaty ratified by the Congress. If we abandon this treaty, it would have drastic consequences in Japan and all over Asia because that would be interpreted as our final withdrawal from Asia and our final withdrawal from our whole postwar foreign policy."[37]

A week later, Kissinger warned North Korea not to make the mistake of questioning the efficacy of the U.S. security commitment to South Korea.[38] Moreover, Secretary of Defense James R. Schlesinger threatened to respond to North Korean armed aggression with massive retaliation and indicated that the United States would not hesitate to use the tactical nuclear weapons stationed in South Korea.[39]

Park was reassured by the announcement of Ford's "Pacific Doctrine" in December 1975: Ford stated that "world stability and our own security depend upon our Asian commitments."[40]

The Ford administration took a series of steps to strengthen South Korea's self-defense capabilities throughout 1975 by issuing National Security Decision Memorandum 282 on "Korean Force Modernization Plan" (January 9, 1975), National Security Study Memorandum 226 on "Review of U.S. Policy Toward the Korean Peninsula" (May 27, 1975), and National Security Decision Memorandum 309 on "Decisions on ROK Air Defense Requirements" (October 9, 1975). In particular, the United States agreed to sell 18 F-4Es and 60 F-E/Fs to South Korea and negotiated a possible sale of U.S. Hawk batteries at a reduced price.

Yet the Ford administration was also determined to halt Park's clandestine program for nuclear weapons development. After receiving U.S. Ambassador Richard Sneider's report that South Korea had entered the initial stage of nuclear weapons development in 1975, Kissinger responded with guidelines for U.S. actions. In a secret memorandum of February 28, 1975, the Department of State explained why South Korea should not be allowed to develop nuclear weapons:

> In the case of Korea our general concerns are intensified by its strategic location and by the impact which any Korean effort to establish nuclear capability would have on its neighbors, particularly North Korea and Japan. ROK possession of nuclear weapons would have major destabilizing effect in an area in which not only Japan but USSR, PRC, and ourselves are directly involved. It could lead to Soviet or Chinese assurances of nuclear weapons support to North Korea in the event of conflict. Further, ROK efforts to secure a nuclear weapon capability will inevitably impact on our bilateral security relationship. . . . Therefore, our basic objective is to discourage ROK effort in this area and to inhibit to the fullest extent any ROK development of a nuclear explosive capability or delivery system.[41]

To achieve this objective, Kissinger proposed (1) to inhibit South Korean access to sensitive nuclear technology and equipment, both through unilateral U.S. action and through the development of common supplier nation policies; (2) to press South Korea to ratify the Nuclear Nonproliferation Treaty (NPT); and (3) to improve U.S. surveillance of South Korean nuclear facilities and to increase U.S. information on the current state of South Korean technical development in this area. Since the South Koreans planned to purchase heavy-water–moderated nuclear reactors from Canada and nuclear reprocessing equipment and technology from France so that they could reprocess the spent nuclear fuel rods into weapons-grade plutonium, the United States strongly urged France and Canada not to supply nuclear technology to South Korea. Under intense pressure as well as inducements (such as a civilian nuclear industry) from the United States, Park was compelled to cancel plans for nuclear weapons development for the sake of preserving its alliance cohesion with the United States.

Against this background, on June 24, 1975, U.S. Ambassador Sneider wrote a long and thoughtful memorandum to provide a new conceptual framework for America's Korea policy. He argued that "our present policy toward Korea is ill-defined and based on an outdated view of [South] Korea as a client state. It does not provide a long-term conceptual approach to Korea, geared to its prospective middle power status. It leaves the ROK uncertain what to expect from us and forces us to react to ROKG [Republic of Korea Government] on an ad hoc basis." The uncertainties of U.S. policy, he said, "lead President Park into preparations for what he sees as our eventual withdrawal, preparations which include internal repression and plans for the development of nuclear weapons." Furthermore, they had the effect of raising optimism on the part of North Korea about the possibility of our withdrawal and creating doubts in Japan about our credibility and about the future of Korea. After criticizing a continuation of the current U.S. policy and rejecting an alternative of deliberate disengagement from Korea, he articulated that "a more feasible, realistic alternative would seek to establish a durable partnership with [South] Korea based on reciprocal obligations, more or less along the lines of our relationships with NATO or Japan." More specifically, he advocated that a durable partnership would include new bilateral consultative machinery, guarantees of a significant U.S. military presence, a well-defined program of technology transfer and limits on South Korean production of sophisticated weapons, a plan to encourage private capital inflow into South Korea, a broad energy agreement, a moderation of South Korean internal policies, the encouragement of a trilateral relationship with Japan, and greater attention to engaging the Soviet Union and China in seeking a stable Korean Peninsula.[42] It remains unclear how the Sneider memorandum played out in the dynamics of bureaucratic politics in Washington, but it was probably forgotten altogether.

As the United States and South Korea hoped, China probably exerted a moderating influence over North Korea following the Communist takeover of Saigon. In their meeting in Wuhan, Mao Zedong reportedly rejected Kim Il Sung's proposal that China and North Korea undertake joint military action to expel U.S. forces from South Korea and Taiwan. The joint communiqué issued by Kim Il Sung and Deng Xiaoping on April 26, 1975, noted that "the new victories the Indochinese peoples have won in their liberation struggles greatly inspire the people of all countries."[43] Just as Mao's victory in the civil war with Chiang Kai-shek in 1949 had en-

couraged Kim's invasion of South Korea, the "new victories" in Indochina might
have emboldened Kim to take aggressive action in Korea. It is most likely, however,
that Mao and Deng counseled against Kim's possible military plans and urged him
to follow a peaceful road to Korean unification. The Chinese attached high priority
to the improvement of relations with the United States and to the relaxation of tension in Asia. Moreover, they were too embroiled in internal factional struggles and
ideological debates at that time to support a risky armed adventure in the Korean
Peninsula. In a meeting with President Ford in Beijing on December 4, 1975, Chinese Vice Premier Deng Xiaoping, who represented the ailing premier Zhou Enlai,
stated that he was not worried about a military attack by North Korea against South
Korea. Instead, Deng asked Ford to "keep an eye on Park Chung Hee" and expressed
his concern about Japan's potentially militaristic ambitions in Korea and Taiwan.[44]

When the promise for inter-Korean reconciliation shattered around the time of
the Vietnam debacle, the venue for the inter-Korean contest shifted to the United
Nations General Assembly. Unlike their earlier cooperation in 1973, the United States
and China now competed to promote the diplomatic interests of their respective
allies at the United Nations in 1975. The ascendancy of radical leaders headed by
Mao's wife, Jiang Qing, in Beijing's power struggles made it difficult for Chinese
diplomats to strike a compromise with their American counterparts on the Korean
question. After heated debates and intense lobbying, the United Nations General
Assembly in November 1975 paradoxically adopted two mutually exclusive resolutions — the pro-Seoul resolution (whose cosponsors included the United States and
Japan) by a vote of 59 to 41 with 29 abstentions, and the pro-Pyongyang resolution
(whose cosponsors included China and the Soviet Union) by a vote of 54 to 43 with
42 abstentions. Whereas the pro-Seoul resolution urged "all the parties directly concerned" (meaning the United States, China, South Korea, and North Korea) to em-
bark on talks as soon as possible so that "the United Nations Command may be dissolved concurrently with arrangements for maintaining the Armistice Agreement,"
the pro-Pyongyang resolution called for the unconditional dissolution of the United
Nations Command and the withdrawal of all foreign troops stationed in South Korea
under the flag of the United Nations and asked "the real parties to the Armistice
Agreement" (meaning the United States and North Korea) to replace it with a peace
agreement. For all practical purposes, the passage of the two contradictory resolutions (3390A and 3390B) ensured that neither resolution would be implemented
and that no further U.N. resolutions on the Korean question would be adopted for
many years to come.

Frustrated by the inability of the United Nations to disband the United Nations
Command and to eject U.S. troops from South Korea, Kim Il Sung decided to mount

a challenge to the sacrosanct neutral area, a visible symbol of the U.S. military presence at Panmunjom. On August 18, 1976, when a United Nations Command work crew attempted to trim a poplar tree in the neutral Joint Security Area because the tree was obstructing the observation of North Korean activities, a group of North Korean security guards obstructed the tree-trimming operation, killing two U.S. officers and wounding several others with axes. The United Nations Command immediately issued a strong protest to North Korea and demanded "explanations and reparations." The UNC sent another work crew to cut down the tree in a show of force by dismissing the objections that it might provoke the North Koreans.[45] The United States, along with South Korea, placed its forces on full alert, deployed F-4 aircraft from Okinawa and F-111 fighter-bombers from Idaho, conducted daily flights of B-52 heavy bombers from Guam to Korea, and dispatched the aircraft carrier USS *Midway* task force to the area. As Assistant Secretary of State Arthur W. Hummel explained, the swift and coordinated U.S. military maneuvers were intended to demonstrate to North Korea that "we are willing and able to move decisively to counter any threat in this area."[46] The U.S. action forced Kim to express "regret" over the incident and to offer a conciliatory proposal for new security measures at Panmunjom, but the United States initially treated this "regret" as insufficient. This was indeed the first time that Kim had expressed his "regret" toward the United States, perhaps because this time he feared U.S. retaliation. As in the case of the EC-121 incident, Secretary of State Kissinger, together with the Joint Chiefs of Staff, advocated punitive military action against North Korea, but President Ford, humiliated by the fall of Saigon in 1975 and facing a difficult presidential election, soon decided to avoid any military action that might lead to another Korean War and to resolve the potentially explosive crisis through negotiations.[47] So Ford decided to accept Kim's "regret."

The South Korean reaction to the incident was predictably angry. In his letter to General Richard G. Stilwell, commander-in-chief of the United Nations Command (CINCUNC), on August 19, Foreign Minister Park Tong Jin denounced this "ugly scheme" of North Korea.[48] On the following day President Park called the incident "collective murder" and said that "a mad dog needs a stick." He added: "Our patience is limited. From now on, if they commit unlawful provocations against us, we will have to take immediate punitive actions, whether small or large, and all responsibility for this shall be borne by North Korean Communists themselves."[49] Once again the United States refused to heed what National Security Adviser Brent Scowcroft called Park's "belligerent measures" toward North Korea and excluded South Korea from a negotiated settlement of the crisis between the United States and North Korea.[50]

CARTER'S MILITARY POLICY

Even before the axe-murder incident at Panmunjom was completely resolved, a dark cloud hovered over the question of the continuation of the U.S. military presence in South Korea. On March 17, 1976, Jimmy Carter, governor of Georgia and a leading contender for the Democratic Party's presidential nomination, told a *Washington Post* reporter that the United States should remove about 7,000 nuclear devices from South Korea. As a front-runner, he delivered a major foreign policy speech on June 23 in Chicago. Among other things, he said that "it will be possible to withdraw our ground forces from South Korea on a phased basis over a time span to be determined after consultation with both South Korea and Japan." He added: "It should be made clear to the South Korean government that its internal oppression is repugnant to our people and undermines the support for our commitment there."[51] His speech combined his profound moral conviction and liberal strategic perspective with shrewd campaign tactics. Disturbed by the Vietnam trauma, he felt that the United States should avoid any situation that might require its automatic involvement in another Asian ground war and favored a policy that would allow strategic flexibility and tactical mobility by giving higher priority to the Navy, Air Force, and Marines than to conventional ground forces. He preferred to shift the U.S. strategic focus from Asia to Europe, where he expected to face a more serious threat from the Soviet Union. In effect, Carter shared the main strategic thrust of Nixon's Guam Doctrine, but with emphasis on moral principles and human rights. Moreover, he aimed at appealing to the antiwar sentiment and neo-isolationist mood of many American voters. And he regarded the planned military pullout as a tangible way to save U.S. taxpayers' money—an approach consistent with his campaign themes of fiscal austerity and a balanced budget.

Carter only had a relatively simplistic grasp of the complexities of the Korean situation and failed to understand the symbolic and psychological importance that South Korea and Japan attached to the continuing U.S. military presence in Asia. In the Pentagon, there had emerged a consensus that U.S. troops stationed in South Korea were indispensable not only to South Korean security interests but also to the overall strategic balance in the Asia-Pacific region. A team of senior military officers completed a detailed report on Carter's Korea policy and submitted it to the Joint Chiefs of Staff in November 1976. In Seoul, General John W. Vessey Jr. (CINCUNC) warned that withdrawal of U.S. ground combat forces would considerably increase the risk of another Korean War and said that he would be very reluctant to withdraw the Second Infantry Division from South Korea.[52] This warning was intended to counter Carter's campaign pledge.

The South Koreans failed to take Carter's policy pronouncements seriously, including his Chicago speech, in part because they did not believe that he could defeat the incumbent Ford. Asked about Carter's Korea policy in the National Assembly in October, Minister of National Defense Suh Jong Chul responded that one individual could not drastically change U.S. military policy and that U.S. forces in South Korea were important to the security interests of other Asian countries as well.[53] Suh and other South Korean leaders continued to get the same message from their American counterparts: that U.S. troops would not be withdrawn from South Korea irrespective of the electoral outcome. Their wishful thinking led to complacency about Carter's campaign rhetoric.

The South Koreans were taken by surprise when Carter defeated Ford, but they still refused to believe that Carter would carry out his promises on Korea. In an appearance before the National Assembly, Foreign Minister Park Tong Jin testified that there would be no significant change in the U.S. security commitment to South Korea under Carter's presidency because campaign promises were not always implemented in the United States.[54] He anticipated a change in the style of U.S. military policy toward South Korea, but not in its substance. He also predicted that if Carter planned to withdraw U.S. forces from South Korea, he would do so only after "prudent and sufficient consultation" with South Korea. In an attempt to alleviate domestic anxieties about Carter's pronouncement on Korea and to discourage military provocations from North Korea, Park declared that "in terms of combat capabilities, the Republic of Korea is almost on level with North Korea."[55] He further explained: "If we are invaded by the North Korean Communists, the United States will automatically support us in view of the presence in Korea of the American troops and the ROK-U.S. Mutual Defense Treaty."

On January 26, 1977, less than a week after his inauguration, President Jimmy Carter issued Presidential Review Memorandum / NSC 13.[56] In it, he directed that "the Policy Review Committee, under the chairmanship of the Department of State, undertake a broad review of our policies toward the Korean Peninsula. The review should be completed by March 7." More specifically, he asked the committee to identify U.S. interests and objectives in the Korean Peninsula, including those deriving from our relationship with Japan, and to examine reductions in U.S. conventional force levels on the peninsula, southward deployment within Korea of U.S. forces, future U.S. military assistance levels for South Korea, diplomatic initiatives to reduce tensions on the peninsula, U.S. relations with North Korea, and the human rights problem in Korea. This memorandum, prepared by National Security Adviser

Zbigniew Brzezinski, called for nothing less than a comprehensive review of U.S. policy toward Korea, including tactical nuclear weapons deployed in South Korea; the only aspect not covered was economic relations.

Equipped with an outline of this memorandum, Vice President Walter Mondale arrived in Tokyo toward the end of January after visiting London, Bonn, Paris, and other major European capitals. In a meeting with Japanese Prime Minister Fukuda Takeo on February 1, Mondale stated that the United States "should and will remain an Asian-Pacific power" and "will preserve a balanced and flexible military strength in the Pacific."[57] Yet he added that "we will phase down our ground forces [in South Korea] only in close consultation and cooperation with the Governments of Japan and South Korea." He was specifically instructed by Carter to inform the Japanese of his decision to withdraw U.S. troops from South Korea but to indicate no possibility of reversing it.[58] After meeting with Mondale, Fukuda moderated his earlier public opposition to the withdrawal of U.S. forces from South Korea. He now insisted that the matter was basically a bilateral issue between the United States and South Korea and said that "the Japanese government does not intend to intervene or mediate between the two."[59]

The South Koreans were not only disappointed by Fukuda's apparent retreat, they were upset by what they regarded as a diplomatic insult and a loss of face. Mondale had failed to include Seoul in his worldwide itinerary, discussed the important Korean question with Japanese officials, and indicated no possibility of a summit meeting between Carter and Park. In fact, Carter had no intention of meeting with Park until human rights conditions improved appreciably in South Korea. The South Koreans refrained from displaying their displeasure publicly so that they would not complicate their relationship with the new Carter administration. The American willingness to slight publicly Park's proud self-esteem was an indication of a profound cultural insensitivity, one that would reappear on several other important occasions.

In a letter delivered to Park by Ambassador Sneider and General John W. Vessey on February 15, Carter discussed a number of bilateral issues.[60] He assured Park that the United States would continue to honor its security commitment for South Korea and promised that the United States would hold "the fullest prior consultations" with South Korea about the withdrawal of U.S. forces. For Park's military modernization programs, he would ask the U.S. Congress to approve $275 million in military assistance for South Korea for fiscal year 1978. And Carter emphasized the importance of improving human rights throughout the world.

In his long response on February 26, Park expressed appreciation for Carter's continuing security commitment but stated bluntly:

> With regard to the problem of reduction of the United States ground combat forces in Korea, mentioned in your letter, my Government has closely followed its developments with keen interest. Needless to say, the United States forces in Korea, both as visible evidence of the Korean-American mutual defense arrangement and as an indispensable factor in the structure of the balance of power in this area, has been playing an important role in deterring the recurrence of war on the Korean peninsula and in ensuring peace and stability in the Northeast Asian region as a whole. . . . At a time when the North Korean Communists have not abandoned their sinister scheme of communizing the whole of Korea by means of force or violence, and when the Republic of Korea's self-defense capabilities have not yet reached the sufficient stage, my Government believes that any reduction in the current level of the United States forces in Korea is not desirable and, therefore, hopes that any such change would not take place for a considerable period of time.[61]

As to human rights, Park said that "I myself subscribe to those lofty political ideals" but criticized those at home and abroad who "insinuate that human rights are being repressed or infringed upon in Korea" and certain "senseless elements" in South Korea who "resort to radical and illegal anti-state actions." He explained that "the overwhelming majority of the Korean people realize that the reservation of some of their rights is unavoidable in order to ensure the security, stability and the very survival of the nation." Of course, Park's defensive but defiant position on human rights did not persuade Carter at all. About the same time, Brzezinski approved an NSC initiative to curtail arms transfers to "egregious human-rights violators" such as South Korea, Argentina, Indonesia, the Philippines, and Thailand but for strategic reasons rescinded it in the case of South Korea.[62]

While Brzezinski supported Carter's premise that with U.S. military assistance and air cover, the South Koreans would be capable of defending themselves against North Korean aggression, Secretary of State Cyrus Vance, Secretary of Defense Harold Brown, and CIA Director Stansfield Turner had varying degrees of reservation about this risky assumption from the beginning. The tension between Vance and Brzezinski, especially in regard to U.S. policies toward the Soviet Union, was well-known. Brzezinski tilted decisively in favor of Beijing over Moscow, but Vance took a more balanced approach toward both Communist countries. Likewise, their differences over the question of U.S. military withdrawal from South Korea were clearly evident.[63] William H. Gleysteen Jr., who served as deputy assistant secretary of state for East Asian and Pacific affairs, recalls that the representatives of State,

Defense, the CIA, and other relevant agencies who were involved in the review of U.S. policy toward Korea reached a consensus that the United States should withdraw a minimum number of U.S. combat troops while withdrawing a larger number of noncombat forces from South Korea, to be followed by a careful review of the Korean situation before any further withdrawals.[64] Yet the Joint Chiefs of Staff presented the strongest resistance to Carter's policy. In their annual military posture report submitted to Congress on January 1977, the JCS argued that "in Korea, American military presence is the tangible manifestation of our commitment to the security of the Republic of Korea. Our presence helps deter North Korean aggression toward the South, thus making a vital contribution to the stability of the Northeast Asian region in general. . . . Our security relationship with Japan requires a continued U.S. force presence and access to bases and facilities."[65] The JCS were reluctant to withdraw all U.S. ground combat forces from South Korea over a period of four to five years. On March 7, in response to PRM/NSC 13, the JCS, with General Vessey's concurrence, recommended to Secretary of Defense Brown a phased partial reduction of 7,000 troops through September 30, 1982, with the condition that the Korean military situation should continue to be reviewed.[66]

On the same day, South Korean Foreign Minister Park Tong Jin stated in New York that the proposed withdrawal or reduction of U.S. forces in South Korea appeared to be premature and unrealistic.[67] He said that the United States had no concrete plan for phasing out its military presence from South Korea. A couple of days later, Carter made an announcement in a nationally televised press conference that completely dismayed Park. In obvious disregard of the JCS recommendation and without any prior consultation with South Korea or Japan, Carter declared that the United States would withdraw its ground troops from South Korea over a period of four to five years, would leave behind "adequate ground forces" under South Korean command, and would provide air cover for South Korea over a long period of time. He also ordered Secretary of State Vance to remove any restrictions on American citizens who wanted to go to Vietnam, North Korea, Cuba, and Cambodia. Park was fully aware that, just like Nixon in 1970, Carter had unilaterally announced his military decision on South Korea as a fait accompli. When Carter explained to Park in the White House why he had decided to withdraw the U.S. troops from South Korea, Park responded that in principle the United States had a sovereign right to dispose of its troops but requested that the two governments have close consultations about the modalities for implementing his decision.[68] To make matters worse, Carter chose this inopportune time to press Park about the human rights violations in South Korea. Park assured Carter that he, too, supported respect for human rights and that the South Korean government was following lawful procedures in the matter.

The peremptory manner with which Carter decided and announced his military decision on South Korea was one of the most humiliating experiences in Foreign Minister Park's long and illustrious diplomatic career. President Park was equally angry, especially since he had believed Carter's earlier promise to make strategic decisions only with the fullest prior consultations with South Korea. The U.S.–South Korean alliance system had suffered yet another crisis of confidence. A high-ranking South Korean diplomat suggested that Minister Park's disillusionment was in part caused by the inability of the South Korean embassy in Washington to understand the active policy review process in the U.S. bureaucracies.[69] At the same time, a prominent general in the South Korean Joint Chiefs of Staff attributed Carter's unilateral decision-making process to his "ignorance" and "inexperience" in foreign affairs.[70] Still another top policy specialist in the Blue House characterized Carter's behavior as "insensitive, discourteous, and arrogant."[71] His assessment probably captured the prevailing feeling of bitterness and betrayal among Park's lieutenants. In order to demonstrate his steadfastness amid adversity, Park proclaimed that "even now, the nation is well-prepared to overwhelm North Korea in any confrontation."[72] Likewise, Minister of National Defense Suh assured the jittery National Assembly that South Korea's military power surpassed that of North Korea at present.[73] Unlike their angry protests against Nixon's military decision, Park and his lieutenants now reacted to Carter's military policy in a more measured and pragmatic manner. They had learned a lesson from the Nixon experience and had gained a greater sense of self-confidence in a matter of six years.

In spite of South Korea's reluctance, the Carter administration hastened the process of finalizing specific plans for U.S. military withdrawal. On April 21, 1977, the Interagency Policy Review Committee, chaired by Secretary of State Vance, discussed the diverse responses to PRM/NSC 13, followed by the National Security Council meeting chaired by Carter on April 27. Carter overruled the reservations expressed by Secretaries Vance and Brown and reaffirmed his determination to remove all U.S. ground forces in five years. Brzezinski refused to support Vance and Brown.[74] On May 5, Carter issued Presidential Directive / NSC 12 on "U.S. Policy in Korea." He directed that "the U.S. 2nd Division and supporting elements shall be gradually withdrawn from Korea," that "final decisions on the precise phasing of ground force withdrawals shall be made following consultations with key Congressional leaders and the governments of South Korea and Japan," and that "U.S. air units will remain in Korea indefinitely."[75]

The unfolding of Carter's military policy toward South Korea met with growing opposition in the United States. In particular, top Republican leaders (such as former president Ford and Senator Charles Percy) and retired generals (such as

Richard Stilwell, CINCUNC in South Korea, and Thomas Moorer, chairman of the JCS) were critical of Carter's approach. The most serious reservation was voiced by Major General John K. Singlaub (chief of staff, U.S. Forces Korea), a tough and feisty veteran of the Vietnam War. In an interview with a *Washington Post* reporter, he said that "if we withdraw our ground forces on the schedule suggested, it will lead to war."[76] He charged that President Carter's decision was based on outdated intelligence reports on North Korea's military capabilities. Angered by Singlaub's outspoken insubordination, Carter recalled him immediately to the White House, reprimanded him, and relieved him of his position in Korea. The president's swift and decisive action thwarted open rebellion from the officers on active duty and asserted the constitutional concept of civilian supremacy over military affairs. He followed the model set by Truman with regard to MacArthur in 1951. For domestic political reasons, however, Carter decided not to dismiss Singlaub altogether but rather to reassign him to the U.S. Army Command in Fort McPherson, Georgia.

On May 16, the Department of Defense submitted to the White House a detailed plan for withdrawing the first two brigades of the Second Infantry Division and a proposal for military assistance to South Korea.[77] The plan envisaged the initial withdrawal of one brigade with appropriate support (6,000 persons) by December 31, 1978, and the second withdrawal of another brigade (9,000 persons) by June 30, 1980, and identified the specific categories, amounts, and schedules of U.S. arms transfers and military assistance to South Korea over the next five years. On the basis of this preliminary plan, Carter dispatched General George S. Brown, chairman of the JCS, and Philip Habib, undersecretary of state for political affairs and former ambassador to South Korea, to Seoul for consultations with President Park. It was reported that in return for his acceptance of Carter's withdrawal policy, Park asked the United States (1) to reaffirm its treaty commitment for South Korea's defense; (2) to provide a package of military assistance to South Korea in advance of the initial pullout of U.S. troops; (3) to keep the headquarters of the Second Infantry Division in South Korea until the final phase of troop withdrawal; and (4) to leave tactical nuclear weapons in South Korea as an ultimate element of effective deterrence.[78]

Shortly after the Habib-Brown mission, the 10th Annual Security Consultative Meeting between the U.S. secretary of defense and the South Korean minister of national defense reached final agreement on the procedures and conditions of U.S. military withdrawal. In his letter in July 1977 delivered by Secretary Brown to President Park, Carter explained that "our ground force withdrawal plans signify no change whatsoever in our commitment to the security of the Republic of Korea" and that "the Mutual Defense Treaty between our two countries remains fully in force."[79] Guided by the letter and spirit of Carter's commitment, Secretary Brown outlined the U.S. decision to withdraw 6,000 soldiers by the end of 1978, to phase out the remaining ground forces by 1982, to maintain the headquarters of the Second Infantry Division until the completion of troop withdrawal, and to strengthen its air force, navy, intelligence units, and logistic support personnel in South Korea for an indefinite period. The Carter administration promised to seek congressional approval for transferring the Second Division's military hardware (worth $500 million) to South Korea, providing a one-time extension of credit ($300 million) for South Korea's five-year force improvement programs (1976–81), and increasing foreign military sales credits ($1.1 billion for five years at an annual interest rate of 8%). In a compromise, the United States agreed to implement the $1.9 billion package "in advance or in parallel with the withdrawals." The two sides agreed to expand joint military exercises and to set up a combined command structure for operational efficiency. Brown committed the United States to retain its nuclear umbrella over South Korea.

The Carter administration used a variety of diplomatic channels to clarify its military policy toward South Korea to Moscow, Beijing, and Pyongyang. In his meeting with Chinese Foreign Minister Huang Hua in Beijing in August, Secretary of State Vance evidently asked his Chinese hosts to exercise their moderating influence over North Korea. This was necessary because another case of North Korean military provocation could easily have torpedoed Carter's withdrawal policy. Vance also mentioned U.S. interest in the resumption of inter-Korean talks and in "four-power discussions of the Korea issue."[80] At times the Chinese expressed concern about the weakening of the American military presence in Asia.[81] Carter reported to the Congress that "we have made it clear to both the People's Republic of China and the Soviet Union that the withdrawal decision signals no weakening of our commitment," adding, "The North Korean Government should be in no doubt about our position."[82] The North Koreans welcomed the announcement of a U.S. military withdrawal from South Korea but remained skeptical, citing a Korean saying about "a cake in a painting": the cake looks appetizing but is not really edible. They also proposed peace talks with the United States, but the Carter administration responded that it would accept the proposal only if South Korea was equally represented.[83]

The agreement reached between Washington and Seoul in July did not prevent the U.S. Congress from taking an increasingly critical view of Carter's military policy toward South Korea. A number of senators launched a concerted attack against it. Sharing Singlaub's assessment, Barry Goldwater (R-AZ) called Carter's policy "ridiculous" and "dangerous." Strom Thurmond (R-SC) accused Carter of committing a "serious mistake" based on a politically motivated campaign promise. Two influential pro-Carter Democratic leaders from the South—John Sparkman (D-AL), chairman of the Senate Committee on Foreign Relations, and John Stennis (D-MS), chairman of the Senate Committee on Armed Services—called upon Carter to exercise extreme caution and to reassess his policy in Korea. Included among those critical of Carter's policy were several other influential Democratic senators—John Glenn, Sam Nunn, Henry Jackson, Daniel Inouye, and Gary Hart.[84] Yet some liberal Democratic senators countered with a defense of Carter's policy. George McGovern (D-SD), who had called President Park a "disreputable tyrant," characterized Carter's approach toward South Korea as "responsible and prudent," and John C. Culver (D-IA) argued that after maintaining a U.S. military presence in South Korea for about twenty-five years, it was the right time to remove the "security blanket."[85] He pointed out South Korea's enormous economic strength and formidable military power, which surpassed that of North Korea. In Culver's opinion, the phased withdrawal of U.S. troops would blunt the criticism that South Korea was a "vassal state" of the United States and could even lead to serious negotiations between Seoul and Pyongyang. He dismissed the possibility of North Korean aggression and contended that neither the Soviet Union nor China would support it.

However, the U.S. Congress clearly let President Carter know that it would aggressively assert its power of oversight in U.S. military policy toward South Korea. As domestic pressure against his Korea policy mounted in a variety of circles— Congress, the military establishment, the federal bureaucracy, and the business community—Carter felt beleaguered in exercising his leadership over other important foreign policy issues, such as the Israeli-Egyptian peace negotiations, the Strategic Arms Limitation Talks with the Soviet Union, diplomatic normalization with China, and the Panama Canal Treaty. He began a carefully orchestrated tactical retreat. In his State of the Union message of January 1978, Carter said, "We are seeking to readjust our military presence in Korea by reducing our ground forces on the Peninsula and undertaking compensatory measures to ensure that an adequate balance of forces remains."[86] It was significant that instead of "withdrawing," he used "reducing," a term he had earlier refused to use in his public statements. A number of his key policy spokesmen opened the door on changing U.S. military policy toward South Korea. Ambassador Richard Sneider said that "nothing is so inflexible that it cannot be changed." In testimony before the House Committee on International Relations, Secretary of Defense Brown conceded that the plan for military withdrawal from South Korea might be modified if North Korea's military capabilities grew faster than those of South Korea or if North Korea assumed a pattern of aggressive behavior. Moreover, Brzezinski admitted his shortcomings (and by implication Carter's) in having paid insufficient attention to Asian problems, especially the issue of the pullout of U.S. troops from South Korea during the previous year.[87]

In early April 1978, the Investigations Subcommittee of the House Committee on Armed Services issued a scathing report on Carter's Korea policy. It concluded that Carter had arrived at his decision to withdraw well before his inauguration and had not sought "advice, assistance, recommendations or estimates of probable impact of his withdrawal decision on U.S. security considerations or stability in the Far East from the Joint Chiefs of Staff."[88] The report claimed that North Korea was superior to South Korea in every key index of military capability except for manpower and that Kim Il Sung was "aggressive" and "irrational." It added: "If South Korea were to fall under Communist control as a direct result of U.S. withdrawal, this would provide conclusive proof to Asian nations of the inability and unwillingness of the United States to prevent further Communist expansion in Asia. Thus, America's influence in the western Pacific would largely come to an end." Shortly after this report was completed, Carter announced an adjustment in the schedule for troop pullout in April—to withdraw only one battalion (800 persons) of the Second Infantry Division in December 1978, to postpone the withdrawal of the other two battalions of a brigade until 1979, and to remove 26,000 noncombat personnel by the end of 1978.[89] The South Koreans were relieved. Foreign Minister Park Tong Jin welcomed Carter's announcement as a "reasonable action."[90]

In fact, the Carter administration solidified its military positions in South Korea throughout 1978. It augmented the U.S. Air Force by 20%, conducted massive joint military exercises with South Korea, and deployed and trained its Air Force combat forces in Japan for the primary purpose of defending South Korea. Although Carter had opposed the introduction of newly developed advanced weapons systems into regional disputes, he authorized the sale of sixty superior lightweight combat aircraft (F-16s) to South Korea. In November, the United States and South Korea set up the Combined Forces Command (CFC). Although it did not completely satisfy the South Koreans' request for a NATO-type command structure in which both sides could enjoy equal and integrated operational status, the new CFC mechanism provided them with a sense of sharing operational responsibilities with their American counterparts. The CFC also allowed the United States to continue its operational control over South Korean armed forces in the event of the UNC's dissolution.

It was important for the United States to keep China and the Soviet Union informed of this change in the U.S.–South Korean military relationship, which was not intended to upset the existing balance of power on the Korean Peninsula. As a result of diplomatic normalization, the United States and China were able to have frequent consultations about Korean questions. In his meeting with Chinese Vice Premier Deng Xiaoping in January 1979, for example, Carter attempted to improve China's relations with South Korea and asked him to use his influence in North

Korea to bring about inter-Korean talks. Deng responded that it was not yet possible to have trade relations or direct communications between China and South Korea and that there was absolutely no danger of a North Korean attack. If China tried to pressure North Korea, he said, it would lose its influence, as the Soviet Union already had.[91]

When U.S. intelligence agencies examined the new data on North Korean military capabilities in December 1978, reaching the consensus assessment that North Korea significantly surpassed South Korea in every major category of military might, it presented the final blow for Carter to suspend his plan for military withdrawal from South Korea—or a convenient excuse. In order to assess the implications of the new intelligence report, on January 22 Carter issued Presidential Review Memorandum 45 entitled "U.S. Policy Toward Korea."[92] On February 9 Carter announced that the United States was holding in abeyance any further reduction in American troop levels until it could assess the new intelligence data on the buildup of North Korean force levels and the impact of U.S.-China diplomatic normalization.[93] So the South Korean leaders expected that during his visit to Seoul toward the end of June 1979, President Carter would officially terminate his unpopular military policy once and for all. The Ministry of Foreign Affairs instructed Ambassador Kim Yong Shik that in his negotiations with U.S. officials about the joint communiqué, an explicit reference to such termination should be included.[94] Yet the summit meeting between Carter and Park on June 30 turned out to be a diplomatic near-disaster, replete with uncomfortable and contentious discussions.

After having been humiliated by Carter's unilateral military decisions and public condemnations of South Korea's human rights situation, Park was determined to deliver a scathing lecture to Carter, despite his aides' pleas for moderation. Although Carter made it known that he preferred not to dwell on the question of a U.S. military pullout from South Korea at the summit meeting because he already knew Park's views, at the first expanded session of the summit Park launched into a long, provocative, and patronizing monologue about security conditions in Asia and the reasons for the U.S. military presence in South Korea.[95] Visibly shaken by his host's 45-minute "sermon," Carter countered with what Ambassador Gleysteen, one of the American participants, later characterized as an "abrasive response."[96] After a brief tension-filled break, Park and Carter had a one-hour private session accompanied only by two assistants—a South Korean interpreter and an American note-taker. When Park requested "no further withdrawal" of U.S. forces from South Korea "until the disparity between North Korea and South Korea is changed and until North Korea changes its policy," Carter bluntly replied that "I can't promise that we will freeze force levels."[97] In response to Carter's question on North Korea's substantial advantage in military capability when South Korea's economy was so prosperous, Park insisted that the North Korean military buildup had not begun until after U.S. policy for military withdrawal was announced in 1977, an assertion Carter criticized as "inaccurate." When Park mentioned that North Korea had over 2,000 tanks to South Korea's 850, Carter disputed the numbers by saying that South Korea had 1,050 tanks. When Carter asked why South Korea spent only 5% of its gross national product on national defense while North Korea spent about 20%, Park responded that "we plan to spend 6% of our GNP."

As a champion of human rights, Carter intended to extract concessions from Park to release political prisoners and to lift the repressive Emergency Measure 9, which severely limited democratic freedoms, but Park, who faced considerable opposition in domestic politics, was quite prepared to defend his position tenaciously, as he had repeatedly been subjected to the Carter administration's public criticisms in the past. The following exchange is typical:

PRESIDENT CARTER: My own wish would be that you could rescind Emergency Measure 9 and release as many prisoners you hold as possible. . . . It is a shame that one of our strongest and most valued allies, and one of the finest nations on earth, should be regarded critically in the U.S. because of this one issue.

PRESIDENT PARK: Every country has unique circumstances. You cannot apply the same yardstick to countries whose security is threatened as to countries whose security is not. Our capital is only 25 miles from the DMZ. Right across the DMZ hundreds of thousands of soldiers are poised. We have suffered a tragic war. We must deal with the situation whether we like it or not, otherwise we might fall into the same situation as the Vietnamese. If dozens of Soviet divisions were deployed at Baltimore, the U.S. Government could not permit its people to enjoy the same freedoms as they do now. If these Soviets dug tunnels and sent commando units into the District of Columbia, then U.S. freedoms would be more limited. We support the human rights policy. Respect for human rights is also our concern. I want as much freedom for our people as possible. But the survival of 37 million people is at stake, and some restraint is required.

PRESIDENT CARTER: Is it your response that you would have to continue to impose EM-9?

PRESIDENT PARK: I hope you will understand, but it is difficult to rescind EM-9 at this point. Of course, we don't intend to maintain it indefinitely. I will heed your advice and do more in that direction, but I cannot take these measures at this time.

The confrontation with Park so infuriated Carter that he lashed out at Ambassador Gleysteen on the way back from the Blue House. Secretary Vance defended Gleysteen but felt that "our Korean policy hung in the balance."[98] Nor was Park pleased with the contentious meeting, especially because he was not prepared to discuss such issues as the defense budget and inter-Korean military comparisons.[99] However, Carter was able to meet with opposition political leaders in the National Assembly, including Kim Young Sam (outspoken critic of Park's policies and future South Korean president), but there was a prior understanding that he would not have a session with Kim Dae Jung (another opposition leader and future South Korean president).

In the joint communiqué issued on July 1, Carter and Park concealed their personal animosity by stating that they had reviewed a variety of subjects of vital mutual interest "in an atmosphere of cordial respect and confidence."[100] Carter reiterated "the firm commitment of the United States to render prompt and effective assistance to repel armed attack against the Republic of Korea in accordance with the Mutual Defense Treaty" and promised to maintain "an American military presence in the Republic of Korea to ensure peace and security." In spite of South Korean discomfort, the communiqué noted the importance of internationally recognized human rights to all respected nations. In his separate meeting with Secretary of State Vance, Park suggested that the disposition of EM-9 should be left to him and promised that South Korea would increase defense expenditures up to 6% of its GNP.[101] Vance delivered a list of about a hundred political prisoners to Foreign Minister Park Tong Jin with the hope that they would be released soon. Acceding to South Korea's adamant request, Carter agreed to affirm that the "United States nuclear umbrella provided additional security for the area." This public pledge was designed to present an effective deterrence against North Korea and to discourage Park's lingering interest in possessing nuclear weapons. Even though Carter's initial plan to hold a joint summit meeting with Park Chung Hee and Kim Il Sung (similar to the Camp David meetings between Egyptian President Anwar Sadat and Israeli Prime Minister Menachem Begin) during his Seoul visit did not materialize in part because of opposition from U.S. Ambassador Gleysteen, Park reluctantly accepted Carter's proposal for three-party talks with the United States, South Korea, and North Korea.[102] Park disliked the idea of three-party talks, largely because he was afraid that it might be a repetition of the Vietnam peace negotiations at Paris, where the South Vietnamese delegation had been reduced to the role of bystanders, but he correctly assumed that the North Koreans would reject this proposal because they insisted on bilateral talks with the United States without South Korea's participation.[103] The South Koreans also assumed that the Soviet Union, one of North Korea's allies, would oppose tripartite talks. Secretary of State Vance and Foreign Minister Park had chosen Indonesia as an intermediary because it had diplomatic relations with both Pyongyang and Seoul. On their way to Kimpo Airport, Carter inappropriately tried to convert Park to Christianity, but without success.[104]

In the aftermath of the summit meeting, both sides implemented their tacit tradeoff over troop withdrawals and human rights. On July 5, the South Korean government informed Ambassador Gleysteen that it would release 180 detainees over a six-month period; on July 17 it released the first group of eighty-six persons convicted under EM-9 and indicated that it would release others in the near future.[105] Park accommodated Carter's "advice" but did not wish to give the impression that he did so under U.S. pressure. A few days later, on July 20, Brzezinski announced Carter's decision:

- Withdrawals of combat elements of the Second Division will remain in abeyance;
- Some reductions of personnel in U.S. support units, including one I-Hawk air defense battalion, will continue until the end of 1980; and
- The timing and pace of withdrawals beyond these will be reexamined in 1981. In that review the United States will pay special attention to the restoration of a satisfactory North-South military balance and evidence of tangible progress toward a reduction of tensions on the peninsula.[106]

In explaining the president's decision, Brzezinski cited the new intelligence reports on North Korean military strength, new diplomatic overtures toward North Korea, and the growth of Soviet military power in East Asia. He made no reference to human rights or tactical nuclear weapons. In contrast to Carter's initial unilateral decision on troop withdrawal from South Korea, it was noted that this decision had been discussed with key U.S. allies in Asia, principal defense and foreign policy advisers, and leaders of Congress. So ended the tortuous saga of Carter's policy of military withdrawal from South Korea. In a brief statement issued on the following day, South Korean Foreign Minister Park welcomed Carter's "reasonable and timely decision."[107] On July 31, President Park expressed similar sentiments to President Carter. In response, Carter expressed his appreciation for the release of the eighty-six prisoners, but he decided not to include the potentially counterproductive sentence, "I hope that you will reintegrate these released persons fully into society and make it possible for them to resume their places as students, professionals, and workers."[108] He also expressed regret that North Korea had rejected the proposal for three-party talks but assured Park that the United States would not agree to any manipulative formula for a bilateral meeting with North Korea that did not include

South Korea as "a full and equal participant." As expected, the North Koreans rejected the proposal for tripartite meetings. As a principal reason for Carter's policy
failure, William H. Gleysteen Jr. candidly pointed out Carter's "ignorance and insensitivity" about East Asia as well as his dangerous disregard for professional and political opinion at home.[109] He added: "There were no rabble-rousing protests [in
South Korea] against the United States, and [South] Korean officials behaved themselves carefully. With hardly an exception, however, they felt that Americans were
once again toying lightly with their fate." As a result, South Koreans' confidence in
their military alliance with the United States suffered irreparable damage.

THE KOREAGATE INVESTIGATIONS

While its military policy toward South Korea was creating serious problems at
home and abroad, the Carter administration was unfortunately saddled with the
diplomatic and legal responsibility of resolving the Koreagate scandals, which had
been evolving since the late 1960s.[110] Committed to upholding high ethical standards, Carter looked with irritation and repugnance on the alleged South Korean
operations to bribe members of U.S. Congress and other top leaders. Yet he had no
choice but to deal with the ongoing congressional investigations and the recalcitrant
South Korean authorities. Together with the swirling controversies over the questions of troop withdrawal and human rights, Koreagate was bound to further strain
the relationship between Washington and Seoul.

The genesis and unfolding of South Korea's influence-buying operations in the
United States were complex and controversial. It was alleged that in 1968 Prime
Minister Chung Il Kwon and KCIA Director Kim Hyung Wook decided to cooperate with Congressman Richard Hanna (D-CA) and businessman Park Tong Son
(a graduate of Georgetown University), who both agreed to share the commissions
from American rice sales to South Korea and to use them to obtain favorable decisions for Seoul in the U.S. Congress.[111] Hanna told Chung and Kim that unlike the
National Assembly in South Korea, Congress played a crucial role in U.S. foreign
relations and he instructed them on how to lobby the U.S. Congress effectively by
emulating the successful models set by Israel and Taiwan. Designated as the exclusive agent for rice sales, Park easily reaped huge commissions and distributed some
of them to Hanna and other members of U.S. Congress. In Washington, Park en-
tertained congressmen, cabinet members, generals, and other influential persons at
the exclusive Georgetown Club, which he had taken over from his social patron,
Anna Chennault. Park joined Hanna in organizing a series of well-financed congressional junkets to Seoul. After heading a 25-member mission to South Korea in

March 1969, House Majority Leader Carl Albert (D-OK) told the House that "we can make no better investment than investing in the strength and prosperity of a friend and ally like Korea."[112] Other members of the Albert delegation praised President Park's political leadership and South Korea's economic achievements. In particular, House Majority Whip Thomas P. "Tip" O'Neill Jr. (D-MA) defended the controversial constitutional amendment that had allowed President Park to run for a third four-year term.[113] The majority whip rejected the view that President Park sought the imposition of personal rule in South Korea. In his report to Prime Minister Chung, Hanna said that members of the Albert mission were helpful in passing a bill for military assistance ($50 million) to South Korea, and he was able to receive cooperation from Secretary of Defense Melvin Laird and Gerald Ford (R-MI), several years before he entered the executive branch.[114] At times U.S. congressmen visiting Seoul were given envelopes containing cash to use in the Walker Hill casino; when all the money was gone, they returned the empty envelopes to receive more cash. This was the extent to which some visiting members of U.S. Congress were seriously compromised in South Korea.

Angered by Nixon's decision to withdraw the Seventh Infantry Division from South Korea, the Park government felt that it was urgent to build support in the U.S. Congress for preserving the remaining U.S. military presence in South Korea and for approving a substantial package of assistance for South Korea's military modernization programs. Apart from its security interests, South Korea intended to dampen or counter the growing criticism of President Park's repressive policies and human rights violations. For this purpose, Park Tong Son made cash payments and campaign contributions or provided services to at least thirty-two congressmen and seven senators. The amounts of his alleged payments ranged from $100 to as much as $200,000 for Richard Hanna. Not all of the payments and services were illegal or improper, but many members of Congress accepted the money and services in unethical ways. In return, a number of those members of Congress who benefited from Park's largesse became active in promoting South Korea's military and economic interests and in blocking resolutions and other legislative maneuvers critical of President Park's policies.

The Department of State recognized the illegal aspects of Park Tong Son's operations in 1970 and informed the South Korean embassy in Washington that his activities in the United States were a "a liability" and "a poison."[115] Even if South Korean Ambassador Kim Dong Jo did resent Park's flamboyant and ubiquitous presence, he found it difficult to constrain a person so politically connected in Seoul. U.S. Ambassador to Seoul William Porter tried to persuade President Park and Prime Minister Chung that Park should be recalled home but to no avail.[116] The

FBI reported that under the direction of KCIA, Park made payments to U.S. congressmen and that some congressional staffers had ties with KCIA. Yet none of the FBI investigations and reports had any significant impact on South Korean lobbying programs. As Ambassador Porter testified later, the official U.S. response was characterized by a "great deal of permissiveness" mainly because the U.S. government did not want to embarrass President Park at a time when South Korea was assisting the U.S. war efforts in Vietnam.[117]

When Philip Habib, who had served as political counselor in Seoul during the 1962–65 period, replaced William Porter as U.S. ambassador to South Korea in October 1971, he wanted to force Park Tong Son to register as a lobbyist for the South Korean government. He was not successful, however. Habib instructed all embassy personnel in South Korea that they should have nothing to do with Park "without my explicit permission."[118] He also warned several visiting congressmen about Park's illegal operations. The Department of Justice, however, was not responsive to the Department of State's allegations regarding Park's influence-buying operations. In fact, Attorney General William Saxby, who maintained close personal relations with Park, informed Park that some individuals in the Department of State were trying to get him. Saxby even accepted a lavish farewell party organized by Park in honor of his appointment as U.S. ambassador to India.

Upon his return to the Department of State as assistant secretary for East Asian and Pacific affairs in 1974, Habib was determined to investigate and terminate Park's improper activities once and for all. Receiving a detailed report from Habib in February 1975, Secretary of State Kissinger discussed the matter with President Ford. As recalled by Kissinger, "The President asked me whether the information was conclusive, and I told him it did not seem to be. He asked me to watch it, and when we had further information to come back to him."[119] On the basis of Habib's further report, Attorney General Edward Levi started a grand jury investigation of the alleged South Korean bribery scandals. When the *Washington Post*, in the middle of the presidential campaign, carried a story on the grand jury investigation, it created a tense and contentious diplomatic problem between Washington and Seoul.[120] The story revealed that under the guidance of the South Korean government, Park had spent from half a million to one million dollars to bribe about ninety U.S. Congressmen and other officials, that the CIA had eavesdropped on the Blue House and had tape-recorded the planning sessions for Park's scheme, and that President Park himself was implicated in the operations. Stunned by the revelation, the South Korean government flatly stated that "Park has never been employed by the Korean government, nor does he have anything to do with President Park." It also denied that President Park even knew the name of Park Tong Son. The Park government imposed a blackout on the *Washington Post* story in South Korea and demanded a clarification from the Department of State. While the United States refrained from commenting on the report about the CIA wiretaps, South Korea threatened to conduct its own investigation and to take "appropriate measures." The Department of State called the veiled threat "not helpful."

The diplomatic sparring between Washington and Seoul was further aggravated by mutual misperceptions and procedural disagreements. The United States adopted a strictly legalistic position and expected South Korea, as an ally dependent on U.S. security commitments and economic aid, to cooperate fully with the Koreagate investigations. On the other hand, many South Korean officials believed that the Koreagate story was concocted by overzealous U.S. journalists who, in collusion with liberal congressmen and anti–South Korea forces, exaggerated and distorted minor cases of private gift-giving, a rather common practice in the Far East. They felt that their ally's legalistic arguments and diplomatic arrogance were part of an anti-Park conspiracy. Still others attributed the Koreagate exposé as a Ford election strategy. In this interpretation, the Ford administration intended to neutralize the Democratic Party's exploitation of the Watergate scandals and Ford's pardon of Nixon as campaign issues by linking a few key Democratic congressmen to the illicit Koreagate operations. According to a memoir by Park Tong Jin, South Korean foreign minister during the Koreagate affairs, Donald Ranard, director of the Office of Korean Affairs in the Department of State, who had served at the U.S. embassy in Seoul during the May 1961 coup d'état, was instrumental in pushing through the investigations because he had long hated President Park.[121] The primary concern of the South Korean government was to establish a clear distance between President Park and Park Tong Son. In his handwritten letter to South Korean Ambassador Hahm Pyong Choon, President Park made it clear that since he had no connection with Park Tong Son, the South Korean embassy in Washington should take a tough posture in its discussions with U.S. officials, both administrative and legislative.[122] In a repeat of the Watergate sensationalism, the U.S. media had a field day with the alleged scandal. The *New York Times* carried reports, editorials, and commentaries on the Korean question on eighty-four occasions through the end of 1976; the *Washington Post* reported on it on about fifty occasions.[123]

The House of Representatives and the Senate authorized their respective ethics committees to investigate the Koreagate allegations in early 1977. Fresh from its successful campaign for higher standards of public morality, the new Carter administration accelerated the grand jury inquiries, but this was awkward given the alleged involvement of key Democratic legislative leaders, including former and present House speakers Carl Albert and Tip O'Neill. In August 1977, the U.S. Department of Justice indicted Park Tong Son, who had already returned home, on thirty-six counts of conspiring to bribe congressmen, defrauding the government, mail fraud, racketeering, and illegal campaign contributions. The indictment did not directly link Park Tong Son to the South Korean government, but it did impose yet another strain on Washington-Seoul relations, which had already been marred by Carter's decisions to withdraw U.S. forces from South Korea and to criticize the human rights violations under President Park. In his long letter to President Park on August 26, 1977, President Carter requested Park Tong Son's extradition to the United States to face criminal charges and expressed his "grave concern" about the South Korean government's unwillingness to arrange Park Tong Son's cooperation with U.S. judicial proceedings.[124] He said that he could not accept Seoul's explanation that it could not influence Park Tong Sun's decision. If Park Tong Son did not cooperate with the U.S. request, Carter warned, public opinion would turn against the U.S.–South Korean relationship. The South Korean reaction was uncooperative. In his reply to Carter on September 12, President Park stated that it was up to Park Tong Son to decide and that the South Korean government could not interfere. He suggested that South Korea's laws and sovereignty as well as the principles of international law should be observed in resolving the Park Tong Son case.[125] At this time there was no extradition agreement between South Korea and the United States. In effect, President Park rebuffed Carter's appeal and adopted a hands-off posture. Adding to this irreconcilable legalistic standoff between Seoul and Washington was the South Korean government's fear that if Park Tong Son were allowed to return to the United States, he might reveal information harmful to President Park. In their meetings with Ambassador Kim, both Secretary of State Vance and Undersecretary of State for Political Affairs Habib continued to press for Park Tong Son's early extradition.

To make matters worse for Seoul, in November 1976 a KCIA representative in New York sought political asylum in the United States, as did the KCIA station chief in Washington in September 1977. They, along with Kim Hyung Wook, former KCIA director, appeared before the Subcommittee on International Organizations of the House Committee on International Relations in 1977 and 1978 and revealed the South Korean government's intricate scheme to buy influence in the United States.

As the combined pressure from the executive and legislative branches of the United States intensified, however, the South Korean government adopted a realistic approach and sought a mutually acceptable compromise, lest the situation deteriorate to the extent of undermining public approval of U.S. military assistance. On the recommendation of Leon Jaworski, an aggressive special counsel of the House

Committee on Standards of Official Conduct who had established his national rep-
utation during the Watergate investigations, the House of Representatives unanimously passed a resolution in October 1977 calling on the South Korean government to cooperate "fully and without reservation" with the Koreagate investigations.
After a series of intense negotiations, South Korean Foreign Minister Park Tong Jin,
U.S. Ambassador Richard Sneider, and Assistant Attorney General Benjamin R.
Civiletti reached an agreement in December 1977 that in exchange for Park Tong
Son's "truthful testimony" in U.S. courts, the Department of Justice would grant
him "full immunity" and drop the criminal charges against him.[126] For this purpose
the South Korean government promised to encourage Park Tong Son's visit to the
United States. This agreement, however, upset the House Committee on Standards
of Official Conduct and the Senate Select Committee on Ethics, both of which intended to secure Park Tong Son's testimony under oath. In particular, Leon Jaworski,
in an overreaching display of his reputation and authority, threatened to call not just
Park Tong Son but also former South Korean Ambassador to the United States Kim
Dong Jo as witnesses. He also hinted that noncooperation might lead to reductions
in U.S. military and economic assistance to South Korea. In an attempt to resolve
the conflict between Congress and Seoul, South Korean Ambassador Kim, a lawyer-
turned-diplomat, met with Speaker O'Neill in January 1978, returned to Seoul for
reports to President Park and Foreign Minister Park Tong Jin, had a discussion with
Assistant Secretary of State for East Asian and Pacific Affairs Richard Holbrooke, and
met with O'Neill a second time.[127] In his shuttle diplomacy, Kim was able to iron
out a consensus among all concerned parties that Park Tong Son would provide a
"voluntary sworn testimony" before both ethics committees but without a subpoena.

As agreed, Park Tong Son made three trips to the United States from February
to September 1978 to appear as a witness before the grand jury proceedings and at
the trials of Richard Hanna, Representative Otto Passman (D-LA), and businessman
Kim Han Cho (who was indicted for another South Korean influence-buying operation). He also testified voluntarily before the ethics committees of both houses of
Congress. In his testimony, Park readily admitted that he had obtained over $9 mil-
lion in commissions for rice sales from 1969 to 1975 and that he had given less than
$1 million in campaign contributions and cash payments to his "personal friends" in
the U.S. Congress. He denied any link with the South Korean government and insisted that he had never met with President Park. Describing himself as an "American success story on a small scale," Park Tong Son claimed that he had befriended
members of the U.S. Congress out of patriotism to South Korea. The Department
of Justice accepted his "truthful testimony" in the criminal cases and granted him
complete immunity. In its report, however, the House Committee on Standards of

Official Conduct concluded that Park Tong Son was "far more interested in paying Congressmen who would help him maintain his status as a rice agent than help the ROK on legislative issues affecting it."[128]

The South Korean government was spared further embarrassment because Park Tong Son had repudiated allegations of his intimate association with South Korean officials, particularly President Park. It successfully resisted Jaworski's full-court pressure to bring Kim Dong Jo as a witness before the House Committee on Standards of Official Conduct on the grounds of sovereign independence and diplomatic immunity as protected by the Vienna Convention. The Department of State tried to mediate between Congress and Seoul but in effect supported Seoul's correct legal position, much to Jaworski's chagrin. In the end, Kim agreed to respond to "written interrogatories" prepared by the ethics committees of both houses. This response was to be voluntary and private, but to be delivered in the form of an intergovernmental aide-mémoire. In denying all allegations of influence-buying activities in the United States, Kim stated, "I never offered or attempted to offer any money directly or indirectly to any U.S. Congressmen or other public officials," with the single exception of Representative Jerome Waldie (D-CA).[129] The Senate Select Committee on Ethics found no evidence to contradict Kim's denial, but the House Committee denounced Kim's written interrogatories as "totally unsatisfactory and insulting." However, Kim was beyond the reach of the U.S. Congress.

The Department of Justice was successful in convicting only two persons—Richard Hanna and Kim Han Cho; its indictment of Otto Passman on tax evasion charges failed. Upon the recommendation of its ethics committee, the House of Representatives voted to reprimand Edward R. Roybal (D-CA), John J. McFall (D-CA), and Charles H. Wilson (D-TX) in connection with Park Tong Son's payments. The House Committee on Standards of Official Conduct took no action against former members of the House such as Richard Hanna (D-CA), Otto Passman (D-LA), and Cornelius E. Gallagher (D-NJ) and exonerated other alleged recipients of Park Tong Son's payments and favors, including Tip O'Neill, Edward J. Patten (D-NJ), John Brademas (D-IN), John Murphy (D-NY), Frank Thompson Jr. (D-NJ), William Minshall (R-OH), and Nick Galifianakis (D-NC). The Senate Select Committee on Ethics reported that the South Korean government had adopted a scheme to influence the Senate by improper and illegal methods and that South Korea's "unregistered agent" Park Tong Son had made substantial campaign contributions to seven or eight senators. Yet it made a rather generous decision about those senators. The Senate Select Committee concluded that Senators Birch Bayh (D-IN) and Joseph M. Montoya (D-NM) had given false information about Park's payments and that Senators Hubert H. Humphrey (D-MN) and John McClellan (D-AK) had failed to report Park's campaign contributions. No disciplinary action against any present or former member of the Senate was recommended.

The entire Koreagate affair—both the judicial decisions and the congressional investigations—proved to be inconclusive and anticlimactic. While Assistant Secretary of State Holbrooke suggested that although "Koreagate had its origins in misperceptions, misguided actions, and lack of timely or adequate remedial measures," it no longer threatened the very fabric of the U.S.–South Korean alliance. One key South Korean official involved in the negotiations over the Koreagate investigations characterized Washington's heavy-handed pressure tactics as a manifestation of "big-nation chauvinism."[130] Apart from the adverse effects of legal and diplomatic conflicts over the Koreagate episode, the United States and South Korea found it difficult to overcome a "little bit of schizophrenia" toward each other for some time to come.[131] According to former foreign minister Park Tong Jin, one of the most important lessons South Korea learned from the Koreagate controversies was the importance of having a clear appreciation of the U.S. legal system.[132]

POLITICAL CRISIS IN SOUTH KOREA

The last year of President Park's 18-year rule was the most traumatic, not only because of his tortuous relations with the United States, but also because of his harsh style of domestic political management. During the summer and fall of 1979, his release of political prisoners, together with the completion of the Koreagate investigations and Carter's proposed suspension of troop withdrawal, did not mitigate the escalating struggle for political democratization and economic justice in South Korea. Influenced by such hardline assistants as Presidential Security Chief Cha Chi Chol, President Park brutally cracked down on labor strikes, took unprecedented steps to expel Kim Young Sam, president of the opposition New Democratic Party, from the National Assembly on insubstantial grounds, and declared "partial martial law" to crush political unrest in Pusan and Masan, the regional base of Kim Young Sam's power. The Carter administration publicly criticized Park's repressive tactics and for a while recalled Ambassador Gleysteen to Washington in protest. On October 18, 1979, Secretary of Defense Harold Brown, who was attending the 12th Security Consultative Meeting in Seoul together with Ambassador Gleysteen, met Park at the Blue House and counseled him to moderate his domestic policies.[133] Park was unwilling to heed Brown's advice—and paid the ultimate price.

When the news that KCIA Director Kim Chae Kyu had assassinated President Park and Cha Chi Chol during a dinner party near the Blue House on October 26, the U.S. Department of State, on Gleysteen's request, promptly issued a statement to reaffirm the U.S. security commitment for South Korea and requested that an air-craft carrier, airborne warning and control system (AWACS) planes, and Navy P3 antisubmarine aircraft be sent to Korea to monitor and deter any military moves by North Korea. U.S. troops were placed on full alert along the DMZ. In the early morning of October 27, Gleysteen went to the residence of Acting President Choi Kyu Ha, expressed his condolences, and discussed the steps to be taken by the two governments.[134] In a letter to Acting President Choi, General John A. Wickham Jr., CFC commander, said, "I assure you that the Combined Forces Command will remain ready and totally dedicated to the security of the Republic."[135] At the same time, President Carter promised Acting President Choi that the United States would "continue to stand firmly behind its treaty commitments to the Republic of Korea." In his response, Choi stated: "Your assurance of the firm treaty commitments of the United States to my country as well as words of sympathy greatly reinforces our determination to overcome with courage and unity the present challenge our nation faces today."[136] It was very important and comforting for Choi and many South Koreans to have the unswerving pledge of support from the United States at this diffi-cult juncture.

At this time of political confusion and uncertainty in South Korea, Gleysteen made the following recommendation to the Carter administration on October 28: "I urge that we resist the temptation to suggest architectural designs to the Koreans in favor of: (A) providing reassurance against the threat from the north, (B) urging the observance of 'constitutional processes' and (C) gently working through all channels toward political liberalization. We should avoid critical public comment or punish-ing actions unless and until the new regime has blotted its copybook. . . . Finally, we should remember that we could easily provoke a very unhealthy anti-American reac-tion if we press too hard, too crassly, and too soon for structural change in the ROK."[137] Gleysteen's careful, moderate, and thoughtful recommendation was quite appropriate. Accordingly, Secretary of State Vance, who was chosen to lead the U.S. delegation to Park's funeral, observed at his press conference on October 31 that "we welcome the preservation of stability in this difficult period and hope that future de-velopments will take place in an orderly manner."[138] If the United States were to be asked to have consultations on the question of a constitutional amendment in South Korea, he said, "we will certainly not be hesitant to express our views."

The United States applauded Choi's decisions to lift Emergency Measure 9, to release political prisoners, to ease press censorship, and to allow democratic political discourse. But there were lingering questions about the assassination. A sizable num-ber of prominent South Koreans and some prominent Americans, including Rep-resentative Clement Zablocki, chairman of the House Committee on International

Relations, suspected U.S. complicity, if not outright instigation or conspiracy, in Park's assassination. In his memoirs, Gleysteen flatly denied all allegations of U.S. complicity but candidly admitted that the assassin, Kim Chae Kyu, "might have misconstrued our words and actions to mean that we anticipated the end of Park's rule and would not be unhappy to see him depart the scene" and wondered "whether the sum total of U.S. actions and words unwittingly contributed in a significant way to Park's downfall."[139] He also speculated whether Kim, who was regarded as a pro-American leader, might have missed the delicate nuances of his critical remarks about Park's repressive policy during their frequent meetings because of the inadequacies of interpretation.[140] Gleysteen's final discussion with Kim had taken place on September 26, a month before Park's death, but it remains unclear exactly what transpired in Kim's intimate talks with Robert G. Brewster, CIA station chief in South Korea. During his interrogation and testimony, Kim indeed implied U.S. complicity but claimed that he had killed Park and Cha in the interest of democracy in South Korea. Soon thereafter Kim Chae Kyu and his security guards were executed.

More disturbing to the Carter administration than the persistent suspicion of U.S. complicity in Park's murder was the coup d'état on December 12, 1979, engineered by Major General Chun Doo Hwan, commander of the Defense Security Command, which was in charge of the inquiry into Park's death. He led a group of "Young Turks" who belonged to a secret military faction called *Hanahoe* (One Association) against another group of senior military officers headed by General Chung Seung Hwa, Army chief of staff and martial law commander; Chung was arrested on the unsubstantiated charge of involvement in the assassination of President Park. The Chun group disregarded both the South Korean army command and the CFC command when it moved some military units, including the Ninth Army Division commanded by General Roh Tae Woo, to Seoul without the prior notification required under the Operational Control (OPCON) of the CFC, which had taken over the UNC's OPCON responsibilities in 1978. Faced with this blatant violation of the CFC Terms of Reference and of the chain of command, General Wickham, furious but powerless, viewed Chun more critically than Gleysteen had. In comparison with Wickham and Gleysteen, Robert Brewster took a more realistic and conciliatory position toward Chun, arguing that Chun was "the only horse in town and we have to work with him."[141]

The U.S. reaction to the coup in South Korea was swift and firm. On the same day the Department of State issued a statement:

During the past few weeks we had been encouraged by the orderly procedures adopted in the Republic of Korea to develop a broadly based government following the assassination of President Park. As a result of events today in Korea we have instructed our Ambassador and the Commander of U.S. Forces in Korea to point out to all concerned that any forces within the Republic of Korea which disrupt this progress should bear in mind the seriously adverse impact their actions would have on the ROK's relations with the United States. At the same time, any forces outside the ROK which might seek to exploit the current situation in Seoul should bear in mind our warning of October 27.[142]

In a hastily arranged meeting with General Chun, who came to the U.S. embassy residence with about forty armed guards on December 14, Gleysteen conveyed U.S. concerns "quickly, bluntly, and directly" to Chun and his "crowd."[143] He told Chun that South Korea had to maintain a civilian government and could not afford to lose the support of the U.S. military and businessmen, who were deeply disturbed by what had happened. Chun responded that his action was not a coup but a patriotic act and that it had been taken because General Chung's complicity in the assassination of the late president needed to be investigated. He disavowed any personal political ambitions on his part and expressed his support for President Choi's program for political liberalization. Just as General Park Chung Hee had done in 1961, Chun promised to return to his military duties. Unlike Marshall Green and Carter B. Magruder in 1961, Gleysteen and Wickham refrained from denouncing the coup publicly but insisted on the preservation of a civilian government under Choi. In fact, Wickham argued for a "hands-off-response" from Washington because he felt that the United States had no reason to interfere in South Korea's domestic problems or to dictate their solutions.[144] He admitted that the United States could exert far less influence in South Korea than it had in 1961 and concluded that "anyone who believed that we were in any position to order a halt to this coup was badly out of date."

When Choi was inaugurated as the new president on December 21, President Carter promptly embraced his leadership and supported his efforts to develop "a broader political consensus" in South Korea.[145] Carter did not forget to praise Choi's earlier decision to repeal EM-9—a decision Park had steadfastly refused to make at the summit meeting in June. The Carter administration was well aware that behind the façade of Choi's civilian government, Chun and his "new military group" wielded the real political and military power and complicated the prospects for political democratization in South Korea. Just as General Park Chung Hee had persuaded President Yun to remain in office in 1961, Chun supported Choi's presidency to demonstrate a semblance of constitutional continuity and civilian rule. Ambassador Gleysteen and General Wickham distanced themselves from Chun and seriously considered supporting a plot for a counter-coup in January and February 1980.

In the end, they discouraged the plot supported by a few disgruntled South Korean generals because of its low probability of success. At the same time the United States urged China to discourage North Korea from exploiting the political instability in South Korea.

As arranged by Brewster, General Wickham agreed to meet with General Chun in late February 1980. As Chun tried to justify his actions of December 12, 1979, and to stress that he had no interest in assuming domestic political leadership, Wickham gave him a lecture: a soldier must support his constitution and legal authorities and confine his purpose to defending the nation.[146] Afterwards, Wickham reported to the Department of Defense and the Joint Chiefs of Staff:

> Chun impressed me as a ruthlessly ambitious, scheming and forceful man who believes he is destined to wear the purple. His manner was cocky and self-assured despite extreme nervousness in smoking almost a pack of cigarettes. I found him unsophisticated in his knowledge of the United States and of the international consequences that could result from instability in his country. There is a hint of anti-U.S. attitude in his intensely nationalistic and conservative views. . . . He is on the make, has a taste for power, knows how to use it, and does not strike me as a man to be trusted.

In spite of this negative view, Wickham recognized the practical necessity of meeting with Chun throughout 1980 and 1981.

After a guardedly optimistic phase of the "Seoul Spring" in early 1980 when the "three Kims"—Kim Jong Pil (president of the governing Democratic Justice Party), Kim Young Sam (president of the opposition New Democratic Party), and Kim Dae Jung (a dissident whose civil rights were fully restored on March 1)—crisscrossed the nation campaigning for the presidency, the spread of massive student protests led to yet another tragic political crisis. On May 17 the Choi administration under Chun's control arrested Kim Dae Jung and placed Kim Young Sam under house arrest, holding them responsible for the political unrest. They also arrested Kim Jong Pil on corruption charges. On the following day the government declared full martial law throughout the country and closed the National Assembly and the universities. A huge protest by students and other citizens erupted in Kwangju, a center of Kim Dae Jung's regional power base.[147] In a statement issued on May 18, the U.S. Department of State said that it was "deeply disturbed" by the deteriorating conditions in South Korea and hoped that "progress toward constitutional reform and the election of a broadly based civilian government, as earlier outlined by President Choi, should be resumed promptly."[148] It added: "The U.S. Government will react strongly in accordance with its treaty obligations to any external attempt to exploit the situation in the Republic of Korea." Subsequently, the United States ordered the aircraft carrier *Coral Sea* and two E-3A early warning aircraft to approach the region as an unmistakable warning to North Korea.

When South Korean military units, including the Special Warfare Command (SWC), were ordered to suppress the demonstrators with brutal force, the United States urged all parties to exercise maximum restraint and to seek a peaceful solution through dialogue. However, the Carter administration did not allow Ambassador Gleysteen to serve as a mediator in Kwangju. Nor did it threaten to impose any sanctions on South Korea's "new military group" led by General Chun in the event of a violent crackdown. By May 27 the military forces had killed several hundred students and other civilians and wounded thousands in Kwangju. The number of civilian casualties exceeded that of those killed and wounded during the April student uprising in 1960. Even if the United States had attempted to counsel restraint and moderation, especially in its discussions with Chun, it felt powerless in the wake of such violent domestic struggles. To make matters worse, the United States was accused of condoning Chun's actions in Kwangju. The Chun group adroitly mobilized the mass media to disseminate disinformation that the United States supported Chun's policies. Anti-American sentiment spread widely in Kwangju and beyond. It seems indisputable, however, that the Carter administration eventually accepted the emerging reality in South Korea—President Choi's resignation and Chun's indirect election as president by the National Conference for Unification in August 1980.[149]

No matter how praiseworthy the Carter administration's idealistic goals—political liberalization, human rights, constitutional reform, free elections, and civilian government—might have sounded in the context of American domestic and foreign affairs, the United States ultimately played no effective role in realizing them in the complex power struggles in South Korea. The assumptions, logical in America, that political democratization would automatically guarantee domestic stability and that domestic stability would provide a sound foundation for the U.S.–South Korean military alliance did not appeal to hard-nosed realists such as General Chun. The United States was reluctant to use its considerable leverage, especially in the form of military and economic assistance, to the maximum extent in South Korea because it was afraid that such extreme measures might further arouse anti-American sentiments, permanently alienate the dominant power group, or even inadvertently encourage dangerous miscalculations on the part of North Korea. The Carter administration, in protest, suspended the annual Security Consultative Meeting and Foreign Military Sales (FMS) credits to South Korea. Although the United States remained a powerful senior partner in the bilateral alliance system, it was constrained in dictating the domestic politics of its junior partner. Moreover, as a result of its impressive economic achievements and resultant self-confidence, South Korea was no longer the docile and submissive client state it once had been. In order to restrain Chun's undesirable behavior, General Wickham at times implied that the United States might negotiate with North Korea without South Korea's participation and that the United States might reconsider the withdrawal of its troops from South Korea, but these veiled threats did not meet with much success. So long as the primary national interests of the United States in South Korea—namely, to preserve the military containment system, to protect economic gains, and to secure a pro-American regime—were assured, other secondary interests such as human rights and the peaceful transfer of power did not, in the end, matter very much. As Ambassador Gleysteen admitted later, the United States was deeply entangled in South Korea, but it was only marginally effective in influencing the course of its domestic development.[150]

The only major domestic issue in which the United States made a notable difference concerned Kim Dae Jung, the symbol of the democratic movement in South Korea. In a case strangely reminiscent of the American role in preventing his death in August 1973, when KCIA agents had kidnapped him from a Tokyo hotel and brought him to Seoul, the United States again helped save his life. In a letter written to Chun on August 27, 1980, the day the National Conference for Unification elected him president, Carter deliberately refused to offer even a customary message of congratulations because he did not want to recognize Chun's legitimacy; instead he expressed his "personal" desire to maintain the basic economic and security relationships between the two countries. He explained that he was greatly troubled by the recent events in South Korea, emphasizing that "we regard free political institutions as essential to sustaining a sound relationship between our two countries." Turning to the main purpose of his letter—namely, the trial of Kim Dae Jung—Carter sternly warned that "Mr. Kim's execution, or even a sentence of death, could have serious repercussions."[151] In response, Chun drew Carter's attention to his Inaugural Address of September 1, in which he stressed the importance of consolidating the South Korean–U.S. mutual defense arrangement and of expanding cooperative relations between the two countries. He defended his recent actions as a necessary step to protect the very foundation of the state and outlined his agenda for guaranteeing "an orderly and broadly based political process" and "a free atmosphere" for fair electoral competition. As to the concern about Kim Dae Jung, Chun firmly stated that "Mr. Kim and his co-defendants are on trial on criminal charges of sedition and activities benefiting North Korean Communists. They are accorded the same fair and due process of law as applicable to any other indicted person, including access to defense lawyers and appeals to the higher courts."[152]

The exchange of letters between Carter and Chun did not prevent the court-martial from sentencing Kim Dae Jung to death on September 17 on the grounds that he not only held a sympathetic position toward North Korea but had also instigated the Kwangju incident to subvert the state. In honor of Carter's demands, the South Korean government had permitted an American government lawyer to observe the trial; he prepared detailed reports on the proceedings. The Carter administration with its high-profile priority on human rights launched an extraordinary campaign to save Kim's life because it had failed to prevent the Pakistani military leaders from executing former prime minister Zulfikar Ali Bhutto in 1979.

In a memorandum prepared for President Carter, National Security Adviser Brzezinski explained that Chun was essentially a Confucian leader trying to find the "virtuous" path that would cause his people to follow him.[153] He added that Chun had been told by some of his advisers that executing Kim Dae Jung and removing him as a disruptive force was in Confucian terms the virtuous thing to do. He assured President Carter that Kim would not be executed. In a concurrent resolution introduced on September 30 by Senators Edward M. Kennedy (D-MA), Paul E. Tsongas (D-MA), Carl Levin (D-MI), Mark O. Hatfield (R-OR), Alan Cranston (D-CA), and Harrison A. Williams Jr. (D-NJ), the U.S. Congress stated that if the sentence of execution of Kim Dae Jung and the harsh sentences for the other defendants were carried out, it would make it increasingly difficult to justify the continuation of a close relationship between the United States and South Korea.[154] The resolution asked President Carter to urge the South Korean government "to fulfill its stated commitments to the democratization of the political life of South Korea" and "to reconsider the process by which Kim Dae Jung and other critics of the [South Korean] government have been tried and convicted." If the South Korean government carried out the sentences, the resolution warned, Congress intended to review the terms of the relationship between the two countries.

Out of desperation, the wife of Kim Dae Jung, Lee Hee Ho, appealed directly to President and Mrs. Carter. Lee had studied at Lambuth College and Scarritt College for Christian Workers in Tennessee and had served as general secretary of the YWCA in South Korea. In a religiously inspired letter dated October 1, 1980, which Robert A. Kinney, a former U.S. official, smuggled out of South Korea, she stressed that Kim Dae Jung was not pro-Communist but rather "a sincere Christian believer devoted to the cause of true democracy." Among other things, she said:

> I have come to believe that God has been directing me through these days of prayer, suggesting that my husband should give up politics and devote himself to a life in the service of proclaiming the Christian gospel. When I shared these thoughts with him

during our recent visiting times at the prison, my husband told me that he also had been thinking along these same lines. But how can a man in prison awaiting the death sentence serve in behalf of spreading the gospel? At this moment I wish to appeal to you both to assist in finding a way for my husband, Kim Dae Jung, to leave Korean politics and travel to the United States, where he can study and also receive needed surgical care on his hip joints.

She argued that Carter had "the full right" to speak out in support of democratic progress and human rights in South Korea. On the margin of this letter, Carter wrote: "Zbig—We will continue our efforts on Kim's behalf."[155]

After the presidential election in November 1980, Richard V. Allen, who as foreign policy adviser for President-elect Ronald Reagan dealt with all important international matters for the incoming administration before the new secretary of state was installed, had consultations with Secretary of State Edmund Muskie, Assistant Secretary of State Holbrooke, Deputy Assistant Secretary of State Armacost, Ambassador Gleysteen, and other senior members of the outgoing Carter administration. The group agreed to send a message to President Chun urging that Kim's life be spared. According to Allen's recollection, Reagan thought that Kim's execution would be a "moral and political disaster."[156] In their meeting to discuss the issues and procedures of administrative transition in late November, Carter expressed his appreciation to Reagan for conveying the timely message to Chun. At that point Reagan admitted that he actually envied the authority that the late president Park had exercised during a time of campus unrest, when he had closed the universities and drafted the demonstrators into military service.[157] (As governor of California, Reagan had met Park in Seoul on October 16, 1971, amid violent campus demonstrations.) Even as a lame-duck president still mired in the hostage crisis in Iran, Carter once again wrote a letter to Chun on December 1, 1980, in which he appealed for "an act of reconciliation and magnanimity."[158] He said: "For the sake of compassion, your own national interest, and for the sake of our mutual relations, I urge you to reverse or commute the court-martial findings. The weakening of ROK-U.S. ties is not in the interest of either of our countries." He decided to omit a more direct and provocative segment in the draft praising Kim as "a symbol of democracy and greater freedom in your country" and positing that there was no evidence to justify the harshness of the sentence. A staff member of the National Security Council proposed to Brzezinski that "if we want to influence the South Koreans, we should begin talks with the North on a bilateral basis."[159] However, Brzezinski refused to use the "North Korean card" as a means for saving Kim Dae Jung's life.

On December 13, 1980, Secretary of Defense Harold Brown delivered the same message to Chun in person. A number of Chun's emissaries, including General Lew Byong Hion (chairman, Joint Chiefs of Staff) and General Chung Ho Yong (commander, Special Warfare Command), apparently went to Washington to persuade Allen that Kim should be executed, but Allen refused to accept their arguments. Minister Sohn Jang Nae of the South Korean embassy, representing the KCIA in Washington, also told Allen that if Kim were left alive, another Kwangju incident might occur.[160] Allen warned that if Kim were executed, its effect would be like "lightning"; public opinion would turn against South Korea so sharply that no American leader could afford to continue supporting it.[161] In his negotiations with General Chung, Allen rejected the proposal to invite Chun to the Reagan inauguration due to a protocol problem but promised that in exchange for sparing Kim's life, Chun would be invited to an early summit meeting with Reagan. Allen explained that this meeting would not be regarded as a state visit, a diplomatic honor, but as an official working visit. The South Koreans wanted to make sure that there would be no demonstrations against Chun during his visit to the United States and that the case of Kim would not be on the agenda for the Reagan-Chun meeting.[162]

Meanwhile, at Chun's request, his secretary general, Kim Kyung Won, who maintained a close liaison with Ambassador Gleysteen, explained to the hardline Young Turks that, apart from a consideration of the future of U.S.–South Korean relations, Kim's execution would inflict long-term damage on Chun's rule, which by this time had stabilized; it would be prudent to avoid any more bloodshed. A similar view was expressed by a few moderate military leaders, such as General Roh Tae Woo, who had played a critical role in the coup on December 12, 1979.[163] On January 24, 1981, Chun commuted Kim's death sentence to life imprisonment and lifted martial law. On February 3, Reagan warmly welcomed Chun to the White House for a summit meeting. He was the second foreign head of state Reagan met after his inauguration. This meeting was important in enhancing the legitimacy of Chun's leadership both at home and abroad. He fully expected to have a better relationship with Reagan than he had with Carter. After all, the lengthy campaign initiated by Carter to save Kim's life was successfully consummated in the first days of the Reagan presidency. A new chapter of very cordial and cooperative relations between Washington and Seoul was about to begin under the auspices of Reagan and Chun.

CHAPTER FOUR

The Passing of the Cold War

The Reagan and Bush Years

Championing a moralistic and militantly anti-Communist foreign policy, President Ronald Reagan, at the time of his inauguration, rejected the liberal premises that had guided Carter's military and diplomatic approaches toward Korea. In his summit meeting with President Chun Doo Hwan in February 1981, Reagan unequivocally declared that "the United States, as a Pacific power, will seek to ensure the peace and security of the region" and that "the United States has no plans to withdraw U.S. ground combat forces from the Korean Peninsula."[1] With this straightforward policy pronouncement, Reagan restored close military and diplomatic cooperation between the two allies, and the new era of collaboration continued throughout Reagan's eight-year presidency, which almost coincided with Chun's rule in South Korea. The personal warmth and rapport between Reagan and Chun sharply contrasted with President Park's uncomfortable and contentious relationship with Presidents Nixon and Carter.

As successor to Reagan's foreign policy, President George H. W. Bush was generally inclined to sustain the strong pro-Seoul posture. In February 1989 he assured President Roh Tae Woo and other South Korean leaders in Seoul that the United States was "a faithful friend and a dependable ally" for South Korea and that "we work together in all things."[2] Yet he was compelled to adapt his policy to the combined effects of three major factors—(1) the passing of the cold war and its regional effects; (2) President Roh Tae Woo's determined pursuit of "northern diplomacy" toward the Soviet Union and China; and (3) a significant change in inter-Korean relations. While preserving its traditional foundation of military containment against North Korea, the Bush administration cautiously modified its policy of diplomatic isolation toward Pyongyang and sustained channels for bilateral talks in Beijing. In view of the unmistakable ascendancy of South Korean capabilities over those of North Korea, the United States supported the expansion of inter-Korean cooperation and explored the possibility of lowering its military profile on the Korean Peninsula. Hence U.S. policy toward the Korean Peninsula began to transcend the narrow ideological boundaries of the cold war era and the predominance of its bilateral relationship with South Korea, commencing a dynamic new period of trilateral interactions with both Seoul and Pyongyang. At the same time, the downfall of the Soviet Union and other East European socialist regimes and the peaceful unification of Germany raised questions as to whether something similar might take place on the Korean Peninsula.

REAGAN'S ANTI-COMMUNIST POLICY

In his seminal book *Diplomacy*, Henry Kissinger observed: "The details of foreign policy bored Reagan. He had absorbed a few basic ideas about the danger of appeasement, the evils of communism, and the greatness of his own country, but analysis of substantive issues was not his forte."[3] Yet Kissinger recognized the positive implications of Reagan's personal convictions and extraordinary consistency in domestic and foreign affairs. It was clear that although Reagan espoused the Wilsonian concept of American moral exceptionalism and focused on what he perceived as the struggle between good and evil in international affairs, he also resorted to expedient realist methods to achieve his unabashed moral crusade. Compared with Nixon, he was less interested in pursuing the détente policy toward the Soviet Union. In fact, he exerted relentless pressure on the Soviet Union as the "Evil Empire," increased the defense budget, started the Strategic Defense Initiative (SDI), deployed intermediate-range missiles in Europe, and supported the anti-Communist insurgency in Nicaragua.

"To Ronald Reagan," recalled George Shultz, who served as Reagan's secretary of state, "South Korea was a stalwart ally and a valiant symbol of resistance to communism."[4] On February 2, 1981, when President Reagan cordially invited the anti-Communist crusader Chun Doo Hwan to the United States, he chose to ignore completely Chun's well-established record of antidemocratic activities. Pointing out the significance of this meeting, U.S. Ambassador to South Korea William Gleysteen Jr., who had resented Chun's undemocratic seizure of power, informed the Department of State that the visit would amount to legitimization of his government and thus was a development of profound importance in terms of consolidating his power domestically, enhancing South Korea's standing vis-à-vis North Korea and paving the way for a more normal relationship between South Korea and the rest of the world.[5] He suggested that while recognizing the overriding importance of U.S. security and economic relationships with South Korea, "we should encourage internal trends toward greater freedom and moderation."

In a memorandum for President Reagan, however, the new secretary of state, Alexander M. Haig Jr., a disciple of the classic realists Richard Nixon and Henry Kissinger, emphasized the primary importance of the U.S.–South Korean security relationship and played down issues of human rights and political liberalization in South Korea. More specifically, Haig reported to the president that his objectives in meeting with Chun were "to restore normalcy to our relations with a valued ally, to underscore the constancy of the American commitment to peace and stability in Northeast Asia, to support recent ROK diplomatic initiatives on North-South issues; and to indicate understanding of ROK economic difficulties without incurring obligations we may be unable to meet." As to the South Korean visitor, Haig explained:

> Chun has come a long way as a national leader in a short time. A highly regarded, rather aggressive career Army officer until December 1979, he has come into political power with little experience of the broader problems of national government outside the security field. He has an impulsive tendency toward quick solutions, and there are many gaps in his knowledge. But he is a fast learner and considerably less self-righteous and rigid than some of his younger supporters. He expects us to be concerned with Korean internal developments and is prepared to consider our advice when it is offered privately and in the context of basic cooperation. His ability and willingness to accommodate foreign concerns over the Kim Dae Jung issue is a measure of how much he has matured.[6]

In his welcoming remarks to Chun at the White House, Reagan hearkened back to the long history of close military cooperation between the two countries, praising General Douglas MacArthur's landing at Inchon and South Korea's participation in the Vietnam War and emphasizing "our special bond of freedom and friendship" and mutual defense against aggression.[7] Immensely moved by Reagan's references to General MacArthur (whom Chun admired) and to the Vietnam War (in which he took part), President Chun responded that he would seek a mature partnership with the United States and an era of dialogue and consensus for building "a freer, more abundant, and democratic society" in South Korea. He was indeed gratified by Reagan's unmistakable cold war rhetoric and mentality.[8]

In a joint communiqué, Reagan and Chun pledged to "strengthen U.S.-Korean cooperation in deterring and defending against aggression as an indispensable contribution to peace and stability in Northeast Asia." Unlike the earlier Carter-Park joint communiqué, Reagan and Chun did not mention three-party talks or human rights. Nor was the political and legal status of Kim Dae Jung high on the agenda for the summit discussions. It was the expressed view of Secretary of State Haig that Carter's approach toward three-party talks had been naive and unrealistic.[9] As did Reagan, Haig sought to mend the "rupture" in U.S. relations with the Chun government caused by Carter's policies on troop withdrawal and human rights. Haig believed that the previous practice of publicly denouncing friendly countries such as South Korea and Argentina on questions of human rights while at the same time attempting to minimize the abuse of those rights in the Soviet Union and other totalitarian countries should end.[10]

Even though Reagan publicly invoked the issues of human rights and democratic liberalization to assail and undermine the Soviet Union, he was relatively reticent about violations of human rights in South Korea and even in China. In this he differed from Carter. Reagan assured Chun that South Korea would be a full participant in any negotiations between the United States and North Korea and that any unilateral steps toward North Korea that were not reciprocated toward South Korea by North Korea's principal allies would not be supported. The two presidents agreed to normalize a wide range of bilateral cooperative arrangements, including the annual Security Consultative Meetings and economic consultations, which had been suspended after the Kwangju incident. Reagan promised that the United States would remain a reliable supplier of nuclear fuel, generation equipment, and power technology. Reagan's unhesitating decision to embrace Chun aggravated anti-American sentiments in South Korea and helped consolidate Chun's political power.

In a meeting with President Chun and Foreign Minister Lho Shin Yong at the Department of State following the Reagan-Chun session on February 2, Haig, a veteran of both the Korean and Vietnam Wars, noted that in Vietnam South Korea had proved to be a true and lasting friend of the United States.[11] He promised to attach top priority to reestablishing "confidence in our security relationships" and to help South Korea secure soft loans from Japan. When Chun complained that unofficial visits to North Korea by American scholars and others gave North Korea the impression that it could deal with the United States over the heads of the South Korean government and could ignore the need for direct dialogue between South Korea and North Korea, Haig responded that the U.S. government frowned on Americans' personal diplomatic activity with hostile regimes but would not and could not attempt to block it. Haig told Lho that although the South Koreans might be uneasy about U.S. ties with China, he would take South Korean views into account while proceeding with the U.S.-Chinese relationship, which to a certain extent had been dictated by American strategic concerns over the Soviet Union. Lho asked Haig to send a distinguished high-level American delegation to Chun's forthcoming presidential inauguration and to publicize such U.S. intentions in order to influence the Japanese, Europeans, and others.

The Department of State reported that the chance coinciding of President Chun's visit to Washington with the annual "Team Spirit" exercise between U.S. and South Korean troops prompted the North Koreans to step up their verbal attacks against President Reagan. They called him a "clown," "an old wolf," and "a gangster on the theatrical stage."[12] While North Korean and Soviet propaganda on the theme of U.S. perfidy had increased, as Robert G. Rich (director of the Office of Korean Affairs, Department of State) noted, "The silence from the Chinese had been almost deafening." In fact, the Chinese took a wait-and-see position toward Reagan, who had advocated a better relationship between the United States and Taiwan during his presidential campaign. When Chun was elected to the seven-year presidency toward the end of February 1981, Reagan, unlike his predecessor, sent his "warmest congratulations" and chose Senator Charles H. Percy (R-IL), chairman of the Senate Committee on Foreign Relations, as his "personal representative" to attend the inauguration on March 3, 1981. In Reagan's view, Chun resembled Park Chung Hee in terms of his strong political leadership, anti-Communist commitment, and emphasis on economic advancement.

The Reagan administration was pleased with the consolidation of a stable rule under President Chun in South Korea. The Department of State reported to Secretary of State Haig in June 1981 that "the situation in South Korea is now fairly normal and President Chun's government is fully functioning. Confidence and full cooperation has been restored to our relationship after a period of some strain."[13] As Reagan's political appointee, U.S. Ambassador to South Korea Richard L. "Dixie" Walker, who had taught political science and Chinese affairs at the University of South Carolina and had developed a wide network of professional and personal ties with his South Korean counterparts, practiced the art of "quiet diplomacy" toward the Chun government. Skeptical of the efficacy of "quiet diplomacy," Senator Edward M. Kennedy (D-MA) continued to push for the release of Kim Dae Jung from prison. He argued in January 1982 that "Mr. Kim has remained in solitary confinement for nineteen months. He is kept now under extremely harsh circumstances in Chungju prison, without adequate heat or food and is denied medical treatment for his swollen legs and infected ears. He is not allowed any visitors except his wife, who may see him under observation for some ten to twenty minutes, once a month."[14] Soon thereafter, the Chun government allowed Kim and his wife to travel to the United States and thus removed a source of friction between the two countries.

Even after Haig resigned in June 1982, in part because of his difficulties with the White House, the new secretary of state George P. Shultz, a marine during World War II and secretary of labor and secretary of the treasury under President Nixon, continued to uphold the importance of the U.S.–South Korean alliance. In a memorandum prepared for Shultz prior to his visit to East Asian countries in January and February 1983, Assistant Secretary of State for East Asian and Pacific Affairs Paul Wolfowitz stated that "our overriding interest in Korea is to preserve the security of the ROK in the face of a formidable threat from the North."[15] However, Wolfowitz noted, South Korea's economic strength and its growing international role added new dimensions to the U.S.–South Korean relationship.

Whenever President Chun faced an international crisis, the Reagan administration promptly rendered its whole-hearted support to South Korea. One such crisis occurred in 1983. On September 1, the South Koreans suffered a major setback in their peaceful overtures toward Moscow when Korean Air Lines Flight 007, on its way from New York to Seoul via Anchorage, strayed into Soviet airspace near Sakhalin Island and was shot down by a Soviet jet fighter. All 269 persons aboard the Boeing 747 jumbo plane were killed (104 South Koreans, 61 Americans, 28 Japanese, 23 Taiwanese, and citizens of eleven other countries). The Soviet Union initially denied that its jet fighter had fired missiles at the South Korean civilian airplane but later contended that Flight 007 had intruded into its territory to gather military intelligence for the United States.[16] The charge was emphatically refuted by both South Korea and the United States.

The South Korean government denounced the Soviet Union's "utterly inhuman act" and "hegemonic behavior." President Reagan, too, assailed the Soviet "massacre" and "savagery" in his public addresses, seizing on the incident to launch a vigorous anti-Soviet campaign.[17] He ordered the flags of the United States flown at half-mast at all federal installations and U.S. military bases around the world. In a confidential directive dated September 5, the U.S. National Security Council decided to "seek maximum condemnation of the Soviet Union in the U.N. Security Council and provide wide dissemination of statements made in these sessions."[18] The directive intended to "assure the government of [South] Korea that we will vigorously support their request to conduct, participate in, or observe salvage operations" and to "indicate our clear willingness and desire to assist the government of Korea in recovering the bodies and flight recorder as appropriate and in accord with international law." Secretary of State Shultz was instructed to develop a coordinated action plan to implement this directive in concert with other relevant leaders. In a meeting with Soviet Foreign Minister Andrei Gromyko during the Madrid Conference on Security and Cooperation in Europe (CSCE), Secretary Shultz lashed out at the Soviet Union for its brutal act and its dishonest justification. Gromyko accused the United States of sending a spy plane over Soviet territory. According to Soviet Ambassador to the United States Anatoly Dobrynin, Shultz and Gromyko exchanged loud and sharp accusations. At one point Gromyko even lost his legendary composure, flinging his glasses on the table, almost breaking them.[19]

At the emergency session of the U.N. Security Council, South Korean Ambassador Kim Kyung Won made five demands on the Soviet Union: (1) to offer a full and detailed account of the incident; (2) to offer a full apology and complete compensation to the families of the dead passengers and crew members and to compensate for the loss of the aircraft; (3) to punish those directly responsible for the tragedy; (4) to guarantee unimpeded access to the crash site to the representatives of impartial international organizations, Korean Air Lines, and the government of the Republic of Korea; and (5) to give credible guarantees against the recurrence of such violent actions against civilian airplanes.[20] None of these demands were acceptable to the Soviet Union. On behalf of South Korea, the United States delivered a diplomatic note to the Soviet Union on September 12 in which the Soviet government was asked to provide "prompt, adequate, and effective compensation for the lives of Korean nationals aboard Korean Air Lines Flight 007 and for any other compensable loss incurred by any Korean national or by the Government of the Republic of Korea or any of its agencies or instrumentalities as a result of the Soviet Union's wrongful action."[21] The Soviet Union simply ignored all the demands.

The United States cosponsored a resolution at the U.N. Security Council deploring the incident and calling for its full investigation by the U.N. secretary-general.[22] The resolution received the necessary minimum of nine affirmative votes, but the Soviet veto killed it. While Poland, too, voted against the resolution, China, Zimbabwe, Nicaragua, and Guyana abstained. Disillusioned by the U.N. impasse, Ambassador Kim warned the Soviet Union that "the civilized world will continue to pursue the matter beyond the walls of this chamber and press the guilty until the Soviet authorities admit their crime and accede to the five demands my government has put forward." Despite its grief and impassioned protests, South Korea had no realistic alternative but to appeal to the amorphous influence of world public opinion. The International Civil Aviation Organization, the International Federation of Air Line Pilots Associations, and the Inter-Parliamentary Union adopted anti-Soviet resolutions, but they had no effect on the Soviet obstinacy. Japan, the United States, and a few other NATO member states suspended commercial flights to and from the Soviet Union for a few weeks. The U.S. and Japanese navies joined in the extensive search for the flight recorders near the crash site, but the failure to find them left many important technical questions unanswered. The Soviet government waited until October 6 to issue a TASS statement openly admitting that the airplane had been mistakenly shot down by a Soviet fighter. And it took eight more years for Soviet Foreign Minister Eduard Shevardnadze to apologize to South Korean Foreign Minister Choi Ho Jung for the Flight 007 tragedy. In Dobrynin's candid assessment, the tragic incident and the way the Soviet government dealt with it constituted "a very serious blunder."[23]

Even before the anger and controversy over Flight 007 had died down, South Korea was plunged into yet another violent crisis that erupted during the first leg of President Chun's 18-day, six-nation trip abroad. On the morning of October 9, 1983, a powerful bomb ripped through the Martyrs' Mausoleum in Rangoon, Burma, which President Chun and his wife were scheduled to visit for a wreath-laying ceremony. They escaped this assassination plot only because a traffic jam had delayed their motorcade. The explosion, however, did kill seventeen South Koreans and four Burmese and wounded several dozen people who were waiting for Chun's arrival at the mausoleum. Among the dead were Chun's most trusted technocrats in the economic and diplomatic fields, including Deputy Prime Minister and Minister of the Economic Planning Board Suh Sok Jun, Minister of Foreign Affairs Lee Bom Sok, Minister of Commerce and Industry Kim Dong Hui, Minister of Energy and Resources Suh Sang Chul, Presidential Secretary General Hahm Pyong Choon, and Senior Secretary to the President for Economic Affairs Kim Jae Ick.[24] Shaken by the loss of his senior aides, Chun canceled his travel plans and hurried home. He lost no time in blaming North Korea for the bombing conspiracy. South Korean armed forces, along with U.S. forces in South Korea, were placed on full alert. An increasing number of South Koreans demanded that their government take punitive military action against North Korea.

The United States denounced the terrorist attack in Rangoon but advised President Chun not to retaliate against North Korea by military means. Kenneth Quinones, a political officer at the U.S. embassy in Seoul, remembers: "The day after the explosion in Rangoon, the U.S. Ambassador dispatched me to the National Assembly to deliver his message to the chairmen of the Foreign and Defense Affairs Committees. Many powerful national assemblymen were retired generals. They demanded armed retaliation against North Korea. My job was to tell them that [the] United States would defend South Korea, but not if it attacked North Korea first."[25] In his memoirs, Secretary Shultz praised the Chun government for exercising "great forbearance" and resisting the temptation to retaliate. He observed: "This tragedy drove home the deep animosity projected by the North Korean government toward South Korea and the necessity for South Korea to be vigilant on security concerns."[26] After a month-long investigation, the Burmese government concluded that North Korean army commandos were responsible for the explosion and decided to sever diplomatic relations with North Korea.

When the South Koreans asked whether President Reagan intended to visit Seoul on November 12 as previously scheduled, he assured them that he was more determined than ever to demonstrate his support for them in person. In a confidential memorandum submitted to Reagan on November 1, Secretary of State Shultz explained that the visit came against the backdrop of the KAL 007 and Rangoon attacks, which had engendered such outrage and frustration in South Korea, and that "our close cooperation with the [South] Koreans helped them to cope with the internal stresses caused by these events and further strengthened their confidence in the United States as a friend and ally." He added that even prior to the twin tragedies, "our ties with [South] Korea had been exceptionally strong. Korean doubts about the reliability of the security commitment, which had been fanned by Carter administration consideration of troop withdrawal, had been eased." On South Korea's domestic affairs, he said that there had been signs of increased respect for human rights and gradual political liberalization and that "we need to signal our strong interest in further progress, and in particular to encourage Chun to carry through his pledge to hand over power in a peaceful transition in 1988."[27] In addition, Reagan was informed of the serious U.S. economic concerns in the area of market access and investment climate in South Korea and was advised to urge Chun to import civil aircraft and nuclear power plants from the United States.[28]

The three-day visit Reagan made to Seoul in November 1983 was a fitting finale to a traumatic year for South Korea. The South Korean government had contained student demonstrators and political dissidents and took extreme measures for Reagan's personal safety. Just as he had done during his first summit meeting with President Chun in 1981, Reagan expressed his strong support for the South Korean host and assured him that the Korean Air Lines tragedy and the bombing at Rangoon did not diminish the U.S. security commitment to South Korea. Speaking before the National Assembly, he assailed both the Soviet Union and North Korea: "Instead of offering assistance to a lost civilian airliner, the Soviet Union attacked. Instead of offering condolences, it issued denials. Instead of offering reassurances, it repeated its threats. Even in the search for our dead, the Soviet Union barred the way. This behavior chilled the entire world. The people of Korea and the United States shared a special grief and anger. . . . We also pledge to work with your Government and others in the international community to censure North Korea for its uncivilized behavior."

Reagan said that the "despicable North Korean attack in Rangoon deprived us of trusted advisers and friends" and that "North Korea is one of the most repressive societies on earth."[29] And he supported goals for human rights and democratic practices and welcomed President Chun's promise for a constitutional transfer of power in 1988. In the joint statement issued on November 14, the two presidents reaffirmed the "importance of defending and strengthening freedom and the institutions that serve freedom, openness and political stability."[30] According to David Lambertson, who as director of the Office of Korean Affairs at the Department of State was instrumental in planning the president's visit to South Korea, Reagan boosted the morale of the depressed South Koreans and showed his "charm at its best."[31]

The only irritant in South Korea's otherwise harmonious relationship with the United States was the continuing disagreement over trade issues. For the 1961–83 period, bilateral trade grew at an average annual rate of 20%. In 1983 the United States was South Korea's biggest trading partner, and South Korea was the ninth-largest market for U.S. exports and the seventh-largest source of U.S. imports. Bolstered by America's economic recovery and the strong dollar, South Korea enjoyed a trade surplus ($1.6 billion) during the first half of 1984. To protect its domestic markets against South Korean penetration, the Reagan administration handed down anti-dumping decisions on South Korean goods (such as color television sets) and sought "voluntary restraints" on steel products and other important South Korean export items. The U.S. Department of Commerce asked the Export-Import Bank not to finance the sale of U.S. materials valuing $100 million for South Korea's steel industries on the grounds that increased South Korean steel exports would be aimed at the U.S. market. The South Koreans argued that America's protectionist practices were unfair, but trade disputes were unavoidable between newly industrializing countries and postindustrial states.

The South Koreans were pleased with Reagan's landslide reelection in November 1984, and no major diplomatic problem emerged to strain Washington-Seoul relations. Summit meetings between Reagan and Chun became routine events. At their summit meeting at the White House in April 1985, Reagan stated that "perhaps nowhere in the world is the contrast between our shared democratic values and communism clearer than it is there on the DMZ. And nowhere is it clearer that strength is the surest path to peace."[32] He expressed his full support for the Asian Games (1986) and the Olympic Games (1988), both to be held in Seoul. The two leaders agreed to defend and expand free trade in their own relationship and multilaterally. No joint communiqué, however, was issued this time. And Vice President Bush, not Reagan, hosted the dinner in honor of the South Korean president.

While continuing to endorse President Chun's staunch anti-Communist posture in the mid-1980s, the Reagan administration gradually assumed a subtle but unmistakable role in improving human rights conditions and in promoting the process of political democratization in South Korea. Unlike President Carter, however, Reagan avoided public criticism of Chun's operations, relying instead upon "quiet diplomacy," which had mixed results. Encouraged by the successful U.S. role in removing Filipino President Ferdinand Marcos from power in February 1986 and in prodding General Augusto Pinochet toward a peaceful transfer of power in Chile, the Reagan administration sought to ensure that President Chun would carry out his pledge to step down in 1988 and thereby guarantee a peaceful transfer of power. Secretary Shultz in particular appeared obsessed by this issue. "When I became secretary of state," he remembered, "I wanted to do all I could to help President Reagan see that President Chun fulfilled his pledge."[33] A few days after a particularly violent demonstration of about 10,000 political dissidents, radical students, and factory workers at Inchon in early May 1986, Shultz visited Seoul to emphasize the importance of an orderly democratic process. Dismissing his assistants' advice to avoid political topics in his public remarks, Shultz spoke out in favor of the peaceful road toward procedural democracy and met with moderate opposition leaders. However, Assistant Secretary of State Gaston Sigur's plan to meet with the two key dissidents—Kim Young Sam and Kim Dae Jung—was cancelled due to intense pressure from the Chun government. In Shultz's recollection, the most difficult trick he had to accomplish in Seoul was to demonstrate firm U.S. support for President Chun while at the same time encouraging the dialogue for political liberalization.[34] Even though he condemned the opposition that had incited the violence at Inchon and voiced support for the government's measures to protect law and order, he was criticized for taking sides in South Korea's domestic politics.

Under mounting pressure from the Reagan administration and opposition forces, President Chun agreed to let the National Assembly consider the issue of constitutional amendments in 1986.[35] The National Assembly set up a Special Committee on Constitutional Revision, but it remained inoperative due to partisan disputes. At issue was the very structure of the governing bodies. While the governing Democratic Justice Party (DJP) intended to adopt a new constitutional framework for a parliamentary-cabinet system of government in which the prime minister, chosen by the National Assembly, would be responsible for the executive branch of government, the opposition New Korea Democratic Party (NKDP) wanted to retain the existing presidential system of government and to hold a direct popular election of the president. When President Lee Min Woo and other top leaders of the NKDP indicated their willingness to reach a compromise with the DJP over this funda-

mental constitutional issue, the two Kims—Kim Young Sam and Kim Dae Jung—
decided in April 1987 to remove their factional followers from the NKDP and to
form a new opposition party, the Reunification Democratic Party (RDP). They reaffirmed their uncompromising stand on the question of direct presidential election.

On April 13, President Chun took advantage of the disarray in opposition circles
and suspended any further negotiations over the constitution. He announced that
the next president would be elected indirectly by an electoral college and that negotiations for constitutional amendments would resume after the Seoul Olympic
Games scheduled for September and October 1988. On June 10, the national convention of the governing Democratic Justice Party endorsed President Chun's hand-
picked nominee—Roh Tae Woo—as its presidential candidate. Coming from Taegu,
Chun and Roh were classmates at the Korean Military Academy in the 1950s. They
had supported General Park's coup d'état in May 1961, served together in combat
during the Vietnam War, organized an exclusive secret society called *Hanahoe* (One
Association) for military officers, and led the coup in December 1979. On Roh's
retirement from military service in 1981, Chun had appointed him as minister of
political affairs, minister of sports, minister of home affairs, chairman of the Seoul
Olympic Organizing Committee, chairman of the Democratic Justice Party, and
member of the National Assembly. Roh became Chun's alter ego.

The unilateral decisions made by Chun ignited a wave of massive prodemocracy demonstrations throughout May and June. An increasing number of students,
opposition politicians, religious leaders, disgruntled intellectuals, and other concerned citizens assailed the Chun-Roh leadership as undemocratic and illegitimate
and demanded a new system of direct and popular presidential elections. They also
accused the United States of condoning or supporting President Chun's antidemocratic measures. Even the politically liberal segment of the growing middle
class joined in the nationwide struggle for political democratization. According to
a Seoul National University survey conducted in May, 52.1% of the middle class responded that political freedom was more important than economic development
and 85.7% said that it was desirable to protect human rights even at the expense of
economic growth.[36]

The Reagan administration was seriously concerned not only about the spread of
anti-American sentiment but also about the distinct possibility that the political turmoil could lead Chun to declare martial law and use armed forces to suppress opposition political forces and that he might renege on his promise to step down in
February 1988. At this critical juncture, Secretary of State Shultz and South Korean
Ambassador Kim Kyung Won agreed that President Reagan should write a confidential letter to President Chun. It was understood that Chun felt a sense of political

indebtedness to Reagan and that both leaders respected each other.[37] On June 19, U.S. Ambassador James Lilley insisted on visiting President Chun at the Blue House and delivering Reagan's letter to him in person.

In this friendly letter, Reagan reaffirmed the U.S. security commitment for South Korea and expressed his appreciation to Chun for his self-restraint in managing the crisis. Then he urged him to avert the use of military forces and to talk to other political leaders in order to ensure a peaceful, unprecedented, and historic transfer of power. He also urged Chun to release political prisoners, encourage freedom of the press, and prosecute police officers who abused their power.[38] Reagan said that such moves would "send to the world a dramatic signal of your interest to break free of what you correctly term the 'old politics.'" He added that "dialogue, compromise, and negotiation are effective ways to solve problems and maintain national unity."[39] Moreover, the imposing and tough-minded Lilley, who as head of the semi-diplomatic American Institute in Taiwan had promoted President Chiang Ching-kuo's democratic reforms in the early 1980s, told Chun that the U.S. embassy in Seoul and the U.S. Forces Korea were united in opposing the declaration of martial law in South Korea. If martial law were declared, Lilley warned, it would undermine the U.S.–South Korean alliance and might provoke another Kwangju uprising.[40] General William J. Livesey, commander-in-chief of USFK, gave no explicit consent to Lilley's statement to Chun, but he was evidently prepared to use U.S. troops to block any South Korean military movements into Seoul.

In addition, Deputy Assistant Secretary of State Michael Armacost proposed that Vice President George H. W. Bush visit Seoul to elaborate on Reagan's message to Chun, but the South Korean government rejected this visit on the grounds that such a high-profile visitor might embolden opposition leaders and put President Chun on the defensive. Instead, Secretary of State Shultz dispatched Assistant Secretary of State for East Asian and Pacific Affairs Gaston Sigur to Seoul to have a series of meetings with all of the major political and civic leaders in South Korea. As director of the Sino-Soviet Institute at George Washington University, Sigur, a moderate and pragmatic conservative, had visited Seoul on several occasions. In a 90-minute conversation with Chun on June 24, Sigur made it clear that a "special relationship" existed between the two allies, that the United States supported the South Korean president's decision for a peaceful transition of power, and that much attention was focused on the process of South Korea's democratization because of its economic prosperity and international prestige as symbolized by the forthcoming Seoul Olympiad.[41] Sigur expressed admiration for the way Chun had handled the difficult situation: Chun had been able to avoid excessive use of force and limit security measures to the police force rather than the army. The only way to resolve the current crisis, Sigur said, was through dialogue and discussion with opposition political leaders.

In response, Chun expressed appreciation for Reagan's earlier letter and said that he had a special regard for Reagan and his administration because of the warmth it had extended to him and because of the public expressions of trust by Reagan, Shultz, and Sigur, who "knew how to deal with a friend—a marked departure from previous administrations." Chun assured Sigur that he would carry out a peaceful transfer of power and that the military forces would be used against external enemies only. He went on to qualify this statement, adding that in the event of the complete disappearance of public safety, his government would be forced to intervene to protect its citizens, although emphasizing that this was a worst-case scenario and that he would do his best to prevent it. In such an eventuality, however, he hoped that "the U.S. must not side with rebels that want to destroy the country." According to Chun, his lame-duck status was being exploited by various forces, including opposition political leaders, North Korean "sleepers" in South Korea, and antigovernment clerics in the church who intended to overthrow his administration. Chun asked Sigur to tell other South Korean political leaders he planned to meet that the United States wanted to see an orderly and peaceful transition of government and that everyone concerned needed to show restraint. Chun added that if the situation spun out of control and his government had to take very harsh measures, it was important for the United States to stand by the South Korean government. Sigur reiterated that Reagan wanted to see a peaceful and orderly transition in South Korea and said that "we would do all we could to support this." At this time the Reagan administration was primarily concerned with preventing Chun's use of military force against demonstrators and with encouraging procedural democracy in the form of free elections for choosing civilian political leaders. If martial law were declared in South Korea, Reagan's persistent support for Chun would appear to have been misguided and would become an easy target for criticism from the Democratic Party.

It was not difficult for Sigur to meet with several top-ranking officials—Prime Minister Lee Han Key, Foreign Minister Choi Kwang Soo, Speaker of the National Assembly Lee Chae Hyong, Stephen Cardinal Kim Sou Hwan, Roh Tae Woo (chairman of the governing Democratic Justice Party and its nominee for the presidency), Kim Young Sam (president of the opposition Reunification Democratic Party) as well as other politicians, intellectuals, and journalists, but his plan to visit Kim Dae Jung met with serious resistance from the Chun government. Foreign Minister Choi conveyed Chun's "strong request" that Sigur should not go through with his plans to meet with Kim Dae Jung.[42] Choi argued that since Chun already intended to make a lenient decision on Kim's status that would lift restrictions on his political activities, the meeting would be counterproductive because it would be misconstrued as U.S. pressure and interference in South Korean domestic affairs. Sigur responded that he was determined to see Kim, who was under house arrest, with or without the South Korean government's concurrence. He said that if he failed to do so, the Reagan administration would appear weak, lose credibility, and receive criticism in domestic political circles. He also invoked Reagan's instructions to meet with Kim. When Choi indicated that if Sigur were to try to approach Kim's residence, South Korean police might "intercept" him, Lilley warned that the damage to U.S.–South Korean relations would be "disastrous." He explained that South Korea had no greater friend than Sigur and that he should answer his domestic critics by seeing Kim; otherwise they would "tear him to pieces on this issue." The U.S. side also rejected Choi's proposal that Sigur's assistant Rust Deming meet with Kim instead of Sigur himself. Sigur changed his initial plan to see Kim prior to the Chun-Sigur meeting but went ahead with a meeting with Kim on the following day. Prior to his departure from Seoul, Sigur issued a statement stressing U.S. support for a democratic and stable society in South Korea and a freely elected government that enjoyed the support of its people and respected their rights. At this tumultuous time, fear and uncertainty gripped many officials, particularly Roh Tae Woo. In a private meeting with Ambassador Lilley on June 25, Roh confided that he found himself in a very difficult position and that he was going too far for Chun's liking. Lilley was informed later that Roh had even considered the possibility of seeking refuge in the U.S. embassy.[43]

After making a report to President Reagan on June 26, Sigur stated at a press conference that "we urge tolerance for peaceful demonstrations, release of people imprisoned for political activities, an end to preemptive arrests and house arrests. . . . Military steps offer no solution."[44] No doubt the Reagan administration's unshakable position was one of the decisive factors in dissuading Chun from using military force against the massive prodemocracy demonstrations in Seoul. In addition, the moderate military commanders were reluctant to inflict bloodshed on civilians in light of the tragic episode at Kwangju. Chun and his associates also had a genuine fear that military intervention would have an adverse effect on the Seoul Olympic Games. In this sense, the Olympiad turned out to be a moderating factor in the government's policy considerations as well as an effective tool used by opposition forces.

As the political confrontation reached the explosive stage, Roh Tae Woo took a dramatic step on June 29, when he announced that he was prepared to listen to the "will of the people" and to solve the "national crisis." For this purpose he proposed an eight-point recommendation package. The most important recommendations were to adopt a direct presidential election system so that a presidential election would be held before 1988, to offer amnesty to Kim Dae Jung and to restore his civil rights, and to release political prisoners except for those charged with violent crimes. He added: "Now that the Olympics are approaching, all of us are responsible for avoiding the national disgrace of dividing ourselves and thus causing the world to ridicule us."[45] On July 1, Chun announced his full acceptance of Roh's recommendations. With this stunning turn of events, the Chun-Roh leadership had dramatically transformed the political landscape in South Korea almost instantly and at the same time had complied with the main thrust of Reagan's advice.

For all practical purposes, the ruling elite led by Chun and Roh had been confronted with a choice between two extreme solutions for political survival toward the end of June. The first was military action to brutally suppress the prodemocracy demonstrations, but its potential consequences both at home and abroad were deemed too costly. Once this option was ruled out, the only other remaining solution was to accommodate popular demands. This drastic move was the only viable, albeit risky, option open to them under the circumstances. The decision was risky because of the possibility that Roh could be defeated in a free and direct presidential election, but he anticipated that the sense of rivalry between the two Kims was so profound that both would eventually run for the presidential election and thus split the opposition forces against Roh.

The immediate reaction to Roh's declaration was almost universally positive. His supporters welcomed it as a "noble decision," a "historic turning point," a "miracle," and a "peaceful coup d'etat." U.S. Ambassador Lilley called Roh a "hero," and others praised him as a brave champion of political democracy. Even his rivals—Kim Young Sam and Kim Dae Jung—initially applauded the Roh recommendations. As soon as Kim Dae Jung regained his political freedom and became the RDP's adviser, however, he argued that the Roh declaration amounted to unavoidable capitulation to popular demands and that the United States had not played a positive role in South Korea's democratic struggles. President Reagan and other top American officials warmly welcomed Roh's visit to Washington in September prior to the presidential election in South Korea, thus giving the impression that the United States favored him over his opponents. Later Roh admitted to Assistant Secretary Sigur that this visit was helpful to his election campaign.[46]

The Reagan administration wanted to make sure that the intensifying maneuvers for the presidential election would not ignite another political crisis in South Korea and that there was no possibility of military disruption of democratic processes. In a meeting with President Chun at the Blue House on September 15, 1987, Assistant Secretary of State Sigur praised the South Korean president's commitment to the democratic process and promised him that the United States would do everything it could to cooperate with the South Korean government to ensure "a safe, secure, and successful Olympics."[47] Sigur told other South Korean leaders that the use of military force, even if the South Korean government thought it justified, would do great damage to South Korea's reputation. In response, South Korean Minister of National Defense Chung Ho Yong, who emerged as one of the most powerful leaders in the country after Chun Doo Hwan and Roh Tae Woo, categorically assured the American visitor that the South Korean military would not intervene in the process of political democratization.[48] In a meeting with Sigur, Kim Young Sam, a major presidential aspirant, explained that in his earlier meeting with his rival, Kim Dae Jung, he had argued that if Kim Dae Jung received the presidential nomination of the opposition Reunification Democratic Party, there was a high likelihood that he would be assassinated, so he had implored Kim Dae Jung to take the "safe" road to democracy by agreeing to Kim Young Sam's nomination by the RDP.[49] Kim Young Sam also informed Sigur that support for Kim Dae Jung among students, workers, and Catholics was eroding and that prominent dissidents were beginning to speak out against him. On the other hand, Kim Dae Jung acted like a prospective presidential candidate in his meeting with Sigur. Kim said that a new president in the post-Chun era should take the three main steps—no retaliation against political opponents, transition from control to autonomy in all fields, and "détente, dialogue, and peaceful coexistence with North Korea." Kim expressed the view that talks with North Korea for national reunification could begin about five years after the establishment of peaceful coexistence between both Koreas.

Meanwhile, four major political leaders—Roh Tae Woo, Kim Dae Jung, Kim Young Sam, and Kim Jong Pil—waged vigorous campaigns for the presidency. United in a political marriage of convenience, Kim Dae Jung and Kim Young Sam lacked trust and respect for each other—a legacy of their competition going back to 1971 and 1980. After Kim Young Sam declared his candidacy for the presidency, Kim Dae Jung and his followers broke away from the RDP and formed a new Party of Peace and Democracy, which nominated Kim Dae Jung as its presidential candidate. Hence the RDP was fatally divided just seven months after its inauguration. Kim Jong Pil, too, set up a new Democratic Republican League and became its nominee for the presidency. The Reagan administration was aware that Roh was the front-runner: a confidential report submitted to the Department of State by Ambassador Lilley had correctly predicted that Roh would emerge victorious in the forthcoming presidential election.[50]

The split in opposition circles did in fact result in Roh's electoral victory, in which he received 35.9% of the popular vote on December 16, 1987. The remaining popular votes were shared by Kim Young Sam (27.5%), Kim Dae Jung (26.5%), and Kim Jong Pil (7.8%). The Reagan administration, which took great pride in encouraging the process of procedural democracy in South Korea, promptly embraced President-elect Roh as a legitimate successor to President Chun and made it clear that he expected to enjoy the continuity of a friendly and cooperative relationship between Washington and Seoul. In addition, President Reagan took every possible opportunity to ensure that the Seoul Olympic Games would take place peacefully and successfully in 1988, especially after the incident in which two North Korean agents had caused the explosion of Korean Air Lines Flight 858 on its way from Abu Dhabi to Bangkok on November 29, 1987. In a meeting on March 23, 1988, President Reagan asked Soviet Foreign Minister Eduard Shevardnadze, "What about the possibility of terrorism from the North during the games?" "Do not worry," Shevardnadze replied. "We [the Soviet Union] will be at Seoul to compete. There will not be any terrorism."[51]

The forthcoming Olympic Games in Seoul became an important topic for discussions in a series of meetings between U.S. and South Korean leaders. When Sigur returned to Seoul in April 1988, he presented a letter of congratulations to the new President Roh Tae Woo and complimented Roh on achieving a "political miracle" in South Korea to equal its economic miracle. Roh expressed his hope that President Reagan would attend the Olympic Games and that Sigur, in his forthcoming meeting with Soviet Vice Minister of Foreign Affairs Igor Rogachev, would have a constructive discussion about the safety of the Olympic Games in view of North Korea's recent "obstructionism."[52] Roh feared that concern about the safety of the Olympic Games might dampen international enthusiasm and keep foreign visitors from attending the games. In a meeting with Secretary of State Shultz in Seoul on July 18, for example, Roh expressed his hope that the United States would help correct negative perceptions about the games in South Korea.[53] He complained that due to such negative perceptions, athletes were now training for the Olympic Games in Japan instead of South Korea. "While the [South] Koreans did all the work," Roh said, "Japanese were gaining the profit." Prior to his departure from Seoul, Shultz told reporters that "I have every confidence that the Olympic Games will go forward in great stride. . . . I think the real gold medal will go to the Korean people."[54] The successful completion of the Olympiad in fact did instill a sense of national pride and a heightened awareness of internationalism among South Koreans. They projected a new national image—that of a vibrant, competent, and efficient modern society—and their leaders, headed by President Roh Tae Woo, gained confidence in their own ability to manage domestic and foreign affairs in an optimistic and constructive way.

THE BEIJING TALKS

As soon as the Seoul Olympic Games were completed, the United States made what appeared to be a promising effort to facilitate contacts and exchanges with North Korea. In response to President Roh's statements of July 7 and October 18 (at the U.N. General Assembly) in which he called upon South Korea's allies and friends to help draw North Korea out of isolation, the U.S. Department of State announced on October 31, 1988, that it would adopt the following steps toward North Korea:

1. Authorize U.S. diplomats to "hold substantive discussions with officials of the Democratic People's Republic of Korea in neutral settings";
2. Encourage "unofficial, non-governmental visits" from North Korea in the academic field, as well as sports, culture, and other areas, so long as prospective North Korean visitors are eligible under U.S. visa laws;
3. Facilitate the travel of U.S. citizens to North Korea by permitting travel services for exchanges and group travel on a case-by-case basis; and
4. Permit commercial exports to North Korea of certain goods that meet basic human needs (food, clothing, medical supplies, etc.), on a case-by-case basis.[55]

The first point reinstated the earlier policy guidelines withdrawn in January 1988 following the destruction of Korean Air Lines Flight 858 by North Korean terrorist agents. The United States had reviewed this four-point initiative with South Korea during President Roh's visit to New York and Washington in mid-October 1988. In a meeting with Reagan on October 20, Roh said that the U.S. undertaking was "entirely appropriate" but asked that the announcement be delayed until a few days after his return to Seoul.[56] The Department of State also gave advance notice to Japan and had discussions with members of the Chinese and Soviet embassies in Washington on October 21.

The United States hoped that its initiative, in conjunction with South Korea's northern diplomacy, would increase "mutual understanding" with North Korea and induce a "positive, constructive response" from North Korea. In its confidential memorandum dated October 28, the Department of State argued that the four "small steps" were designed to encourage North Korea to end its hostile policy in favor of dialogue and integration into the world community, to abandon its periodic terrorist actions, and to support further Soviet and Chinese contact with South Korea in the direction of eventual cross-recognition.[57] It instructed U.S. embassies in Moscow and Beijing to ask for assistance from the Soviet Union and China in conveying messages to North Korea that the door was open for an improvement of bilateral relations if it abandoned "belligerence, confrontation and terror in favor of dialogue" and that if the North Koreans had any questions about U.S. regulations and procedures, the U.S. government was prepared to meet with them in a neutral setting, such as the United Nations, to clarify the nature and scope of the U.S. initiative. As Deputy Assistant Secretary of State Desaix Anderson later explained, the U.S. decision was also intended to give "encouragement to those in North Korea who may advocate more open policies."[58] In the economic area, however, the United States refused to lift comprehensive sanctions against North Korea. The Foreign Assets Control Regulations, the Export Administration Act, and the Trading with the Enemy Act prohibited almost all commercial and financial transactions with North Korea. U.S. citizens were not allowed to use credit cards in North Korea or to bring home more than $100 worth of North Korean merchandise for personal use.

As a specific application of its four-point initiative, the United States agreed with North Korea to hold talks with their respective political counselors in Beijing. The talks began in December 1988 at the International Club, a neutral Chinese venue. Just as the Warsaw Ambassadorial Talks had sustained a useful, albeit intermittent, dialogue between the United States and China from 1954 to the early 1970s, so too were the Beijing Talks an important new opportunity for Washington and Pyongyang to discuss a wide range of issues formally and directly. Since the North Koreans had always wanted to hold such meetings without the presence of South Korea, they were hopeful for a possible breakthrough in their hostile relations with the United States. In February 1989 President George H. W. Bush told his South Korean audience that "we must complement deterrence with an active diplomacy in search of dialogue with our adversaries, including North Korea."[59] And Secretary of State James Baker testified before the Senate Committee on Foreign Relations in February 1990 that "we are looking for a steady, reciprocal process toward better relations both between North and South Korea and between the United States and North Korea."[60]

Yet the Bush administration was careful not to heighten North Korea's expectations or to undermine South Korea's northern diplomacy and unification policy. The United States made it clear that the Beijing Talks were just that—and were not for "negotiations." In the ensuing talks, the U.S. side asked North Korea to take the following measures:

1. Adopt positive, tangible, and reciprocal steps for improving North-South relations;
2. Sign a full-scope nuclear safeguards agreement with the International Atomic Energy Agency (IAEA);

3. Account for about 8,200 U.S. soldiers still listed as missing in action during the Korean War and return their remains, if found, to the United States;

4. Accept confidence-building measures, including restraint in the sales of arms abroad;

5. Cease its anti-American propaganda; and

6. Give credible evidence that North Korea did not pursue or support international terrorism.[61]

In addition, the U.S. political counselor urged Pyongyang to stop the export of ballistic missiles to the Middle East and to improve human rights in North Korea. The State Department's annual reports on human rights routinely accused North Korea of denying its citizens even the most fundamental human rights, persecuting religious activities, conducting a pervasive indoctrination program, and detaining about 150,000 political prisoners and their family members in maximum security camps. Upholding the principle of reciprocity in improving its relations with North Korea, the United States suggested that if North Korea made progress on any of the requests and concerns made at the Beijing Talks, the United States would be prepared to take reciprocal steps favorable to North Korean interests.[62]

Among other things, the North Koreans asked the United States to transform the Korean Armistice Agreement into a bilateral peace treaty, to suspend its joint military exercises with South Korea, to withdraw its military forces and facilities from South Korea, and to accept the proposal for a nuclear-free zone on the Korean Peninsula. They also requested that the United States agree to upgrade the Beijing Talks to regular high-level negotiations, to exchange liaison offices between the two countries, to lift economic sanctions against North Korea, and to remove North Korea from the State Department's list of states supporting international terrorism. Evidently they also indicated that a high-level U.S. delegation, including members of U.S. Congress, would be welcome to travel to Pyongyang for the purpose of receiving the remains of U.S. soldiers killed during the Korean War. A senior member of the North Korean embassy in Beijing complained that "nothing important can be discussed or achieved at such low levels of talks" and insisted that the Beijing Talks should be elevated to the level of ambassadors or cabinet ministers.[63]

The United States, along with South Korea, regarded the nuclear issue as a litmus test to determine whether North Korea was serious about entering into peaceful and constructive relations with Washington and Seoul. Assistant Secretary of State Richard Solomon stated: "Pyongyang's continuing refusal to conclude a safeguards agreement quite naturally fuels suspicion about the objectives of its unsafeguarded nuclear program, casting doubt among North Korea's neighbors about its intentions. These doubts and suspicions can only increase tensions in Northeast Asia and limit Pyongyang's welcome in the international community."[64] In the aftermath of the Persian Gulf War, the United States equated the danger of Kim Il Sung's nuclear program with that of Saddam Hussein's nuclear ambitions. The North Koreans insisted that they had no plans to develop nuclear weapons and that their nuclear facilities at Yongbyon were strictly intended for peaceful use. In turn, they demanded that the United States withdraw its nuclear weapons from South Korea, stop nuclear war exercises directed against North Korea, and give "legally binding" assurances not to use nuclear weapons against North Korea. Yet the United States refused to disavow its nuclear umbrella for South Korea, viewing it as an effective deterrent against North Korea's chemical and biological weapons.

While the United States and North Korea continued to discuss nuclear issues and other matters at the Beijing Talks, a number of influential U.S. senators and representatives accelerated their pressure upon the Bush administration to scale down the U.S. military presence in South Korea. First, they argued that the reduction in cold war confrontations, the decline of the Soviet Union, and China's open-door policy challenged the earlier assumption that U.S. military presence in South Korea was necessary to contain the outward expansion of the Soviet and Chinese military forces. The United States was more interested in seeking arms control and confidence-building measures with the Soviet Union and China than in escalating the endless arms race and military hostilities. Second, they contended that North Korea would not attack South Korea because neither the Soviet Union nor China would approve or would agree to supply military weapons to North Korea. The two Communist countries were expected to exercise a moderating influence over their North Korean ally. Third, they noted that since South Korea's GNP was eight times that of North Korea, South Korea was strong enough to defend itself, even with a substantial reduction of U.S. troops. In light of all this, they concluded, the United States should no longer spend $2.6 billion per year to maintain its troops in South Korea but rather save the American taxpayers' money.

In order to stem the rising legislative criticism of his military policy toward Korea, in November 1989 President Bush accepted the moderate Nunn-Warner Amendment, which directed the president to reassess the U.S. military presence in South Korea and to develop a five-year military plan that would address a number of policy options.[65] Senator Sam Nunn (D-GA), the powerful chairman of the Senate Committee on Armed Services, believed that it was possible for the United States to implement "partial and gradual reductions" in its troops stationed in South Korea but that it should not lead to the total withdrawal of U.S. troops. Obviously he did not wish to repeat the policy blunder made by his fellow Georgian, President Carter, in regard to U.S. military policy toward Korea. He also suggested that in view of its "prosperous economy," South Korea should offset more of the direct costs incurred by U.S. forces there.

Mandated by the Nunn-Warner Amendment, the Bush administration submitted to Congress on April 18, 1990, a report titled, "A Strategic Framework for the Asian Pacific Rim: Looking Toward the 21st Century."[66] The report outlined the U.S. intention to retain its forward deployed forces, overseas bases, nuclear umbrella, and bilateral security arrangements in the Asian and Pacific region for the foreseeable future but also to reduce incrementally the overall U.S. military presence in South Korea, Japan, and the Philippines. More specifically, the report stated that "the Korean Peninsula will remain one of the world's potential military flashpoints" and that North Korea was devoting an extraordinary percentage of its national wealth to maintain a favorable military balance with over a million men in uniform at the expense of the welfare of its citizens. The United States defined its security objectives in South Korea as (1) deterring North Korean aggression or defeating it if deterrence were to fail; (2) reducing political and military tensions on the peninsula by encouraging North-South talks and instituting a confidence-building measures (CBM) regime; and (3) transforming U.S. forces on the peninsula from a leading to a supporting role, including some force reductions.

In the initial phase (from one to three years), the United States envisioned a modest force reduction of about 7,000 personnel—2,000 Air Force personnel and 5,000 ground force personnel—and promised to support "steady improvements" in South Korea's defense capabilities. For the second phase (from three to five years), the United States indicated the possibility of further adjusting its combat capability by assessing the North Korean threat, the state of inter-Korean relations, and the improvement of South Korea's military capabilities; the United States would possibly restructure the Second Infantry Division during this period. And in the final phase (from five to ten years) a smaller deployment of U.S. forces was projected to remain in South Korea because by the year 2000 the South Koreans should be ready to take the lead role in their own defense. The United States did not intend, however, to revise or abrogate the mutual defense treaty with South Korea. Gone were the days when President Park bitterly opposed Nixon's and Carter's decisions to withdraw U.S. troops from South Korea. The United States and South Korea enjoyed a high degree of policy coordination with respect to a number of security issues.

For its phased military plan, the United States encouraged the South Koreans to increase their defense spending, not only to compensate for U.S. force reductions but also to increase their contribution to the cost of the remaining U.S. in-country presence, especially the expenditures for indigenous labor (about 22,000 South

Koreans) and military construction. Given the economic problems and mounting congressional pressure in America, South Korea agreed to increase its cost-sharing responsibility for the U.S. military presence and to assume a third ($900 million) of all won-based costs for U.S. military forces in South Korea by 1995. In January 1991 the two governments amended the "Agreement on the Status of United States Armed Forces in the Republic of Korea" (SOFA) so that South Korea's burden-sharing obligations as well as the legal status of U.S. soldiers in South Korea would be clarified.

In order to reduce North Korea's fear of a U.S. nuclear attack and to encourage its nuclear disarmament, Assistant Secretary of State Solomon clarified in January 1991 that the United States posed no nuclear threat to North Korea.[67] Since the relatively low level of the Beijing Talks made no progress in resolving international doubts about the North Korean nuclear program, Arnold Kanter (undersecretary of state for political affairs) planned to meet with Kang Sok Ju (North Korea's senior vice minister of foreign affairs) for the purpose of delivering an "authoritative message" that would reach the top leadership in Pyongyang in "unfiltered form." The South Koreans opposed this top-level intergovernmental meeting but urged Kanter to talk to Kim Yong Sun (secretary for international affairs, Korean Workers' Party), who did not hold a government position.[68] In Seoul, the South Korean ministers of foreign affairs and national defense (Lee Sang Ock and Lee Chong Koo, respectively) joined U.S. Ambassador Donald Gregg and General Robert W. RisCassi (commander-in-chief, USFK) in coordinating their respective views on the Kanter-Kim meeting. It was agreed that the meeting would be held only once, not as the beginning of a high-level diplomatic dialogue, and that Kanter would not negotiate with Kim but would simply explain the firm American position to Kim. Foreign Minister Lee reconfirmed this understanding in his discussions with Secretary of State Baker and Undersecretary of State Kanter in Washington.[69]

On January 22, 1991, Kanter and Kim met in the morning and over lunch at the U.S. Mission to the United Nations in New York. This was the highest-level bilateral official meeting ever held between the United States and North Korea. After the meeting, Kanter characterized it as a "cordial, frank, and useful" opportunity to articulate each other's views.[70] On the following day Assistant Secretary of State Richard Solomon, Assistant Secretary of Defense James Lilley (former ambassador to South Korea), and other U.S. participants in the meeting briefed Foreign Minister Lee in person. It was important for both the United States and South Korea to have a common stand on this sensitive and controversial matter. At the Senate Committee on Foreign Relations, Kanter further explained that he had asked Kim to take actions to allay concerns about North Korean nuclear program and lead to an improvement in U.S.–North Korean relations and stressed the fundamental importance of North-South dialogue in resolving the problems of the Korean Peninsula.[71] He also reported that the North Koreans affirmed their intention to accept IAEA inspections of their nuclear facilities and to develop and implement a bilateral nuclear inspection regime with South Korea. However, he rejected Kim's proposals to issue a joint statement and to continue meeting on a regular basis.[72] It was learned later that Kim had expressed North Korea's willingness to accept the continuing presence of U.S. troops in Korea to counterbalance Japanese influence, but some members of the U.S. delegation, such as James Lilley, did not take Kim's statement seriously.[73]

In appreciation of the Kanter-Kim discussion and the Beijing Talks, the North Koreans softened their militant anti-American rhetoric. After the collapse of socialist regimes in Eastern Europe and the disintegration of the Soviet Union, Kim Il Sung evidently believed that as the only strategic superpower, the United States held a key to the resolution of the Korean problems and was a potentially attractive partner for North Korea's economic and technological development. As a ruler who had learned a juggling act by playing Moscow off against Beijing so as to extract the maximum benefits from both countries, Kim now attempted to drive a wedge between the United States and South Korea and to create a sense of competition and balance between the United States and Japan. His southern diplomacy was intended to counter the success of President Roh's northern diplomacy. In his interview with *Asahi Shimbun* editors in March 1992, Kim said that "the end of the Cold War has created a new atmosphere for improving [North] Korea-U.S. relations" and that "there is no longer any excuse or necessity for the United States to continue its old and erroneous policy toward [North] Korea."[74] Moreover, in an interview with *Washington Times* reporters a month later, he said that he was ready to "bury the hatchet" and to welcome an American embassy in Pyongyang "as quickly as possible."[75] About this time North Korea delivered the ratified instrument of the nuclear safeguards agreement to the International Atomic Energy Agency, but the U.S. government was not yet prepared to accommodate Kim's diplomatic overtures.

ROH'S NORTHERN DIPLOMACY

In order to break out of the deadlock on the Korean Peninsula and to relax the regional environment prior to the Seoul Olympic Games, President Roh Tae Woo decided to launch an ambitious northern policy, or northern diplomacy, in 1988. This northern policy was also referred to as *Nordpolitik*, akin to West German Chancellor Willy Brandt's celebrated *Ostpolitik* (eastern policy) initiated in 1969. In his

Inaugural Address on February 25, Roh promised to intensify South Korea's diplomatic efforts to promote international peace and cooperation with "all nations in the world."[76] Moreover, in his Special Declaration on July 7, 1988, he announced that South Korea would seek "improved relations with the Soviet Union, China and other socialist states" and would not oppose an improvement in North Korea's relations with the United States and Japan.[77] On October 18 at the United Nations General Assembly, he said, "I welcome as an encouraging development the fact that socialist countries such as China and the Soviet Union are showing a forward-looking attitude in recent months concerning mutual exchanges and cooperation with the Republic of Korea in a number of fields."[78] He favored the proposal for the simultaneous admission of South Korea and North Korea to the United Nations and envisioned the prospect of cross-recognitions—in exchange for the Soviet Union's and China's recognition of South Korea, the United States and Japan would recognize North Korea. He proposed to hold a "consultative conference for peace" that would include six parties—both Koreas, the United States, the Soviet Union, China, and Japan. As to the main thrust of his new diplomatic offensive, Roh succinctly explained: "The northern policy of the Republic of Korea will serve to convince socialist countries of the effectiveness and efficiency of freedom and democracy and help them carry out reforms. The ultimate objective of our northern policy, however, is to induce North Korea to open up and thus to secure stability and peace on the Korean Peninsula. The road between Seoul and Pyongyang is now totally blocked. Accordingly, we have to choose an alternative route to the North Korean capital by way of Moscow and Beijing. This may not be the most direct route, but we certainly hope it will be an effective one."[79]

Encouraged by the successful completion of the Seoul Olympic Games and equipped with economic assistance as a main incentive, South Korea initially directed its northern policy toward East European countries. As secretly negotiated by Roh's special political assistant, Park Chul Un, Hungary became the first socialist state to establish diplomatic relations with South Korea on February 1, 1989. In protest, North Korea promptly downgraded its diplomatic relations with Hungary. On November 23, President Roh paid a state visit to Budapest during his European tour. Soon thereafter, other East European countries (Poland, Yugoslavia, Czechoslovakia, Bulgaria, and Romania) followed Hungary's lead, as did Mongolia. For the sake of maintaining good relations with the United States, Roh sought advice and suggestions from Ambassador Lilley in regard to his northern policy.[80] U.S. assistance was helpful for South Korea's diplomatic adventures in virgin territory. For his first diplomatic reception at Belgrade in March 1990, South Korean Foreign Minister Choi Ho Jung borrowed a guest list from the U.S. embassy. In Prague, U.S.

Ambassador Shirley Temple Black hosted a party in Choi's honor so that he could meet a large number of Czechoslovakian leaders. When Choi stopped at Beijing Airport on his way to Pakistan in March 1990, U.S. Ambassador James Lilley welcomed him at the airport and briefed him on current Chinese affairs.[81]

Although the Soviet Union and China shared a common interest in maintaining full diplomatic relations and security commitments with North Korea, they had tactical and procedural differences in responding to South Korea's northern diplomacy. Ever since his Vladivostok Declaration in July 1986, Mikhail Gorbachev, general secretary of the Communist Party, applied his "new thinking" to the Asia-Pacific region, issuing a series of purposeful statements and undertaking measures for improving Moscow-Seoul relations.[82] While he viewed North Korea as an increasingly burdensome liability, he regarded South Korea as an attractive economic partner at a time when his own reform programs were less than successful. He was impressed by South Korea's excellent organizational and technological ability demonstrated during the Seoul Olympic Games. As a pragmatist, Gorbachev was prepared to recognize the reality of the Korean Peninsula and to adopt a two-Korea policy in diplomatic and economic fields. He hoped that by accepting South Korea's diplomatic overtures, he would be able to exercise an even-handed role in dealing with the Korean question and to use South Korea as an instrument for influencing Washington's and Tokyo's policies toward the Soviet Union. In a joint communiqué issued by South Korea's governing party, the Democratic Liberal Party led by Kim Young Sam, and the Soviet Institute for World Economy and International Relations (IMEMO) headed by Yevgeni Primakov in March 1990, the two sides stated that the normalization of relations between the Soviet Union and South Korea would be essential to the peaceful unification of Korea and to peace in East Asia. When Anatoly Dobrynin, a senior foreign policy adviser to Gorbachev and former Soviet ambassador to the United States (1962–86), went to Seoul to attend a meeting of the nongovernmental Inter-Action Council in May 1990, he secretly visited with President Roh at the Blue House in the late evening of May 22 for the purpose of arranging a summit meeting between Roh and Gorbachev. Roh preferred to see Gorbachev, his title now president of the Soviet Union, in Vladivostok, but Dobrynin conveyed Gorbachev's wish to hold the meeting in San Francisco during his planned trip to the United States.[83] In exchange for diplomatic normalization, Roh promised to offer $3 billion in economic assistance to the Soviet Union. Dobrynin had follow-up discussions with Roh's secretary general, Dr. Ro Jai Bong, at the Shilla Hotel.[84] As a former professor of international relations at Seoul National University with a great deal of knowledge of Soviet affairs, Ro, along with Kim Chong Whi (senior secretary for foreign affairs and national security), took part in the Roh-

Dobrynin meeting and provided useful and confidential assistance for the president's northern diplomacy. At this time Gorbachev, due to the difficulties of his ambitious *perestroika* (restructuring) and *glasnost* (openness) programs, desperately needed $20–25 billion to buy goods for consumption in the Soviet Union and expected much help from West German Chancellor Helmut Kohl.[85]

For the Gorbachev-Roh summit meeting, the United States and South Korea maintained close cooperation and frequent consultations. The Bush administration made Assistant Secretary of State Richard Solomon and U.S. Ambassador to the Soviet Union Jack Matlock available to brief Roh in San Francisco on the current Russian situation, especially Boris Yeltsin's political ascendancy, prior to the summit meeting. Former secretary of state George Shultz, now back at Stanford University and the Hoover Institution, agreed to assist Gorbachev's and Roh's activities in the San Francisco area. Ambassador Donald Gregg urged his South Korean counterpart to place the highest priority on getting the Soviets to pressure North Korea on the IAEA inspections.[86] The South Korean official agreed with Gregg's suggestion, explaining that promoting North-South dialogue was the other top priority. Gregg observed that "the obvious U.S. cooperation in making possible the San Francisco meeting will help us put to rest the tenacious theory that we are discomfited by any improvement in ROK-Soviet relations, a broadly held view that happens to fit snugly with the extreme left's line that we are in Korea only for reasons of superpower strategy vis-à-vis the USSR."

At his summit meetings with President Bush in the White House and in Camp David on May 31–June 2, 1990, Gorbachev was anxious to prevent a unified Germany from remaining in NATO and to sign a trade agreement, in which the United States would grant most favored nation (MFN) status to the Soviet Union. The presidents also discussed the Korean question.[87] Upon his arrival at San Francisco, President Roh met both former president Ronald Reagan and former secretary of state Shultz. When Shultz cautioned Roh that it was not wise to push for diplomatic normalization with the Soviet Union, Roh made it clear that at the meeting he nonetheless planned to clarify his hopes for early normalization between the Soviet Union and South Korea. On June 4, Gorbachev met with President Roh for a little over an hour at the Fairmont Hotel (where both Soviet and South Korean delegations were staying) in San Francisco instead of at the Soviet consulate general, which the South Koreans opposed. Afterwards, Gorbachev politely declined Roh's proposals to issue a joint statement or to hold a joint press conference and only reluctantly agreed to have his photograph taken with Roh. Gorbachev avoided the spotlight and then quietly slipped away.[88] He appeared to be uncomfortable with the highly publicized event, which he considered to be a necessary step to obtain the substantial loans from South Korea. In his own press conference, Roh praised Gorbachev as a "man of courage and forthrightness" and described their meeting as "very productive talks" and an "epoch-making event."[89] In his explanation, the two presidents shared the view that the efforts to normalize bilateral relations would lead to establishment of diplomatic relations and would expand economic, scientific, technological, and cultural exchanges between the Soviet Union and South Korea. He declared his goals to be the development of peaceful coexistence, common prosperity, and co-operation between Seoul and Pyongyang. And he expressed his gratitude to the United States for having solidly supported his northern policy.

According to a confidential report submitted to the Department of State by Ambassador Gregg, a top official of the South Korean Ministry of Foreign Affairs briefed Gregg on the Gorbachev-Roh meeting, which addressed three main topics: (1) reform and openness; (2) inter-Korean relations; and (3) Soviet–South Korean relations.[90] The two presidents agreed that reform and openness contributed greatly to stability and peace in other regions but that South Korea and the Soviet Union should make joint efforts to encourage a similar movement on the Korean Peninsula. Roh told Gorbachev that he saw no such changes taking place in China or North Korea and expressed the hope that the San Francisco meeting would encourage those countries to move toward reform. Gorbachev shared that view but noted that reform in Northeast Asia was moving more slowly than in Eastern Europe.

Gorbachev expressed concern over the continued division of the peninsula and asked if South Korea could accommodate any North Korean proposals, some of which he found "noteworthy." Roh responded that North Korea's proposals were propagandistic and oriented toward maintaining its isolation. Roh said that South Korea would not attempt to isolate North Korea but would instead try to induce it to play a responsible role in the world community. When Gorbachev asked if Roh had a message for Kim Il Sung, Roh asked Gorbachev to convey three points. The North should (1) agree to a meeting of "responsible authorities," especially a Roh–Kim Il Sung meeting; (2) adopt openness and reforms; and (3) end military and political confrontation. Roh assured Gorbachev that South Korea would not seek military and political superiority over North Korea. Gorbachev asked Roh if the presence of U.S. nuclear weapons in South Korea was a factor in North Korean policies. Roh responded that the South Korean government respected the U.S. policy of neither confirming nor denying the presence of its nuclear weapons in South Korea and that it was not appropriate for him to discuss the nuclear weapons issue. However, Roh added that as a matter of principle, he would like to see the abolition of nuclear weapons.

The two presidents agreed that working-level officials should take up the question of normalizing diplomatic relations. Gorbachev told Roh that the two governments should proceed gradually, working step by step until the process was completed. Gorbachev told Roh that when ice melted, water would flow and that relations between the Soviet Union and South Korea should follow the same pattern. When Roh said that it was about time to harvest the fruit (read: diplomatic normalization), Gorbachev responded that one could not eat the fruit until it was ripe. Roh stated that he was known for his patience and that when he said the fruit was ripe, it could be eaten.[91] Roh said that overcoming economic difficulties was the essence of *perestroika* and suggested that the Soviet Union might look to South Korea as a model of economic success. Gorbachev said that the several hundred economic advisers he had in Moscow were useless and jokingly asked Roh to lend the Soviet Union one of South Korea's economic advisers. Responding in kind, Roh offered Senior Secretary for Economic Affairs Kim Chong In to Gorbachev.[92] The South Koreans described the atmosphere of the summit meeting as "cordial and friendly," but the two presidents did not have enough time to develop much of a personal relationship. Gregg's report did not refer to something he had regarded as a top priority — namely, Soviet assistance with respect to the IAEA inspections of North Korean nuclear facilities.

Immensely pleased with the successful summit, Roh traveled to Washington to have breakfast with President Bush and expressed his appreciation to the United States for its support of the San Francisco meeting. Roh felt that it was important to demonstrate that his reconciliation with the Soviet Union would in no way undermine or downgrade the continuing importance of the U.S.–South Korean alliance. The summit meeting generated a great deal of excitement and a media frenzy in South Korea, spurred a pro-Russian bandwagon, and also exalted Roh's status as an able practitioner of northern diplomacy. Yet his domestic detractors contended that his offer of massive economic aid to the Soviet Union (and other East European countries) was excessive and unnecessary.

In his memoirs, Gorbachev explained that he met Roh because the Soviet Union could not, for obsolete ideological reasons and because of its ties with North Korea, continue opposing the establishment of normal relations with South Korea, which showed an exceptional dynamism and had become a force to be reckoned with, both in the Asia-Pacific region and in the wider world.[93] On September 2 and 3, 1990, Foreign Minister Shevardnadze made a "working visit" to Pyongyang and broke the news to North Korean Foreign Minister Kim Yong Nam that the Soviet Union would establish diplomatic relations with South Korea on January 1, 1991, and would convert barter trade with North Korea into a cash payment of hard (convertible) currency. Unhappy with this decision, Kim Yong Nam warned Shevardnadze that if the Soviet Union did not change its mind, North Korea would develop nuclear weapons, support Japan's position on the northern territorial issue, and recognize the independence of some Soviet republics (presumably, the three Baltic republics).[94] Shevardnadze bluntly told Kim that, as a sovereign state, the Soviet Union had the right to make independent diplomatic decisions and did not require approval from any other country. In contrast with his friendly discussions with Shevardnadze in December 1988, the furious Kim Il Sung refused to see the Soviet foreign minister at this time.

After Shevardnadze's unceremonious departure, North Korea publicized an extraordinary government document that scathingly denounced the forthcoming diplomatic relationship between the Soviet Union and South Korea and argued that it would be detrimental to the process of Korean reunification. Among other things, the document contended that Moscow-Seoul diplomatic normalization would mean the formation of a "tripartite alliance," with the Soviet Union joining the United States and South Korea in a conspiracy to topple the socialist system in North Korea. More ominously, it declared: "If the Soviet Union establishes diplomatic relations with South Korea, the [North] Korean-Soviet alliance treaty will automatically be reduced to a mere name. This will leave us no other choice but to take measures to provide us for ourselves some weapons for which we have so far relied upon the alliance."[95]

The North Korean threats did not prevent Shevardnadze from signing an agreement with South Korean Foreign Minister Choi Ho Jung at the United Nations to set up diplomatic relations between Moscow and Seoul. In fact, Shevardnadze was so angry at North Korea's threats that he agreed to move the date for diplomatic normalization up from January 1, 1991 to September 30, 1990.[96] This diplomatic accord completed the implementation of South Korea's northern policy in Europe. The North Koreans condemned the Soviet Union's "betrayal and hypocrisy" and accused the Soviet Union of "openly joining the United States in its basic strategy aimed at freezing the bipartite division of Korea, isolating us internationally and guiding us to 'opening' and thus overthrowing the socialist system in our country."[97] The North Koreans refrained from taking any drastic action against the Soviet Union, such as suspending diplomatic relations, but the Soviet–North Korean relationship was extremely strained and even hostile at times.

Meanwhile, South Korea and the Soviet Union expanded their cooperative relations in diplomatic and economic areas. After their second summit meeting in Moscow in December 1990, Presidents Roh and Gorbachev declared that the two countries would respect each other's sovereign equality, territorial integrity, and political independence; renounce the threat or use of force; and settle international controversies and regional conflicts through peaceful means.[98] The "Moscow Declaration" categorically ruled out the likelihood of armed confrontation between South Korea and the Soviet Union and, in effect, amounted to nullifying the application of the Soviet–North Korea Treaty of Friendship, Cooperation, and Mutual Assistance to South Korea. In a separate meeting, Shevardnadze apologized to South Korean Foreign Minister Choi Ho Jung for the Korean Air Lines 007 incident. Moreover, at the third summit meeting on Cheju Island in April 1991, Presidents Roh and Gorbachev discussed the possibility of concluding a "treaty of friendship and cooperation" between South Korea and the Soviet Union. They also took the identical position that North Korea should accept a full-scope nuclear safeguards agreement with the International Atomic Energy Agency (IAEA). Gorbachev informed Roh that the Soviet delegate at the U.N. Security Council would not veto South Korea's application for admission to the United Nations.

To counter the successful implementation of President Roh's northern diplomacy, Kim Il Sung embarked on his version of "southern diplomacy" toward Japan and the United States. On the heels of Shevardnadze's disastrous visit to Pyongyang, Kim welcomed to North Korea Kanemaru Shin, a kingpin of Japan's Liberal Democratic Party, and Tanabe Makoto, vice chairman of the Japan Socialist Party; the two men headed a mammoth delegation of eighty-nine Japanese political leaders and government officials. Vice Minister of Foreign Affairs Kuriyama Takakazu saw members of the Kanemaru party off at Narita Airport and expressed the hope that Kanemaru would be able to obtain the release of two Japanese seamen seized in 1983 as "spies."[99] In a meeting in the scenic Myohyang Mountains, Kanemaru delivered a letter to Kim from Prime Minister Kaifu Toshiki (written in his capacity as the president of the LDP). Kaifu's letter indicated that Japan was prepared to offer an official apology and compensation for damages inflicted by Japan during the 1910–45 period. He also expressed the hope for improving relations between Japan and the Democratic People's Republic of Korea. Kim in turn praised Japan as an "economic giant that is also becoming a political power" and promised to let the two Japanese seamen return home.

On September 27, 1990, Kanemaru and Tanabe signed an eight-point joint declaration with Kim Yong Sun, a secretary of the Korean Workers' Party.[100] They agreed that "there is only one Korea" and then recommended that Japan and North Korea negotiate to establish diplomatic relations "as soon as possible." The declaration stated: "Japan must officially apologize and compensate the Democratic People's Republic of Korea for the misfortune and damage inflicted upon the Korean people during 36 years [of colonial rule between 1910 and 1945] and the losses the

Korean people suffered in the 45 years of the postwar era." Kanemaru suggested that Japan should provide some compensation to North Korea even before diplomatic relations were established between the two countries. In addition, the three political leaders accepted the principle of eliminating the threat of nuclear weapons from all regions. Other recommendations included (1) permission for North Korea to use Japanese satellite communications to expand its links with the rest of the world; (2) creation of a regular and direct air route between Tokyo and Pyongyang; and (3) elimination of the ban on travel to North Korea that was stamped on passports issued to Japanese citizens.

The Japanese explained that their diplomatic initiative toward North Korea had been taken in response to President Roh's declaration issued on July 7, 1988, and that the initiative was intended to support the process of peaceful Korean reunification and to promote peace and stability on the Korean Peninsula. They also argued that Japan–North Korea diplomatic normalization was one of the two postwar issues that remained unsettled and that it was abnormal for North Korea to be Japan's only neighboring country without diplomatic relations. In addition, however, there were probably a number of other reasons for the Japanese diplomatic overtures toward North Korea. First, the Japanese had publicly welcomed the success of South Korea's northern diplomatic activities, but they were nonetheless privately concerned about the manner in which that policy was pursued and consummated. They suspected that there was potentially an anti-Japanese element in South Korea's growing ties with Russia and China. Hence Japan's approach toward North Korea was viewed as a conscious effort to counterbalance South Korea's vigorous diplomatic maneuvers. Second, the Japanese undertook diplomatic negotiations with North Korea so that they would not lag behind the United States in dealing with the Korean question. They did not forget the embarrassing consequences of the "Nixon shock," in which Washington's sudden rapprochement with China had taken them by surprise. Once the United States had begun the Beijing Talks with North Korea, the Japanese felt free to move beyond America's policy of diplomatic isolation toward North Korea. Third, the Japanese wished to assume an active role in sustaining the balance of power in Korea and in influencing the direction of inter-Korean relations.

The three-party joint declaration stunned both the United States and South Korea. Even though both countries publicly welcomed Japan's efforts to de-isolate North Korea, the United States and South Korea pointedly requested that the Japanese government act "prudently" in its negotiations with North Korea and insisted on North Korea's acceptance of the nuclear safeguards agreement with the IAEA. The South Koreans feared that if Japan were precipitously to agree to normalize diplomatic relations and to extend substantial economic assistance to North Korea, Kim Il Sung might have no incentive for improving inter-Korean relations.

Jolted by the Kanemaru mission, U.S. Ambassador to Japan Michael Armacost felt that it was unprecedented for the Japanese to undertake such a wide-ranging initiative in Korea without consulting the United States and South Korea; he found Kanemaru's evident readiness to discuss compensation for unspecified sins of commission or omission in the postwar period even more astonishing. "Moreover," he argued, "reparations in the absence of IAEA safeguards on nuclear activities and military force reductions—not mentioned in the communiqué—could be regarded as indirectly supporting North Korea's threatening military posture."[101] Faced with protests from Washington and Seoul, Prime Minister Kaifu distanced himself from the three-party joint declaration and explained that it was not an official position of the Japanese government. On October 8 Kanemaru expressed his regrets to President Roh in Seoul and promised not to bypass South Korea in his future dealings with North Korea. Roh bluntly stated that Kanemaru had been taken in by the shrewd and unreliable North Koreans.[102] On the following day, Kanemaru visited Ambassador Armacost in Tokyo and apologized for not consulting with the United States prior to his Pyongyang visit.[103] He explained that his visit to North Korea was a party-to-party undertaking designed to establish an atmosphere of mutual trust for the opening of government-to-government negotiations. At his meeting with President Roh in Seoul on January 9, 1991, Prime Minister Kaifu emphasized the importance of maintaining close contacts with South Korea and promised to honor Seoul's concerns and interests in future Japanese negotiations with North Korea. He also explained that the Japanese government was not necessarily bound by the 1990 joint declaration signed by Kanemaru, Tanabe, and Kim.

Soon after Kaifu's Seoul visit, Japan and North Korea held the first round of full-dress normalization talks in Pyongyang on January 30 and 31, 1991. This time the Japanese government consulted closely with South Korea and the United States. As the talks continued throughout 1991 and 1992, the two sides articulated their divergent positions on several major issues. Most important, in view of Seoul's and Washington's concerns and because of strong antinuclear sentiment in Japan, the Japanese government decided that the satisfactory resolution of North Korea's nuclear issue was a necessary precondition to diplomatic normalization between the two countries. The Japanese leaders assured their South Korean and American counterparts that Japan would refuse to establish diplomatic relations with Pyongyang until North Korea not only signed the nuclear safeguards agreement but also fulfilled the IAEA's full-scope inspections. They also insisted that North Korea should accept a bilateral nuclear inspection regime with South Korea. Another troublesome issue was the amount of Japan's economic assistance to North Korea. Whereas the Japanese government was reportedly prepared to offer a package of property settlements and economic cooperation funds worth about $2 billion—the estimated current value of the $500 million aid package Japan had committed to South Korea at the time of Tokyo-Seoul diplomatic normalization in 1965—North Korea was expected to request as much as $10 billion in view of Japan's wealth.[104] The two sides failed to make any tangible progress in their negotiations, entering into a prolonged stalemate after the eighth round of talks at Beijing in November 1992. Seoul expected as much as Washington did that Japan would not normalize diplomatic and economic relations with North Korea until the suspicions about Pyongyang's nuclear weapons program were satisfactorily resolved.

As had been apparent in the case of the Gorbachev-Roh summit meeting in San Francisco, the United States welcomed and supported Seoul's assertive northern diplomacy because it contributed to peace and stability on the Korean Peninsula. At a luncheon held in honor of President Roh on July 2, 1991, Secretary of State Baker observed that by effectively pursuing *Nordpolitik*, South Korea was beginning to melt the last glacier of the cold war. He added: "The establishment of full diplomatic relations with the Soviet Union, the exchange of trade offices with China, and the ascension to the United Nations—which we expect this fall—all clear the path for reducing tensions on the Korean Peninsula and ultimately for reunification—a good goal that our two peoples have shared for over four decades."[105] The United States and South Korea jointly undertook an active diplomatic campaign to secure South Korea's "ascension" to the United Nations. President Roh preferred to realize the simultaneous admission of both South Korea and North Korea to the United Nations in 1991, but if North Korea continued to oppose this plan on the grounds that it would perpetuate the legal division of the Korean Peninsula, he would then seek South Korea's single admission. The first step in this process took place in a speech at the U.N. General Assembly on October 1, 1990, when President Bush stated for the first time that the United States, while supporting South Korea's admission to the United Nations, would not oppose North Korea's entry to the world organization.

Since the Soviet Union had already promised not to veto South Korea's application to the United Nations, the United States and South Korea turned their attention to China. The atmosphere for intergovernmental cooperation between Seoul and Beijing had improved with the opening of South Korea's semi-diplomatic Trade Office in the Chinese capital. And the United States had already decided to improve its relations with Beijing, which had been strained since the Tiananmen Square incident, so that it could obtain China's tacit support for the Persian Gulf War. At a meeting with Chinese Foreign Minister Qian Qichen on November 30,

1990, Secretary of State Baker asked China to support South Korea's admission to the United Nations, but Qian responded that it was not possible in 1990. He left the door open, however, for 1991. South Korean Foreign Minister Lee Sang Ock orchestrated a meticulously planned campaign to obtain support from permanent and nonpermanent members of the U.N. Security Council. In an attempt to ensure that China would not veto South Korea's bid to join the United Nations, Minister Lee met with Chinese Vice Minister of Foreign Affairs Liu Huaqiu, who was in Seoul in April 1991 to attend the Economic and Social Council for Asia and the Pacific. Lee expressed the hope that China would persuade Kim Il Sung to change his opposition to the simultaneous admission of the two Koreas.[106] Liu made no such commitment, however.

Efforts to persuade China eventually met with success after the Bush administration made an effective diplomatic representation to the Chinese leaders on behalf of South Korea. In his meetings with Kim Il Sung in Pyongyang on May 3 through 6, 1991, Chinese Premier Li Peng apparently indicated that China would not veto the application for South Korea's entrance to the United Nations and that it would be better for North Korea to join it too.[107] After Li's return to Beijing, a spokesman for the Chinese Ministry of Foreign Affairs reported that Li and his North Korean hosts discussed "the question of joining the United Nations by both North and South Korean sides of Korea" and that Li stated his wish that the two Korean sides would find an acceptable solution through dialogue and consultation.[108] On May 28, the North Korean Ministry of Foreign Affairs announced its decision to apply for admission to the United Nations by reversing its opposition to the simultaneous admission of both Koreas.[109] On the same day the South Korean Ministry of Foreign Affairs and the U.S. Department of State welcomed the North Korean decision. So did China, the Soviet Union, and Japan. As a result of the closely coordinated efforts by South Korea and the United States, the Security Council (on August 8) and the General Assembly (on September 17) of the United Nations unanimously voted to admit North Korea and South Korea as the 160th and 161st member states.

An even more unprecedented development came later that year. The two Korean governments achieved a historic milestone in their relations on December 13, 1991, when the two Korean prime ministers—Chung Won Shik and Yon Hyung Muk—signed a comprehensive 25-article "Agreement on Reconciliation, Nonaggression, and Exchanges and Cooperation" in Seoul. This so-called Basic Agreement, which expanded and refined the joint communiqué of July 4, 1972, was a functional equivalent of the Basic Treaty signed by the Federal Republic of Germany and the German Democratic Republic twenty years earlier (May 26, 1972). Among other provisions, the two Korean governments declared that "both parties shall not use armed force against each other" and that "differences of views and disputes arising between the two sides shall be resolved peacefully through dialogue and negotiation." They agreed to preserve the Korean Armistice Agreement until a solid state of peace could be realized. For implementation of the Basic Agreement, both sides promised to establish liaison offices at Panmunjom, a South-North political committee, and a joint military commission. The United States, along with other major powers, enthusiastically applauded and endorsed the inter-Korean Basic Agreement.

Meanwhile, the Bush administration fully cooperated with President Roh's intention to assume a positive and pivotal role in denuclearizing the Korean Peninsula. The North Koreans continued to propose the establishment of a nuclear-free zone on the Korean Peninsula, and Roh wanted to respond to the North Koreans' argument that so long as U.S. nuclear weapons remained in South Korea, it would be difficult for them to disavow nuclear options completely. The United States maintained its usual "neither confirm, nor deny" policy in regard to the presence of American nuclear weapons in South Korea and did not wish to link the two issues — namely, U.S. nuclear weapons in South Korea and the IAEA inspections of North Korean nuclear facilities. The United States and South Korea had a common interest in promoting the idea of a nuclear-free Korean Peninsula. Although the presence of tactical nuclear weapons in South Korea was no longer regarded as essential to preserving extended nuclear deterrence because of advanced technology and strategic mobility, the United States was concerned about how North Korea would perceive American intentions if nuclear weapons were removed. In their joint memoirs, Bush and Scowcroft remembered: "In connection with its efforts to engage North Korea, South Korea was suggesting the removal of the U.S. nuclear weapons stationed there. We did not wish to make such a move solely in Korea, concerned that the North might take our actions as the beginning of a U.S. withdrawal."[110] They were nonetheless enthusiastic about the possibility of removing nuclear weapons in part because the passing of the cold war and the unification of Germany had rendered short-range nuclear weapons undesirable in Europe. The United States had already decreased the number of its nuclear warheads deployed at Kunsan Air Base in South Korea from 763 in 1972 to about 100 in 1989. This issue was thoroughly discussed at a secret meeting between Paul Wolfowitz (undersecretary of defense for policy) and Kim Chong Whi (senior secretary to the president for foreign affairs and national security) in Honolulu on August 6 and 7, 1991, and followed up at the summit meeting between Bush and Roh in Washington on September 23.[111] A few days later (September 29), Bush unilaterally announced a series of sweeping measures to withdraw and destroy all U.S. tactical nuclear weapons (except for air-delivered ones).[112]

This decision differed from other agreements on nuclear issues—such as the Limited Test Ban Treaty, the Nuclear Nonproliferation Treaty (NPT), the Strategic Arms Limitation Treaty (SALT), the Intermediate-Range Nuclear Forces (INF) Treaty, and the Strategic Arms Reduction Treaty (START)—requiring prolonged negotiations, elaborate contents, and ratification processes. And Bush expected that Gorbachev would do the same despite his rapidly deteriorating political status in the Soviet Union. The Bush announcement enabled President Roh to declare unilaterally on November 8 that South Korea would refrain from producing, possessing, or storing nuclear weapons; use nuclear power only for peaceful purposes; and allow the IAEA's inspections of its nuclear facilities. A few domestic critics of Roh's nonnuclear policy, however, argued that he had unconditionally abandoned South Korea's "nuclear sovereignty" forever and that it was rather naive for him to expect reciprocal action by North Korea. It was also viewed by some analysts as submission to U.S. pressure for a nuclear-free South Korea. As soon as the removal of all U.S. tactical nuclear weapons was completed, Roh categorically stated on December 18 that not a single nuclear device existed anywhere in South Korea.

In order to assist South Korea with respect to the issues of nuclear nonproliferation, a number of U.S. officials and specialists, including Paul Wolfowitz and Ronald Lehman (director of the U.S. Arms Control and Disarmament Agency), visited Seoul to share intelligence on North Korean nuclear programs, to discuss nuclear reprocessing facilities and highly enriched uranium (HEU) programs, to suggest a set of specific ideas for inspection procedures, and to train South Korean inspectors in the United States.[113] According to South Korean Foreign Minister Lee Sang Ock, the United States emphasized the importance of "challenge inspection" between both Koreas. The United States had no evidence of North Korean interest in HEU programs but wanted to cover all possible ways of manufacturing nuclear weapons. The United States was very careful to educate South Korean inspectors on the technical complexities of inspections without transferring nuclear technology to them, which was prohibited by the NPT provisions.[114] On December 31, 1991, the two Korean sides initialed the "North-South Joint Declaration on the Denuclearization of the Korean Peninsula" in Panmunjom. This six-point agreement included the following aspects:

1. The South and the North shall not test, manufacture, produce, receive, possess, store, deploy, or use nuclear weapons;
2. The South and the North shall use nuclear energy solely for peaceful purposes;
3. The South and the North shall not possess nuclear reprocessing and uranium enrichment facilities; and

4. The South and the North shall establish and operate a South-North Joint Nuclear Control Commission.

In addition, the two sides agreed to conduct mutual inspections of nuclear facilities as determined by the Joint Nuclear Control Commission. While North Korea agreed to ratify its full-scope nuclear safeguards agreement with the International Atomic Energy Agency, South Korea joined the United States in deciding to suspend the annual Team Spirit exercises in 1992. Following necessary ratification processes in Seoul and Pyongyang, both the Basic Agreement and the Joint Declaration went into effect on February 19, 1992. The North-South committees for political and military affairs and the Joint Nuclear Control Commission were duly set up to carry out both agreements.

The North-South Joint Declaration on the Denuclearization of the Korean Peninsula, along with the Basic Agreement and the simultaneous admission of the two Korean governments to the United Nations, made it easier for China to take concrete steps to accommodate South Korea's persistent efforts for diplomatic and economic normalization. Even if the Chinese lagged appreciably behind the Soviet Union and East European states in establishing its embassy in Seoul, they had long recognized South Korea's outstanding economic achievements and had aggressively sought its cooperation for their ambitious Four Modernizations program designed to develop China's agriculture, industry, science and technology, and national defense in a rapid fashion. Geographic proximity and cultural similarities between China and South Korea lowered the barriers and costs of transportation and communications. The South Koreans were particularly interested in China's nearby coastal areas, such as Shandong and Laoning Provinces. Moreover, South Korea relied upon a large number of highly educated and linguistically equipped Koreans in China who were ready to facilitate Seoul-Beijing exchanges and cooperation.[115]

The economic imperative had become important in China's evolving relationship with South Korea. Attracted by South Korea's capital, technology, and managerial expertise, a growing number of Chinese government and business delegations had visited South Korea to explore the possibilities of economic collaboration back in the 1980s. An even greater number of South Koreans had gone to China to discuss a variety of cooperative plans, ranging from joint ventures and technology transfer to resource development and cultural exchanges. The volume of bilateral trade reached about $3 billion per year in 1988 and 1989, about six times that of trade between China and North Korea. When the United States, the Western European states, and Japan imposed economic sanctions against China in the aftermath of the Tiananmen Square tragedy in June 1989, the South Korean government decided not to follow suit and instead actively penetrated the China market, assisted China's flagging tourist industries, and provided substantial funds for the Asian Games held in Beijing in the fall of 1990. As soon as the Asian Games were successfully completed, the South Korean Trade Promotion Corporation (KOTRA) and the China Chamber of International Commerce (CCOIC) agreed to exchange trade offices with consular functions between Seoul and Beijing. Much to North Korea's chagrin, this was a positive step toward full diplomatic normalization between the two governments.

As their economic cooperation increased in the early 1990s, the mutually reinforcing diplomatic contacts between Beijing and Seoul intensified. On October 2, 1991, the Chinese and South Korean foreign ministers—Qian Qichen and Lee Sang Ock—met for the first time at the United Nations and briefly discussed the future of their bilateral relations. In response to Lee's inquiry, Qian expressed interest in promoting functional relations with South Korea in a quiet and unobtrusive manner. A month later, Qian, together with Li Lanqing (minister of foreign economic relations and trade), went to Seoul to attend the Asia-Pacific Economic Cooperation (APEC) conference; Qian expressed appreciation for South Korea's role in ironing out a delicate matter concerning the representation of China, "Chinese Taipei," and Hong Kong in APEC. On November 12, Qian paid a courtesy call on President Roh, who expressed a strong interest in establishing diplomatic relations with China, explained that South Korea had no intention of absorbing North Korea, and asked Qian to transmit his views to North Korea. A couple of days later, Lee and Qian discussed the problems of bilateral relations, but Qian remained noncommittal about the prospect of diplomatic normalization. In a meeting with Qian during his visit to Beijing on November 15 through 17, 1991, Secretary of State Baker urged China to establish diplomatic relations with South Korea. Qian asked whether the United States would recognize Pyongyang in return for China's recognition of Seoul, and Baker said that it would be difficult for the United States to do so unless North Korea accepted the IAEA's full inspection of its nuclear facilities.[116] The United States in effect rejected the concept of cross-recognitions—which South Korea still favored.

When Lee visited Beijing on April 12, 1992, as the outgoing president of the U.N. Economic and Social Commission for Asia and the Pacific (ESCAP), he arrived in a plane flying the flag of the Republic of Korea and was invited to meet with President Jiang Zemin and Premier Li Peng. At a one-on-one meeting on April 13, Qian and Lee reached an agreement to begin secret negotiations for diplomatic normalization. The Chinese had finally decided to adapt to the changing political and economic realities on the Korean Peninsula and to transcend their earlier commitment for a one-Korea formula. They also intended to thwart Taiwan's aggressive diplomatic offensive and to counter the growing U.S. influence in the Asia-Pacific region following the end of the cold war. In addition to the success of President Roh's northern diplomacy toward the Soviet Union (Russia) and Eastern Europe, they recognized the ascendancy of South Korea's international diplomatic and economic status vis-à-vis North Korea. In July Qian made a secret trip to North Korea to explain to Kim Il Sung China's decision to normalize diplomatic relations with South Korea. The South Korean government, too, kept the United States fully informed of the progress of Seoul-Beijing diplomatic negotiations.

On August 24, 1992, Foreign Ministers Qian and Lee signed a joint communiqué in which China and South Korea agreed to recognize each other and to establish immediate diplomatic relations.[117] The communiqué declared that the government of the Republic of Korea "recognizes" the government of the People's Republic of China as the sole legal government of China and "respects the Chinese position that there is one China and Taiwan is part of China." The South Koreans were pleased with the successful consummation of their northern diplomacy toward China. President Roh visited Beijing toward the end of September 1992. He joined Chinese President Yang Shangkun in issuing a joint press communiqué, which stated that "relaxation of tension on the Korean Peninsula will not only serve the interests of the whole Korean people but also be favorable for the settlement of peace and stability of the Northeast Asian region as well as the whole of Asia." Yang expressed "hope for early realization of the goals set forth in the Joint Declaration on the Denuclearization of the Korean Peninsula."[118]

The South Koreans had secured a friendly and cooperative international environment in Asia and established diplomatic relations with all five permanent members of the U.N. Security Council. The conclusion of Seoul-Beijing diplomatic ties was a major setback for the North Koreans and further weakened the political foundation of the China–North Korean mutual security treaty. Gone were the days when Kim Il Sung enjoyed the benefits of the Soviet and Chinese one-Korea policy and relied upon a coalition of Communist countries against the U.S.-led containment system in the region. While South Korea had succeeded in establishing diplomatic relations with Moscow and Beijing, North Korea's diplomatic overtures toward Washington and Tokyo remained unfulfilled. The failure of cross-recognitions meant a clear asymmetry of diplomatic relations on the Korean Peninsula and further increased the sense of isolation and frustration on the part of North Korean leaders.

In general, the Bush administration had endorsed and assisted President Roh's effective northern diplomacy because it normalized Seoul's relations with Moscow and Beijing, had a sobering effect upon North Korea, and promoted the interests of peace and stability in Northeast Asia. It also reduced, if not eliminated, an important diplomatic source of disagreements and contentions among the major powers over the Korean Peninsula. The United States may have been concerned that South Korea would be tempted or persuaded to invest heavily in Siberia's and China's industrial projects, to export strategically sensitive high technology to China or Russia, or to purchase Russian or Chinese military hardware. The Bush administration hoped that South Korea would pursue its policy toward China and Russia in a manner consistent with the long-term strategic and diplomatic interests of the United States in the Asia-Pacific region. As South Korea diversified the scope of its diplomatic activities and gained a greater sense of self-confidence, there was a fear in Washington that Seoul would feel less dependent on U.S. support and protection and that the United States might have a diminishing influence over Korean affairs. A number of high-level visitors and close consultations between Washington and Seoul throughout 1992, especially President Bush's visit to Seoul in January and President Roh's trip to the United States in September, were intended to solidify bilateral alliance cohesion and to prevent Beijing, Moscow, and Pyongyang from driving a wedge between the United States and South Korea.[119]

ECONOMIC RELATIONS

The unfolding of generally cooperative and mutually supportive relations between the United States and South Korea on such issues as security commitments, political democratization, and northern diplomacy sharply contrasted with their growing disagreement over economic issues in the late 1980s and early 1990s. This disagreement reflected the profound structural change in their bilateral economic relations. As a result of its effective economic development plans during the 1960s and 1970s, South Korea had graduated from U.S. economic assistance and compiled a remarkable record in economic growth and foreign trade (see tables 1 and 2). The gross national product (GNP) had increased at an average annual rate of 10% since the early 1960s and per capita GNP grew from $88 in 1962 to $6,200 in 1990. Its exports expanded from $50 million to $65 billion during the same period. The United States absorbed about 30% of South Korea's total exports. South Korea emerged as the seventh-largest trading partner for the United States and the second-largest market for American agricultural products. The United States no longer regarded South Korea as a poor, dependent, and burdensome country but as an interdependent and competitive economic partner.

As their economic and commercial relations became more complex and competitive, disputes and conflicts inevitably arose between the United States and South

Korea. In the 1970s, the United States had attempted to protect its domestic industries from inexpensive goods made in South Korea. This protectionist policy stemmed from the collapse of U.S. hegemony in the world economy and the declining competitiveness of its industries in such important areas as textiles, steel, electrical appliances, automobiles, and electronics. The United States forced South Korea to accept the Orderly Marketing Agreements (OMA) and the Voluntary Export Restraints (VER), which limited its penetration into American markets.

When the United States accumulated an increasing deficit in its trade with South Korea in the 1980s, reaching a high of $9.8 billion in 1987 and $8.7 billion in 1988, it focused on the issues of fair trade and market access to South Korea. Armed with a set of retaliatory legal devices such as Super Section 301 of the Omnibus Trade and Competitiveness Act (1988), the United States demanded that South Korea open its domestic markets to U.S. agricultural products (tobacco and beef) and service industries (banking, insurance, advertising, communications, and stock brokerage) and honor foreign intellectual property rights (copyright, patents, and computer software). An increasing number of U.S. senators and congressmen threatened to impose a stiff protectionist legislative mandate against South Korea, Japan, Taiwan, and other major trading partners of the United States. U.S. Ambassador to South Korea James Lilley argued in 1987 that "we are not asking for any special favors, but we insist on the opportunity to compete on fair terms."[120]

In the case of U.S. cigarette exports, for example, the South Korean government offered an initial concession in 1986 by opening the door to foreign cigarettes but imposed high prices on them. In 1987 imported cigarettes represented only 0.27% of South Korea's domestic tobacco market. Dissatisfied with this situation, the United States pressed its demands for complete market access in South Korea, pointing out that foreign cigarettes amounted to about 10% of tobacco consumption in Japan and Taiwan. The South Koreans argued that unrestricted imports of American cigarettes would jeopardize their own tobacco growers and cigarette companies. This resistance was buttressed by a broad coalition of tobacco growers, religious organizations, radical students, and opposition political parties, which organized a campaign to boycott American cigarettes. They criticized the "hypocrisy" and "immorality" of U.S. trade policy by pointing out that while the U.S. Surgeon General was warning that cigarette smoking was harmful to public health, the U.S. government was championing cigarette exports to other countries. Moreover, Dr. SaKong Il (former South Korean finance minister) suggested that American cigarettes represented many of the social evils that had existed in South Korea during the Korean War—smuggling, illegal activity, conspicuous consumption, and so forth.[121]

Sensing that no further concessions would come from South Korea, the U.S. Cigarette Export Association used Section 301 of the Trade Act to file a petition against the South Korean government and the state-run Korean Monopoly Corporation (KOMOCO) in January 1988. The association estimated that if the South Korea market were completely open and prejudicial pricing removed, American cigarettes would account for as much as 25% ($500 million) of South Korean tobacco consumption per year. A group of powerful legislators from the tobacco-growing southern states maneuvered to draft a protectionist bill aimed at South Korea. In anticipation of this legislation and possible U.S. retaliation, South Korean Ambassador Park Tong Jin and U.S. Trade Representative Clayton Yeutter signed an agreement in May 1988 to open the South Korean market to the import, distribution, and promotion of American cigarettes. The agreement stipulated that American cigarettes would be subject to the same excise tax levied on quality South Korean cigarettes but that importers of American cigarettes had to be approved by KOMOCO.

An equally contentious case involved U.S. efforts to export beef to South Korea. When the Reagan administration, sensitive to the cattle industry in the midwestern states and its political sponsors in Congress, asked South Korea to open its markets to American beef and other agricultural products in 1987, the South Korean Ministry of Agriculture, Forestry, and Fisheries categorically responded, "We are not in a position to allow U.S. farm products at this time when Korean farmers are beset with difficulties."[122] The Dairy and Beef Farmers Association, the National Livestock Cooperatives Federation, and other interest groups organized mass rallies and protest activities against the United States and urged their government not to capitulate to U.S. pressure. The American Meat Institute filed a Section 301 petition against South Korea, and the United States, together with Australia and New Zealand, asked for a GATT investigation of South Korea's beef import restrictions. Then the Ministry of Foreign Affairs and the Ministry of Trade and Industry overcame their interbureaucratic policy differences and advocated a partial concession to the United States. In the summer of 1988, the South Korean government agreed to import a limited amount of high-quality American beef for use by tourist hotels and restaurants.[123] The government explained to the angry South Korean beef breeders that had it defied the GATT rule, it would have faced legal retaliation not only from the United State but also from other GATT member states. It also argued that beef imports were needed to control rising beef prices and accommodate unhappy consumers in South Korea. In November 1989, South Korea agreed to expand the amount of beef imports from the United States, which amounted to about 25% of South Korea's beef consumption per year.

In his speech before the South Korean National Assembly in February 1989, President Bush praised South Korea's economic progress as "an inspiration for developing countries throughout the world" and stated that "[South] Korea has become an industrial power, a major trading power, and a first-class competitor."[124] Yet he stated that South Korea should join the United States in rejecting protectionism and in removing barriers to international trade. The Bush administration fought against the rising protectionist sentiment in U.S. Congress but was unhappy about the slow pace of economic liberalization taking place in South Korea.

In an address before the joint session of U.S. Congress in October 1989, President Roh clarified that South Korea was "moving vigorously toward a more open, liberalized and self-regulating economy" and that in the next four or five years South Korea would achieve "the same degree of openness as is found in the OECD [Organization for Economic Cooperation and Development] countries."[125] In the case of agricultural imports from the United States, he asked for more time to avert adverse political and social consequences to South Korean farmers. When President Bush complained that U.S. workers and companies did not have the same access to South Korean markets that South Korean workers and companies had to America's open markets, President Roh responded that "if an apple is picked before it's ripe, it can be a bit tough and sour. When it's ripe, however, it's nice and sweet." Bush replied, "We don't want the ripening to take so long that we're too old to enjoy the food."[126] This humorous but pointed exchange demonstrated the seriousness of the trade disputes between the two countries. Yet South Korea grudgingly agreed in 1989 to phase out or bring into conformity with GATT more than 270 agricultural restrictions over seven and a half years. The U.S. Trade Representative claimed that "this landmark agreement resulted almost entirely from patient and consistent U.S. pressure."[127]

Faced with ever-mounting pressure from the United States, the South Koreans argued that their economy was still fragile, with many infant industries and high defense expenditures, and heavily dependent on the expensive imports of raw materials and crude oil. They pointed out that they were incurring large foreign debts and suffering from a chronic trade deficit with Japan. They also suggested that in light of growing anti-American sentiment in South Korea, they could not afford to give the appearance of submitting to high-profile U.S. pressure tactics. In this regard, Assistant Secretary of State Richard H. Solomon warned in January 1991 that an anti-import campaign directed against foreign goods and services would only further stimulate a protectionist mood in the United States.[128] He hoped that the robust economic ties between the United States and South Korea would continue to be a "fundamental pillar" of their relationship and would endure long after the confrontation between North and South Korea was resolved.

The Roh government took a series of additional steps to lower tariff and nontariff barriers against imports from the United States and to gradually accept U.S. service industries in South Korea. In fact, U.S. Trade Representative Carla Hills expressed her general satisfaction with the overall implementation of South Korea's liberalization, with the single exception of agricultural products. During his visit to Seoul in January 1992, President Bush noted that in recent years the U.S. trade deficit with South Korea had decreased from $9 billion to $1 billion per year and that U.S. exports to South Korea had increased at a pace of more than 7% annually, but he still criticized South Korea's "frugality campaign" as a form of protectionism.[129] He preached the advantages of a free, fair, and open international trading system and reminded his South Korean audience that trade was not a zero-sum game.

At the same time, the United States recognized the importance of its bilateral partnership with South Korea in dealing with multilateral economic issues. "As an emerging economic power," Bush said, "[South] Korea must now shoulder with other trading nations the burden of leadership on behalf of the multilateral trade regime."[130] More specifically, he elicited South Korea's active role in moving the Uruguay Round of GATT negotiations to a successful conclusion. The United States greatly valued South Korea as a strong pro-American country in promoting the APEC framework that included the United States, Canada, Australia, and New Zealand and in resisting a Malaysian proposal to exclude these four countries from a new Asian trading bloc. Even if their bilateral trade disputes could not be resolved easily to their mutual satisfaction, the United States and South Korea shared the view that their economic ties were bound to expand in the years ahead and that they needed each other in managing the challenges posed by regional and global economic dynamics. They also agreed that the continuation of South Korea's economic prosperity was essential to protecting the interests of peace and stability on the Korean Peninsula.

CHAPTER FIVE

From Containment to Engagement

Clinton's Policy

As discussed in the preceding chapter, the end of the global cold war marked a sea change in the international strategic and economic order. As a principal beneficiary and custodian of this changing world order, President William J. Clinton was faced with the challenge of meeting the commitments made by his predecessors in a world that had dramatically changed. When he took office in the early 1990s, a mood of uncertainty and optimism prevailed. The disintegration of the Soviet Union and the Warsaw Pact had left the United States as the only remaining hegemonic superpower, and the emerging unipolar strategic system began to change the way America approached global and regional conflicts. The United States had come to assume the immense responsibility of managing and even leading diplomatic activities and sought to do so through multilateral venues such as the United Nations. At the same time, however, the United States was clearly suffering from a relative decline in its economic capabilities, especially in comparison with Japan and the European Community. This triangular economic relationship tended to determine and limit the choice of means and instruments for implementing Clinton's foreign policy goals. His electoral victory gave him a popular mandate for renewing America's economic health.

In the Asia-Pacific region, however, the effects of the cold war lingered. Unlike their counterparts in Europe, several socialist regimes in Asia—China, North Korea, Vietnam, and Laos—not only withstood the wave of "peaceful evolution" but also adopted varying strategies to ensure their survival. The U.S.-led military containment system, including the U.S.–South Korean Mutual Defense Treaty, remained largely intact, and regionwide collective security systems and transparent confidence-building measures were conspicuously absent. National divisions and ideological confrontations persisted in China, Korea, and Cambodia. On the Korean Peninsula, expectations for North-South reconciliation and cooperation were overshadowed by escalating tensions and mistrust between Seoul and Pyongyang. Hence the new Clinton administration was saddled with a complicated and seemingly contradictory mixture of global and regional trends in the strategic, diplomatic, and economic fields.

ENGAGEMENT POLICY

In his Inaugural Address, Clinton declared that "as an old order passes, the new world is more free but less stable" and promised that "when our vital interests are challenged, or the will and conscience of the international community defied, we will act—with peaceful diplomacy when possible, with force when necessary."[1] He firmly believed that new security threats to the United States and its allies were posed by renegade dictators, terrorists, and international drug traffickers and by the local armed conflicts that could endanger the peace of entire regions. In order to deal with the growing possibility of regional armed conflicts, the United States planned to enhance its rapid deployment capabilities and military technology and to maintain sophisticated, accurate, and timely intelligence facilities. The incoming secretary of defense, Les Aspin, said that regional threats to U.S. interests in places like Korea, Iraq, and Africa would replace the former Soviet Union as the major focus of U.S. military policy.[2] As demonstrated in the Persian Gulf War, the United States preferred to respond to regional crises with multilateral military measures and to rely upon the peace-keeping functions of the United Nations and other international organizations as far as possible.

Yet the Clinton administration did not completely rule out the possibility of unilateral use of its own armed forces. The new secretary of state, Warren Christopher, argued that "the discreet and careful use of force in certain circumstances, and its credible threat in general, will be essential to the success of our diplomacy" and that "when our vital interests are at stake, we will always reserve our option to act alone."[3] This did not necessarily mean that the United States was prepared to use its unipolar strategic advantages as an instrument to solve all international and regional problems. The Clinton administration expressed its firm commitment to halting the spread of nuclear weapons and other weapons of mass destruction, to strengthen the functions of the International Atomic Energy Agency (IAEA), and to enforce strong sanctions against governments that violated international agreements. Warren Christopher declared, "One of the main security problems of this era will be the proliferation of very deadly weapons—nuclear, chemical, biological, and enhanced conventional weapons—as well as their delivery systems. . . . We must work assiduously with other nations to discourage proliferation through improved intelligence, export controls, incentives, sanctions, and even force when necessary."[4] The U.S. government assumed that if a country withdrew from the Nuclear Nonproliferation Treaty (NPT) and developed nuclear weapons, that country might (1) use or threaten to use them for aggressive purposes; (2) cause its neighboring countries to possess nuclear weapons; and (3) export nuclear weapons technology to rogue states, such as Iran and Libya. More important, the United States believed that if a country successfully withdrew from the NPT system without incurring any cost, it might encourage other signatories to follow suit and might eventually destroy the integrity of the nuclear nonproliferation regime that the United States had assiduously nurtured since 1968.

In this context, the first direct challenge to the United States took place on the Korean Peninsula. When the North Koreans rejected the request made by the IAEA to make special inspections of suspected nuclear facilities at Yongbyon (about 90 kilometers north of Pyongyang) and announced on March 12, 1993, that they would withdraw from the NPT after the required waiting period of three months, President Clinton, despite his initial preoccupation with domestic economic issues, was compelled to turn his attention to the North Korean crisis. In close consultation with the new South Korean government under President Kim Young Sam, the Clinton administration decided not to employ military force against North Korea but to seek a diplomatic solution through the IAEA and the United Nations.

This decision signified an essential continuity in U.S. policy from Bush to Clinton. Since the Bush administration had already started to modify aspects of the traditional American framework of military containment and diplomatic isolation toward North Korea, the new Clinton administration found it relatively easy to pursue a policy of constructive engagement with North Korea for the purpose of furthering the goal of nuclear nonproliferation. This conciliatory posture was based on the classic liberal assumption that even with dictatorial countries, mutually beneficial discussions could be conducted and reasonable compromises could be reached in good faith. In their meetings in Washington in late March, Secretary of State Christopher and South Korean Foreign Minister Han Sung Joo, a sophisticated and cosmopolitan scholar, reached an agreement on "step-by-step" and "carrot and stick" approaches to the North Korean nuclear issue.[5] They assumed that by offering tangible benefits to North Korea, such as economic assistance and cancellation of the joint military exercises, the issue could be resolved through diplomatic means. If North Korea refused, however, they envisaged diplomatic and economic sanctions against North Korea through the U.N. Security Council. Han also obtained the same agreement from Japanese Prime Minister Miyazawa Kiichi and Foreign Minister Watanabe Michio in Tokyo. Compared with his American and Japanese counterparts, Han appeared to be more careful and moderate toward North Korea at this time mainly because South Korea would suffer most if the crisis escalated.

The United States and South Korea agreed to mobilize international diplomatic pressure on North Korea and to support Dr. Hans Blix (former foreign minister of Sweden), director general of the IAEA (which had already conducted ad hoc inspections in North Korea six times since May 1992) in asking for special inspections designed to ascertain how much weapons-grade plutonium North Korea had already produced and whether North Korea's report on this question was accurate or not. On April 1 the 35-member IAEA Board of Governors in Vienna found North Korea in noncompliance with its obligations under its nuclear safeguards agreement with the IAEA and called upon North Korea to remedy its noncompliance. China and Libya did not participate in this decision. The North Koreans rejected the IAEA's request on the grounds that it impinged upon the principle of state sovereignty and was designed to probe for military secrets. However, there was a strong suspicion in the IAEA and in the U.S. government that North Korea was concealing its possession of weapons-grade plutonium. Upon receipt of a report submitted by Blix, the president of the U.N. Security Council, as the first step for gradual escalation, issued a statement on April 8 expressing concern and reaffirming the importance of the NPT system. More important, in a meeting with Chinese Vice Minister of Foreign Affairs Tang Jiaxuan on April 15, U.S. Ambassador to China Stapleton Roy asked Tang to inform Pyongyang that the United States proposed to hold a dialogue between the United States and North Korea.[6] On May 11, the U.N. Security Council adopted a resolution by a vote of thirteen in favor and two abstentions (China and Pakistan) asking North Korea to reaffirm its commitment to the NPT, to honor its nonproliferation obligations under the treaty, and to comply with its safeguards agreement with the IAEA.[7] This resolution was the first important step taken by the world organization serving notice to North Korea that the U.N. Security Council might take other measures, including economic sanctions, in the event of a North Korean refusal.

In response to Roy's earlier proposal transmitted by China and other similar peace feelers from Washington, a senior member of the North Korean Mission to the United Nations (Deputy Ambassador Ho Jong) called C. Kenneth Quinones, a specialist in Korean affairs at the Department of State, to begin bilateral talks.[8] After several low-level preparatory meetings, Robert Gallucci (assistant secretary of state for political-military affairs) started the first round of talks with Kang Sok Ju (North Korea's first vice minister of foreign affairs) in New York on June 2. A veteran of nuclear issues under the Bush administration, Gallucci had dealt with Russia and Iraq but had never met a North Korean official before.[9] Gallucci and Kang achieved a significant breakthrough in the frozen relations between the two erstwhile enemies. The joint statement issued by them on June 11, a day before the North Korean withdrawal from NPT was to become effective, spelled out their agreement on three principles:

- assurances against the threat and use of force, including nuclear weapons;
- peace and security in a nuclear-free Korean Peninsula, including impartial application of fullscope safeguards, mutual respect for each other's sovereignty, and non-interference in each other's internal affairs; and
- support for the peaceful reunification of Korea.[10]

They expressed support for the North-South Joint Declaration on the Denuclearization of the Korean Peninsula initialed in December 1991. In return for America's negative security assurance, Kang promised to suspend North Korea's withdrawal from the NPT regime "as long as it considers necessary." This was the first official document in which the United States and North Korea disavowed any hostile intention toward each other. Since Kang adamantly opposed the inclusion of "special inspections" in the joint statement, the all-encompassing term, "fullscope safeguards" (to be implemented by the IAEA), was adopted as a convenient compromise. Both sides understood this provision to include both regular and special inspections. The phrase "impartial inspection" was inserted to address the North Korean position that the past IAEA inspections were less than impartial. The U.S. negotiators cited the Charter of the United Nations as a basis for this document, but there is, of course, no reference to nuclear weapons in the relevant sections of the U.N. Charter.[11] They believed that this negative security assurance was essential in persuading North Korea to agree to nuclear disarmament but refused to accept the North Korean proposal that Gallucci and Kang sign the joint statement. The North Koreans gained a sense of legitimacy after being accepted by the United States, and the joint statement represented an almost equal degree of relative gains for both Washington and Pyongyang.

The South Korean Ministry of Foreign Affairs expressed its endorsement of the joint statement and hoped that North Korea would promptly clear up international suspicions about its nuclear program, contribute to peace and stability on the Korean Peninsula and in the world, and make tangible progress in inter-Korean reconciliation and cooperation.[12] Unlike the earlier disputes over the *Pueblo*, EC-121, and the axe-murder at Panmunjom, the nuclear program in North Korea posed a potentially lethal security threat to South Korea. The South Koreans, however, had once again been excluded from negotiations between the United States and North Korea, and their suggestions were not fully accommodated.[13] This was particularly galling for President Kim Young Sam, who had promised his voters that he would attach higher priority to the promotion of inter-Korean reconciliation than to the maintenance of alliance cohesion with the United States and had even released a long-term pro–North Korean prisoner, Li In Mo, to Pyongyang as a goodwill gesture, over objections from the Agency for National Security Planning (formerly the Korean Central Intelligence Agency).[14] As a self-confident and assertive leader, Kim, unlike his two predecessors — Presidents Chun Doo Hwan and Roh Tae Woo — took great pride in being the first popularly elected civilian president since 1960. Even though he had agreed to the U.S.–North Korean negotiations in New York, Kim Young Sam still felt marginalized and did not want to appear weak in the eyes of South Koreans. Not always happy with Foreign Minister Han's conciliatory diplomatic approach, he had only grudgingly accepted the proposition that the United States was representing his country's interests at the bilateral talks with North Korea.

In an interview with the *New York Times* that appeared on July 2, 1993, President Kim warned that North Korea was manipulating its negotiations with the United States to "buy time" to finish its nuclear weapons program and claimed that by early 1994 North Korea would be able to produce plutonium in large enough quantities to manufacture several weapons. He implied that the Clinton administration had been naive and gullible and had been taken in by shrewd North Korean tactics. The interview served as a wake-up call to the Clinton administration, implying that unless it carefully accommodated Kim's sensitivities, Clinton could end up damaging the credibility of U.S. policy and provide a convenient issue for the Republicans to attack. Foreign Minister Han attempted to control the damage by explaining that his president had no misgivings about the joint statement but that his remarks were intended to mollify his conservative critics at home. The Department of State made its displeasure clear by indicating that Clinton's planned visit to Seoul might be reconsidered, but it eventually relented.[15]

After attending the G-7 meeting in Tokyo, Clinton paid a two-day visit to Seoul on July 10 and 11. At their first summit meeting, Presidents Clinton and Kim had an opportunity to discuss a wide range of issues with special emphasis on their respective policies toward North Korea. In a joint news conference, Kim urged North Korea to remain in the NPT regime and to fulfill its inspections agreement with the IAEA. He emphasized the importance of mutual inspections by both Koreas as prescribed by the North-South Joint Declaration on the Denuclearization of the Korean Peninsula and warned that if North Korea did not agree to a peaceful solution of its nuclear issue, "the international community will inevitably have to come up with appropriate countermeasures to deal with the issue." Yet he added that "we will keep the door open for South-North dialogue." In response, Clinton promised to continue "our very close cooperation" in dealing with North Korea. He reaffirmed his "strong intention to have no further reduction in our military presence in this region, as long as there is any outstanding question of security." The two leaders agreed to cooperate at the Uruguay Round negotiations and the Asia-Pacific Economic Cooperation (APEC) meetings.[16]

In a speech before the National Assembly in Seoul, Clinton said that "the time has come to create a new Pacific community built on shared strength, shared prosperity, and a shared commitment to democratic values."[17] He identified four priorities for the security of this new Pacific community: (1) a continued American military commitment; (2) stronger efforts to combat the proliferation of weapons of mass destruction; (3) new regional dialogues on the full range of common security challenges; and (4) support for democracy and more open societies throughout this region.

Speaking in more detail, Clinton said:

> As the Cold War recedes into history, a divided Korea remains one of its most bitter legacies. Our nation has always joined yours in believing that one day Korea's artificial division will end. We support Korea's peaceful unification on terms acceptable to the Korean people. And when the reunification comes, we will stand beside you in making the transition on the terms that you have outlined. But that day has not yet arrived. The demilitarized zone still traces a stark line between safety and danger. North Korea's million men in arms, most stationed within 30 miles of the DMZ, continue to pose a threat. Its troubling nuclear program raises questions about its intentions. Its internal repression and irresponsible weapons sales show North Korea is not yet willing to be a responsible member of the community of nations. So let me say clearly, our commitment to Korea's security remains undiminished. The Korean Peninsula remains a vital American interest. Our troops will stay here as long as the Korean people want and need us here.

The two new leaders agreed to launch a "Dialogue for Economic Cooperation" and to set up a round-the-clock hotline between the White House and the Blue House. When Clinton visited the demilitarized zone (DMZ) and the Joint Security Area (JSA) at Panmunjom, he declared that if the North Koreans ever used nuclear weapons, "it would be the end of their country." Upset by this statement, Kang Sok Ju threatened to cancel the second round of talks with the United States, but he did not carry out his threat.[18] The first encounter between Presidents Clinton and Kim turned out to be a useful opportunity to share views on important issues and to develop what Clinton called a "very good personal relationship."[19]

On July 14 through 19, Gallucci and Kang held a second round of talks at Geneva, a neutral place that was more convenient for both sides than noisy and congested New York. As he had indicated at the first round of talks in New York, Kang proposed that if the United States were really so concerned about the possible production of weapons-grade plutonium by North Korea's five-megawatt (MW) graphite-moderated nuclear reactor at Yongbyon and two additional nuclear reactors under construction with capacities of 50 and 200 MW, respectively, it should replace them with light-water moderated reactors (LWRs), which were less prone to extraction of weapons-grade plutonium. In his initial reaction, Gallucci laughed aloud as if it were a joke and said that this proposal was not acceptable.[20] Kang, however, went on to explain that Russia had agreed to construct a LWR at Kumho in 1985 in return for North Korea's safeguard agreement with the IAEA but had reneged in 1988. After consultation with North Korea experts in Washington and with the South Korean government, Gallucci recognized a window of opportunity to strike a bargain with North Korea.

In a press statement issued on July 19, 1993, Gallucci and Kang both acknowledged the desirability of replacing North Korea's reactors with LWRs, and the United States promised to explore the ways of obtaining LWRs for North Korea.[21] In addition, North Korea agreed to begin discussions on nuclear inspection with the IAEA "as soon as possible" and to start the North-South talks on bilateral issues—including the nuclear issue—"as soon as possible." In his unilateral statement announced on the same day, Gallucci made it clear that the United States would not engage in any peaceful nuclear cooperation with North Korea until it "has unambiguously complied with its nonproliferation obligations, including the NPT, IAEA, and the bilateral North-South declaration" and that the United States would not begin a third round of talks with North Korea until "serious discussion" with the IAEA and the Republic of Korea had begun.[22] As to the principle of refraining from the threat or use of force as announced in the joint statement of June 11, he added the qualification that the United States would preserve "our obligation and ability to assist the Republic of Korea in its self-defense, including the right to conduct defensive exercises." At Geneva, Gallucci rejected Kang's proposal to stop the annual joint military exercises (Team Spirit) between the United States and South Korea but apparently indicated that the United States and South Korea would consider such a possibility. This time the United States made a special effort to be attentive to the South Koreans' positions and sensitivities and kept them informed about the progress of the bilateral discussions. Gallucci, for example, had frequent telephone discussions with Foreign Minister Han.

Their agreement to hold a third round of talks at Geneva in September 1993 notwithstanding, Gallucci and Kang were unable to resume their talks for the next ten months mainly because North Korea failed to allow the IAEA's full and impartial inspections at Yongbyon and to conduct a constructive dialogue with South Korea. Aside from North Korean recalcitrance, the United States found it increasingly difficult to coordinate its negotiating tactics with the complex IAEA bureaucracies and the South Korean government, which was deeply divided between the liberals and the conservatives in regard to North Korea. The IAEA and the CIA suspected that the operational 5-MW reactor had already produced enough plutonium for at least one nuclear device and had a load of spent fuel rods that could generate enough plutonium (25 to 30 kilograms) for four to five nuclear bombs. Moreover, if the two other reactors were completed, North Korea could produce plutonium for about a dozen nuclear bombs per year. On October 1, the IAEA General Conference adopted a resolution in which it expressed "grave concern" over North Korea's failure to accept the agency's scheduled ad hoc and routine inspections at Yongbyon and urged North Korea to cooperate immediately with the agency in the full implementation of the safeguards agreement. A month later (November 1), the United Nations General Assembly also passed a resolution for the same purpose by a vote of 140 to 1, with 9 abstentions. It also commended the IAEA's director general, Dr. Hans Blix, and the secretariat of the IAEA for their "impartial efforts" to implement the safeguards agreement with North Korea. The North Koreans, who accused the IAEA and its director general of being under the control of the United States, cast the only negative vote on this resolution and thereafter simply ignored the recommendations made by the IAEA and the United Nations.

On NBC's "Meet the Press" program on November 7, President Clinton, whose engagement policy toward North Korea had come under harsh criticism from the Republican Party, categorically declared that any military attack on South Korea "is an attack on the United States" and warned that if North Korea produced nuclear weapons and used them against South Korea, the United States would mobilize its overwhelming military power to obliterate North Korea.[23] This rhetoric was intended not only to warn North Korea but also to quell criticism of his policy in South Korea and in the U.S. Congress. American public opinion was divided on the problems of nuclear proliferation and armed conflict in Korea. According to a CNN/Gallup poll conducted from November 19 to 21, 1993, 59% supported U.S. military action to destroy North Korean nuclear facilities and 33% were opposed. However, the American public remained averse to the prospect of fighting another war abroad: when asked if the United States should enter the war in the event of North Korean aggression against South Korea, 31% said yes and 63% no.

The North Korean nuclear question was addressed during the summit meeting between Presidents Clinton and Kim Young Sam at the White House on November

23, 1993. Clinton expressed his concern about North Korea's refusal to grant IAEA inspectors full access to its nuclear sites and about North Korea's concentration of forces near the DMZ. He explained: "My administration has made it clear to North Korea that it now faces a simple choice. If it abandons its nuclear option and honors its international non-proliferation commitments, the door will be open on a wide range of issues—not only with the United States, but with the rest of the world. If it does not, it risks facing the increased opposition of the entire international community."[24] He promised to take "a thorough, broad approach" toward North Korea to discuss a number of issues, including the nuclear question. Even though the Principals Committee had decided to pursue a "comprehensive approach" toward North Korea on November 15 and even though President Clinton had used the same term during his November 20 press conference during the APEC summit meeting in Seattle, Clinton reluctantly yielded to Kim's strong recommendation that the phrase "thorough, broad approach" should replace the old terms "comprehensive approach" or "package deal," presumably because President Kim's political rival, Kim Dae Jung, as well as North Korea, had already appropriated the old terms.[25] The new phraseology was recommended by Anthony Lake (assistant to the president for national security affairs) and Chung Chong Wook (senior secretary for foreign affairs and national security).[26]

This last-minute semantic replacement inadvertently undermined the agreement that Secretary of State Christopher and Foreign Minister Han had carefully worked out prior to the summit meeting. Kim spoke for about forty minutes, to Clinton's visible dismay, vehemently insisting that North Korea would not behave "comprehensibly." Clinton accepted Kim's proposals that South Korea, not the United States, should announce the temporary suspension of the Team Spirit exercises (if both countries agreed on it) and that the United States should closely consult with South Korea about the talks with North Korea. As a step toward inter-Korean reconciliation and cooperation, Kim stressed the importance of exchanging special envoys between Seoul and Pyongyang. Clinton agreed to make the resumption of North-South dialogue a precondition for the third round of U.S.–North Korean negotiations. In this way was the linkage between the two issues established. The two sides agreed to set up "hot lines" between Presidents Clinton and Kim and between Anthony Lake and Chung Chong Wook for direct and effective communications.

From the beginning, Kim was determined to break away from what he regarded as an established pattern of South Korean submission to unilateral U.S. decisions and to assert a degree of independence and nationalistic pride in U.S.–South Korean relations. Extremely sensitive to domestic public opinion and critics, Kim wanted to appear strong and assertive in dealing with the United States. And as a relatively inexperienced leader in foreign affairs, he was instinctively more inclined to listen to the advice of his hardline aides than that of his moderate and pragmatic diplomats, including Foreign Minister Han. Moreover, Kim appeared to take North Korea's nuclear program less seriously than Clinton did and assumed that North Korea was merely using the nuclear issue as a bargaining chip to extract concessions from the United States. Confident that he knew more about North Korea than Clinton did, Kim wanted to teach his younger host a lesson. He lectured Clinton, telling him that the United States should not trust North Korea and that North Korea would eventually violate any agreement concluded with the United States. In order to develop good personal relationship with Kim, Clinton graciously stated at a press conference: "I have a great deal of admiration for President Kim, who for decades has worked tirelessly to broaden Korea's democracy at great personal cost to himself. His democratic passage to the presidency is an inspiring measure of Korea's progress—proof that freedom knows no regional bounds."[27] At the first state dinner held in his honor, Kim spoke to First Lady Hillary Clinton so intensely for three hours that he barely interacted with the other guests. (Yet he missed the opportunity to dance with her because he would not agree to Clinton's request to dance with the South Korean First Lady.)[28]

While Kim was satisfied with his accomplishments at the summit meeting, Clinton found working with such a strong-willed, independent-minded, and supremely self-assured political leader difficult and uncomfortable. The personal relationship between the two leaders was bound to deteriorate in the subsequent months. Even a decade later, Joel S. Wit, Daniel B. Poneman, and Robert L. Gallucci, who had served as Clinton's key officials responsible for the resolution of the North Korean nuclear crisis, offered a disparaging comment on Kim's "theatrics" in the Oval Office.[29] A former U.S. diplomat who was intimately involved in the summit meeting characterized President Kim as "very emotional and unreasonable," a description reminiscent of Assistant Secretary of State Robertson's view of President Syngman Rhee in 1953 and of Cyrus Vance's opinion of President Park Chung Hee in 1968.

The Clinton-Kim meeting did not prevent further escalation of saber-rattling rhetoric between the United States (and by extension South Korea) and North Korea throughout the spring of 1994. Even though North Korea allowed the IAEA's limited inspections at Yongbyon and the annual Team Spirit exercise was suspended, no progress was made in the North-South preliminary negotiations in Panmunjom, which were held to agree on the methods for exchanging special envoys between Seoul and Pyongyang prior to the third round of U.S.–North Korean talks at Geneva. In an ensuing heated debate at Panmunjom on March 19, a chief North Korean delegate even warned that should war break out on the peninsula, Seoul would become a "sea of blood."

This inflammatory rhetoric not only terminated the dialogue between the two Korean sides, it also elevated North Korea's image as a dangerous pariah in the international community. On March 21, 1994, the IAEA Board of Governors passed a resolution by a vote of 25 to 1 with 5 abstentions holding North Korea to be in "further non-compliance" with its safeguards agreement and referring the matter to the Security Council and the General Assembly of the United Nations.[30] At the IAEA, France, Britain, and other European countries took a more aggressive position against nuclear proliferation than the United States or South Korea did. It was significant that the Chinese, who favored a nuclear-free Korean Peninsula, abstained in the vote because they too were frustrated by North Korea's unwillingness to cooperate with IAEA inspections. The South Korean Ministry of Foreign Affairs supported the IAEA's decision and called upon North Korea to implement fully the safeguards agreement with the IAEA and to accept confidence-building measures on the Korean Peninsula. In his letter to Clinton on March 23, President Kim mentioned that although international pressure on North Korea should be intensified, South Korea and the United States needed to cooperate closely at the U.N. Security Council so that the situation would not escalate to an "extreme level." He also accepted the deployment of Patriot missiles in South Korea and the resumption of Team Spirit exercises.

At the U.N. Security Council, China played an active role in blocking the U.S.-sponsored resolution on the North Korean issue, which threatened to "consider further action" (read: sanctions) in the event of North Korea's continuing noncompliance, but it was ready to support a consensus statement to be issued by the president of the Security Council on March 31, 1994.[31] Once again the statement called upon North Korea to allow IAEA inspections of its nuclear facilities, invited the IAEA director general to submit a report on the inspections to the U.N. Security Council, and asked North Korea and South Korea to renew discussions for implementing the Joint Declaration on the Denuclearization of the Korean Peninsula. The North Koreans denounced the statement as containing "unjustifiable demands," thus defying the unanimous position of the U.N. Security Council. And they threatened to regard any sanctions resolution at the U.N. Security Council as a declaration of war against them and to take appropriate action.

The Clinton administration undertook the delicate process of finding a unified strategy that accommodated both the "safeguards-firsters" represented by the Department of State and the "dismantlement-firsters" led by the Department of Defense, and in the early months of 1994 it intensified diplomatic pressure on North Korea.[32]

Appearing before the House Committee on Foreign Affairs in March, Assistant Secretary of State for East Asian and Pacific Affairs Winston Lord declared that "we will not stand idly by if we can't continue to make progress" on the North Korean nuclear issue and that the United States would resort to whatever measures were required to ensure a nonnuclear Korean Peninsula.[33] In his address to the Asia Society on May 3, 1994, Secretary of Defense William Perry said that the biggest threat to peace and stability in Asia emanated from North Korea, because it had an "excessive military force" deployed along the DMZ, including Scud missiles, and a dangerous missile and nuclear program. He stated: "An unchecked nuclear capability—coupled with North Korea's large conventional military forces—could put North Korea in a position to subject South Korea to extortion in establishing its terms for unification. It could undermine the security of the whole Northeast Asia region and tempt other countries to seek their own nuclear weapons in self-defense. A nuclear North Korea could be in a position to export nuclear technologies and weapons to terrorist or rogue regimes around the world, unleashing a nightmare spread of nuclear threats." In an attempt to deter any precipitous military action by North Korea, Perry made it clear that South Korean forces were well trained, well fed, highly motivated, and equipped with high-quality weapons and that "there also can be no confusion about the military preparedness of the combined U.S.–Republic of Korea military forces and their ability to decisively defeat any attack from the North."[34]

At the same time, Perry authorized joint military exercises between U.S. and South Korean forces and augmented U.S. offensive capabilities. The United States had already deployed new Apache attack helicopters, Bradley fighting vehicles, Stinger antiaircraft missiles, and Patriot missile batteries in South Korea despite North Korea's vociferous protest. Secretary of Defense Perry asked General John Shalikashvili (chairman, Joint Chiefs of Staff) and General Gary Luck (commander, U.S. Forces Korea), a veteran of the Vietnam War and the Gulf War, to update Operation Plan 5027, a blueprint for a massive U.S. and South Korean counterattack to capture Pyongyang and to destroy the North Korean system. He also asked them to develop a contingency plan, which could be implemented with only a few days' alert and at a low risk of casualties, for a surgical attack to destroy the nuclear facilities at Yongbyon. During his visit to East Asia, Perry discussed America's military preparedness with President Kim in Seoul and obtained the Japanese government's commitment to support U.S. war efforts, if necessary. He was determined not to repeat the ignominious disaster of the Task Force Smith at the initial stage of the Korean War, when Lieutenant Colonel Charles B. Smith led the first contingent of unprepared and ill-equipped U.S. troops from Japan only to be routed by the superior North Korean forces and tanks.

General Luck projected that a war in Korea would kill or wound as many as 52,000 U.S. troops and 490,000 South Korean military forces and would cost $61 billion in the first ninety days; a prolonged full-scale war would kill or wound about a million people, including 80,000 to 100,000 U.S. troops at a cost of $100 billion — about one-third of the annual U.S. defense budget.[35] According to both Perry and Anthony Lake, this demonstrable contingency step was taken as a defensive measure, to be used only in the event of armed North Korean provocations. They preferred to attach priority to seeking U.N. sanctions against North Korea but took seriously the North Korean threat that the U.N. sanctions would mean a declaration of war.[36] Perry said that he had never presented the president with a recommendation for a surgical attack against nuclear facilities in Yongbyon and that in any event South Korea would undoubtedly have rejected it. And he added that military preparedness was demonstrated to make coercive diplomacy credible.

The contingency planning of military actions was accompanied by a U.S. diplomatic offensive in June. At the U.N. Security Council, the United States, in cooperation with South Korea and Japan, drafted a resolution to impose economic and diplomatic sanctions against North Korea.[37] The draft resolution asked all states to:

- Suspend all technical and scientific cooperation with North Korea that could contribute to its nuclear activities;
- Deny aviation connections with North Korea except for regularly scheduled commercial passenger flights;
- Stop all economic development assistance to North Korea;
- Suspend mutual assistance treaties with North Korea;
- Significantly reduce the number and level of the staff at North Korea's diplomatic and consular offices in their territories and restrict the movement of the remaining North Korean staff;
- Prevent import and export of "all nuclear, chemical, biological, strategic, and conventional weapons, missiles, and missile delivery systems, including dual use items" with North Korea; and
- Suspend all cultural, technical, scientific, commercial, and educational exchanges and visits and sporting events with North Korea.

If North Korea further developed its nuclear capabilities through withdrawal from the NPT, resumed nuclear reprocessing, or obstructed the IAEA's conduct of safeguard activities, the resolution stipulated additional sanctions:

- Freeze North Korean funds and financial resources; and
- Prohibit remitting or transporting any other funds to North Korea.

Excluded from this list were normal commercial transactions and payments for medical or humanitarian purposes, journalistic activities, informational materials, and personal travel.

The Korean Peninsula stood on the brink of another major armed conflict. Confidently insisting that the sanctions effort would have no effect on them whatsoever because of their self-reliant economy, North Korea threatened to wage war rather than yield to international condemnation and economic pressure. Most Americans (61%) surveyed in the poll taken on June 17 felt that a military conflict between the United States and North Korea was "very likely" or "somewhat likely" and only 31% of them approved of the way Clinton was handling the North Korean situation, with 42% disapproving.[38] Among those who supported Clinton's policy, 76% advocated tighter economic sanctions on North Korea, 44% favored U.S. air strikes on suspected nuclear facilities in North Korea, and 28% supported a U.S. invasion of North Korea. The survey indicated that Americans were anxious about the North Korean nuclear crisis but held a diversity of views on its resolution.

Alarmed by the escalating crisis in Korea, the Chinese accepted Washington's and Seoul's requests to urge North Korea to resume negotiations with the United States in good faith. After a meeting between Chinese Foreign Minister Qian Qichen and South Korean Foreign Minister Han Sung Joo at Beijing in early June, China modified its posture at the U.N. Security Council, changing its old formula of "opposing economic sanctions" against North Korea to "not favoring economic sanctions."[39] This subtle change implied to North Korea that China might abstain from the sanctions resolution. The expected removal of a Chinese veto, coupled with Clinton's and Kim Young Sam's close consultations with Russian President Boris Yeltsin, indicated possible passage of the sanctions resolution at the Security Council, which would be devastating to North Korea's international status and economic interests. The Japanese government expressed its willingness to impose sanctions on North Korea even without a U.N. sanctions resolution so that the transfer of significant remittances from pro-Pyongyang Korean residents in Japan to North Korea could be blocked.

As tensions over North Korea's nuclear program reached a potentially explosive stage in mid-June, former U.S. president Jimmy Carter decided to travel to Pyongyang with the Clinton administration's tacit approval. He spoke to President Clinton and Vice President Gore over the phone and received extensive briefings from several individuals—Gallucci in Plains, Georgia; Anthony Lake at the Washington National Airport; Korea specialists at the Department of State; South Korean Ambassador Han Seung Soo in Washington; U.S. Ambassador James Laney; and, of course, General Gary Luck in Seoul.[40] Secretary of State Christopher and Lake were apprehensive about what they regarded as Carter's interference in a sensitive diplomatic matter, and Carter received a thinly veiled critical reaction from South Korea.[41] In fact, President Kim had called President Clinton to say that the Carter visit was a mistake and that he might spoil a carefully calibrated diplomatic campaign to enact the U.S. sanctions on North Korea. Other South Korean officials, who remembered Carter's abortive decision to withdraw U.S. troops from South Korea, were suspicious of his ulterior motives in going to North Korea. After a two-day stopover in Seoul, Carter crossed the DMZ to travel to Pyongyang on June 15. He characterized his visit as that of a "private citizen," but he was accompanied by a U.S. diplomat fluent in Korean (Richard A. Christenson) and a former U.S. ambassador (Marion Creekmore).

At their meetings, President Kim Il Sung suggested to Carter that if the United States made a commitment not to launch a nuclear attack against North Korea and agreed to provide LWRs, he would freeze the nuclear program, allow IAEA inspectors to remain at Yongbyon, and resume the third round of negotiations at Geneva. He also accepted President Kim Young Sam's proposal for a summit meeting. In response, Carter assured Kim that the sanctions effort at the United Nations would be "held in abeyance"—a commitment that the Clinton administration, however, was not yet ready to offer. Confronted with the potentially disastrous consequences of Washington's coercive pressure—both military maneuvers and economic sanctions—Kim Il Sung took advantage of the former U.S. president's visit as a timely and convenient opportunity to retreat from the edge of brinkmanship and to defuse the crisis. President Clinton correctly viewed Carter's visit as "an escape hatch, some way to climb down without losing face." Kim was well aware of America's overwhelmingly superior military technology, which had recently been on display during the Persian Gulf War. The Carter mission served to enhance Kim's legitimacy and prestige and also satisfied his ego. Speaking authoritatively to Carter, Kim probably silenced whatever reservations hardline North Korean leaders, especially in the Korean People's Army, might have had about the negotiations at Geneva. Carter found Kim to be "vigorous, alert, intelligent, and remarkably familiar with the issues." He also reported: "Throughout our visit, our hosts were open, friendly, and remarkably reticent about making abusive or critical comments against the South Koreans. The North Koreans expressed concern about misunderstandings and lack of progress on the peninsula, but would acknowledge that these had been caused by mutual mistakes."

The initial South Korean reaction to Carter's activities was one of skepticism and confusion, especially in regard to his facile commitment to table the sanctions resolution at the United Nations. The Ministry of Foreign Affairs took the position that there was no reason for changing the U.N. efforts to impose sanctions on North Korea and that any change in the efforts required consultations among the five permanent members of the U.N. Security Council. Upon Seoul's request for clarification, both Assistant Secretary of State Lord and Gallucci informed South Korean Ambassador Han Seong Soo in Washington that Carter's statement was "incorrect." The situation changed, however, when Carter met President Kim at the Blue House. Reading from his pocket diary, Carter briefed Kim on the details of his North Korean visit and revealed that Kim Il Sung had agreed to a proposal for an inter-Korean summit meeting. The South Korean president readily accepted it and immediately announced his decision at a press conference. He then praised Carter's efforts at mediation between Seoul and Pyongyang. Kim was enthusiastic about a historic meeting with Kim Il Sung. Carter emerged as a peace broker between Seoul and Pyongyang and ameliorated his largely negative image in South Korea.

On June 24, the two Korean delegates—Lee Hong Koo (South Korean deputy prime minister of national unification) and Kim Yong Sun (secretary of the Korean Workers' Party)—had a preparatory meeting at Panmunjom and agreed to hold the summit meeting in Pyongyang on July 25 through 27.[42] Lee quickly relinquished his initial proposal to have the first meeting in Seoul, even though it was a logical choice, since historically it had been the capital of the entire Korean Peninsula during much of the Choson Dynasty and during the Japanese colonial rule. Nor did he insist on a North Korean commitment for a return visit to Seoul by Kim Il Sung because Kim Young Sam was especially accommodating, eager not to miss this rare opportunity. At this time President Kim had been strongly urging President Clinton and Ambassador Laney not to take any precipitous military action against the nuclear facilities at Yongbyon because he believed that it would certainly lead to another Korean War with destruction on an enormous scale.[43] He was also concerned that any hint of war might have adverse economic effects, particularly when it came to foreign investments in South Korea. After Clinton received a letter from Kim Il Sung confirming the accuracy of the agreements between Kim and Carter, the United States suspended the sanctions effort at the United Nations, halted further military deployments, and opened a third round of talks between Gallucci and Kang at Geneva on July 8.[44]

On the very next day the sudden death of Kim Il Sung was announced. On receiving this information, Quinones transmitted it to the North Korean delegates in Geneva, who had not yet learned of Kim's death. While staying in Naples, Italy, during the G-7 meeting, Clinton immediately issued sincere condolences to the "people" of North Korea and expressed the hope that North Korea would carry on with the late president Kim's decision to conduct a dialogue with the United States. Invited by his North Korean interlocutors, Gallucci, over South Korea's objections, went to the North Korean mission at Geneva to convey the condolences in person.[45] Kang left for Pyongyang to attend the funeral of Kim Il Sung. Meanwhile, President Kim Young Sam, unlike Clinton, refused to express his condolences, but rather criticized the late Kim's legacy and assailed him for starting the fratricidal war in 1950. This unsympathetic and vitriolic statement was probably intended to dampen any expressions of condolence and sympathy toward Kim Il Sung in South Korea. Stung by President Kim's criticism, the grieving Kim Jong Il, Kim Il Sung's son and successor, abandoned the agreement for an inter-Korean summit meeting during Kim Young Sam's presidency.

The public expression of condolences by Clinton and Gallucci made it easier for Kang to return to Geneva in a relatively short span of time. After resuming their negotiations on August 5, Gallucci and Kang moved swiftly to reach a provisional "Agreed Statement" on August 12, 1994.[46] While Clinton was eager for this agreement so that he could publicize the success of his foreign policy prior to the midterm congressional elections in November—especially in view of the questionable record of his policies in Somalia, Haiti, and Bosnia—Kim Jong Il embraced his father's legacy and sought to demonstrate the positive consequences of his political succession. The United States had not informed the South Koreans in advance that Gallucci and Kang would "sign" the Agreed Statement because they wanted to circumvent any objections by Seoul, for the U.S. negotiators often felt that South Korean diplomats assigned to monitor U.S.–North Korean talks in New York and Geneva were almost actively unhelpful.

On August 12, a chief South Korean diplomat (Kim Sam Hoon) who had remained at Geneva to maintain a liaison with U.S. negotiators became visibly upset because Gallucci briefed diplomats from other permanent member states of the U.N. Security Council first and kept him waiting.[47] Even more serious, however, were the deficiencies of the Agreed Statement pointed out by the South Koreans: it failed to include any provision for "special inspections" or "impartial application of fullscope safeguards" as mentioned in the joint statement of June 11, 1993. Even though the implementation of the North-South Joint Declaration on the Denuclearization of the Korean Peninsula was included, there was no reference to the resumption of a North-South dialogue. The South Koreans were also unhappy about the agreement to establish liaison offices in Washington and Pyongyang within two months after the freeze of North Korean nuclear programs. They suggested that the exchange of liaison offices should take place only after the completion of IAEA's special inspections; until then, any indication of diplomatic normalization between Washington and Pyongyang was to be resisted. Signs of mutual distrust and of the erosion of alliance cohesion between the United States and South Korea appeared. While U.S. negotiators at times deliberately withheld sensitive information from their South Korean allies because they suspected that it would be leaked to the press, thereby complicating negotiations with North Korea and prompting Republican criticism in Congress, the South Koreans felt that the United States promoted its own agenda at the expense of their important national interests.

In early September, South Korean Foreign Minister Han visited Washington to discuss with Secretary Christopher and National Security Adviser Lake how to iron out their differences over the Agreed Statement. Among other things, Han emphasized the concept of parallelism between the Geneva negotiations and North-South talks. This concept was particularly important to President Kim in the context of criticism from South Korea's conservative forces. Han's visit was soon followed by Gallucci's travels to Tokyo and Seoul. Gallucci attempted to soothe the ill will on the part of South Korean leaders, including President Kim, and to finalize the precise formula for South Korea's assistance to the LWR project. In the end, President Kim wrote a letter to President Clinton promising to provide financial contributions (about 70% of the cost) for the construction of two LWRs in North Korea. The letter specified two conditions to his financial commitment—the LWR project should use the South Korean model and North Korea should fulfill its agreed responsibilities, including special inspections. Thomas Hubbard, who had ably assisted Gallucci in Geneva, insisted that the South Korean side had initiated the idea for assuming 70% of the cost and that it had not come as a result of U.S. pressure.[48] In Tokyo, Japanese Prime Minister Murayama Tomiichi, who as chairman of the pro-Pyongyang Japan Socialist Party led a multiparty coalition government, had agreed to share the cost for the LWR project by overruling the reservations of the Ministry of Finance.[49] If South Korea and Japan had proven unwilling to assume the major portions of funds for the LWR project, the Clinton administration might have faced a serious dilemma because the United States was prohibited by law from providing nuclear reactors to North Korea.

While Gallucci and Kang were intensely engaged in the last stage of negotiations in Geneva, President Kim publicly aired his frustration and bitterness toward the United States, in part because he suspected that he was not fully consulted about the progress of the U.S.–North Korean compromises and the U.S. concession to defer the timing of special inspections in North Korea. Contrary to the understanding reached at his meeting with Clinton in November 1993, Kim had been forced to give up the resumption of a North-South dialogue as a precondition for the nuclear settlement. More important, his earlier hope for an inter-Korean summit meeting, which was a positive by-product of the U.S.–North Korean dialogue, was irretrievably shattered by the death of Kim Il Sung. In a brutally candid and provocative interview with the *New York Times* on October 8, he castigated the Clinton administration for ignorance, inexperience, and gullibility in its negotiations with North Korea. He charged that, in allowing themselves to be manipulated by North Korea, U.S. negotiators had been "naïve" and "overly flexible." He expressed grave doubts that the North Koreans would live up to the agreement, which would only bring even "more danger and peril." This accusation was more direct and serious than that of his earlier interview in July 1993. Just as President Rhee had sought to manipulate the United States during the Eisenhower administration, so too did Kim when he brandished his unpredictability and flamboyance as a tool to reveal his true feelings and to constrain U.S. diplomacy so that the Clinton administration would become more circumspect about South Korea's national interests and policy recommendations.

It was probably true that America's nonproliferation functionaries, unlike regional specialists, were more concerned about the global implications of North Korean nuclear programs than local issues (such as the North-South dialogue) and that they were not sufficiently sensitive to the domestic political difficulties faced by President Kim or to cultural nuances. Gallucci readily admitted that he had little knowledge of the history, politics, and culture of Korea. He repeatedly mispronounced his North Korean counterpart Kang Suk Ju's name as *kaeng*, instead of *kahng*, a blunder Kang did not appreciate.[50] Nor did Gallucci understand how decisions were made in Seoul and Pyongyang. However, he turned out to be a skillful and effective negotiator with humor and grace, and he applied his rich experience with Russian and East European nuclear issues to North Korea.

The Kim interview wrought havoc on Washington-Seoul relations.[51] In the middle of the night, Secretary of State Christopher called Foreign Minister Han from London and lodged a protest on behalf of Clinton. The embarrassed Han explained that the interview was meant to be off the record.[52] In a subsequent telephone conversation with Clinton, Kim reiterated his view that the North Koreans would never carry out the agreement with the United States. The *New York Times* interview had disturbed the Clinton administration but did not diminish its determination to consummate a deal with North Korea before the congressional elections.

On October 21, Gallucci and Kang signed the Agreed Framework at Geneva.[53] The two governments agreed to replace North Korea's graphite-moderated reactors and related facilities with light-water reactor (LWR) power plants at a total generating capacity of approximately 2,000 MW(e) by a target date of 2003, to reduce barriers to trade and investment, to open a liaison office in each other's capital, and to upgrade bilateral relations to the ambassadorial level "as progress is made on issues of concern to each side." More specifically, North Korea promised to:

1. freeze its graphite-moderated reactors and related facilities and allow the IAEA to monitor this freeze;
2. remain a party to the NPT and allow implementation of the safeguards agreement;
3. dismantle the graphite-moderated reactors and related facilities when the LWR project is completed;
4. store safely the spent nuclear fuel and dispose of the fuel in a safe manner;
5. take steps to implement the North-South Joint Declaration on the Denu-clearization of the Korean Peninsula; and
6. engage in North-South dialogue "as this Agreed Framework will help create an atmosphere that promotes such dialogue."

In retrospect, it was very important that the Agreed Framework specifically included the North-South Declaration not only because it satisfied one of South Korea's persistent requests, but also because the North-South Joint Declaration was explicit in banning any facilities for highly enriched uranium (HEU). According to Thomas Hubbard, the U.S. delegation at Geneva, preoccupied with the immediate question of weapons-grade plutonium, did not pay sufficient attention to the possibility of a HEU program, which was destined to become a major bone of contention in October 2002.[54]

The Agreed Framework failed to mention the IAEA's "special inspections" or "fullscope safeguards" specifically, but it stated: "When a significant portion of the LWR project is completed, but before delivery of key nuclear components, the DPRK will come into full compliance with its safeguards agreement with the IAEA, including taking all steps that may be deemed necessary by the IAEA, following consultations with the agency with regard to verifying the accuracy and completeness of the DPRK's initial report on all nuclear material in the DPRK." Since the United States had decided that special inspections designed to determine the past production of weapons-grade plutonium by North Korea were not that urgent and could be deferred for about five years, it was satisfied with the above provision for North Korea's "full compliance" [read: special inspections] in the future. As far as Gallucci was concerned, insisting on special inspections up front could force the United States to choose between a nuclear North Korea and another Korean War.[55] If North Korea failed to comply with this provision, the United States could stop completion of the LWR project. In return, the United States agreed to organize and lead an international consortium to finance and supply the LWR project and to deliver heavy oil to

North Korea at a rate of 500,000 tons annually until completion of the first LWR unit. This commitment was clearly confirmed in President Clinton's letter addressed to "His Excellency Kim Jong Il, Supreme Leader of the Democratic People's Republic of Korea" on October 20, 1994. The Clinton letter fell short of the North Korean demand for a legally binding agreement, but Kim's preeminent status in the post–Kim Il Sung era was publicly recognized. At Geneva, Gallucci and Kang signed the ten-point "Confidential Minute" to clarify the specific terms—such as the schedule for fuel delivery, inspection procedures, the construction of two nuclear power plants, and an agreement for peaceful nuclear cooperation—for implementing the Agreed Framework.[56] However, Gallucci rejected North Korea's proposals that the United States should withdraw its troops from South Korea, provide one million tons of grain to North Korea through the Food for Peace Program (Public Law 480) as well as a cash compensation of $1.2 billion for forgoing three present and future nuclear reactors, sign a bilateral peace agreement, establish diplomatic relations at the ambassadorial level, terminate the annual Team Spirit exercises, and completely lift economic sanctions imposed on North Korea.

The Agreed Framework was a major turning point not only for the interests of nuclear nonproliferation on the Korean Peninsula but also for the expansion of official contacts between the United States and North Korea. While the North Koreans capitalized on the nuclear issue to extract a host of benefits from the United States, the accord enhanced Clinton's status in domestic and foreign affairs. He jubilantly stated: "This agreement will help to achieve a long-standing and vital American objective—an end to the threat of nuclear proliferation on the Korean Peninsula.... It reduces the danger of the threat of nuclear weapons spreading in the region."[57] He did not forget to mention America's "unshakable commitment to protect our ally and our fellow democracy—South Korea." Writing in 1998, Warren Christopher proudly remembered that "the Agreed Framework stands out as one of the major achievements of our foreign policy.... This was an occasion on which the United States rose to the challenge of its indispensable leadership role."[58] Yet Vice President Albert Gore, Lake, and other U.S. officials represented a prevailing view in Washington (and Seoul) that the North Korean regime would collapse before the completion of the LWR project.[59]

The South Korean Ministry of Foreign Affairs promptly issued a statement welcoming the Agreed Framework, which addressed a couple of important matters directly relevant to Seoul's interests—namely, the Joint Declaration on the Denuclearization of the Korean Peninsula and North-South dialogue.[60] The statement also urged North Korea to fulfill its obligations under the Agreed Framework and to take a "positive and sincere" step for improving South-North relations. This official reaction did not overcome a sense of disappointment and frustration that remained strong in Seoul, and President Kim and Foreign Minister Han came under criticism from legislators and the mass media in South Korea. Rep. Park Chung Soo, a senior member of the governing Democratic Liberal Party, complained that the government's goal to establish nuclear transparency prior to the construction of the LWRs in North Korea was now lost. A few members of the National Assembly went so far as to demand the reshuffling of Kim's foreign and unification policy team. An official at the Blue House admitted that the Agreed Framework was "the second best policy" and that "the United States pushed ahead with the logic of a superpower."[61] President Kim agreed to cancel the Team Spirit exercises scheduled for November but refused to share the costs of delivering heavy fuel oil to North Korea. Public opinion in South Korea was evenly divided about the utility of the Agreed Framework, but about 74% supported President Kim's promise to assist the LWR project in North Korea. In December 1994, however, Foreign Minister Han was forced to step down as a result of his moderate policy, which was frequently at odds with President Kim's conservative political instincts.

On March 9, 1995, the United States, South Korea, and Japan signed the Agreement on the Establishment of the Korean Peninsula Energy Development Organization (KEDO) to carry out the terms of the Agreed Framework.[62] It appointed an executive director (American) and two deputy directors (South Korean and Japanese). The Clinton administration took great pains to satisfy Seoul's adamant demands that the South Korean model, originally from the United States, should apply to the LWRs in North Korea and that the Korea Electric Power Corporation (KEPCO), the state-run power monopoly, should be named as a prime contractor for the construction at Kumho. This demand was made to ensure that South Korea would exercise firm control over the project.[63] Many officials in Seoul, including President Kim, agreed with those in Washington and Tokyo who believed at the time that the North Korean regime without Kim Il Sung would collapse within ten years due to economic difficulties and that the LWRs to be constructed in North Korea would eventually become a major source of energy for a unified Korea. In this sense, South Korea's financial contributions were regarded as a long-term investment. While the United States assumed responsibility for the funds to supply heavy fuel oil to North Korea, South Korea and Japan pledged to share a significant portion of the funds for the LWR project, which was projected to cost about $5 billion. In September 1997, the European Atomic Energy Community in the European Union became a member of KEDO and joined the United States, South Korea, and Japan on KEDO's executive board. The KEDO Office at Kumho was set up to oversee the LWR construction project on site and to serve as a liaison with North Korea.

Nine other countries subsequently joined KEDO. Neither China nor Russia provided any financial assistance to KEDO, however.

Refusing to honor their commitment made in Geneva, the North Koreans stubbornly resisted undertaking a meaningful dialogue with their South Korean counterparts throughout 1996. The Clinton administration took every opportunity to encourage inter-Korean contacts and exchanges. When heralding a major achievement in U.S.–North Korean negotiations—the agreement to use the South Korean model for the LWR project—the Department of State pointed out that "the resumption of North-South dialogue is essential not only for the full implementation of the Agreed Framework, but also to the continuing effort to build lasting prosperity and a stable peace on the Korean Peninsula."[64] The same issue was discussed at the summit meeting between Presidents Clinton and Kim Young Sam on July 27, 1995, at the White House, and the concept of linkages was again made explicit. To demonstrate his solidarity with Kim, Clinton made it clear that "the United States regards North Korea's commitment to resume dialogue with the South as an integral component of the [Agreed] Framework."[65] At the same time Kim reiterated that "improvement of relations between the United States and North Korea should proceed in harmony and parallel with the improvement of relations between the Republic of Korea and North Korea." The two leaders attended the dedication ceremony for the Korean War Veterans Memorial and reaffirmed their mutual security commitment. However, Kim's persistent efforts to reach out to Pyongyang via Washington did not bear fruit.

The Agreed Framework and the KEDO operations became the subject of partisan wrangling in Washington. The Republicans, who captured the majority of seats in the U.S. Congress in November 1994, seized on the North Korean nuclear issue to criticize Clinton's foreign policy, claiming that the United States had offered too many concessions to North Korea in return for its less-than-full compliance with the IAEA's full-scope safeguards agreement. The amendment that Representative Benjamin Gilman (R-NY), chairman of the House Committee on International Relations, introduced to the American Overseas Interests Act (1995) stipulated that President Clinton should only take further steps toward upgrading diplomatic relations with North Korea if and when North Korea entered into a dialogue with South Korea on several issues—such as the reduction of military tensions, the expansion of trade relations, cooperation in science and technology, and the establishment of postal and telecommunications services. It was ironic that the Republican Party attempted to articulate Seoul's preferences more aggressively than the Clinton administration had in its negotiations with North Korea. Other critics of Clinton's policy argued that light-water moderated reactors were not necessarily "proliferation-resistant." James A. Baker III, secretary of state under President George H. W. Bush, complained that "our policy of carrots and sticks gave way overnight to one of carrots only—fuel oil to help run North Korea's beleaguered economy, two new nuclear reactors, and diplomatic ties."[66] He criticized Clinton's abrupt policy "flip-flop" and predicted that the Agreed Framework would prove to have been a mistake that would make stability on the Korean Peninsula less, not more, likely. Still others questioned why Gallucci agreed to provide an expensive program for reactors that would generate 2,000 MW of electricity in return for the suspension of three North Korean reactors with a total capacity of 275 MW.

So long as North Korea kept its pledge to freeze the nuclear program at Yongbyon under the IAEA's inspection mechanism, the Clinton administration continued to deliver 500,000 tons of heavy fuel oil to North Korea each year and to facilitate the construction of two LWRs in North Korea "by a target date of 2003." The exchange of liaison offices, however, had yet to take place. Evidently, bilateral expert-level discussions had settled most consular and other technical issues for exchanging liaison offices between Washington and Pyongyang, but no final decision had been made. The Clinton administration, eager to open its liaison office in Pyongyang, concluded a "Memorandum of Understanding" with North Korea in December 1994, but the North Koreans responded less than enthusiastically to this semi-diplomatic mechanism. A senior State Department official explained that you can lead a horse (North Korea) to water (liaison office), but you can't make it drink.[67] The North Koreans argued that since there was no significant breakthrough in their substantive relations with the United States, especially in economic fields, the mere presence of their liaison office in Washington would not be very useful.[68] From their perspective, they could easily rely upon their permanent mission to the United Nations in New York for diplomatic communications with the United States. This New York channel had, in effect, replaced the Beijing Talks. They were probably apprehensive about the likelihood of intrusive functions, such as sophisticated intelligence-gathering operations, by a U.S. liaison office in Pyongyang. The Clinton administration was somewhat hesitant to upgrade its fledgling diplomatic relations with North Korea too quickly without commensurate improvement in inter-Korean relations because South Korea continued to insist on "linkages" and "parallelism" in this regard. Assistant Secretary of State for East Asian and Pacific Affairs Winston Lord clarified the central role that the concept of linkages played: "In the Agreed Framework the DPRK made a commitment to engage in North-South dialogue. This commitment was so central that the U.S. would not have concluded the Framework without it. North-South dialogue is an essential aspect of the Agreed Framework and a prerequisite for its full implementation."[69] For the United States, alliance cohesion and smooth cooperation with South Korea were more important than a newly developing relationship with North Korea.

On January 20, 1995, the State Department announced its initial measures to ease economic sanctions against North Korea:

- to authorize transactions related to telephone and telecommunications connections, credit card use in connection with personal travel, and the opening of offices by journalists;
- to authorize North Korea's use of the U.S. banking system and to release frozen assets unrelated to the North Korean government's interests;
- to authorize U.S. imports of North Korean magnesite (a refractory material used in the steel industry); and
- to authorize transactions related to liaison offices and to the implementation of the Framework.[70]

Soon AT&T became the first U.S. company to install direct-dial service to North Korea. Mineral Technology signed a contract to import magnesite. The New York–based Stanton Group, a power plant developer, concluded a joint venture with North Korea to operate a power plant and oil refinery in the Rajin-Sonbong area. A relatively modest door for bilateral commercial relations had opened.

Yet U.S. businessmen quickly found it rather frustrating to conduct economic transactions with North Korea because of inefficient bureaucracies, an outdated infrastructure, widespread energy shortages, delayed delivery schedules, and abrupt unilateral cancellations. A spokesman for the U.S. Treasury Department candidly admitted: "The situation is sufficiently unstable there to give great pause to any smart American businessman or businesswoman seeking to invest eggs in various baskets. This is a basket which is still rife with risk."[71] In spite of North Korea's active promotion of the Tumen River Development Project, not many U.S. companies showed interest in the Rajin-Sonbong area because of its uncertain commercial prospects. Another discouraging factor was the lingering effect of U.S. economic sanctions against North Korea. Winston Lord explained that the timing and extent of further sanctions reduction measures would in large part depend on DPRK willingness to engage constructively on the issues of missile proliferation, the return of war remains, the reduction of tensions, and, most important, North-South dialogue.[72] The United States did not intend to give away all the economic sanctions that could be used as tangible methods of reward and punishment for North Korea.

For humanitarian purposes, however, the United States joined South Korea and Japan in expanding economic assistance programs to North Korea. After floods devastated large areas of North Korea in the summer and fall of 1995, for example, the U.S. government donated $225,000 to the United Nations Children's Fund (UNICEF) for a vaccination program and for a program to give nutritional support to young children and nursing mothers in North Korea. In response to North Korea's unprecedented appeal for assistance, the governments of South Korea and Japan shipped a sizable amount of rice to North Korea in 1995. Even if the Clinton administration could not use the Public Law 480 program to assist North Korean flood victims directly (because of South Korean objections), it decided in February 1996 to donate $2 million in food assistance to North Korea through the United Nations World Food Program. In contrast with their ungrateful response to South Korean rice deliveries, the North Koreans publicly expressed their appreciation to President Clinton. In view of the risk of a serious famine in North Korea, Clinton announced in June 1996 that the United States would give additional emergency food aid ($6.2 million) to Pyongyang.[73] Skeptics of Clinton's food-aid program for North Korea insisted that, as had been the case for the Hoover Mission to the Soviet Union in the 1930s, the United States should control the distribution of food in North Korea and prevent its diversion to the [North] Korean People's Army (KPA). The South Koreans, too, were concerned about the problem of transparency in U.S. food assistance to North Korea.

Reports of severe food and energy shortages in North Korea, which had occurred in the aftermath of the demise of the Soviet Union, East Germany, and other East European socialist regimes, touched off an intense interbureaucratic debate over North Korea's viability—most notably between the intelligence and military leaders and the Department of State in the United States. In testimony before the Senate Select Committee on Intelligence in February 1996, CIA Director John Deutch asserted that under Kim Jong Il, "North Korea remains isolated, xenophobic, militaristic, and resistant to reform and its hostility toward the South is unabated."[74] He explained that the North would find it harder to maintain military capabilities and to insulate the armed forces from worsening economic problems. "If food shortages should spread to front-line military units," he predicted, "it could undermine regime stability." Moreover, the outgoing commander of U.S. Forces Korea, General Gary Luck, told a subcommittee of the House of Representatives in March 1996 that "we worry that, in a very short period, this country [North Korea] will either collapse or take aggressive actions against the South in a desperate attempt to divert attention from its international situation." The question, he said, is not "will this country disintegrate?" but rather "how will it disintegrate—by implosion or explosion? And when?"[75] In order to dampen the excitement generated by the testimony of Deutch and Luck and to soften its adverse effects on U.S.–North Korean relations, both Secretary of State Christopher and Assistant Secretary of State Lord made it clear that there were no signs of "imminent collapse" of North Korea. They further relaxed economic sanctions against North Korea in March 1996, a move designed to authorize exports of commercially supplied goods that met basic human needs and donations of funds for humanitarian assistance to victims of natural disasters.

President Clinton had high political stakes in ensuring that the Agreed Framework and the KEDO operated smoothly because he needed to prevent his North Korean policy from becoming a potentially explosive campaign issue readily exploitable by his Republican opponents. Severely constrained by its fiscal and legal limits, however, the Clinton administration could not play a decisive leadership role in KEDO-related developments; instead it was relegated to coordinating the wishes of the principal financial providers (South Korea and Japan) and to relying on Japan for assisting with the delivery of heavy oil to North Korea.

Within the Clinton administration, however, there was general satisfaction with KEDO's pragmatic and businesslike working relationship with North Korea, but in other quarters there was considerable skepticism and apprehension about the future of nuclear nonproliferation in Korea. In criticizing the Agreed Framework, a leading candidate for the Republican Party's presidential nomination, former senator Robert Dole (R-KS), declared that "a bad deal is often much worse than no deal at all," but he fell short of calling for nullification of the arrangement. He asserted: "The greatest immediate security threat in Asia is the Stalinist regime in North Korea, armed to the teeth, determined to develop weapons of mass destruction and the means to deliver them. . . . President Clinton failed to hold North Korea to its 1991 commitments to resume bilateral North-South talks and to work with South Korea for a nuclear-free Peninsula. His accommodation of North Korea, and his neglect of our ally's well-founded concerns, set a pattern that has continued to this day: appeasing the North, slighting the South, and ignoring the strategic consequences."[76] Another critic of the Agreed Framework argued that North Korean leaders retained "a latent ability" to break out of the agreement if they felt it was unsatisfactory.[77]

In spite of the partial improvement of its relations with North Korea following the Agreed Framework, the Clinton administration was reluctant to abandon its system of military containment toward North Korea altogether or to accept Pyongyang's desire to change the Korean Armistice Agreement into a bilateral peace agreement by excluding South Korea. The North Koreans had long contended that since the Korean Armistice Agreement was a temporary ceasefire arrangement, the United States should negotiate and conclude a peace treaty with North Korea, and that since South Korea was not a signatory to the Korean Armistice Agreement, it should have no role in this process whatsoever. In addition to this legalistic argument, the

North Koreans probably had other objectives in mind when they insisted on U.S.–North Korean negotiations. First, influenced by their hierarchical view of world politics, they believed that for all practical purposes the United States was the true master of military affairs in South Korea, and they attempted to perpetuate the myth that South Korea was a mere puppet of the United States. Second, they wished to drive a wedge between the United States and South Korea, to loosen the U.S.–South Korean alliance system, and to transform the United States from a military adversary into a security guarantor for North Korea. A U.S. diplomat engaged in negotiations with North Korea asserted that his North Korean counterparts were willing to accept the continuing presence of U.S. forces in South Korea as insurance against any northward military action by South Korea. Hence the concept of "double containment" for U.S. military policy in Korea came into being. Third, by concluding a peace treaty with the United States, the North Koreans anticipated elevating their status and legitimacy in the international community and emerging as nationalistic champions of peace and cooperation at the expense of South Korea.

Aware of North Korea's ulterior motives and South Korea's extreme sensitivity, the United States rebuffed a series of North Korean proposals for bilateral peace negotiations. About the time when the negotiations for the Geneva Agreed Framework were underway in 1994, the North Koreans maneuvered to deactivate the Military Armistice Commission (MAC) at Panmunjom and the Neutral Nations Supervisory Commission and forced the Chinese government to recall its representatives from the MAC. They also set up the Panmunjom Mission of the Korean People's Army (KPA) to replace the MAC. Alarmed by these maneuvers, the United States reminded North Korea that the inter-Korean "Agreement on Reconciliation, Non-aggression and Exchanges and Cooperation" clearly confirmed that it was the responsibility of the two Korean governments to change the armistice regime into a firm state of peace and that both Koreas should honor the present armistice agreement until a stable peace system could be established. A spokesman for the Department of State declared in February 1995 that if Pyongyang hoped that its attempts to destroy the mechanism set up by the armistice agreement would lead the United States to enter into bilateral talks on a peace treaty, it was badly mistaken.[78] Yet the United States, along with China, was unsuccessful in persuading the North Koreans that both Korean governments should bear primary responsibility for negotiating a permanent system of peace on the peninsula.

On February 22, 1996, the North Koreans proposed a stopgap measure that would be effective until such time as a comprehensive peace agreement could be concluded. They suggested a tentative agreement between the United States and North Korea that would create a joint U.S.–North Korean military body at Panmunjom to manage the military demarcation line (MDL) and the demilitarized zone (DMZ).[79] When the United States flatly rejected this proposal, the North Koreans escalated their militant rhetoric and orchestrated armed demonstrations in March and April 1996. They also publicized Kim Jong Il's frequent inspection tours to the DMZ area. A North Korean commentator accused the United States of clinging to a hostile policy toward North Korea and of staging daily war exercises, warning that U.S. belligerence was leading to the brink of war. Speaking at the People's Palace of Culture in Pyongyang on April 4, Yang Hyong Sop, chairman of the North Korean Supreme People's Assembly, defiantly proclaimed: "Instigated by the U.S. ultrarightist conservative forces, the Kim Yong Sam ring adopts a confrontation and war maneuver, driving the situation of the Korean peninsula to the brink of war. Actually, due to the war threat from the South, a war on the Korean peninsula is not out of the question, only the timing is the remaining question."[80] Claims of the inevitability of war were repeated in other North Korean statements and public commentaries. Citing an imminent military threat from the United States and South Korea, the Korean People's Army announced on April 4 that it would give up its duty to maintain and control the DMZ and would remove the distinctive insignia and markings from its personnel and vehicles in the joint security area. For three successive days, it dispatched several hundred armed soldiers to the northern section of the DMZ, violating the demilitarized status of the section. A spokesman for the North Korean Ministry of Foreign Affairs blamed the United States for its systematic violation of the Armistice Agreement.[81] The North Koreans probably wanted to compel the United States to heed and accept their peace proposals. For they had learned from the nuclear disputes that brinkmanship by threat and intimidation could effectively gain attention and concessions from the United States. It was also conceivable that the North Koreans dramatized the theme of an inevitable war to divert attention from their own internal predicaments or as a way of acceding to the KPA's growing militancy. And the Panmunjom incident may have been aimed at the National Assembly elections in South Korea or at the summit meeting between Presidents Clinton and Kim Young Sam in Cheju Island. The North Koreans assailed Clinton's Cheju visit as an encouragement to the "war maniacs" in South Korea.

The United States, characterizing the North Korean violation of the DMZ as "provocative," heightened military alertness and intelligence surveillance in Korea and let the president of the United Nations Security Council issue a mildly worded admonition to North Korea.[82] The United States, together with South Korea, refused to panic in response to these latest North Korean provocations, to be taken in by North Korea's ploy. Yet President Clinton did not want to face another explosive military crisis with the potential of hurting his chances for reelection in November 1996.

THE FOUR-PARTY TALKS

Since the Agreed Framework was basically a product of bilateral negotiations between the United States and North Korea, the South Koreans, who had been left on the sidelines, intended to claim a legitimate and equal role in any further discussions on the Korean questions and to find a way to resume direct official contact with North Korea. The North Koreans had repeatedly failed to fulfill their commitment made in the Agreed Framework to implement the North-South Joint Declaration on the Denuclearization of the Korean Peninsula and to "engage in North-South dialogue." This was a subject for intensive and constructive discussions between Anthony Lake (assistant to the president for national security affairs) and Yoo Chong Ha (senior secretary to the president for foreign affairs and national security), a seasoned career diplomat with extensive experience in U.S. and U.N. affairs, at Cheju Island for three days in February 1996. At the beginning of their meeting, Lake told Yoo that a visit by President Clinton to South Korea was "out of the question" because of his busy schedule for reelection campaign. Yoo told Lake that President Kim would be extremely upset if Clinton skipped South Korea during his planned visit to Japan. Even for Clinton's reelection strategy, Yoo argued, it would be important for the U.S. president to demonstrate that he was maintaining good relations with his South Korean counterpart and had a clear plan for a new peace mechanism on the Korean Peninsula. About a month thereafter, Lake informed Yoo that President Clinton reversed his initial decision to skip South Korea on his state visit to Japan and that he would hold a brief summit meeting with President Kim at Cheju Island and would join him in proposing a new multilateral venue for discussing the problems of peace on the Korean Peninsula.[83] Agreeing to a summit meeting provided an opportunity to placate the unpredictable and potentially explosive South Korean president.

At their one-day meeting held on Cheju Island on April 16, 1996, Presidents Clinton and Kim reconfirmed "the fundamental principle" that "establishment of a stable, permanent peace on the Korean Peninsula is the task of the Korean people" and that "separate negotiations between the United States and North Korea on peace-related issues cannot be considered."[84] This was intended to satisfy Kim's strong view on national self-determination—an attempt to transcend what he called past tendencies toward a "passive and dependent" approach to the United States. However, they proposed to convene a four-party meeting of representatives of South Korea, North Korea, China, and the United States as soon as possible and without preconditions for the purpose of initiating a process aimed at achieving a permanent peace agreement. The four-party format would actually serve as a means of facilitating direct contact between North and South Korea, Kim explained. According to Kim's plan, after the Four-Party Talks began, South Korea would then be able to conduct a bilateral meeting with North Korea; in this sense, it was not a "two-plus-two" formula but rather a "four-minus-two" scheme.[85] In a confidential letter written to Chinese President Jiang Zemin on April 14, Kim had given advance notice to China about the forthcoming proposal for the Four-Party Talks and had asked him to convey the proposal to North Korea. On April 20, Jiang expressed China's willingness to participate in the talks.[86] Japan was persuaded to support the proposed multilateral venue, but for a while Russia continued to insist on six-party talks (i.e., including Russia and Japan).

This initiative marked a significant departure from the earlier U.S. position that the issues of peace and reunification must be resolved by the Korean people themselves. It was a serious attempt to bring North Korea to the conference table with South Korea. Unlike the tripartite conference that Presidents Jimmy Carter and Park Chung Hee had proposed in their joint statement of 1979, this proposed meeting was set up to include China. The United States and South Korea wished to solicit China's direct participation in a new venue so that China, as a signatory to the Korean Armistice Agreement, could exert a positive influence over North Korea and could help bring about a satisfactory implementation of any agreement that might be concluded.

Although the initial North Korean reaction appeared to be negative, a spokesman for the North Korean Ministry of Foreign Affairs announced on April 18 that "we are now examining the proposal of the U.S. side to see whether it seeks another purpose and whether it is feasible."[87] He intentionally ignored the fact that the United States and South Korea had jointly proposed the meeting. On May 7 the same North Korean spokesman complained that since "we have not received any official explanation [from the United States] about the proposal, we are increasingly doubtful about it with the passage of time."[88] While the North Koreans preferred not to abandon their consistent position that only the United States and North Korea, "the real parties" to the Armistice Agreement, should negotiate a peace agreement, they did not wish to miss a potentially useful opportunity to terminate the Korean Armistice Agreement, change the U.S. policy of military containment, and erect a new system of peace on the peninsula. Above all, they expected to obtain substantial economic assistance from the United States and South Korea in return for their participation in the Four-Party Talks.

The Clinton administration accepted a South Korean proposal to hold a joint briefing session with North Korea so that the procedures and agenda for the Four-Party Talks could be clarified. The South Koreans requested this joint undertaking because they recognized the possibility that they could be excluded from preparatory meetings for the talks. Yet the North Koreans swiftly rejected the idea of a joint briefing session on the grounds that South Korea had no qualifications or justification to participate in a dialogue on ensuring peace in Korea; in effect, they urged South Korea not to interfere in their bilateral contacts with the United States. The prospect for the Four-Party Talks was further threatened by two unexpected events — a North Korean submarine incident in September 1996 and the defection of a senior North Korean leader in February 1997.

When a North Korean submarine with twenty-six armed commandos ran aground near the east coast of South Korea on September 18, 1996, the South Korean government declared it an act of military provocation in violation of the Korean Armistice Agreement and decided to bring its grievance before the international community. While conducting a massive manhunt for fifteen surviving North Korean infiltrators and threatening to stop humanitarian assistance programs for North Korea, the South Korean government referred the matter to the U.N. Security Council, which urged both countries on the Korean Peninsula to settle their outstanding issues through dialogue.[89] Since South Korea was unable to have a dialogue with North Korea at that time, it let the United States negotiate with North Korea to find a peaceful solution to the incident. On November 24, Presidents Kim and Clinton discussed the incident on the sidelines of an APEC summit meeting in Manila and reaffirmed their support for the Four-Party Talks. Under intense pressure from the United States and the United Nations, the North Korean Ministry of Foreign Affairs at last issued a statement toward the end of December in which it expressed "deep regret" over the incident and promised to ensure that "such an incident will not recur." This was the first time North Korea had ever apologized to South Korea, even indirectly. In response, South Korean Foreign Minister Yoo Chong Ha announced that "the North Korean statement is one that the people of the Republic of Korea can accept, because it recognizes the incident, apologizes and promises to prevent a recurrence."[90] President Clinton, too, issued a statement to welcome North Korea's expression of deep regrets and to praise President Kim's patient and positive efforts. So ended the first submarine crisis.[91]

About forty days later, a high-ranking North Korean political leader, Hwang Chang Yop, defected to the South Korean consulate general in Beijing on his way from Tokyo to Pyongyang. While North Korea claimed that he was kidnapped by South Korean intelligence agents and that China should immediately repatriate him to Pyongyang, South Korea insisted that since he had defected of his own free will, China should allow his safe and direct passage to Seoul. The Chinese rejected both demands, conducted patient and even-handed negotiations with the two Korean governments, and finally decided to "expel" him to a third country.[92] This shrewd stratagem enabled Hwang to stay in the Philippines for a month before traveling to Seoul. As a result, China minimized the damage to North Korea, respected Hwang's right to choose, and ultimately satisfied South Korea's expectations.

The United States and South Korea feared that because of these two incidents, North Korea would be less interested in the Four-Party Talks than before. After receiving food assistance from Seoul and Washington, however, North Korean Vice Minister of Foreign Affairs Kim Gye Gwan joined South Korean Deputy Foreign Minister Song Yong Shik and U.S. Deputy Assistant Secretary of State Charles Kartman in holding briefing sessions in New York on March 5, April 16 through 21, and June 30, 1997.[93] Kim insisted that in order to create a favorable environment for the talks, the United States should lift economic sanctions against North Korea. He also requested that they have more preliminary sessions with the United States and South Korea without Chinese participation. Kim went on to argue that it was "unfair" that North Korea had no diplomatic relations with the United States while South Korea had diplomatic relations with China, and that the United States had its troops in South Korea whereas there were no foreign troops in North Korea. In addition to his concerns about the diplomatic asymmetry and military imbalance between Seoul and Pyongyang, Kim probably suspected that, in view of the way the Hwang Chang Yop case was handled, China might not only refrain from supporting North Korea's positions, it might also join with the United States and South Korea against North Korea. At one point the North Koreans even suggested a "three-plus-one" formula: the three principal parties (both Koreas and the United States) would conduct the peace negotiations, and China would join them later to endorse the outcome. The United States was initially amenable to this formula, but South Korea opposed it and wanted China's full participation in the Four-Party Talks. Just as they had done in 1979, the South Koreans resisted the ominous implications of tripartite peace talks reminiscent of the Paris peace negotiations on Vietnam. And they expected that China, because of its two-Korea policy, would play a constructive role in the negotiations. It is conceivable that the Chinese had already expressed their displeasure to their North Korean "comrades" and assured them that China would not take a position harmful to Pyongyang's basic interests. As a further incentive, China had announced in early June that it would donate 80,000 tons of food to North Korea, thereby bringing China's total aid to 127,000 tons in 1997.[94]

On August 5 through 7, 1997, Chinese Assistant Minister of Foreign Affairs Chen Jian joined Kim Gye Gwan, Song Yong Shik, and Charles Kartman at Columbia University to discuss the agenda, venue, and other related matters for the Four-Party Talks. The North Koreans proposed that the talks should focus on two agenda items: (1) a bilateral peace agreement between the United States and North Korea and (2) the withdrawal of U.S. troops from South Korea. They did not want to recognize China's and South Korea's roles in the peace agreement. On November 21, all four parties agreed on a broadly defined but ambiguous agenda: (1) "the establishment of a peace regime on the Peninsula" and (2) "issues concerning tension reduction there." The Chinese were helpful in persuading North Korea to accept this consensus.

On December 9 and 10, 1997, the first full-dress session of the Four-Party Talks was held in Geneva. It was the first multilateral diplomatic meeting on the Korean question since the failure of the Geneva Conference twenty-three years earlier. The United States and South Korea had close consultations prior to each session. Yet they did not have a clear road map for the talks. Nor did they reach an agreement on the specific contents of a new peace mechanism for Korea. While Lee Si Young (ambassador to France and former vice foreign minister), who had long experience in multilateral diplomacy at the United Nations, led the South Korean delegation, the North Korean side was headed by Kim Gye Gwan (vice minister of foreign affairs and former deputy ambassador to the United Nations) and Ri Gun (deputy ambassador to the United Nations). Stanley Roth (assistant secretary of state for East Asian and Pacific affairs) and Tang Jiaxuan (vice minister of foreign affairs, a Japan specialist) represented the United States and China, respectively (see table 3). The chairman's statement issued on December 10 noted that the talks "successfully inaugurated the negotiation process" and proceeded "in a cordial and productive atmosphere."

Lee, Roth, and Tang were apparently satisfied with the initial encounter, but Ri Gun complained that the talks failed to address the "real issue." A spokesman for the North Korean Ministry of Foreign Affairs insisted that it was necessary to have a peace agreement concluded between North Korea and the United States and for U.S. troops to be withdrawn from South Korea.[95] He claimed that China supported North Korea's longstanding positions on U.S.–North Korean relations and inter-Korean issues but accused South Korea and the United States of pushing for the inter-Korean agreements signed in 1991 being implemented before a more permanent peace mechanism could be established on the Korean Peninsula. In fact, the South Koreans criticized North Korea's failure to carry out the Basic Agreement of 1991 and the Joint Declaration on the Denuclearization of the Korean Peninsula.

Enthusiasm for the Four-Party Talks in South Korea began to dwindle in 1998, mainly because of the demoralizing effects of the financial crisis and the inauguration of President Kim Dae Jung on February 25, 1998. At the end of 1996 South Korea's total foreign debts had reached $157.5 billion (33% of its gross domestic product), and its banking system had assumed as much as $500 billion in failed loans.

Total debts incurred by the top 30 *chaebol* (business conglomerates) increased by 32.4% from the end of 1996 to the end of 1997; the average debt-equity ratio grew from 386.5% to 518.9% during the same period. After the escalating financial and currency crisis in Southeast Asia during the summer of 1997, the rapid exodus of capital from South Korea drastically devalued the local currency against the dollar, caused stock prices to nosedive, and substantially drained foreign exchange reserves.[96] The reasons for South Korea's financial meltdown toward the end of 1997 were complex, but Paul Krugman correctly pointed out that banks, depositors, lenders, and shareholders in South Korea had suffered from "extreme moral hazard," hoping that the government would bail them out in the event of trouble.[97] Without a prudent regulatory and supervisory mechanism, the banks had failed in their domestic and international operations. In return for its massive bailout package, the International Monetary Fund (IMF) stipulated a set of rigorous conditions: the South Korean government was required to execute a disciplined fiscal and monetary policy, to restructure financial institutions, to manage the labor market efficiently, and to make the *chaebol* more transparent, productive, and responsible. The IMF's stringent conditionality triggered anti-American sentiment among many South Koreans because they assumed that the United States was exploiting the IMF to open up South Korean markets and to make their lives more difficult.[98] Robert Manning asserted that the financial crisis made South Korea "tumultuous, inward-focused, resentful and economically nationalistic as it copes with the pressures of globalization."[99] As a result, the South Koreans were more worried about the possible collapse of North Korea than ever, because they did not want to assume any additional financial burdens.

More important, President Kim Dae Jung, unlike his predecessor, who had had a conservative outlook, adopted a distinctly liberal and conciliatory "sunshine policy" toward North Korea. As the first president to achieve a peaceful transfer of power from the governing political party to the opposition group and as someone with expertise on inter-Korean relations, he enunciated the three principles of his new policy: (1) South Korea would not tolerate armed provocation by North Korea; (2) South Korea had no intention of undermining or absorbing North Korea; and (3) South Korea would actively pursue reconciliation and cooperation with North Korea, beginning with areas in which mutual cooperation was possible.[100] He decided to pursue a "two-plus-two-plus-two" formula, which placed the primary focus on direct bilateral contacts with North Korea. Once a breakthrough was made in inter-Korean relations, he planned to bring the United States and China into a multilateral dialogue and eventually to seek Japan's and Russia's endorsement of the outcome of such a dialogue. For this endeavor, he was ably assisted by Lim Dong Won (senior secretary for foreign affairs and national security), who had played a pivotal role in negotiating the Basic Agreement and the Joint Declaration on the Denuclearization of the Korean Peninsula with North Korea in 1991.[101] Departing from his predecessor's rigid position, Kim Dae Jung did not adhere to the principle of linkages, which tied improvement in U.S.–North Korean relations to that of inter-Korean relations. He urged the United States and Japan to lift economic sanctions against North Korea and to normalize diplomatic relations with Pyongyang. Hence a participant in the first summit meeting between Presidents Clinton and Kim Dae Jung on June 9, 1998 in the White House noticed that the Four-Party Talks were not even a major subject for their discussions.[102]

The U.S. government recognized the conceptual and practical compatibility between Kim's sunshine policy and Clinton's engagement policy toward North Korea and expected to enjoy a high degree of mutual support between the two allies. In fact, Clinton called Kim brave and visionary; compared him to Nelson Mandela in South Africa, Lech Walesa in Poland, and Vaclav Havel in Czechoslovakia; and praised him as "a human rights pioneer, a courageous survivor, and America's partner in building a better future for the world."[103] Clinton knew that the United States was instrumental in saving Kim's life twice—after his abduction by KCIA agents at Tokyo in 1973 and after he had received a death sentence in 1980. The two leaders promised to cooperate closely in a number of areas, including South Korea's financial recovery, North Korean nuclear disarmament, the LWR project at Kumho, and U.S.–South Korean security relations. In response to a question at their joint press conference, Kim said that the two Korean governments should take the lead in settling their own problems with support from the Four-Party Talks.[104]

At the third plenary session on October 21 through 24, 1998, the four parties had "useful and constructive discussions" in a "business-like manner" and agreed to set up two subcommittees to discuss, respectively, the establishment of a peace regime and tension reduction. They also adopted a "Memorandum on the Establishment and Operation of the Subcommittees."[105] Much procedural progress on the institutional framework was made, and the South Koreans believed that the Four-Party Talks would become a regular channel for discussing the goals of permanent peace and tension reduction on the Korean Peninsula.[106] Yet the North Koreans were still unhappy that the talks did not directly discuss the withdrawal of U.S. forces from South Korea and a peace agreement between the United States and North Korea.

The Chinese were generally sympathetic with the North Korean arguments but were not prepared to argue for the immediate termination of the U.S. military presence on South Korea and for U.S.–North Korean negotiations on a peace agreement without their participation. They stated that the talks would improve North

Korea's relations with South Korea and the United States and promised to play a constructive role in the talks. As South Korea expected, China attempted to bring about mutual concessions on procedural matters, to mediate the differences among the three delegations, and to iron out a consensus among them as much as possible. At the sixth plenary session on August 5 through 9, 1999, China presented a draft peace agreement on the Korean Peninsula.[107] It envisaged a legal termination of the Korea War, a commitment to nonaggression, a principle of noninterference in domestic affairs, military confidence-building measures, and arms reduction. In spite of Chinese enthusiasm, the diplomatic momentum for the Four-Party Talks dissipated by the end of 1999, in part because President Kim Dae Jung intended to take a central role in dealing with North Korea without depending on America's mediation, as had been the case in the Agreed Framework. The North Koreans, too, abandoned any remaining interest in the Four-Party Talks and wanted to have bilateral discussions with the United States and South Korea, respectively, for they were basically suspicious of the functional utility of multilateral meetings on Korea. Even though the Four-Party Talks failed to realize the goal of transforming the Korean Armistice Agreement into a new mechanism for peace, the four participating countries nonetheless had an important opportunity to articulate their respective views and proposals and to come to understand each other's policy preferences. The experience allowed each delegation to have a realistic perspective about the promises and limits of future multinational conferences on the Korean questions. And China's full participation in the talks demonstrated its willingness to play a positive and even-handed role in diplomatic activities relevant to the Korean Peninsula.

THE PERRY PROCESS

At times the Clinton administration found it more difficult to deal with the Republican critics of his Korea policy in Congress than with North Korean negotiators. A number of conservative Republican legislators continued to constrain Clinton's flexibility in managing the Agreed Framework and the KEDO operations. Most notably, they were successful in inserting a new provision in the "Omnibus Consolidated and Emergency Supplemental Act" (Public Law 105-277) in October 1998; it mandated that "not later than January 1, 1999, the President shall name a North Korea Policy Coordinator, who shall conduct a full and complete interagency review of United States policy toward North Korea, shall provide policy direction for negotiations with North Korea related to nuclear weapons, ballistic missiles, and other security related issues, and shall also provide leadership for United States participation in KEDO."[108] It made a fund of $35 million available for KEDO under several stringent conditions, including the requirement that the president certify that "the United States is fully engaged in efforts to impede North Korea's development and export of ballistic missiles." The issue of North Korean ballistic missiles had emerged as a vexing bone of contention in U.S.–North Korean relations, especially after North Korea launched a long-range missile (Taepodong I) over Japanese territory toward the end of August 1998.

Clinton appointed former Secretary of Defense William Perry as his North Korea policy coordinator in late 1998, and the new nominee immediately found himself caught between the wishes of the administration and the interests of his critics in the U.S. Congress. The outspoken views of the Republican Party were so sharply divergent from the Clinton administration's engagement policy that mutual consensus on a new policy was highly unlikely. Representative Gilman criticized the Agreed Framework as a "deeply flawed accord that has failed to change North Korea's behavior as it was predicted it would."[109] He believed that "North Korea has used the Agreed Framework as a cover for their real goal: the ability to deliver nuclear weapons against the United States by the end of the century." He also condemned the Four-Party Talks as "so ineffective and so meaningless to North Korea that there has been great difficulty in even arranging a date for the next meeting." Representative Dana Rohrabacher (R-CA) even went so far as to call the Clinton administration's policy of engagement with North Korea "the most nonsensical program [he had] ever heard of."[110] Going far beyond calls for containment and deterrence, he declared that "when it comes to [North] Korea, our goal should not be the status quo, it should not be stability; our goal should be the overthrow of that government and the replacement of that government with something that is more consistent with the democratic values our country is supposed to represent." The rising criticism of Clinton's North Korea policy was not, however, confined to the Republicans in the U.S. Congress. A group of influential policy analysts headed by Richard L. Armitage (former assistant secretary of defense for international security affairs) issued a report, "A Comprehensive Approach to North Korea," in March 1999, in which Clinton's "fragmented," "reactive," and "politically unsustainable" policy toward North Korea was scrutinized. It applauded Perry's appointment as an important step and advocated a more comprehensive and integrated approach tempered with an appropriate mixture of diplomacy and deterrence. If diplomacy failed, the report recommended, the United States should take a more ready and robust posture, including a willingness to interdict North Korean missile exports on the high seas, and the United states should also consider the option of preemption, based on "precise knowledge of [North Korean] facilities, assessment of probable success, and clear understanding with our allies of the risks."[111] It was indeed a tough and risky prescription for U.S. action.

Perry not only assumed the daunting task of maintaining close consultations with Clinton's persistent opponents in the U.S. Congress but also that of formulating a united front with South Korea and Japan. He correctly believed that no U.S. policy toward North Korea could be successful if it did not enjoy the support of U.S. allies in the region. Whereas the South Koreans took a relatively benign position toward North Korea's long-range missiles, which would not necessarily upset the military balance on the Korean Peninsula because North Korea already possessed enough short- and medium-range missiles (Nodong I and II) to cover all of the Korean Peninsula, Japan adopted a very rigid approach toward North Korea's ballistic missiles, since they could pose a direct threat to Japan's national security. The Japanese suggested that if North Korea launched another long-range missile, it would be difficult for them to finance the LWR construction in North Korea. The United States found itself caught in the middle between divergent positions held by its two East Asian allies.

Perry did not deny that there was a serious policy cleavage on North Korea's long-range missiles among the United States, South Korea, and Japan, but he explained that all three allies were able to reach a common strategy prior to his trip to Pyongyang on May 25 through 28, 1999.[112] On that trip he carried a letter from Clinton addressed to Kim Jong Il; the letter mentioned that Perry represented the president and that the United States wished to improve its relations with North Korea. In order to demonstrate the unity among the three allies, he also brought similar letters from South Korean President Kim Dae Jung and Japanese Prime Minister Obuchi Keizo.[113] On this visit he was accompanied by several members of the National Security Council and the Department of State, including a Korean-American official (Philip Yun).[114] Perry had "very intense, extremely substantive, and quite valuable" discussions with senior North Korean officials, including Kang Sok Ju. His hope to see Kim Jong Il, however, was not realized. In Pyongyang, Perry noticed that North Korean military leaders made "disparaging remarks" about members of the North Korean Ministry of Foreign Affairs. It was not clear, however, whether there existed a serious policy cleavage between civilian pragmatists and military hardliners or whether the remarks were a calculated negotiating tactic. In Perry's words, he took neither a "check book" nor a "package deal" to North Korea. Yet he understood that North Korea's interest in nuclear weapons and ballistic missiles was undertaken to defend itself against what it regarded as a threat from the United States, to enhance its international status, and to earn hard currencies. Meeting at the White House on July 2, 1999, Presidents Clinton and Kim Dae Jung fully endorsed Perry's important efforts.[115] Moreover, Secretary of State Madeleine Albright joined South Korean Foreign Minister Hong Soon Young and Japanese Foreign Minister Koumura

Masahiko in calling on North Korea to seize the opportunity presented by Perry, to build a new and positive relationship with its neighbors and potential partners, and to accept the comprehensive and integrated approach, which would build on the engagement policy.[116]

In early September 1999 Perry submitted his confidential report to President Clinton and the U.S. Congress; he also testified before the relevant committees of both houses.[117] The Perry Report was based on a "two-path" strategy. If North Korea accepted the path of cooperation by providing "complete and verifiable assurances" that it did not have a nuclear weapons program; by ceasing to test, produce, and deploy missiles exceeding the parameters prescribed by the Missile Technology Control Regime (MTCR); and by terminating the export of such missiles, the report recommended that the United States should normalize relations with North Korea, relax economic sanctions, and take other "positive steps." If, however, North Korea chose the alternate path, the path of collision, by rejecting the strategy for cooperation and normalization, the report recommended that the United States should take measures to contain the North Korean threat. The unclassified version of the Perry Report did not reveal those measures in order not to upset North Korea. The report was not particularly favorable to Kim Jong Il's rule because it characterized North Korea as isolated, reprehensible, enigmatic, suspicious, and vulnerable and referred to its longstanding record of blackmail, threats, and provocations.

One of Perry's major accomplishments was to foster and institutionalize close policy coordination with South Korea and Japan; the Trilateral Coordination and Oversight Group (TCOG) was set up for this purpose. His gentle manner, superb diplomatic skills, and military and technical expertise were well suited for the Asian cultural milieu. A senior U.S. official acknowledged that Perry undertook his operations in such close cooperation with his South Korean and Japanese counterparts that "they consider the Perry Report as much theirs as ours."[118] In fact, a high-ranking South Korean official claimed that his government had prepared an outline of the Perry Report and had proposed his visit to Pyongyang.[119] The report hoped that a senior North Korean official would visit Washington in the fall of 1999 to continue the Perry process.

Even though the Perry Report originated in a congressional mandate and incorporated the views articulated by both the Clinton administration and the Republican Party, it failed to mollify the deeply entrenched critics of Clinton's North Korea policy. A few weeks after the release of the Perry Report, the nine-member North Korea Advisory Group in the House of Representatives chaired by Benjamin Gilman (R-NY) submitted a lengthy report to Speaker J. Dennis Hastert (R-IL).[120] The Gilman Report sharply contrasted with the Perry Report in several important areas.

The Gilman Report concluded that the comprehensive threat posed by North Korea to U.S. national security interests had in fact increased since the Agreed Framework was signed and pointed out that Clinton's policy did not adequately address other North Korean issues—such as human rights, political and economic liberalization, international terrorism, narcotics trafficking, political prisoners, and counterfeiting. It claimed that U.S. economic assistance (totaling $645 million over the previous five years) had been delivered to help sustain a repressive and authoritarian regime in North Korea. Most importantly, in view of the dramatic improvement in its missile capabilities and its undeclared nuclear weapons program, the Gilman Report declared, "North Korea can now strike the United States with a missile that could deliver high explosive, chemical, biological, or possibly nuclear weapons." Since the Perry Report was limited to a narrow scope of nuclear weapons and ballistic missiles, the Gilman Report in effect suggested that the Perry Report was unsatisfactory in assessing other important problems with North Korea. Hence the Perry process was expected to encounter continuing obstacles in the U.S. Congress. In addition to the conservative Republican criticism of the Perry Report, Selig A. Harrison, a liberal journalist who was sympathetic to North Korea, questioned the underlying assumption of Perry's approach, that economic incentives and political recognition would be sufficient to bring about North Korean concessions on nuclear weapons and ballistic missiles.[121]

A MISSED OPPORTUNITY

While the Perry process was underway, the Clinton administration, in cooperation with South Korea and Japan, made concerted efforts in 1999 and 2000 to resolve all of North Korea's nuclear and missile issues and to normalize diplomatic and economic relations. No doubt Clinton hoped to reach a milestone in the search for lasting peace on the Korean Peninsula and in the Middle East, leaving a legacy of diplomatic triumph as his tenure drew to a close. Even though his Secretary of State Madeleine Albright had expressed her critical views on North Korea's lack of transparency and trust and had crafted the abortive economic sanctions resolution against North Korea at the United Nations in 1994, she continued trying to resolve the North Korean issue at Clinton's insistence. In return for lifting economic sanctions against North Korea, providing humanitarian assistance, and removing North Korea from the list of terrorist states, she wanted North Korea to commit to a far-reaching agreement on America's major concerns—its nuclear and missile issues.[122]

The United States continued to adhere to the Geneva Agreed Framework and the KEDO arrangements, but its annual delivery of heavy fuel oil to North Korea encountered restrictions and delays because the Republican majority in the U.S. Congress was increasingly skeptical of the wisdom of Clinton's engagement policy toward North Korea. This partisan rancor became particularly pronounced in regard to a new suspected nuclear site at Kumchangri because the Republicans capitalized on it as another indication of Clinton's policy failure. On March 16, 1999, the United States and North Korea released a joint statement in which North Korea agreed to "provide the United States satisfactory access to the site at Kumchangri by inviting a U.S. delegation for a initial visit in May 1999 and allowing additional visits to remove U.S. concerns about the site's future use." The United States responded with a promise to "take a step to improve political and economic relations between the two countries" and to give humanitarian assistance to North Korea. The team of fourteen American technical experts arrived in North Korea in May 1999 and found an "unfinished site, the underground portion of which was an extensive, empty tunnel complex." It concluded that the site did not violate the Geneva Agreed Framework.[123]

In order to reward North Korea for its cooperation over the Kumchangri site and its moratorium on long-range missile tests and to support the Perry process, the Clinton administration announced on September 17, 1999, its decision to relax the economic sanctions against North Korea administered under the Trading with the Enemy Act, the Defense Protection Act, and the Export Administration Regulations.[124] The decision was intended to allow a wide range of exports and imports of commercial and consumer goods, direct personal and commercial financial transactions, commercial flights between the United States and North Korea, and U.S. direct investments in North Korea. However, the easing of the sanctions did not change U.S. counterterrorism or nonproliferation controls on North Korea, which still prohibited exports of military and sensitive dual-use items and most types of U.S. government assistance and loans by international financial institutions to North Korea.

After the discussions held by Charles Kartman (special envoy for the North Korea Peace Talks) and Kim Gye Gwan (vice minister of Foreign Affairs) in Berlin in January 2000, North Korea accepted the U.S. invitation to send a high-level delegation to Washington to discuss the Perry Report. It was expected that this visit would take place in about two months. It took nine months before the visit was consummated, however, in part because both sides failed to settle several pending issues—especially, the questions of terrorism and economic sanctions. Meanwhile, the second U.S. visit to the Kumchangri site was satisfactorily completed in May 2000. For a while the North Koreans were probably preoccupied with the inter-Korean summit meeting.

For the purpose of realizing the summit meeting, President Kim made an extraordinarily concerted effort to apply his celebrated sunshine policy toward North Korea throughout 1999 and in the spring of 2000. In spite of rising domestic criticism about his "softness" on North Korea, Kim contained the political fallout of several bloody clashes between South Korean and North Korean naval vessels along the Northern Limit Line (a practical extension of the borderline) in the West Sea (Yellow Sea). He decided not to refer the incidents to the U.N. Security Council as his predecessor had done in 1996, nor did he hold Kim Jong Il directly responsible for them. He repeated his disavowal of any interest in absorbing North Korea; praised Kim Jong Il as a reasonable and competent political leader; expanded the delivery of food, chemical fertilizer, and other humanitarian aid (from $11 million in 1998 to $28 million in 1999 and $79 million in 2000) to North Korea; and promised to invest heavily in the improvement of North Korea's dilapidated economic infrastructure. He encouraged South Korean *chaebol* groups to invest in North Korea and subsidized the Hyundai Asan Corporation's tourism programs at the Kumgang (Diamond) Mountains. In a series of secret negotiations with North Korean officials in Shanghai, Beijing, and Singapore, Kim's trusted emissaries — Park Jie Won (minister of culture and tourism) and Lim Dong Won (director, National Intelligence Service) — and Chung Mong Hun (chairman, Hyundai Corporation) struck an illegal deal to provide a sizable amount of funds (at least $500 million) to North Korea prior to the summit meeting.[125]

On June 13, 2000, President Kim made a historic visit to Pyongyang and held meetings with Chairman Kim Jong Il. In their joint statement issued on June 15, the two leaders agreed that "the South and North, as masters of national unification, will join hands in efforts to resolve the issue of national unification independently" and that the two countries would "pursue a balanced development of their national economies and build mutual trust by accelerating exchange in the social, cultural, sports, health and environmental sectors"[126] (see table 4). They also agreed to seek a commonality between their respective proposals for unification and to arrange the reunion of dispersed family members and their relatives. This statement inherited the spirit of the inter-Korean joint communiqué (July 4, 1972), but largely ignored the contents of the Agreement on Reconciliation, Nonaggression, and Exchanges and Cooperation (December 13, 1991). The North Koreans believed that they had made too many concessions in the 1991 pact. On his return from Pyongyang, President Kim triumphantly declared that as a result of the summit meeting, the possibility of another Korean War had disappeared and that Kim Jong Il had agreed to the continuing presence of U.S. troops in Korea even after its unification. Evidently Kim Dae Jung had convinced his North Korean counterpart that U.S. military forces in Korea would counterbalance the temptations of its neighboring countries and that they could serve as a guarantor of peace and stability in a unified Korea. The euphoria for inter-Korean peace and cooperation that swept the country enabled a large number of South Koreans, especially the youth, to develop strong national-istic sentiments and a high level of self-confidence in dealing with North Korea. The more cooperative their relations with North Korea became, the less emphasis they placed on the importance of U.S.–South Korean relations and of the U.S. security commitment. At the same time there was an underlying possibility that North Korea would turn around and manipulate the promises of inter-Korean exchange in an at-tempt to carry out its united front strategy toward South Korea and to drive a wedge between the United States and South Korea.

Yet the South Korean government maintained close consultations with the United States both before and after the inter-Korean summit meeting. For example, Minister of Unification Park Jae Kyu frequently met U.S. Ambassador Thomas Hubbard to review the progress of inter-Korean contacts and negotiations.[127] After the summit, President Kim dispatched his senior secretary for foreign affairs and na-tional security, Hwang Won Tak, to brief President Clinton at the Waldorf Astoria Hotel in New York. Clinton listened intently to Hwang's generally uplifting report, but he appeared to be somewhat skeptical about the assertion that Kim Jong Il had agreed to welcome the U.S. military presence in Korea even after its unification.[128] The inter-Korean summit meeting had, however, justified and buttressed Clinton's own engagement policy toward North Korea. The United States, along with China, Japan, and Russia, enthusiastically endorsed the promising outcome of the summit meeting. Secretary Albright stated: "Today is a new day of hope for the future of the Korean Peninsula. The historic summit between the leaders of South and North Korea represents a bold step toward resolving a half-century of conflict there."[129] At this opportune moment the United States seized the momentum to accelerate its cooperative overtures toward North Korea. On June 19 it implemented the relax-ation of economic sanctions against North Korea (as announced in September 1999) by publishing the new regulations in the Federal Register. Clinton made it clear that this step was taken on Perry's recommendations and in close coordination with South Korea and Japan. The North Koreans welcomed this implementation but insisted that "the United States should give up a hostile policy against us and make a complete and realistic removal of all restrictions as soon as possible."[130]

About a month thereafter, Secretary Albright met with North Korean Foreign Minister Paek Nam Sun in Bangkok during their participation in the Seventh ASEAN Regional Forum (ARF). This was the first bilateral meeting at the ministe-rial level ever held between the two countries. They hit it off well: when Paek said that Albright looked younger this year than before, Albright called him "a very nice man."[131] They discussed a possible restraint on the North Korean missile program in exchange for commercial space technology and a visit by a high-ranking North

Korean official to Washington. After the meeting she said that it constituted "a substantively modest but symbolically historic step away from the sterility and hostility of the past and towards a more direct and promising approach to resolving differences and establishing common ground." She was "somewhat more hopeful" than before about the prospect for long-term stability in Korea. The North Koreans were equally satisfied with the meeting. They reported that the two leaders had had a "serious discussion" to normalize and expand bilateral relations.

The rapid pace of U.S.–North Korean reconciliation, coupled with the bandwagon for cooperation generated by the inter-Korean summit meeting, prompted the Republican Party to launch a sharp attack against what they called the Clinton-Gore administration's "appeasement policy" toward North Korea. This attack clearly had partisan overtones, coming in the context of the presidential contest between Gore and George W. Bush. Republican leaders in the U.S. Congress maneuvered to increase the restrictions on the U.S. delivery of heavy fuel oil to North Korea as well as on the U.S. transfer of nuclear facilities and materials necessary for the LWR project in North Korea. They also attempted to pass the "North Korea Nonproliferation Act of 2000" (H.R. 4860, July 19, 2000), which was intended to require a mandatory re-imposition of economic sanctions against North Korea if North Korea launched a long-range missile again or transferred missiles or missile technology to any country included in the U.S. list of state sponsors of terrorism. A report prepared by the 39-member House Policy Committee chaired by Christopher Cox (R-CA) defined the North Korean leadership as "a uniquely monstrous tyranny that has tormented the Korean people for half a century, creating the most completely totalitarian and militarized state in human history" and declared that "along with Clinton-Gore foreign aid, [North Korea's] long-range missile development continues to this day." This report castigated the Perry Report as an extension of an appeasement policy and criticized the Clinton-Gore administration's naiveté in using U.S. taxpayers' money to meet North Korea's "most brazenly extortionate demand."[132]

For their part, the North Koreans did not pay much attention to the legislative dynamics in the U.S. Congress, instead focusing their efforts on using a high-level North Korean delegate's visit to Washington as an opportunity to obtain U.S. concessions on the question of international terrorism. They insisted that the United States should agree to remove North Korea from the list of terrorist states because it was harming their national image and because it imposed a legal restriction on bilateral economic transactions. The United States replied by requesting that North Korea demonstrate its commitment against terrorism by ceasing to harbor such international terrorists as the members of the Japanese Red Army faction who had hijacked a JAL plane to North Korea in 1970. After a series of negotiations in October

2000, Michael Sheehan (the State Department's coordinator on counterterrorism) and Kim Gye Gwan were able to issue a joint statement on international terrorism.[133] The North Koreans promised to refrain from organizing, instigating, facilitating, financing, encouraging, or tolerating terrorist activities; to become a party to all twelve U.N. counterterrorism conventions; and to refrain from providing safe haven to terrorists and terrorist groups. If North Korea "satisfactorily addresses the requirements of U.S. law," the United States agreed to remove North Korea from the list of state sponsors of terrorism. This joint statement fell short of meeting the North Korean demand, but it paved the way for its possible resolution.

Once the last hurdle to the Perry process was at least partially out of the way, Vice Marshal Jo Myong Rok (first vice chairman, National Defense Commission; director, general political department, Korean People's Army) visited Washington from October 9 to 12, 2001, as Kim Jong Il's special envoy. He was the second most powerful leader in North Korea; he had played a prominent role during President Kim Dae Jung's visit to Pyongyang in June and had delivered a farewell speech during the summit meetings. Accompanied by Kang Sok Ju, Jo, dressed in a gold-braided military uniform with numerous medals, met Clinton at the White House with a leather-covered letter from Kim Jong Il. Upon reading it, Clinton said that it was a "good letter."[134] Jo had a lengthy talk with Albright. In welcoming Jo to the United States, Albright hoped that the two countries could "seize the opportunity to take the concrete steps required to open a new and more hopeful chapter in our relations."[135] In response, Jo asked for dramatic and positive changes in U.S.–North Korean relations and requested "strong and concrete security assurances" from the United States. He acknowledged Perry's "important contributions" and praised the recommendations made by the Perry Report. Yet Perry, who had welcomed Jo at Stanford University on his way to Washington, was uncomfortable because Jo visited the White House wearing his military uniform, which reinforced a negative stereotypical image of North Korea in the United States.

In a joint communiqué issued on October 12, 2000, the United States and North Korea agreed that they would disavow any "hostile intent" against each other, work to build mutual confidence, and uphold the principles of respect for each other's sovereignty and noninterference in internal affairs.[136] The North Koreans promised not to launch long-range missiles of any kind "while talks on the missile issue continue." It was also agreed that Albright would visit North Korea "to prepare for a possible visit by the President of the United States." Since the Korean-language text of the joint communiqué (which was displayed on the front page of the North Korean official paper *Rodong Sinmun* in bold type) mentioned a "visit" without being preceded by "possible," the North Koreans presumably assumed or expected that Clinton's visit to Pyongyang had been decided.[137] This demonstrated their eagerness for Clinton's visit, which would enhance Kim Jong Il's international status and complete the Perry process before the election of a new U.S. president.

The Albright visit from October 23 to 25 was promptly arranged because both sides knew that there was not much time left before the end of Clinton's tenure. Upon her arrival at Pyongyang in the early morning of October 23, Albright and her entourage paid their respects to the late president Kim Il Sung at the Kumsusan Memorial Palace.[138] She delivered a personal letter from Clinton to Kim Jong Il and had six hours of talks with him over two days. She was the highest-ranking American official ever to visit North Korea; Carter had gone there as a private citizen. Kim accompanied her to a mass gymnastic spectacle performed by over 100,000 participants, which had been organized for the fifty-fifth anniversary of the Korean Workers' Party.[139] Kim revealed his enthusiasm for American movies and added that the only American movie he could not see more than once was *Titanic* because he could not bear to watch its tragic ending again.[140] Albright gave him gifts (a basketball autographed by Michael Jordan and Nike shoes) and had separate meetings with Vice Marshall Jo Myong Rok, Kim Yong Nam (president of the Presidium of the Supreme People's Assembly), and Foreign Minister Paek Nam Sun, whom she had met earlier in Bangkok. She found Kim Jong Il intelligent, confident, knowledgeable, and "not uninformed," just as Kim Dae Jung had described him to her earlier.[141] He seemed to believe sincerely "in the blarney," but was not a desperate or even worried man. She also characterized him as "a good listener and a good interlocutor" and "very decisive and practical and serious." In order to show that Albright did not ignore the problems of human rights in North Korea, she was accompanied by Harold H. Koh, assistant secretary of state for democracy, human rights, and labor and a Korean-American legal scholar. He testified later that she raised a wide range of issues, including human rights, in her discussions with Kim.[142] The Albright mission by far overshadowed the visit of Qi Haotian (China's minister of national defense and a veteran of the Korean War), who was in North Korea at the same time.

Evidently Kim Jong Il put forward what Wendy Sherman (who had replaced Perry as North Korea policy coordinator in 2000) described as "landmark commitments" regarding North Korea's missile program:

- not to produce, test, or deploy missiles with a range of more than 300 miles;
- not to provide missiles, missile components, technology, and training to other countries; and
- not to ask for compensation in cash payments (estimated at $1 billion per year).[143]

In return, Kim apparently requested a significant package of economic assistance and a commercial satellite program for North Korea.

Albright described her talks with Kim Jong Il as "serious, constructive, and in-depth discussions of proposals and diplomatic relations, missile restraint, and security issues." In the end, she concluded, "We made important progress, but much work remains to be done." On her way back from Pyongyang, she visited Seoul and briefed President Kim Dae Jung, who had recently been awarded the Nobel Peace Prize. After profusely praising his vision and accomplishments, she told him: "I stood on the shoulders of a giant [Kim Dae Jung] in order to be able to have the discussion with Kim Jong Il." Gratified by her remarks, Kim once again expressed his hope that Clinton should visit North Korea.[144] Albright then held a trilateral meeting with South Korean and Japanese Foreign Ministers Lee Joung Binn and Kono Yohei to brief them on her Pyongyang visit and to coordinate their respective approaches toward North Korea.

In the immediate aftermath of the Albright mission, Robert J. Einhorn (assistant secretary of state for nonproliferation) held an expert-level talk with his North Korean counterparts in Kuala Lumpur. He presented a draft of an agreed framework on missile issues and a confidential letter outlining each side's obligations, as Gallucci had done in Geneva six years earlier. The United States proposed that North Korea agree not to test, manufacture, or export missiles exceeding the MTCR parameters (a range of more than 180 miles and a payload of more than 1,100 pounds); to provide information about the types and numbers of missiles in its arsenal; and to destroy its existing stocks of missiles beyond the MTCR limits.[145] The two sides probably discussed the procedures for on-site verification, the compensation package, and a commercial satellite program for North Korea. Even if the range of missiles were agreed upon, Einhorn recognized that there were no assurances about the capability and quality of North Korean missiles.[146] At this time North Korea sold missiles to Iran, Syria, and Libya, but there was no evidence of missile exports to Iraq. In spite of their strong desire to welcome Clinton to Pyongyang, the North Koreans remained noncommittal on the question of on-site verification and suggested that Clinton and Kim should resolve this thorny question at their summit meeting. They told Einhorn that Kim would make all important decisions and that Clinton would not be disappointed during his visit to Pyongyang. Kim Jong Il may have hoped that Clinton would visit Pyongyang just as Nixon had visited China eighteen years earlier, with a "white flag."

A number of Clinton's senior assistants, led by National Security Adviser Samuel Berger, felt that it was too risky for the president to travel all the way to Pyongyang without a firm and verifiable agreement on missile issues in advance.[147] In particular, Berger assumed that even if Clinton reached an agreement on ballistic missiles with Kim Jong Il, the incoming Bush administration might reject it. Clinton also considered a sensitive trip abroad unwise at that time because the prolonged electoral controversies in Florida over the U.S. presidential election could still have resulted in a constitutional crisis. A number of Republican legislators—such as Senators Jesse Helms (R-NC) and Trent Lott (R-MS)—urged Clinton to defer any further decision on North Korean missiles to the new administration. The mass media turned decisively against his possible trip to Pyongyang. An editorial in the liberal *New York Times*, for example, pointed out that "Clinton's visit would lend prestige to the North Korean leader, one of the world's last Stalinist dictators and a brazen violator of his people's human rights."[148] Most important, the Bush foreign policy team took the deliberate public posture of neither opposing nor endorsing Clinton's trip, but in effect it indicated its reservations about it.

As a last-ditch effort to salvage a U.S.–North Korean summit meeting, the Clinton administration invited Kim to come to Washington, but the North Koreans rejected this initiative.[149] On December 28, Clinton finally admitted that "there is not enough time while I am President to prepare the way for an agreement with North Korea that advances our national interest and provides the basis for a trip by me to Pyongyang."[150] In his memoir, Clinton recalled that Secretary of State Albright, after her visit to Pyongyang, was convinced that if he went to North Korea, he could have made the missile agreement, but he attributed his decision solely to his desire to visit the Middle East in the event of a major breakthrough in the negotiations between Israeli Prime Minister Ehud Barak and Yasir Arafat. He recalled: "Although I wanted to take the next step [toward North Korea], I simply couldn't risk being halfway around the world when we were so close to peace in the Middle East, especially after Arafat had assured me that he was eager for an agreement and had implored me not to go [to North Korea]."[151] Clinton instead urged the new Bush administration to continue his policy of engagement toward North Korea and to "build on the progress we have made." To his great chagrin, Clinton had been compelled to abort his coveted journey to North Korea and to miss a promising opportunity for solving North Korea's missile proliferation problems once and for all. Aside from his failure to resolve the Middle Eastern problems toward the end of his tenure, Clinton later told William Perry that it was his "biggest regret" that he did not visit North Korea.[152] Albright also recalled that there had been a chance to change the dynamics in Korea, saying, "Do I regret that we did not go forward? I personally do. I wish we could have."[153]

In retrospect, it was remarkable that, as a candidate who had once criticized President George Bush for coddling dictators, Clinton had effectively transformed U.S.

policy toward North Korean dictators—both Kim Il Sung and Kim Jong Il—moving away from the constraints of containment toward a policy with promises of engagement. As a result of constructive negotiations with them, he was able to freeze the North Korean nuclear programs at Yongbyon and to sustain bilateral and multilateral diplomatic dialogues with Pyongyang. In return, he provided negative security assurances, humanitarian assistance, and heavy fuel oil to North Korea. He had welcomed the North Korean vice marshal to the White House and had sent his secretary of state to North Korea.

The North Koreans, recognizing the growing influence of the United States as the only remaining strategic superpower in the post–cold war era, softened their longstanding hostility toward Washington and sought a pragmatic adaptation to the changing international context. In addition to their dismay at the demise of the Soviet Union, they were disillusioned with receiving less than full help from China. Toward the end of his eight-year presidency, Clinton eagerly planned to hold a summit meeting with Kim Jong Il in Pyongyang, but he just narrowly missed that opportunity due to a combination of unforeseen circumstances. Yet the controversies over North Korean ballistic missiles remained unsolved, liaison offices were not exchanged between Washington and Pyongyang, and the LWR project at Kumho was delayed considerably in part because of disputes over the wages for North Korean workers.[154]

On the other hand, Clinton was able to overcome initial difficulties with the self-confident and independent-minded President Kim Young Sam and went on to develop an excellent rapport with the liberal and populist President Kim Dae Jung, both in personal contacts and in policy coordination. Clinton and Kim Dae Jung admired each other enormously and nurtured a mature, positive, and interdependent relationship between the two countries. The mutually reinforcing elements of Clinton's engagement policy and Kim's sunshine policy toward North Korea went a long way in the direction of reducing the earlier misperceptions and paranoia between Washington and Seoul and also limited North Korea's efforts to drive a wedge between the United States and South Korea. The U.S.–South Korean military alliance was on a solid footing, but there also emerged strong nationalistic sentiments in South Korea that held that the imperative of inter-Korean cooperation was more important than the preservation of alliance cohesion. Prospects for inter-Korean reconciliation and exchange were guardedly optimistic. Restored to a prosperous economic status again under Clinton's effective tutelage (in sharp contrast to Japan and the European Union), the United States had less friction with South Korea over such economic issues as fair trade, market liberalization, intellectual property, and technology transfer. Kim himself presided over South Korea's successful financial recovery, thanks in part to support from the IMF and the United States. Gone were the days when the United States and South Korea were locked in serious disagreements over a number of sensitive issues, including troop withdrawal, human rights, political democracy, and lobbying activities. The two allies cooperated well in global and regional institutions—such as the APEC, the WTO, the United Nations, the ARF, and KEDO. The overall state of affairs between the United States and the Korean Peninsula toward the end of 2000 never looked better, but it was perhaps too good to last. Confident that Vice President Albert Gore would win the presidential election, the Kim administration did not heed the explicit recommendation, made as early as September 1999, that it should choose a prominent and sophisticated nongovernmental emissary to establish a policy liaison with the foreign policy advisers working for Texas Governor George W. Bush.[155] Just how much the new Bush administration would change its trilateral relations with South Korea and North Korea—that question still loomed on the horizon.

CHAPTER SIX

In Search of
Hegemonic Diplomacy
Bush's Policy

Dashing President Clinton's hopes that his Republican successor, George W. Bush, would continue his carefully crafted policies of constructive engagement with North Korea and close cooperation with South Korea, the incoming Bush administration was inclined to change both the philosophical foundations and the substantive direction of the U.S. approach toward the Korean Peninsula. In terms of foreign policy priorities and specific methods for their implementation, the transition from Clinton to Bush was as pronounced as that from Carter to Reagan. Initially driven by a realist paradigm and coercive posture, the Bush administration deliberately sought to distance itself from President Clinton's liberal tendencies in foreign affairs— his emphasis on the primacy of democratic peace, human rights, and diplomatic accommodation—and instead articulated a new set of strategic concepts and doctrines that directly confronted the aggressive and irresponsible behavior of "rogue states." The United States now sought an assertive position of hegemonic global leadership rather than offering concessions and compromises to such countries. President George W. Bush and his lieutenants criticized the basic assumptions and actual record of Clinton's engagement policy toward North Korea and believed that, with respect to North Korea's tactics of blackmail and brinkmanship, the Clinton administration had used tactics of "appeasement" and succumbed to "extortion."[1]

In the process of shifting his foreign policy priorities, President Bush met with cognitive dissonance and policy cleavages in his dealings with Presidents Kim Dae Jung and Roh Moo Hyun, both of whom pursued a liberal "sunshine policy" seeking a period of peaceful coexistence, mutual reconciliation, and economic cooperation with North Korea. In spite of frequent exchanges and consultations with his South Korean and Japanese counterparts, Bush was less than successful in developing a genuine sense of trilateral cooperation. This was particularly apparent when it came to managing a host of new troublesome developments, such as the trauma of September 11, 2001, the threat of international terrorism, the proliferation of weapons of mass destruction (WMDs), the war in Iraq, North Korean nuclear programs, and the status of U.S. troops stationed in South Korea and Japan. While the United States pursued a multilateral approach toward North Korean nuclear issues and promoted the Three-Party Talks (the United States, North Korea, and China) and the Six-Party Talks (the United States, North Korea, South Korea, China, Japan, and Russia) in 2003 and 2005, the growing wave of anti-American sentiment in South Korea, together with the expansion of South Korea's economic and diplomatic capabilities, the unfolding of inter-Korean rapprochement, and the ascendancy of Chinese power and influence—all of this in fact undermined the traditional framework of alliance cohesion and diplomatic coalition between Washington and Seoul and prompted a fundamental restructuring of the U.S. military presence in Korea. This profound military transformation was based less on the concepts of containment, deterrence, and isolation than on the Rumsfeld Doctrine, which stressed the advantages of advanced technology, rapid mobility, and strategic flexibility. Hence agonizing reassessment and an uncertain trajectory came to characterize the outline of U.S. policy toward the Korean Peninsula under President Bush.

BUSH'S NEW DOCTRINES

Since President Bush, unlike his two predecessors George H. W. Bush and Bill Clinton, had little interest or experience in foreign affairs prior to his inauguration, he tended to rely heavily on his aides, such as Condoleezza Rice, a specialist in Russia, in articulating and implementing his diplomatic and military policies. Almost a year before Bush's election, Rice had openly criticized the "Wilsonian thought" and "multilateral solutions" in Clinton's foreign policy and unabashedly advanced political realism as the foundation of Bush's international outlook. She identified Bush's key priorities: "to ensure that America's military can deter war, project power, and fight in defense of its interests if deterrence fails" and "to deal decisively with the threat of rogue regimes and hostile powers, which is increasingly taking the forms of the potential for terrorism and the development of weapons of mass destruction." And she lambasted North Korea: "The regime of Kim Jong Il is so opaque that it is difficult to know its motivations, other than that they are malign. But North Korea also lives outside of the international system. Like East Germany, North Korea is the evil twin of a successful regime just across its border. It must fear its eventual demise from the sheer power and pull of South Korea. Pyongyang, too, has little to gain and everything to lose from engagement in the international economy. The development of WMD thus provides the destructive way out for Kim Jong Il." Even though North Korea and Iraq were "living on borrowed time," she said, "if they do acquire WMD, their weapons will be unusable because any attempt to use them will bring national obliteration."[2]

This new hardline approach suggested that the incoming Bush administration would reverse Clinton's policy of constructive engagement toward North Korea. After the election, Rice, now assistant to the president for national security affairs, joined Vice President Dick Cheney and Secretary of Defense Donald Rumsfeld in advocating the missile defense system against rogue regimes, including North Korea. Even the relatively moderate secretary of state, Colin Powell, did not hesitate to label Kim Jong Il a "dictator" whose regime was unable to feed its own people or to denounce North Korea as a repressive, anachronistic, and unreliable "failed state." He stated in his confirmation hearings at the Senate that he was not afraid to engage North Korea and that he would not seek normalization of bilateral relations with "any sense of haste."[3]

In an immediate reaction to Powell's denunciation, a spokesman for the North Korean Ministry of Foreign Affairs countered in early 2001: "He dared make such reckless remarks going against the elementary common sense as slandering our supreme leadership as dictator."[4] He threatened that North Korea "will not remain a passive onlooker to the U.S. hatching up a plot to stifle the DPRK, its dialogue partner, by force of arms." The North Koreans even went so far as to hint that if the Bush administration continued its position of hostility and confrontation, they might reconsider their nuclear freeze and missile test moratorium.

In an effort to avert further deterioration of U.S.–North Korean relations and to sustain momentum for his sunshine policy toward North Korea, President Kim Dae Jung sought an early summit meeting with President Bush and ignored the U.S. advice that he should not come to Washington until the new Bush administration had a few top foreign policy personnel in place and had an opportunity to formulate its approach toward North Korea.[5] He became the first Asian leader to meet the new U.S. president in March 2001. Kim was probably poorly advised by his foreign policy aides, who had insisted that the Bush administration would have no other alternative but to support Seoul's sunshine policy and to continue Clinton's policy of engagement toward North Korea. After his first meeting with Secretary of State Powell in February 2001, South Korean Foreign Minister Lee Joung Binn had indicated that the United States and South Korea had "no differences" in regard to North

Korean issues and that both sides would be able to fine-tune their positions on North Korea's missile threat.[6] It is also likely that President Kim, in view of his elevated international status as a recipient of the Nobel Peace Prize and his seasoned political leadership, was confident that he could persuade the young and inexperienced Bush to accept his positive views of Kim Jong Il and North Korea.

After their summit meeting at the White House on March 7, 2001, Presidents Bush and Kim declared that reconciliation and cooperation between South and North Korea would contribute to peace on the Korean Peninsula and lasting stability in Northeast Asia.[7] Bush expressed support for South Korea's engagement with North Korea and President Kim's leading role in resolving inter-Korean issues. Notwithstanding this diplomatically correct language, Bush apparently refused to accept President Kim's arguments that change for reform in North Korea was not a matter of choice but of survival, that Kim Jong Il's "new thinking" and his recent visit to Shanghai indicated his willingness to emulate the Chinese model for modernization, and that Kim Jong Il recognized the utility of a continuing U.S. military presence in Korea even after unification. Bush was also reluctant to accommodate President Kim's suggestions that the United States resume high-level dialogue with North Korea as soon as possible, seize the opportunity to assist North Korea change, further relax economic sanctions against North Korea, remove North Korea from its list of terrorist states, and permit North Korea's entry into the Asian Development Bank and other international financial institutions.

After characterizing Kim Jong Il as an intelligent and reasonable person with whom the United States could do business, Kim Dae Jung was taken aback by the severity with which the U.S. president criticized the North Korean leader.[8] The South Korean president was unprepared for Bush's deep-seated animosity and mistrust of Kim Jong Il. At their joint press conference, Bush bluntly stated that he was skeptical about the North Korean leader and his commitment to the current and future arms deals and that any negotiation with North Korea would require "complete verification" of a potential agreement.[9] Seeing the wisdom in "trust but verify," Reagan's celebrated dictum about the Soviets, Bush felt that any arms control and disarmament agreement with North Korea would be pointless without a strict system of verification. Bush pointed out the problems of transparency and verification in a country that did not enjoy freedom, especially a free press. "When you make an agreement with a country that is secretive," he asked, "how are you aware as to whether or not they are keeping the terms of the agreement?" Yet he also characterized President Kim Dae Jung as a "realist" who was "under no illusions" about North Korea.

Confronted with Bush's tough stand, Kim was unable to play a role of mediation between the United States and North Korea and instead promised to "consult with the United States every step of the way" in dealing with North Korea. He also acknowledged that "without progress between the United States and North Korea, advances in South-North Korean relations will be difficult to achieve." Thus the notion of linkage between the two issues was reconfirmed. The South Korean president also abandoned his earlier plan to sign a peace treaty or at least a peace declaration with North Korea at the time of Kim Jong Il's future visit to Seoul. President Kim shared Bush's view that countering the new types of threats posed by weapons of mass destruction and missiles required "a broad strategy involving a variety of measures, including active nonproliferation diplomacy, defense systems, and other pertinent measures." Even though Kim was asked to express his public support for Bush's national missile defense policy, the South Korean president did not explicitly endorse Bush's policy but rather agreed to consult with the United States in regard to the latter's missile defense system. He was not bitter about Bush but was profoundly disappointed with the failure of their summit meeting.[10]

In fact, the Bush administration had seized on the summit meeting as an opportunity to suggest that Kim's peace initiatives had moved too fast and to stress that the United States would play a vital role in influencing not only the problems of war and peace on the Korean Peninsula, but also the scope and speed of inter-Korean relations.[11] On the heels of the summit meeting, Powell quickly retreated from his earlier promise to resume a dialogue with North Korea by picking up where the Clinton administration had left off, and he assumed a more rigid posture toward North Korea. He now declared that "in due course, at a time and at a place of our choosing, we will decide and determine how best to engage with the North Korean regime."[12] He added that "there is a huge [North Korean] army poised on the demilitarized zone that is probably as great a threat to South Korea and Seoul and regional stability as are weapons of mass destruction." This new emphasis on North Korea's conventional forces was to complicate the Bush administration's approach toward North Korea.

Key Republicans, including Senator Jesse Helms (chairman, Senate Committee on Foreign Relations), Representative Henry Hyde (chairman, House Committee on International Relations), Representative Christopher Cox (chairman, Republican Policy Committee), and other participants in the Gilman Report exerted a continuing influence on the president: their support was indispensable to Bush's ambitious legislative agenda in light of the Republican Party's slim majority in the U.S. Congress. On the eve of the Bush-Kim summit meeting, Representatives Hyde, Cox, and Edward J. Markey (D-MA) had even signed a joint letter to the president in which they pointed out the deficiencies of the Geneva Agreed Framework. They urged him "to avoid making any commitments to foreign governments that would prejudice your ability to refine U.S. policy toward North Korea."[13] The Bush administration remained sensitive to the strong anti–North Korean sentiments in the U.S. Congress.

The dynamic shift of interbureaucratic politics in favor of neoconservatives and hardliners, including Vice President Cheney, Secretary of Defense Rumsfeld, and Deputy Secretary of Defense Paul Wolfowitz, left Secretary Powell and other pragmatists and moderates far behind. And functional specialists led by the archconservative John Bolton (undersecretary of state for arms control and international security) at times became more influential than regional veterans in the Department of State. Likewise, the military establishment assumed a more assertive role in influencing U.S. policy toward North Korea than during the Clinton administration. In his testimony before the Senate Committee on Armed Services in March 2001, General Thomas A. Schwartz (CINCUNC, commander of USFK) warned that despite a "wave of reconciliation" generated by the inter-Korean summit meeting, "North Korea still poses a major threat to stability and security in the region" and that Kim Jong Il's "military forces are bigger, better, closer, and deadlier" than ever before. He insisted that North Korea continued to enhance its Scuds so as to threaten the entire peninsula, to produce and deploy medium-range Nodong missiles capable of striking Japan and U.S. bases there, and to develop a multistage missile that could even strike the continental United States. He asserted that North Korea continued to proliferate missiles, technology, technicians, transporter-erector-launchers, and underground facility expertise and had reportedly sold at least 450 missiles to Iran, Iraq, Syria, and Pakistan, among other states. In view of what he characterized as a tense, unpredictable, and serious security situation in Korea, he advocated "tangible military confidence-building measures that are verifiable and reciprocal."[14] This alarmist report undermined President Kim Dae Jung's assurances that, as a result of the inter-Korean summit meeting, there would be no more danger of war in Korea and supported the Bush administration's plan for missile defenses.

On May 1, 2001, President Bush argued that the old concept of deterrence based on the nuclear balance of terror during the cold war was no longer applicable and that a new concept of deterrence was required to build missile defenses against a small number of missiles in the hands of the world's least responsible states for whom "terror and blackmail are a way of life." He said: "Like Saddam Hussein, some of today's tyrants are gripped by an implacable hatred of the United States of America. They hate our friends. They hate our values. They hate democracy and freedom and individual liberty. Many care little for the lives of their own people. In such a world, Cold War deterrence is no longer enough. . . . We need new concepts of deterrence that rely on both offensive and defensive forces. Deterrence can no longer be based solely on the threat of nuclear retaliation. Defenses can strengthen deterrence by reducing the incentive for proliferation."[15] Bush did not name Kim Jong Il in his speech, but there could be no doubt that Kim was included in the list of "today's tyrants." The new deterrence policy, predicated on the threats posed by tyrants, however, would be difficult to justify if Kim Jong Il, Saddam Hussein, and other "tyrants" happened to disappear or suddenly become peaceful and reasonable.

Exactly three months after his unsatisfactory and unproductive meeting with President Kim Dae Jung, Bush completed a long-awaited review of U.S. policy toward North Korea. On June 6, 2001, he announced: "I have directed my national security team to undertake serious discussions with North Korea on a broad agenda to include: improved implementation of the Agreed Framework relating to North Korea's nuclear activities; verifiable constraints on North Korea's missile programs and a ban on its missile exports; and a less threatening conventional military posture." He called for a "comprehensive approach" toward a "constructive relationship" between the United States and North Korea. For all practical purposes, the formula of "a thorough, broad approach" that Presidents Clinton and Kim Young Sam had adopted in November 1993 was abandoned. "If North Korea responds affirmatively and takes appropriate action," he promised, "we will expand our efforts to help the North Korean people, ease sanctions, and take other political steps." He did not specify what the United States might do in the event that North Korea refused to take "appropriate action."[16] He emphasized the importance of close policy cooperation with South Korea and Japan but made no reference to the Perry Report or the U.S.–North Korea joint communiqué issued in October 2000, which had been adopted under Clinton's engagement policy.

However, Bush introduced new, sensitive issues to his agenda for a comprehensive approach—namely, conventional military forces and "improved implementation" of the Geneva Agreed Framework. In this way he actually raised the bar for mutual accommodation much higher than ever before and showed his doubt about President Kim's ability to deal with North Korea's conventional military issues. In contrast with the Republican hardliners in the U.S. Congress, Bush did not repudiate the Geneva Agreed Framework altogether, but he did make it clear that, unlike Clinton's use of conciliatory "carrots," he would not offer material incentives to North Korea prior to seeing tangible evidence of its affirmative response and appropriate action.

It was widely assumed that Powell, who was pragmatic and politically astute, was able in the interagency review process to overcome the powerful conservative coalition of Cheney, Rumsfeld, and CIA Director George Tenet and to redirect Bush's initial hardline stance a little toward the moderate position.[17] For all practical purposes, however, the Bush administration had no other viable option but to propose the resumption of a dialogue with North Korea. Otherwise it would have come under criticism for practicing an inept foreign and security policy, undermining President Kim's sunshine policy, and alienating the European Union, which advocated a constructive engagement policy toward North Korea.[18] At this time Bush was still amenable to the concept of multilateral diplomacy with emphasis on close cooperation with European countries. Just as had been the case with Clinton, Bush could not afford to ignore the opposition party's criticism of his Korea policy, especially after the Democratic Party had captured a narrow majority of seats in the Senate following the defection of Senator James Jeffords (Vermont) from the Republican Party. Indeed, in welcoming Bush's announcement, Senator Joseph R. Biden Jr. (D-DE), who had replaced Jesse Helms as chairman of the Senate Committee on Foreign Relations, commented that "I am pleased that the administration has concluded that the best way to promote peace and reconciliation on the Korean Peninsula is through a comprehensive engagement strategy, one that enjoys the strong support of our South Korean and Japanese allies."[19] The Bush administration appointed Charles "Jack" Pritchard, who had accompanied Albright to Pyongyang as director for Asian affairs at the National Security Council, as the special envoy for the North Korea peace talks. On June 13 Pritchard met Ri Hyong Chol (North Korean permanent representative to the United Nations) in New York. This was the first high-level talk between the two countries after the inauguration of President Bush. A State Department official described the meeting as "useful" and "businesslike," but no agreement was reached on the agenda or the venue for U.S.–North Korean negotiations.[20]

Soon thereafter, the North Koreans escalated their verbal attacks against the Bush administration's "hostility," beclouding the prospects for high-level dialogue with the United States. Contrary to President Kim's assurances to Bush in March 2001, North Korea demanded the withdrawal of U.S. forces from South Korea and accused the United States of including the question of conventional forces in the agenda unilaterally. They charged that this inclusion was an attempt to disarm North Korea through negotiation. They also demanded compensation for their loss of electricity — 2,000 MW(e) — from the year 2003 because the light-water reactor (LWR) construction had been delayed. A North Korean commentator declared that if the United States decided against compensation, it would possibly create a situation where North Korea would have to reoperate the graphite-moderated reactors.[21] When a spokesman for the North Korean Foreign Ministry insisted that this issue of compensation should be a top priority in U.S.–North Korean negotiations, the Department of State flatly rejected the idea altogether.

When Secretary of Defense Rumsfeld met with South Korean Defense Minister Kim Dong Shin in Washington on June 21, 2001, he grudgingly acquiesced in the understanding that South Korea should assume a leadership role in discussing the issues of conventional forces and confidence-building measures with North Korea.[22] Yet the United States continued to argue that conventional forces would ultimately be included in the agenda for U.S.–North Korean talks. As Powell explained earlier, the United States had a vital interest in the potential threat posed by North Korean conventional forces near the DMZ because the United States had 37,000 troops stationed in South Korea, exercised operational control over South Korean forces in time of war, and headed the United Nations Command and the Combined Forces Command. Unlike South Korea, the United States had accumulated both experience and expertise in negotiating and implementing the Treaty on Conventional Forces in Europe (CFE).

The North Koreans blamed the Bush administration not only for blowing a "cold wind of tension" on their bilateral relations but also for obstructing inter-Korean governmental contacts and exchanges. This charge was part of their time-honored strategy of driving a wedge between the United States and South Korea and mobilizing nationalistic sentiments and movements against U.S. "imperialism" and "interference" in South Korea. In this contentious climate it was a delicate task for President Kim to exercise a moderating influence over the United States and North Korea and to resuscitate the momentum for peaceful cooperation and functional integration between Seoul and Pyongyang. In his meeting with President Kim in Seoul on July 27, 2001, Secretary Powell made a conciliatory gesture when he supported South Korea's sunshine policy and called for a "comprehensive dialogue without preconditions" between the United States and North Korea.[23] Contrary to his earlier statements, he declared that "we can meet at a time and a place of North Korea's choice."

Meanwhile, North Korea remained unresponsive to Powell's overtures and decided not to send Foreign Minister Paek Nam Sun to the annual meeting of the ASEAN Regional Forum (ARF), where he and Powell could have met for the first time. In an apparent attempt to counterbalance U.S. influence over Korea, Kim Jong Il met with President Vladimir Putin in Moscow during his 24-day visit to Russia in August and with President Jiang Zemin at Pyongyang in September.[24] He obtained promises from Putin and Jiang for economic assistance and solidified a united front with them in opposing Bush's missile defense policy. He also agreed to resume the inter-Korean cabinet-level meeting in September in Seoul after a six-month hiatus. More important, after the terrorist attacks on the World Trade Center and the Pentagon on September 11, the North Koreans expressed sympathy, describ-

ing the attacks as a "shocking" and "regrettable" incident. Yet they severely criticized the U.S. military action in Afghanistan.[25]

THE "AXIS OF EVIL"

The unprecedented tragedy on September 11 reaffirmed Bush's firm stand
against terrorist groups and states and further bolstered his hardline approach toward
North Korea. As a result, tension and rhetoric between Washington and Pyongyang
inevitably escalated. In his State of the Union address on January 29, 2002, President
Bush characterized North Korea as "a regime arming with missiles and weapons of
mass destruction while starving its citizens" and denounced Iran and Iraq as supporters of international terrorism. He declared:

> States like these, and their terrorist allies, constitute an axis of evil, arming to threaten
> the peace of the world. By seeking weapons of mass destruction, these regimes pose a
> grave and growing danger. They could provide these arms to terrorists, giving them the
> means to match their hatred. They could attack our allies or attempt to blackmail the
> United States. In any of these cases, the price of indifference would be catastrophic. . . .
> We'll be deliberate, yet time is not on our side. I will not wait on events while dangers
> gather. I will not stand by as peril draws closer and closer. The United States of America
> will not permit the world's most dangerous regimes to threaten us with the world's most
> destructive weapons.[26]

The "axis of evil" reference conjured up popular memories of the aggressive Axis
Powers (Germany, Italy, and Japan) during World War II and Ronald Reagan's condemnation of the Soviet Union as the "Evil Empire." A majority of Americans were
presumably receptive to the demonization of Iraq, Iran, and North Korea as the
most dangerous terrorist states in the aftermath of the 9/11 trauma. A number of
Bush's domestic critics, however, asserted that it was wrong to equate the three states
and to suggest a linkage among them. Still others, including former secretary of state
Madeleine Albright, argued that the United States should deal with North Korea
independently of Iraq and Iran because the problems and challenges presented by
Pyongyang were unique.

Evidently, in Bush's eyes Kim Jong Il was even worse than Saddam Hussein because of the stark contrast between "opulence and poverty" in North Korea.[27] David
Frum, the presidential speechwriter who coined the term the "axis of evil," later
identified a "culture of modern Evangelicalism" and "upright and hygienic local
norms" as distinguishing features of the Bush White House.[28] Bush went so far as
to invoke the biblical concepts of "good and evil" in foreign affairs. His simplistic,

moralistic, and messianic outlook prevented him from taking a nuanced approach and led him to divide the world into "friends and enemies," "black and white," and "right and wrong." Viewed from his one-dimensional perspective, any compromise between good and evil was inconceivable and repugnant. The 9/11 national tragedy had further solidified his stubborn convictions. He declared later that "either you are with us, or you are with the terrorists." Like Reagan, Bush now espoused an element of Wilsonian idealism, notably the notion of American moral exceptionalism with a universal dimension. As far as the goals of U.S. foreign policy were concerned, he now transcended Rice's earlier criticism of Wilsonian ideals. Supremely confident of his moral clarity and flush with Evangelical zeal, he redefined America as the beacon of hope and freedom in the world and readily accepted the global mission of crusading against evildoers and spreading the gospel of democracy. To further his religiously inspired and self-righteous goal, he was prepared to use America's hegemonic power unilaterally, if necessary. In this regard, Bush distanced himself both from the amoral and expedient realist policies practiced by Nixon and Kissinger and from his father's moderate and nuanced pragmatism.

In his book *Bush at War*, Bob Woodward revealed that Bush became very emotional when he spoke about the North Korean leader. "I loathe Kim Jong Il," Bush shouted, waving his finger in the air. He added: "I've got a visceral reaction to this guy, because he is starving his people. And I have seen intelligence of these prison camps— they're huge—that he uses to break up families, and to torture people."[29] His religious beliefs were cited as a possible basis of these intense feelings. The president wondered how the civilized world could stand by and coddle Kim Jong Il. He disagreed with the argument that since the collapse of North Korea would cause great financial burden, the United States should be careful about removing him from power. On the contrary, Bush definitely wanted to help bring about the downfall of the "evil regime" in North Korea. His personal animosity toward Kim Jong Il was displayed on many occasions. For instance, at a private gathering of Republican senators in the Mansfield Room of the Capitol on May 23, 2002, the agitated president talked about Yasir Arafat and then abruptly began accusing Kim Jong Il of starving his own people and imprisoning intellectuals in "a gulag half the size of Austin," the capital of Texas. Referring contemptuously to Kim as a "pygmy," Bush compared him to "a spoiled child at a dinner table." Stunned by the president's impromptu diatribe, the senators remained silent.[30]

The North Korean reaction to Bush's "axis of evil" address was predictably swift and hostile. A spokesman for the Ministry of Foreign Affairs stated on January 31 that the Bush address was "little short of declaring a war" against North Korea.[31] He argued that the crisis faced by the United States was "entirely attributable to the unilateral and self-opinionated foreign policy, political immaturity and moral leprosy of the

Bush Administration" and that the heroic Korean People's Army and people would never tolerate the U.S. attempt to stifle the DPRK by force of arms.

The Bush speech met with a mixed response in South Korea. While conservative political leaders welcomed his assertion as correct and appropriate, other political leaders with liberal, progressive, or nationalistic orientations criticized his harsh rhetoric. In the National Assembly, a member of the governing Millennium Democratic Party (MDP), Song Sok Chan, even asserted that Bush himself was "evil incarnate," a statement representing the strong sentiments among some South Koreans that Bush's speech had denigrated all Koreans and could lead to increased tensions on the Korean Peninsula. After President Kim rebuked the MDP leadership over Song's statement, which had made it more difficult for the South Korean government to maintain cooperative relations with the Bush administration, Song was forced to apologize.[32] The escalation of accusations between Washington and Pyongyang had adverse effects on inter-Korean relations. And despite his desire to improve relations with North Korea and to avoid offending Kim Jong Il, President Kim Dae Jung was compelled to recognize the universal imperative of opposing weapons of mass destruction and the spread of international terrorism.

In a summit meeting in Seoul on February 20, 2002, Presidents Kim and Bush managed to patch up their differences over North Korea and to establish a modus operandi. Bush publicly endorsed Kim's sunshine policy toward North Korea and moderated his public utterances on the "axis of evil," and Kim supported Bush's campaign against terrorism and WMD. They agreed to seek a peaceful resolution of the WMD controversies and other related issues with North Korea.[33] Faced with about 4,000 student activists, union members, and demonstrators in Seoul shouting "No Bush! No War!" in unison, Bush appeared surprisingly tame and even mild-mannered.[34] A participant in the Kim-Bush meeting observed that President Bush gained a new appreciation of the Korean situation from his visit, becoming more sympathetic with President Kim's domestic and foreign policies.[35]

At a joint press conference with Kim, Bush reiterated that the United States had no intention of invading or attacking North Korea and that his goal was peace. Yet he made it clear that he was "troubled by a regime that tolerated starvation. . . . I am deeply concerned about the people in North Korea." He added: "I worry about a regime that is closed and not transparent." "I will not change my opinion on Kim Jong Il," he declared, "until he frees his people and accepts genuine proposals from countries like South Korea and the United States for dialogue." On his tour of the DMZ, he could not resist the temptation to use the word *evil* again. When he was informed that the axes used to kill two U.S. officers and wound nine U.S. and South Korean soldiers at the DMZ in August 1976 were prominently displayed in a North

Korean museum, Bush said, "No wonder I think they're evil."[36] This remark was not widely reported in South Korean media, however.

The North Koreans escalated their verbal abuse against the United States, countercharging that it was, in fact, the "evil empire" and comparing Bush to "a puppy knowing no fear of the tiger" and "a politically backward child."[37] The president's visit to South Korea, they argued, was "a war junket to finally examine the preparations for a war on the spot." The North Koreans were particularly incensed by the Bush administration's confidential contingency plan entitled the "Nuclear Posture Review," which envisaged a possible use of nuclear weapons against North Korea, because the report identified a North Korean attack on South Korea, along with an Iraqi attack on Israel or its neighbors and a military confrontation over the status of Taiwan, as cases of immediate contingency.[38] They warned that a nuclear war imposed by the United States would lead to its own ruin in nuclear disaster and threatened to reconsider all prior agreements (including the Geneva Agreed Framework) with the United States.[39] Yet despite these threats the North Koreans did not take steps to unfreeze their nuclear programs or to resume missile tests. Nor did they completely close the channels for low-level contacts with the United States.

Meanwhile, the Bush administration formulated and announced a new doctrine — that of preemptive attack against rogue states. In a speech at West Point in late May 2002, President Bush declared that "the war on terror will not be won on the defensive." He told the graduating class of cadets that "we must take the battle to the enemy, disrupt his plans and confront the worst threats before they emerge. In the world we have entered, the only path to safety is the path of action, And this nation will act." More specifically, in its National Security Strategy issued on September 17, 2002, the Bush administration made it clear that

> given the goals of rogue states and terrorists, the United States can no longer solely rely on a reactive posture as we have in the past. The inability to deter a potential attacker, the immediacy of today's threats, and the magnitude of potential harm that could be caused by our adversaries' choice of weapons, do not permit that option. We cannot let our enemies strike first. . . . The United States has long maintained the option of preemptive actions to counter a sufficient threat to our national security. The greater the threat, the greater is the risk of inaction and the more compelling the case for taking anticipatory action to defend ourselves, even if uncertainty remains as to the time and place of the enemy's attack. To forestall or prevent such hostile acts by our adversaries, the United States will, if necessary, act preemptively.[40]

This strategic assertion, in effect, nullified the negative security assurance that the United States had promised to North Korea in their joint statement (June 11, 1993), the Geneva Agreed Framework (October 21, 1994), and the U.S.–North Korea Joint Communiqué (October 12, 2000). Critics charged that the Bush Doctrine was unprecedented, dangerous, and illegal.

THE HEU PROGRAM

Equipped with this new doctrine of preemptive attack, James A. Kelly (assistant secretary of state for East Asian and Pacific affairs) led a high-level U.S. delegation to Pyongyang from October 3 to 5, 2002. It was the first such meeting in the twenty-one months since the start of the Bush administration. His earlier plan to visit North Korea in mid-July had been cancelled because of a clash between South Korean and North Korean naval vessels on the West (Yellow) Sea on June 29, 2002. Kelly had a series of meetings with Kim Yong Nam (president, Supreme People's Assembly), Kang Sok Ju (first vice minister of foreign affairs), and Kim Gye Gwan (vice minister of foreign affairs). It was revealed on October 16 that when Kelly had presented intelligence reports about North Korea's secret program to enrich uranium for nuclear weapons on October 3, Kim Gye Gwan had flatly denied the reports. On the following day, however, an agitated Kang Sok Ju had presumably admitted to Kelly that North Korea possessed not only the highly enriched uranium (HEU) program but also more powerful things as well, and he blamed the hostile U.S. policy for necessitating North Korea's self-defense measures. He added that the Geneva Agreed Framework had been "nullified."[41]

In response to Kang's admission, the Bush administration concluded that North Korea had blatantly violated the Geneva Agreed Framework, the Nuclear Nonproliferation Treaty (NPT), the safeguards agreement with the IAEA, and the North-South Joint Declaration on the Denuclearization of the Korean Peninsula; hence it publicly demanded that North Korea should immediately dismantle its HEU program in verifiable ways. When the South Korean Ministry of Foreign Affairs issued a statement on October 17 in which it obliquely referred to a "suspicion" about a North Korean nuclear program and asked North Korea to "continue" to comply with all the agreements, including the Inter-Korean Joint Declaration, the Bush administration expressed its displeasure with South Korea's tentative and hesitant response.[42] In this connection, it was reported that South Korean Minister of Unification Jeong Se Hyun suggested that Kelly had misunderstood Kang's remarks and that Kang had not actually admitted the existence of an HEU program in North Korea.[43] The United States flatly rebuffed North Korea's proposal for a bilateral nonaggression treaty and indicated that it would not resume any high-level dialogue with North Korea until the latter clearly and unconditionally accepted an unmistakable plan for nuclear nonproliferation to be verified by the IAEA or another reliable method.[44] And the United States decided to suspend delivery of heavy fuel oil to North Korea and intended to reassess a program for constructing two light-water nuclear reactors at Kumho.

Seen from the perspective of President Bush's neoconservative lieutenants, North Korea's new nuclear program proved how correct they had been in maintaining a profoundly skeptical view of Kim Jong Il and of the Geneva Agreed Framework and how wrong President Kim Dae Jung had been in regarding Kim Jong Il as a reasonable and reliable partner for peaceful cooperation. The relative moderates in the Bush administration were now compelled to support the hardline posture toward North Korea. In this context, Secretary Powell lamented that "no North Korean child can eat enriched uranium. . . . It is fool's gold for North Korea."[45] Once again James A. Baker III, secretary of state under former president George H. W. Bush, denounced the Clinton administration for its failures: pursuing "an abrupt policy flip-flop" and signing the Agreed Framework on the basis of "accommodation, compromise, and appeasement." He called upon the U.N. Security Council to impose political and economic sanctions on North Korea and proposed to "beef up our forces in South Korea to whatever extent necessary."[46] The Democratic Party's key foreign policy experts, including Madeleine Albright, Zbigniew Brzezinski, Anthony Lake, and Robert Gallucci, criticized North Korea's secret nuclear weapons program. While defending the Agreed Framework, recognizing the North Korean negotiating style as "clumsy brinkmanship," and advocating a combination of carrots and sticks, Anthony Lake and Robert Gallucci, who had spearheaded Clinton's engagement policy toward North Korea, now felt cheated by North Korea and recommended that the United States persuade its allies to suspend economic and political engagement with North Korea except for vital food aid, suspend its performance under the Agreed Framework, seek immediate initiation of full-scope inspections by the International Atomic Energy Agency, and reserve the possibility of a preemptive military strike against North Korea.[47] Moreover, Bush's unprecedented victories in the midterm congressional elections in November strengthened his domestic political position in dealing with all rogue states and in reducing the Democratic Party's opposition to his foreign policies in the U.S. Congress.

For his North Korea policy, Bush solicited Chinese President Jiang Zemin's assistance. In their friendly meeting in Crawford, Texas, on October 25, 2002, Bush and Jiang expressed a common concern about North Korea's program to enrich uranium and agreed to work toward a nuclear-free Korean Peninsula. It is conceivable that in return for Bush's commitment to uphold a one-China policy and to discourage the movement for Taiwan's independence, Jiang promised to help Bush with respect to the North Korean nuclear issue. Yet the Bush administration was not particularly pleased with President Kim Dae Jung's initial reluctance to link nuclear issues with inter-Korean economic cooperation and to abandon the Geneva Agreed Framework. It was also concerned with Japanese Prime Minister Koizumi Junichiro's efforts to normalize diplomatic and economic relations with North Korea. In an attempt to demonstrate a semblance of trilateral policy unity, President Bush held a meeting with President Kim and Prime Minister Koizumi on October 26, 2002, during the APEC summit in Los Cabos, Mexico. In a joint statement, they asked North Korea to dismantle its program to enrich uranium for nuclear weapons "in a prompt and verifiable manner" and to come into full compliance with all its international obligations. They also agreed to seek a peaceful resolution of the North Korean nuclear crisis "in close trilateral consultation and with other concerned nations around the globe."[48] In addition, Bush reiterated his commitment not to invade North Korea and suggested the possibility of pursuing a "bold approach" for transforming U.S. relations with North Korea.

The APEC summit meeting unanimously adopted a joint statement on October 27, which upheld the importance of a nuclear weapons-free Korean Peninsula and called upon North Korea to visibly honor its commitment to give up nuclear weapons programs. The United States was hard-pressed to overcome the temptation to resort to hegemonic and coercive diplomacy and to iron out its policy cleavages with South Korea and Japan. The disagreement between Washington and Seoul became particularly apparent when KEDO's operations were under consideration. The South Koreans preferred to continue the delivery of heavy fuel oil to North Korea for a while, but the United States insisted on immediately turning back an oil tanker with 42,500 tons of heavy fuel bound for North Korea, on the grounds that it was no longer justified because of North Korea's clear violation of the Agreed Framework. The Japanese proposed delivering the November portion of heavy fuel to North Korea and then reassessing the situation in December. The Republican-dominated Congress moved to cut the funding for the heavy oil supply. On November 14, KEDO's executive board, which had condemned North Korea's pursuit of a nuclear weapons program, decided to suspend the heavy fuel oil delivery beginning with the December shipment, but the LWR project was sustained. The KEDO stated: "Future shipments will depend on North Korea's concrete and credible actions to dismantle completely its highly-enriched uranium program." In response, the North Koreans ordered IAEA inspectors to leave Yongbyon by the end of December 2002 and announced their intention to resume nuclear programs.

The escalating confrontation between the United States and North Korea took place during a heated contest for the presidential election in South Korea. As a candidate of the governing Millennium Democratic Party, Roh Moo Hyun, a maverick labor lawyer and diplomatic novice, promised to carry on President Kim Dae Jung's sunshine policy and criticized the Bush administration's hardline stance toward North Korea. His main rival, Lee Hoe Chang, a candidate of the opposition Grand National Party, advocated a realist approach, seeking modification of the sunshine policy with emphasis on the principles of reciprocity and transparency, and he proposed that South Korea should halt economic assistance programs to North Korea until the nuclear issue was satisfactorily resolved. Compared with Lee's conservative positions, Roh's liberal, populist, and nationalistic orientation was less compatible with Bush's policy toward North Korea.

Moreover, Roh's campaign was significantly bolstered by a rapidly growing anti-American movement after a U.S. military jury acquitted two American soldiers charged with the accidental death of two South Korean schoolgirls by an armored vehicle. The soldiers hurriedly left South Korea a day after their acquittal, over the objections of the South Korean government, because they were afraid of harassment or assault by angry South Koreans.[49] Many South Koreans, especially young people, viewed this acquittal as yet another example of U.S. hubris and lack of accountability for offenses by the U.S. military against innocent civilians.

In retrospect, it seems clear that the United States failed to handle the matter in the most sensitive and effective way, leaving the impression that U.S. soldiers could injure South Koreans with impunity. On behalf of President Bush, U.S. Ambassador Thomas Hubbard read an apology for the accident and offered financial compensation to the families of the two dead girls. It might have been better if President Bush himself had apologized in a press conference (as President Clinton had done in connection with the rape of a Japanese girl by U.S. soldiers at Okinawa in 1995) or if he had dispatched a high-level emissary to Seoul for the same purpose. President Bush eventually called President Kim to express his apology, but by then it was too little, too late. A large number of South Koreans, for the most part led by college students, had already organized massive demonstrations in protest, held a candlelight vigil in Seoul every night throughout 2002, argued for a drastic revision of the Status of Forces Agreement (SOFA), and went so far as to demand the withdrawal of U.S. troops from South Korea. Many South Korean critics complained that the United States had not held anyone accountable for the death of the two schoolgirls. Asked about this complaint, Ambassador Hubbard responded that the senior officers of the unit to which the two acquitted U.S. soldiers belonged had in fact been reprimanded, but the decision had not been publicized because of the confidentiality of military personnel policy.[50] When the widespread misunderstanding in South Korea with respect to the actual circumstances of the accident and the American system of decision by jury was mentioned, he maintained that all of the information was available on the U.S. embassy website. The Bush administration was disappointed that President Kim, albeit a lame-duck leader, did not do more to discourage the anti-American movement. It is conceivable that Kim was reluctant to do anything significant to dampen the anti-American sentiment because this very sentiment was helpful to the candidate of his party. In a subtle but shrewd way, Roh Moo Hyun harnessed the high-pitched emotional fervor of the mass demonstrations, particularly among young voters, as part of an effective campaign strategy. Public display of his critical stance toward the United States turned out to be among his major assets.

As soon as Roh defeated Lee by a slim margin (48.9% vs. 46.7%) on December 19, 2002, the United States moved quickly to downplay the differences between President-elect Roh and the Bush administration. Ari Fleischer, the president's spokesman, stated: "The United States continues to have very strong and good relations with the people and the government of South Korea. . . . We are friends and we are allies. It is the role of America's great democracy to honor and respect the elections of every nation in the world and work with those leaders." Assistant Secretary of State Kelly viewed Roh's election "as an opportunity to work with him and his government to build an even stronger relationship between our two countries."[51] On December 20, President Bush called Roh to offer him warm congratulations and invited him to visit Washington at his convenience. They agreed to work closely together to promote peace on the Korean Peninsula and to strengthen the U.S.– South Korean military alliance.

No doubt the United States was quite uneasy about the possibility of strained relations with the new South Korean government under Roh. When Bush told reporters on February 7, 2003, that "all options are on the table" in regard to the North Korean nuclear issue—a clear reference to the possibility of military action—and Secretary Rumsfeld denounced North Korea as a "terrorist regime" and put twenty-four long-range bombers on alert in around the same time, President-elect Roh and the Millennium Democratic Party publicly rebuffed the Bush administration's bellicose stance.[52] Meanwhile, at a seminar in Washington, a senior foreign policy adviser to Roh candidly admitted that if it were forced to choose, the incoming South Korean government would prefer that North Korea had nuclear weapons to seeing the regime collapse.[53] To make matters worse, on January 10, 2003, North Korea announced its decision to withdraw from the NPT immediately and declared that its safeguards agreement with the IAEA was no longer in effect.

In his Inaugural Address on February 25, 2003, President Roh enunciated his policy for peace and prosperity on the Korean Peninsula. Setting forth the four principles of this policy, he promised (1) to resolve all pending issues through dialogue;

(2) to give priority to building mutual trust and upholding reciprocity; (3) to seek international cooperation on the premise that South and North Korea are the two main actors in inter-Korean relations; and (4) to enhance transparency, expand citizen participation, and secure bipartisan support. He emphasized that the North Korean nuclear issue should be resolved peacefully through dialogue. And he also stated: "This year marks the 50th anniversary of the Korea-U.S. Alliance. It has made a significant contribution in guaranteeing our security and economic development. The Korean people are deeply grateful for this. We will foster and develop this cherished alliance. We will see to it that the alliance matures into a more reciprocal and equitable relationship."[54] In the afternoon following his inauguration, Roh met with Secretary of State Powell. They agreed to pursue a multilateral approach on the North Korean nuclear issue. Powell dismissed the significance of North Korea's testing a short-range missile, which had landed in the East Sea (Sea of Japan) on the same day. Roh asked Japanese Prime Minister Koizumi Junichiro to normalize diplomatic relations with North Korea, and he told Chinese Vice Premier Qian Qichen that China should be more active in the U.N. Security Council in regard to the North Korean nuclear issue. This suggestion, in effect, reflected his hope that China would constrain the United States from introducing another sanctions resolution against North Korea at the world organization. Unlike his predecessor, who had accumulated a great deal of knowledge and experience in foreign affairs with emphasis on the United States and North Korea, Roh was a novice in these areas and tended to apply his own populist and nationalistic preconceptions to foreign relations and to rely upon a group of like-minded young liberal staff members of the greatly expanded National Security Council in the Blue House. He appointed Yoon Young Kwan, a liberal academic, as foreign minister; Ra Jong Il, former ambassador to Britain, as senior secretary for national security affairs; and Han Sung Joo, former foreign minister and a moderate conservative, as ambassador to the United States. As a clear sign that he would continue the sunshine policy toward North Korea that he had inherited from his predecessor, Roh reappointed Jeong Se Hyun as minister of unification. He was the only cabinet member of the previous administration retained by the new president. In addition to his long experience in negotiations with North Koreans, Jeong was known to be a tough-minded bureaucrat.

From the beginning Roh faced the dilemma, with all of the inherent tensions, of maintaining an alliance with the United States while at the same time promoting national reconciliation with North Korea. No less serious was the emerging conflict between the idealistic, liberal, and reform-minded young staff members in the Blue House and the pragmatic, experienced, and conservative bureaucrats in his government. As far as North Korea was concerned, Roh adopted a rather charitable and optimistic outlook. He argued: "If we give them [North Koreans] what they desperately want—regime security, normal treatment, and economic assistance, they will be willing to give up their nuclear ambitions. We should not, therefore, treat them as criminals but as partners in negotiations."[55] He tended to question the realists' contention that North Korea was determined to develop nuclear weapons and ballistic missiles at any cost, and he favored the liberal assumption that Kim Jong Il only intended to use nuclear and missile issues as a bargaining chip for obtaining concessions from the United States, South Korea, Japan, and other concerned countries.

MULTILATERAL DIPLOMACY

On February 12, 2003, a special session of the IAEA's 35-member board of governors adopted a resolution that expressed "deep concern" about North Korea's noncompliance with its safeguards agreement and referred the matter to the Security Council and the General Assembly of the United Nations. The IAEA pointed out that despite North Korea's withdrawal from the NPT, its safeguards agreement with the IAEA was still in effect. The IAEA resolution was adopted by a vote of 31 to 0 with 4 abstentions and absences: the United States and China voted for it, Russia and Cuba abstained, Panama was absent, and Sudan was not eligible to vote. South Korea was not a member of the board of governors. This resolution was reminiscent of the scenario enacted at the IAEA session nine years earlier (March 1994), in which China had abstained in voting for an almost identical resolution and Russia had voted for it. This reversal of China's and Russia's voting decisions from 1994 to 2003 suggested that China had become dissatisfied with North Korea's recalcitrance and that Russian President Putin now intended to woo North Korea. However, Chinese Ambassador Zhang Yan stated at the IAEA meeting that the involvement of the U.N. Security Council at this time might not necessarily contribute to the diplomatic settlement of the North Korean nuclear issue. In so doing, he was heeding North Korea's vehement opposition to any U.N. resolution against its interests. In this connection, President Roh shared his predecessor's view that the United Nations should refrain from taking any provocative action toward North Korea lest it exacerbate the situation.

On March 2, 2003, another potentially explosive incident between the United States and North Korea occurred when four North Korean fighter jets (two MiG-29s and two MiG-23s) closely shadowed an unarmed U.S. reconnaissance plane, an RC-135S "Cobra Ball," for twenty-two minutes in international airspace near Wonsan over the East Sea (Sea of Japan).[56] This was the most serious challenge from North Korea to the U.S. aerial reconnaissance programs since the destruction of the EC-121 in 1969. The incident was reminiscent of the Chinese action to force another U.S. spy plane (EP-3E) to make an emergency landing on Hainan Island on April 1, 2001. This time, however, the RC-135S returned safely to Kadena Air Base in Okinawa. The North Koreans complained that "the U.S. imperialist RC-135 strategic recon-naissance plane" was illegally intruding into their skies almost every day. The Bush administration lodged a formal protest with the North Korean government and de-cided to carry on the RC-135 missions escorted by U.S. fighter aircraft. On March 3 President Bush told reporters that he hoped to persuade China, Russia, South Korea, and Japan "to join us in convincing North Korea that it is not in their nation's in-terest to be threatening the United States, or anybody else for that matter, with a nu-clear weapon."[57] He said that all options for the United States were on the table, adding that the military option was his last choice.

As usual, every major turn of events on the Korean Peninsula generated acrimo-nious partisan confrontations in the U.S. Congress. In the spring of 2003 the Demo-crats pointed out the contradiction in Bush's policies toward Iraq and North Korea: Bush, obsessed with the removal of Saddam Hussein, even going so far as to advo-cate unilateral military action, paid far less attention to the North Korean nuclear crisis, which was being approached multilaterally. They warned that North Korea posed a more direct and imminent threat to the United States and its allies than Iraq did and that Bush should assume an active role in addressing this threat.[58] Senate Minority Leader Tom Daschle (D-SD) complained: "We have repeatedly urged the administration to get off the sidelines and face up to the developing crisis. The White House continues to sit back and watch, playing down the threat, and appar-ently playing for time. But time is not on our side." Senator Robert C. Byrd (D-WV) observed that North Korea "presents a far more imminent threat than Iraq to the security of the United States." And Senator Biden complained that Bush's policy to-ward North Korea was paralyzed by interbureaucratic infighting.[59] On the other hand, a number of Republican senators and representatives maneuvered to block U.S. assistance for the KEDO operations and LWR projects in Kumho, to condemn the violations of human rights in North Korea, to admit North Korean refugees to the United States, to seek the return of the *Pueblo*, and to increase Radio Free Asia's broadcasting with respect to North Korea to twenty-four hours a day. In particular, the North Korea Democracy Act of 2003 (S. 145) cosponsored by Republican sena-tors Jon Kyl (Arizona), John McCain (Arizona), Elizabeth H. Dole (North Carolina), and five other colleagues prescribed a wide range of restrictions and sanctions in U.S. relations with North Korea. It stipulated: "It is the sense of Congress that the United States, in conjunction with the Republic of Korea and other allies in the Pacific region, should take measures, including military reinforcements, enhanced defense exercises and other steps as appropriate, to ensure—(1) the highest possible level of deterrence against the multiple threats North Korea poses; and (2) the highest level of readiness of United States and allied forces should military action become necessary."[60] The toughness of the proposed act reflected the prevailing view of the Republican majorities in both houses of the U.S. Congress. If this legislation were enacted, it could have substantially tied Bush's hands in handling the North Korean nuclear issue.

It was revealed in February 2003 that President Bush became furious when Deputy Secretary of State Richard Armitage testified before Congress that the United States would have to talk to North Korea. The president was favorably inclined toward the hawkish members of his administration, including Cheney and Rumsfeld, who pushed for a military strike against North Korea if diplomacy failed.[61] At that time the hawks were worried that if it were not stopped soon, North Korea would be able to produce about sixty nuclear devices annually and could then easily export them to the governments of Iraq, Iran, Libya, and Syria and the extranational terrorist organization Al Qaeda. In a response typical of unilateralism, they argued that the United States should be prepared to launch a surgical strike against North Korean nuclear facilities, even without South Korean consent, and that Kim Jong Il would be reluctant to resort to a suicidal retaliation.

With the United States and North Korea at an impasse, it was up to China and South Korea to mediate between them so that a dialogue could begin on the North Korean nuclear issue. The Chinese were increasingly concerned that the Bush administration might expand its new doctrine of preemptive attack from Iraq to North Korea. Evidently they were also disturbed by North Korea's belligerent rhetoric and inflexible posture. Shi Yinhong, an international relations specialist at the Chinese People's University in Beijing who was well connected with the Chinese government, publicly stated that "without question, the North Korean government has been the main provocateur."[62] In a flurry of diplomatic contacts with other relevant countries, both China and South Korea attempted to defuse the pent-up tensions on the Korean Peninsula and to find a suitable venue for U.S.–North Korean negotiations. In this process, neither South Korea nor China supported North Korea's adamant insistence on bilateral talks with the United States only but instead promoted a compromise formula in which the United States and North Korea would talk to each other in a multilateral setting. Prodded by the United States, South Korea, and Japan, the Chinese at last decided to pressure North Korea by suspending the delivery of crude oil to North Korea for a few days in February, citing "technical difficulties." Evidently this maneuver served notice on North Korea of China's vital leverage over North Korea's economic survival. For North Korea depended on

China for more than 90% of its oil imports, and the Chinese oil supply had become all the more indispensable after the United States terminated its deliveries of heavy fuel oil to North Korea in November 2002. China provided a significant amount of economic assistance to North Korea and accounted for about a third of North Korea's total foreign trade. In addition, China absorbed a growing number of illegal economic refugees (between 140,000 and 300,000 in 2003) from North Korea. In view of the seriousness of the situation, the Chinese Communist Party set up a new "Leadership Small Group on the [North] Korean Question" under Hu Jintao's leadership. On March 7 this group dispatched Vice Premier Qian Qichen to North Korea for a meeting with Kim Jong Il; they explored a diplomatic way to resolve the crisis over the North Korean nuclear issue.[63]

On April 9, the U.N. Security Council held a closed-door meeting to discuss the North Korean nuclear question. The Chinese, together with the Russians, opposed the U.S. attempt to adopt a resolution or a statement that would reprimand North Korea, arguing that it would be better to seek a dialogue with North Korea outside the United Nations. The Roh government, too, quietly lobbied the member states of the U.N. Security Council not to criticize North Korea, lest it further aggravate the situation.[64] This marked a sharp departure from the Kim Young Sam government that had supported the U.N. Security Council in passing a series of statements and resolutions against North Korea in 1993 and 1994. At about the same time, in April 2003, South Korean Foreign Minister Yoon Young Kwan met with his Chinese counterpart, Li Zhaoxing, in Beijing.[65] They agreed to seek realistic ways to bring North Korea to a multilateral negotiating table.

In response to China's growing pressure and persuasion after the beginning of the Iraqi War, a spokesman for the North Korean Ministry of Foreign Affairs announced on April 12 (a few days after the U.S. military occupation of Baghdad) that if the United States were willing to change its hostile policy toward North Korea, it was prepared to talk to the U.S. delegation irrespective of the format of the meeting.[66] This was a significant concession that paved the way for the Three-Party Talks in Beijing with the United States, North Korea, and China. The North Koreans made it clear that although China would assume an appropriate role as the host of the meeting, the United States and North Korea would hold bilateral talks on "substantive matters."[67] This interpretation of the arrangement was designed to rationalize North Korea's participation in a multilateral setting, which the United States had requested all along. The Chinese did not dispute the North Korean interpretation, but the United States still wanted to have China's full participation in the tripartite talks.

Although the South Koreans preferred to take part in the multilateral talks, they accepted their exclusion because they were eager to promote a trilateral dialogue on the North Korean nuclear issue. In a series of diplomatic consultations, including Foreign Minister Yoon's meeting with Secretary of State Powell in Washington on March 29, they had actively campaigned for the early beginning of a multilateral dialogue on the North Korean nuclear issue. Through various formal and informal channels they had also urged North Korea to be flexible. In response to the critics who pointed out President Roh's diplomatic abdication, South Korean Ambassador Han Sung Joo stated that "South Korea and Japan can join multilateral talks when the issue of economic cooperation arises, and Russia may also be included for consultations on energy matters."[68] It was most likely that the United States and South Korea reached an understanding that the tripartite talks in Beijing would be a prelude to a larger meeting that would eventually include South Korea and Japan.

At the Diaoyutai State Guest House on April 23, Chinese Vice Minister of Foreign Affairs Wang Yi, who had attended the Four-Party Talks in 1998, chaired the opening session of the Three-Party Talks and welcomed the three delegations headed by James A. Kelly (U.S. assistant secretary of state), Ri Gun (deputy director for American affairs in the North Korean Ministry of Foreign Affairs), and Fu Ying (director of Asian affairs in the Chinese Ministry of Foreign Affairs), respectively. In the absence of Chinese delegates, Ri revealed to Kelly that North Korea had almost finished reprocessing 8,000 spent nuclear fuel rods, had nuclear weapons, would not dismantle them, and might transfer or demonstrate them. Kelly cautioned Ri against any escalation.[69] It is unclear whether Kelly took the information from Ri at face value or as another attempt at blackmail. He reacted passively because he was ordered to follow an NSC-approved script and because his actions and remarks were being carefully monitored by Michael Green from the National Security Council and Richard Lawless from the Department of Defense. Upon learning of Ri's statement, President Bush complained to NBC News that North Korea was "back to the old blackmail game" and that he would not be intimidated.[70] This was all taking place at a time when North Korea was arguing that the Iraqi War was imparting the lesson that a "strong deterrent capability" was required to prevent a war and to protect a nation's sovereign right.[71]

At the Beijing Talks, Ri also presented what North Korea called a "bold plan" for simultaneous and cumulative steps to resolve the North Korean nuclear and missile issues. Kelly, however, continued to insist that North Korea must first agree to dismantle its nuclear facilities in a verifiable and irreversible way before discussing other matters—such as the resumption of heavy oil delivery, a legally binding commitment for nonaggression, economic assistance, and diplomatic normalization. Since North Korea had already violated the bilateral system of the Agreed Framework, Kelly explained that a multilateral approach was the only realistic method for guaranteeing North Korea's full compliance with any agreement that could be concluded. The Chinese, who had attracted the North Koreans to the Three-Party Talks by promising that a bilateral meeting with the United States would take place, appealed to Bush's National Security Adviser Rice for permission to arrange a meeting between Kelly and Ri, but the appeal was denied. Kelly was ordered to cancel a dinner that he had planned to host for North Korean participants.[72] So ended the Three-Party Talks, without even an agreement to meet again.

As a result of the initial success of the U.S. military campaign in Iraq, the relative influence of hardline advocates such as Cheney, Rumsfeld, Wolfowitz, and Bolton increased in the Bush administration. They seized on the failure of the Three-Party Talks, arguing that it was useless to talk to North Korea, bilaterally or multilaterally. In a confidential internal memorandum, Rumsfeld reportedly explored the possibility that the United States should work together with China to bring about regime change in Pyongyang.[73] Evidently he did not yet advocate an Iraq-type preemptive attack against North Korea.

Embarrassed by the hasty termination of the talks they had carefully and patiently brokered, the Chinese hosts attempted to put a positive spin on the meeting and called upon the United States and North Korea to seek reconciliation. On April 25, Li Zhaoxing and Wang Yi had separate meetings with Kelly and Ri Gun and explained that the talks represented a good beginning and that it was not unusual to have differences on major issues.[74] They hoped that the relevant parties would continue to work toward a peaceful settlement of the North Korean nuclear issue and expressed their willingness to help facilitate a settlement. On the following day President Bush called Chinese President Hu Jintao to convey his appreciation for China's contribution to the Beijing Talks. Because of the key role the Chinese had assumed, it was important for Bush to secure China's continuing cooperation. Faced with the stalemate in the U.S.–North Korean dialogue, the Chinese had taken on the difficult responsibilities of preventing any further escalation of tension and conflict on the Korean Peninsula and of discouraging the United States from imposing economic sanctions or launching a preemptive attack against North Korea. They also cooperated with South Korea and North Korea to keep the idea of multilateral talks alive.

For his first visit to the United States in May 2003, President Roh was eager to eradicate his image as an anti-American demagogue and to hold a successful summit meeting with President Bush. Unlike Kim Dae Jung, who had nurtured a vast network of friends and supporters among American politicians, academics, journalists, and religious leaders and in the Korean-American communities, Roh was a complete stranger in terms of cultivating friendly ties with the United States. As late as 1990, Roh had demanded the pullout of U.S. troops from South Korea. He had taken great pride in the fact that, unlike other South Korean politicians, he had never been to America. In his presidential campaign, he had declared that he would not visit Washington merely for photo opportunities. This was an indirect criticism of his rival, Lee Hoe Chang, who had met with Vice President Cheney and other top U.S. officials in Washington in 2002. When characterized as an anti-American, Roh had responded, "So what?" He had also said that if the United States and North Korea were to wage war, he would rather mediate than participate. This statement was inconsistent with the reciprocal obligations pledged by the United States and South Korea in their defense treaty. He had voiced criticism of Bush's policies toward North Korea, Afghanistan, and Iraq, and, above all, he had coasted to his electoral victory on a wave of massive anti-American demonstrations in the second half of 2002.

On his way to Washington, Roh paid a two-day visit to New York City, where he was ushered through ceremonious activities—he opened the stock market, visited the site of the World Trade Center, and then met with U.N. Secretary General Kofi Annan and Henry Kissinger. In an overly pro-American speech at the Korea Society on May 12, 2003, he acknowledged the healthy state of the fifty-year old U.S.–South Korean alliance and assured his American listeners that they should not worry about the future of the alliance. He promised: "The Korean government and I will continue to work hard to develop a more mature and full partnership with the United States." He expressed his appreciation to the United States for its sacrifices during the Korean War. If the United States had not intervened to rescue South Korea at that time, he said, he might have ended up in a North Korean political prison. This comment, which was not included in the prepared text of his speech, received much attention, both positive and negative, in the South Korean media. He urged North Korea to find a peaceful solution for its nuclear issue. Echoing Bush's familiar theme, he said that "North Korea has two alternatives: it can go down a blind alley or it can open up."

In an interview with the New York Times (May 13), Roh admitted that he had been mistaken in demanding the pullout of U.S. forces from South Korea throughout the 1980s, and he obliquely expressed his concern about the hardline members of the Bush administration. He also said that he did not trust North Korea much, thus distancing himself from Kim Dae Jung. While Roh was still in New York, the North Koreans announced that because of America's "sinister and hostile" policy, they might decide to abrogate the North-South Joint Declaration on the Denuclearization of the Korean Peninsula, which prohibited the production and use of nuclear weapons and the possession of nuclear reprocessing and uranium enrichment facilities. North Korea was threatening to remove yet another legal ground for opposing its nuclear programs in order to complicate the forthcoming summit meeting between

Roh and Bush. However, Roh did not lodge a public protest against North Korea's announcement, mainly because he did not want to antagonize Kim Jong Il.

On May 13 Roh visited several monuments, including the Lincoln Memorial, where he demonstrated his respect for the sixteenth U.S. president, for whom he had expressed admiration in his book *Roh Moo Hyun Meets Lincoln*, published in 2001. He repeated his pro-American commitments in a meeting with U.S. senators and at other events, including a luncheon cosponsored by the U.S. Chamber of Commerce and the U.S.-Korea Business Council in Washington and a dinner co-hosted by the Woodrow Wilson Center for International Scholars and the Center for Strategic and International Studies. He praised the United States as a very good country where freedom and justice always prevailed. After making it clear that he intended to follow his predecessor's sunshine policy toward North Korea, he observed that the North Korean nuclear issue would be peacefully resolved if all parties concerned should engage in the dialogue with sincerity.

The same issue was high on the agenda for the summit meeting between Presidents Bush and Roh on May 14. After a relatively brief session (less than forty minutes) at the White House, they issued a joint statement, in which they reaffirmed that "they will not tolerate nuclear weapons in North Korea."[75] They reiterated their strong commitment to work for the complete, verifiable, and irreversible elimination of North Korea's nuclear weapons program through peaceful means and agreed that South Korea and Japan were essential for a successful and comprehensive settlement of the North Korean nuclear question. The two leaders also noted that increased threats to peace and stability on the peninsula would require consideration of further steps, but they did not specify what this meant and when and how the steps would be taken. It was an ambiguous compromise reached by both sides prior to the summit meeting. While Deputy Assistant Secretary of Defense Richard Lawless wanted to include a phrase in the joint statement implying that "all options" (including military ones) were on the table, South Korean Deputy Minister of Foreign Affairs Lee Soo Hyuck opposed the idea because it might provoke North Korea too much.[76] (The formula of "further steps" was milder than that of "tougher measures," which was to be used by Bush and Japanese Prime Minister Koizumi at their joint press conference nine days later.) Evidently, Bush did not accept Roh's suggestion that the United States should rule out a military option toward North Korea. In accord with Bush's request, Roh promised that "future inter-Korean exchanges and cooperation will be conducted in light of developments on the North Korean nuclear issue." It was an important commitment for linkages between the two issues, but the specific methods for implementing linkages were left unclear.

Another issue high on the agenda for their discussions was the future of the U.S. military presence in South Korea. Even though Bush rejected Roh's plea that the United States not relocate the Second Infantry Division from the DMZ area until the North Korean nuclear issue was settled, the joint statement said:

> President Bush reaffirmed the U.S. commitment to a robust forward presence on the peninsula and in the Asia-Pacific region. The two leaders pledged to work closely together to modernize the U.S.-ROK alliance, taking advantage of technology to transform both nations' forces and enhance their capabilities to meet emerging threats. . . . The two leaders agreed to work out plans to consolidate U.S. forces around key hubs and to relocate the Yongsan garrison at an early date. President Bush pledged to consult closely with President Roh on the appropriate posture for USFK during the transition to a more capable and sustainable U.S. military presence on the peninsula. They shared the view that the relocation of U.S. bases north of the Han River should be pursued, taking careful account of the political, economic and security situation on the peninsula and in Northeast Asia.

This statement indicated that the Bush administration had already decided to abandon the concept of the "trip-wire effects" of U.S. troops deployed in the DMZ area and to remove them from harm's way. The only remaining question was how this decision could be implemented in cooperation with South Korea without causing an overreaction on the part of North Korea. Yet no reference was made to Roh's campaign promises to seek a revision of the SOFA and a change in the U.S. commander's operational authority over South Korean armed forces.

In their joint news conference, Bush called Roh "an easy man to talk to. He expresses opinions very clearly and it's easy to understand." In response, Roh said, "When I left Korea, I had both concerns and hopes in my mind. Now, after having talked to President Bush, I have gotten rid of all my concerns, and now I return to Korea only with hopes in my mind." He added that "we have become to trust each other and have confidence in each other." These were wishful and premature observations, but it is fair to conclude that Roh's weeklong visit to the United States did lessen U.S. anxiety about his liberal orientations and fostered a mutually supportive working relationship between him and Bush. However, Bush's use of the phrase "an easy man to talk to" stirred objections among those South Koreans who felt it was a manifestation of his condescending attitude toward their president. The furor over this semantic episode, symptomatic of the fragility of the emotional ties between the United States and South Korea, illustrated the intensity of the South Korean response to what was perceived as a slight to President Roh and underscored the important role the mutual perceptions played in their relationship. Conversely, some of Roh's domestic supporters who held anti-American views criticized him for being too sycophantic and submissive toward the United States. In fact, he had demonstrated a remarkable degree of tactical, if not substantive, adaptation to the reality of America's hegemonic power. This pragmatic adaptation indicated the temporary triumph of his moderate and practical advisers over his hard-core liberal aides. According to a public opinion survey conducted a few days after Roh's return from the United States, 55.7% of South Korean respondents made a positive assessment of his American visit and only 31.2% had a negative view. Support for his performance as president stood at 55.2%.

THE SIX-PARTY TALKS

It was a difficult task for Bush and Roh to translate their agreement on the North Korean nuclear issue into a concrete diplomatic resolution. They intended to include South Korea and Japan (and Russia, if necessary) in a new format for multilateral talks and again called upon China to exercise its constructive influence over the reluctant North Korean leadership. For this purpose President Bush requested Chinese President Hu Jintao's cooperation when they were in Evian, France, on June 1, 2003, for the G-8 meeting; Bush also had consultations with Japanese Prime Minister Koizumi and Russian President Putin. At the Trilateral Coordination and Oversight Group (TCOG) meeting on June 13 in Honolulu, James Kelly, Lee Soo Hyuck, and Yabunaka Motoji (director-general of the Bureau of Asian and Oceanic Affairs, Japanese Ministry of Foreign Affairs) insisted that South Korean and Japanese participation in the Beijing talks was "indispensable" and expressed concern about the question of Japanese abductees and North Korea's illegal activities abroad. In his summit meeting with Chinese President Hu Jintao in Beijing on July 7, President Roh asked China to mediate between the United States and North Korea and to bring North Korea to another round of multilateral talks.

The Chinese diplomats undertook busy shuttle diplomacy. Most important, Chinese Vice Minister of Foreign Affairs Dai Bingguo, who, as director of the Department of International Liaison of the Chinese Communist Party had cultivated a close working relationship with North Korea over many years, met with Kim Jong Il in Pyongyang on July 14. In a letter delivered by Dai to Kim, Chinese President Hu Jintao apparently suggested that North Korea should halt the programs for weapons of mass destruction, improve its relations with other countries, and make efforts for a diplomatic resolution of nuclear issues. Kim most likely accepted Dai's proposal to resume the Three-Party Talks in principle. Afterwards, Dai traveled to Washington for a meeting with Secretary Powell on July 18. Dai proposed to reopen the Three-

Party Talks in Beijing, but Powell requested that South Korea and Japan also be included in the talks.[77] The North Koreans preferred to include Russia in a multilateral meeting as a counterweight to the United States and China. In order to finalize details for the Six-Party Talks, China played a pivotal role in a series of intense diplomatic consultations with all five capitals in July and August, including Chinese Foreign Minister Li Zhaoxing's visits to Tokyo and Seoul and Wang Yi's trip to Pyongyang. On August 13 and 14, James Kelly met with Lee Soo Hyuck and Yabunaka Motoji in Washington for policy coordination. They agreed on a general outline of their policies, understanding that each delegation would exercise a degree of flexibility in preparing its specific views and proposals in Beijing. When there was a suggestion that John Bolton, a leading neoconservative spokesman who had called Kim Jong Il a "tyrannical rogue," described life in North Korea as a "hellish nightmare," and denounced Kim's "extortionist demands," might lead the U.S. delegation to Beijing, the North Koreans registered their opposition, vilifying Bolton as "rude human scum" and a "bloodsucker."[78] The Bush administration decided to designate Kelly as head of the U.S. delegation instead. In protest, Jack Pritchard, the special envoy for the North Korea Peace Talks who had served in the National Security Council under President Clinton, tendered his resignation because he had been so marginalized and frustrated.[79] Senator Kyl, chairman of the Republican Policy Committee, had urged Powell to dismiss Pritchard, who was viewed as too soft on North Korea.[80] The episodes with Bolton, Pritchard, and Kelly were indicative of the complexity of policy cleavages and personal tensions in the Bush administration.

The Six-Party Talks, like the Three-Party Talks, opened at the exclusive Diaoyutai State Guest House on August 27. The delegations were headed by Wang Yi, James Kelly, Lee Soo Hyuck, Yabunaka Motoji, Kim Yong Il (North Korean deputy minister of foreign affairs), and Alexander Losyukov (Russian deputy minister of foreign affairs), respectively (see table 5). As host, Wang presided over the proceedings. It was the first "two-plus-four" meeting, with both Koreas and the four major powers convening to discuss the North Korean nuclear question. The South Koreans were particularly pleased with their full and equal participation in the multilateral discussion of an issue so vital to their security interests. This had been made possible by the steady improvement in inter-Korean relations ever since the summit meeting in June 2000. In the morning, each chief delegate made a keynote speech. During a break in the afternoon, Wang encouraged an informal side meeting between Kelly and Kim, which lasted less than an hour. The other delegates observed their agitated exchange of words and gesticulations from a distance. Exactly what transpired in this meeting remains unclear, but it is most likely that they candidly explained their respective policies to each other. The Chinese tactfully seated the U.S. and North

Korean delegations next to each other in a hexagonal table arrangement and in having Kelly and Kim at the same table in a banquet hosted by Foreign Minister Li Zhaoxing. The United States, however, attempted to play down the importance of its bilateral encounters with North Korea.

As expected, Kelly again insisted that North Korea should first pledge to dismantle its nuclear facilities in a complete, verifiable, and irreversible way before they could begin to address other important matters. He repeated President Bush's promise not to invade North Korea but rejected North Korea's proposal for a nonaggression treaty or agreement. He promised to provide humanitarian assistance to North Korea. Yet he also raised sensitive issues such as human rights, narcotics trafficking, and counterfeiting activities. A compromise between the hardline and moderate forces in the Bush administration, Kelly's statements and responses were strictly constrained, revealing an unusual degree of inflexibility and circumspection. Equally adamant was Kim Yong Il's stance. He felt uncomfortable in a multilateral setting because the North Koreans were apprehensive about the possibility that the other five delegations might join together in an effort to exert pressure on his country. Adhering to the same script that the North Koreans had presented at the Three-Party Talks four months earlier, Kim argued that the United States should first change its hostile and aggressive policy toward North Korea before discussing Pyongyang's commitment for nuclear disarmament, and he reiterated a package of simultaneous measures to be taken by North Korea and the United States.

Compared with Kelly, South Korea's Lee Soo Hyuck took a more conciliatory approach. He presented a "three-step" plan for reciprocal and simultaneous measures: (1) North Korea declares its intention to abandon its nuclear weapons program, and other countries express their willingness to assure North Korean national security; (2) while North Korea begins to dismantle its nuclear facilities, other countries provide North Korea with security assurances in writing and offer economic aid and energy to North Korea; and (3) as North Korea completes its nuclear disarmament, all parties begin to discuss the ways for resolving ballistic missiles and other related issues and for normalizing relations among them.[81] Lee urged North Korea to stop reprocessing spent nuclear fuel rods and to freeze its nuclear programs. In turn, he promised to provide massive economic aid to North Korea and to support the World Bank and other international financial institutions in assisting North Korea. Lee also had an informal bilateral meeting with Kim lasting a half hour; they agreed to cooperate for the success of the Six-Party Talks. Yabunaka, too, mentioned that if the nuclear issue were to be peacefully resolved, Japan would consider delivering heavy oil, electricity, and other economic benefits to North Korea. Yet he brought up the problems of Japanese abductees and the North Korean ballistic missiles—issues that North Korea regarded as irrelevant to the agenda of the talks. Generally sympathetic with North Korean positions, Wang and Losyukov suggested that the two central issues—North Korea's nuclear nonproliferation and security concerns—should be addressed simultaneously.

On the following day, Kim suddenly announced that North Korea intended to declare itself a nuclear nation and to test nuclear devices. He said that North Korea also had the means to deliver them, adding still more tension to the negotiations. Kim's confrontational behavior not only stunned all the other delegates, it also made Wang Yi "visibly angry." The more provocative the North Koreans became, the better America's policy of isolating North Korea diplomatically in the multilateral forum and mobilizing international pressure on North Korea appeared. A U.S. official bluntly stated: "We are letting them [North Koreans] dig their own grave."[82]

The meeting adjourned earlier than expected. Since North Korea refused to issue a joint statement, Wang Yi announced on behalf of all of the delegations what he called a six-point consensus on August 29:

- to resolve the nuclear issue peacefully through dialogue and maintain peace and stability on the Korean Peninsula;
- to have a nuclear-free Korean Peninsula, while there is a need to consider and address the North Korean concerns in a wide range of areas, including its security concerns;
- to explore an overall plan that is fair and reasonable in approach, aimed at producing a solution with "phased in and synchronized, or parallel, stages of implementation";
- to refrain from saying anything or taking any action that may escalate tensions or aggravate the situation;
- to continue dialogue to establish trust, reduce differences, and broaden common ground; and
- to continue the Six-Party Talk whose specific date and venue should be decided through diplomatic channels as soon as possible.[83]

He admitted that there were substantial differences between the United States and North Korea but noted that the United States had confirmed its intention not to threaten, attack, or invade North Korea, which in turn had expressed its willingness to peacefully coexist with the United States. He added that this six-point consensus demonstrated a spirit of understanding and cooperation and laid a solid and necessary foundation for the next round of talks, which were expected to be held within two months. It was difficult to have a serious and sustained discussion in a meeting of six delegations, twenty-four interpreters, and many recorders, and personal relationships in extended contacts should be nurtured to have a successful dialogue with North Korea.[84]

Even before the first round of the Six-Party Talks ended, the North Koreans had made it clear that there was no point in holding another round of multilateral discussions. Wang was disappointed by North Korea's recalcitrance and America's rigidity. He complained in Manila on September 1 that the United States was the "main obstacle" to a peaceful settlement of the North Korean nuclear issue because of its reluctance to concede anything.[85] The South Koreans, too, were unhappy about the inflexibility of the United States. On September 3, Powell unexpectedly accompanied South Korean Foreign Minister Yoon Young Kwan to the White House for a brief meeting with President Bush. This was an unusual goodwill gesture toward the Roh administration, but it could not conceal the serious policy cleavage between Washington and Seoul. At their discussion back in the Department of State, Yoon informed Powell that South Korea might not dispatch combat troops to Iraq if the United States refused to become more forthcoming toward North Korea. Disappointed with Yoon's remarks, Powell was quoted as saying: "That is not how allies deal with each other."[86] This sharp exchange was characterized as a "minor rebellion"—a clear indication as to how far the U.S.–South Korean alliance had degenerated under Presidents Bush and Roh. In a joint press conference, however, Powell promised to consult with South Korea "in the closest possible manner," saying, "As partners, we have an open relationship where we can share ideas in full candor and with the desire of reaching a common understanding on the way forward." He also assured Yoon that the United States would not be frightened by North Korea's threats and truculent statements. Yoon had little to say at the press conference.

In view of the linkage promised between the resolution of the North Korean nuclear issue and the progress of inter-Korean cooperation, President Roh was frustrated by the stalemate in the U.S.–North Korean dialogue. This situation undermined his ambitious plan to expand Kim Dae Jung's sunshine policy and to carry out his policy of "peace and prosperity" on the Korean Peninsula. A major breakthrough in inter-Korean relations could have boosted his popularity in South Korea and fulfilled his campaign pledge to make South Korea the "hub" of economic cooperation in Northeast Asia. Disillusioned with the Bush administration, Roh then attempted to forge a diplomatic united front with China and Japan. On October 7, he joined Chinese Premier Wen Jiabao and Japanese Prime Minister Koizumi for a trilateral summit session in conjunction with the ASEAN+3 meeting in Bali, Indonesia. For the first time, the top leaders of three Northeast Asian countries issued a joint statement in which they agreed, among other things, to seek a peaceful resolution of the North Korean nuclear issue and to cooperate for the second round of the Six-Party Talks.[87]

In fact, the South Koreans felt more comfortable and compatible with their new Chinese friends than with their old American allies, both in the policy arena and in cultural exchanges. It was no accident that at Seoul National University in 2003 there were more applicants to the Department of Chinese Literature than to the Department of English Literature, one of the most prestigious and coveted programs. Learning the Chinese language and studying in Chinese institutions of higher learning became fashionable among South Koreans. This tendency was closely associated with the steady increase in economic relations between China and South Korea and with the appreciable deterioration in U.S.–South Korean relations. China was South Korea's top investment market in 2001, its top export market in 2002, and its top trading partner in 2003. The volume of two-way trade between South Korea and China (including Hong Kong) reached $74 billion ($57 billion without Hong Kong) in 2003, surpassing South Korea's trade with the United States ($59 billion) and Japan ($54 billion).

Bogged down in Iraq, the Bush administration did not wish to modify its fundamentalist position that North Korea should not be rewarded for its violation of international agreements and that its blackmail and brinkmanship should not be tolerated. Although President Bush continued to recognize the political liabilities of Clinton's policies of engagement and appeasement toward North Korea (as the Republican Party described it), he realized that a somewhat more flexible diplomatic overture toward North Korea was necessary to accommodate the wishes of South Korea and China and to respond to the growing criticism of his Korea policy in the United States prior to the approaching presidential election. After meeting with Thai Prime Minister Thaksin on October 19 during the APEC summit in Bangkok, Bush said that he was willing to put into writing assurances that the United States would not attack North Korea, but he categorically rejected any formal treaty with North Korea. The following day he had a further discussion with President Roh Moo Hyun. They stressed the importance of the Six-Party Talks for achieving the goal of the complete, verifiable, and irreversible elimination of North Korea's nuclear weapons programs and urged North Korea to respond positively to the other parties' diplomatic efforts and to refrain from any action that would exacerbate the situation. Roh announced that he had decided to dispatch additional South Korean troops to Iraq after carefully considering such factors as the U.S.–South Korean alliance and South Korea's national interests. South Korea also committed $260 million for Iraqi reconstruction over three years. Bush expressed his gratitude to Roh for making a "principled determination." They agreed to pursue the question of relocating U.S. bases after careful consideration of the Korean security environment. The North Koreans, however, were quick to rebuff Bush's offer of a written security assurance: "It is laughable and does not deserve even any consideration that the United States gives a security guarantee on the condition that we drop our nuclear development."[88]

Nevertheless, when Kim Jong Il met Wu Bangguo (chairman of the Standing Committee of the National People's Congress) on October 30 in Pyongyang, the two sides agreed in principle to "continue" the Six-Party Talks for a peaceful resolution of the "[North] Korean-U.S. nuclear issue."[89] Accompanied by Wang Yi, Wu presented Kim with a large jade tablet with his name inscribed in Chinese characters and promised to provide a new grant-in-aid to North Korea. In addition, Wu paid his respects at the Kim Il Sung mausoleum and laid a wreath at "the Tower of [North] Korean-Chinese Friendship." In a joint announcement, the North Koreans expressed their willingness to attend the Six-Party Talks only if a "comprehensive settlement" under the "principle of simultaneous actions" could be achieved. In turn, the Chinese emphasized that the concerns of both countries—North Korea and the United States—should be resolved at the same time.

The United States and South Korea welcomed the news from Pyongyang but nevertheless joined Japan and the European Union in suspending the light-water reactor project for a period of one year, beginning December 1, 2003. The United States preferred to terminate the project altogether, but South Korea argued that it could serve as a useful instrument for solving the North Korean nuclear questions. After costing about $1 billion and with almost a third of its work finished, this centerpiece of the Geneva Agreed Framework was on the verge of complete collapse unless a breakthrough could be found on the North Korean nuclear issue (see table 6). In an angry response to the suspension, the North Koreans announced that they would impose "ten temporary measures" on the Korean Peninsula Energy Development Organization operations in Kumho, in effect nullifying a series of agreements and protocols reached between KEDO and North Korea. They planned to apply North Korean laws and regulations to about 120 KEDO personnel, who remained in Kumho. At that time the KEDO became engaged in negotiations with North Korea to ease the "ten temporary measures," to guarantee free movement of the KEDO personnel, and to preserve and maintain the facilities and materials at the construction site in Kumho. While the North Koreans called the LWR site a "museum of failure," KEDO Assistant Director Robert Carlin, who had played an important role in U.S.–North Korean negotiations during the 1993–94 period, described it as a "stable platform" for future cooperation between the United States and North Korea.[90] Administrative costs for maintaining the KEDO operations both in New York and in Kumho were about $14 million per year. The United States, South Korea, and Japan each shared 30% of this amount; the European Union assumed 10%.

Yet support for U.S.–North Korean dialogue and cooperation was dwindling even further in the Republican-dominated U.S. Congress. In November 2003, for example, Senator Samuel Brownback (R-KS), the influential and outspoken conservative chairman of the Subcommittee on East Asian and Pacific Affairs, introduced the North Korean Freedom Act to the U.S. Congress.[91] He pointed out that the North Korean government had imprisoned about 200,000 persons for political reasons, that as many as 3.5 million North Koreans had died from hunger or famine-related disease since 1994, and that estimates of the number of North Korean refugees living in China ranged from 100,000 to 300,000. Brownback's bill was designed to grant the right to "humanitarian parole" status to North Korean refugees, to provide funds ($32 million per year) for nongovernmental organizations or foreign government organizations assisting North Korean refugees, to encourage nongovernmental organizations to arrange the adoption of North Korean orphans by U.S. families, and to distribute clandestine radios (at $11 million per year) into North Korea so that North Korean citizens could listen to U.S. broadcasts of Radio Free Asia and the Voice of America. It also stipulated that "any negotiations between the United States and North Korea should include the human rights of North Korean citizens as a key item in a dialogue on political freedoms, prison systems, and religious freedoms." Even though the bill was couched in the universal principles of human rights, its hidden political agenda was to bring about regime change in North Korea. It also exerted powerful pressure on the moderates in the Bush administration who were eager to seek a compromise with North Korea via the Six-Party Talks.

In order to arrange the second round of the Six-Party Talks, the Chinese again conducted intense shuttle diplomacy with the other five countries and attempted to generate a consensus about the text of a joint communiqué to be issued following the meeting. They did not want a repeat of the embarrassing situation in which Wang Yi had read the six-point consensus after the abrupt end of the first round. In early December 2003 the United States rejected a Chinese draft of the text at a meeting between Fu Ying (director of Asian Affairs, Chinese Ministry of Foreign Affairs) and Deputy Secretary of State Armitage because it represented North Korean points of view, but joined South Korea and Japan at TCOG in drafting a "statement of principles" that was transmitted to North Korea via China.[92] This statement envisaged a coordinated set of steps in which the five countries would collectively offer a security guarantee and economic assistance to North Korea in return for its commitment to dismantle all its nuclear facilities, including the HEU program, in a verifiable and irreversible way. It apparently did not ask North Korea to return to the NPT regime but fell short of accommodating North Korea's well-known proposals for a bilateral nonaggression treaty with the United States or some other legally binding agreement outlining a U.S. renunciation of the threat or use of military force, including nuclear weapons, against North Korea. Lee Soo Hyuck admitted that there were disagreements on specific issues among the three participants in the TCOG session and that "indirect and implicative" language was used to accommodate the differences.[93]

Although South Korea was prepared to offer specific economic benefits to North Korea as tangible incentives or face-saving devices for nuclear disarmament, the United States did not want to reward North Korea's bad behavior. In a fashion that had become all too familiar, the North Koreans rebuffed the draft and dampened any hopes for the early resumption of the Six-Party Talks. On December 9, a spokesman for the North Korean Ministry of Foreign Affairs said that in return for freezing North Korea's nuclear activities, the United States should satisfy three preconditions: (1) remove North Korea from the list of states sponsoring international terrorism; (2) lift political, economic, and military sanctions; and (3) provide heavy fuel oil, electricity, and other assistance.[94] On the same day, Bush in effect rejected the North Korean preconditions by declaring at his joint press conference with Chinese Premier Wen Jiabao that "the goal is to dismantle a nuclear weapons program in a verifiable and irreversible way." Wen made no comment.[95] At the White House, Bush praised Wen as a partner in diplomacy and asked for Chinese assistance in reaching a peaceful resolution of the North Korean nuclear issue. At the same time he confirmed Washington's adherence to a one-China principle and opposed Taiwan President Chen Shui-bian's move to change Taiwan's legal status vis-à-vis China. Wen expressed appreciation for Bush's statement. As Bush and Jiang Zemin had done in October 2002, the discussion between Bush and Wen suggested a possible connection between U.S. disavowal of Taiwan's independence and Chinese opposition to North Korean nuclear proliferation. It was not clear whether a confidential deal for mutual assistance between the two sides was made.

By the end of 2003 the importance of domestic political considerations loomed even larger in Bush's and Roh's policies toward North Korea. In terms of U.S. politics, it was important for Bush to demonstrate that his multilateral diplomacy with respect to North Korea was underway and to keep a lid on the potentially dangerous problem on the Korean Peninsula while simultaneously developing an exit strategy from the chaotic Iraqi situation. Moreover, he continued to maintain the moral high ground in domestic politics by denouncing the "evil regime" under Kim Jong Il and by refusing to give in to what he regarded as North Korea's blackmail and diatribes. So long as China was willing to bear a major responsibility for resuming the Six-Party Talks, the Bush administration did not have to devote much of its time and resources to the North Korean issue. It hoped that the widely publicized capture of Saddam Hussein and the capitulation of Libya's Moammar Kadafi in giving up nuclear, biological, and chemical weapons as well as long-range ballistic missiles in December 2003 might have a sobering or chilling effect on Kim Jong Il.[96] The Democratic Party, mired in internal struggles over the presidential nomination, was less than effective in challenging Bush's Korea policy. However, Jack Pritchard, who had visited North Korea as a member of an unofficial American delegation in January 2004, continued to criticize President Bush's "failed policy" toward North Korea and claimed that it was based on a string of serious intelligence failures.[97] He argued that the United States should step out from behind China's diplomatic skirts and take the leadership in solving the North Korean crisis.

Just as President Bush's foreign policy was being subjected to growing criticism both at home and abroad, President Roh, faced with his own domestic political crisis, remained ineffective in managing the ongoing problems with the United States and North Korea. When his close aides and personal friends became implicated in serious corruption charges in October 2003, Roh apologized for "this shameful and unsavory situation" and called for a "vote of confidence" from the people.[98] A coalition of three opposition political parties in the National Assembly—the Grand National Party, the Millennium Democratic Party, and the Liberal Democratic League—passed legislation by a vote of 184 to 2 with 7 abstentions to appoint a special prosecutor to investigate the charges; 47 members of the new Uri Party, a pro-Roh splinter group from the Millennium Democratic Party, boycotted the vote altogether. After Roh vetoed the legislation, on December 4 the National Assembly overrode his veto by an overwhelming vote of 209 to 54 with 3 abstentions. The New Uri Party constituted a distinct minority in the 272-member National Assembly, thus crippling Roh's legislative agenda. His political life hung in balance.

Less than a year after assuming power, President Roh had failed to carry out his campaign promises in domestic and foreign affairs. Public support for his presidential performance hovered around 30%. An even more serious problem confronted him: a dramatic upsurge in anti-American sentiment among South Koreans. When asked in January 2004 which country posed the most serious threat to South Korea's national security, 39% of the respondents picked the United States—more than even North Korea, at 33%. China and Japan received 12% and 8%, respectively. Russia was no longer a source of much concern in South Korea.[99] As table 7 shows, there was a significant generational gap in the perceptions of the threat. Among those in their twenties, more than three times as many viewed the United States as more threatening than North Korea. The exact opposite was the case among those who were fifty and older. The fear was not that the United States would directly threaten South Korean security but rather that an American preemptive attack against North Korea might ignite another Korean War. Anti-American sentiment was particularly strong among college students, white-collar workers, and women. This weakened and complicated the domestic basis of Roh's diplomatic and military relations with the United States and challenged the status of the U.S. military presence on the Korean Peninsula.

After six months of hectic diplomatic maneuvers and consultations led by China, the second round of the Six-Party Talks was finally held in Beijing on February 26, 2004. It was telling that North Korea chose a delegation of seasoned diplomats with extensive experience negotiating with the United States. Vice Minister of Foreign Affairs Kim Gye Gwan replaced Kim Yong Il as chief delegate. The new chief had participated in the nuclear negotiations (1993–94) in New York and Geneva, headed the North Korean team throughout the Four-Party Talks (1997–99), maintained the New York channel of liaison with the United States (1999–2000), and hosted Kelly's visit to Pyongyang (October 2002). He was assisted by two other American affairs specialists—Ri Gun and Han Song Ryol (deputy ambassador to the United Nations). The leaders of the other five delegations remained the same as in the first round.

On the sidelines of the six-party meeting, Kelly and Kim held an informal bilateral discussion for about two hours. Even though it was not immediately revealed what transpired in this meeting, it appeared that it was a less contentious, more businesslike session than Kelly's meeting with Kim Yong Il six months earlier. Kelly was quick to brief the four other parties, so as to make the dialogue transparent. As a champion of the principle of a multilateral approach to the North Korean nuclear issue, he did not want to leave the impression that the discussion between the United States and North Korea was more important than the Six-Party Talks. Later, Kelly testified that in talking to Kim Gye Gwan and his colleagues, he brought up the Libyan example of voluntary nuclear disarmament in the hopes that "they understand its significance."[100] Once North Korea's nuclear problem was resolved, he told them, "discussions would be possible on a wide range of issues that could lead to an improvement in relations" between the United States and North Korea.

Yet the positions and views publicly articulated by Kelly and Kim in Beijing remained as far apart as ever. Kelly reconfirmed the U.S. position that it had no intention of instigating a military attack on North Korea and that North Korea should first agree to dismantle all nuclear weapons programs, including a clandestine project for highly enriched uranium, in a complete, verifiable, and irreversible way before undertaking other measures for U.S.–North Korean cooperation. Kim denied that North Korea had an HEU program and demanded that the United States should first stop its hostile policy against North Korea.

In order to break the deadlock between the United States and North Korea, Lee Soo Hyuck took the initiative in presenting a more detailed version of his earlier proposal for a three-step procedure.[101] In the first phase, all five parties would agree to guarantee North Korea's security in return for a declaration renouncing its nuclear weapons programs. Once North Korea took measures to freeze and dismantle its nuclear weapons programs and facilities, the second phase, which envisaged that the United States, Japan, and South Korea would take reciprocally coordinated steps for diplomatic and economic normalization with North Korea, would begin. In the third phase following the resolution of the North Korean nuclear issues, all relevant parties would conclude a comprehensive peace mechanism on the Korean Peninsula to address such other issues as ballistic missiles, human rights, and international terrorism. In the interim period, Lee proposed that if North Korea agreed to freeze its nuclear programs, other countries would supply it with energy. China and Russia endorsed this proposal, but the United States took a "neutral position," indicating its reluctance to resume delivery of heavy fuel oil to North Korea anytime soon. Kelly instinctively disliked the very concept of a "freeze" because it was a central feature of the failed Geneva Agreed Framework. Nor was North Korea prepared to suspend all of its nuclear-related activities as a means of obtaining energy assistance from abroad. At the second round of the Six-Party Talks, Lee distanced himself from Kelly and Yabunaka and moved closer to Wang Yi in an attempt to encourage them to serve as facilitators between the United States and North Korea. Unlike Lee, Yabunaka did not deviate from the position of diplomatic solidarity with Kelly on the North Korean nuclear issue. The Japanese delegate also brought up the question of the Japanese who had been abducted by North Korea, but in a less confrontational manner than before. The United States, South Korea, and Japan tried to maintain a semblance of trilateral unity in Beijing, but the growing fissure in America's military alliance and diplomatic coalition with Seoul was all too apparent.

One important issue on which the six delegations failed to agree was whether North Korea had a clandestine HEU program or not. While the United States argued that it had enough evidence to prove the existence of an active North Korean HEU program and that Kang Sok Ju had already admitted its existence to Kelly in October 2002, the North Koreans were adamant that Kang had never made any such admission and that they had no HEU program at all.[102] Lee Soo Hyuck refrained from supporting the U.S. position completely, conspicuously maintaining an ambiguous stand. Like his Chinese and Russian colleagues, Lee knew that Dr. Abdul Qadeer

Khan, the Pakistani scientist, had sold HEU designs and technology, including high-speed centrifuges, to North Korea (and Libya and Iran), but he assumed that North Korea had not yet reached the stage of actually producing weapons-grade enriched uranium.[103]

In spite of China's earnest efforts, the Six-Party Talks once again failed to issue a joint press release, primarily because of North Korean opposition. After representatives of the six delegations agreed on the draft of this release, the South Koreans feared that the Bush White House might veto it. However, Secretary Powell was able to obtain President Bush's approval of the draft; it was, after all, North Korea that also demanded too significant revision to be acceptable to other delegations.[104] As he had done on August 30, 2003, Wang Yi issued the chairman's statement. On February 28, 2004, he said that "the parties expressed their commitment to a nuclear-weapons-free Korean Peninsula, and to resolving the nuclear issue peacefully through dialogue in a spirit of mutual respect and consultations on an equal basis, so as to maintain peace and stability on the Korean Peninsula and the region at large." According to Wang, all six parties agreed to coexist peacefully and to take coordinated steps to address the nuclear issue and related concerns.[105] Two aspects of this announcement were a little more positive than his earlier statement: the six parties agreed to resume the third round of the Six-Party Talks by the end of June 2004, and they also planned to hold a working group meeting in the interim. Even though South Korea was disappointed that its modest initiative—the exchange of a North Korean commitment to a nuclear freeze for energy assistance—had failed, Lee expressed satisfaction with a commitment for continuing dialogue among all six countries, especially at a working-level meeting.[106] While the North Koreans continued to accuse the United States of attempting to disarm and stifle them, the Bush administration sounded most positive and optimistic about the prospects for the Six-Party Talks. Kelly explained that the second round of the Six-Party Talks had made "significant progress" on several fronts.[107] Most importantly, he said that the North Koreans had heard what they needed to do in sessions with all parties represented, and they had heard it from him in direct encounters on the margins of the formal sessions. In addition, he said that the six-party approach had the potential to transcend the North Korean nuclear issue and to evolve into a regular security forum for the Northeast Asian region.

Following a meeting with the new South Korean foreign minister Ban Ki Moon in Washington on March 4, 2004, Secretary of State Powell stated that "we are both quite satisfied with the way those talks went. We have come out of those talks with an institutionalized process to move forward in further discussions at working group and plenary level." Emphasizing that there was "no sense of urgency," he added,

"We have shown patience. And as long as we are seeing progress, we are going to continue to work with the six-party format and our friends to achieve our CVID [complete, verifiable, and irreversible dismantlement] objectives." He took the opportunity to state that the bilateral relationship between the United States and South Korea was "very strong" and thanked the South Korean government for its contributions in Iraq.[108] After a brief visit with President Bush at the White House, Foreign Minister Ban also recognized the "generally positive result" of the second round of the Six-Party Talks and supported the CVID formula. In an attempt to reconfirm the importance of alliance cohesion and policy coordination between Washington and Seoul, he explicitly denied the widespread report that South Korea had maneuvered to serve as an "intermediary" between the United States and North Korea in Beijing. In doing so, he intended to dispel the suspicion that South Korea was not fully supportive of the U.S. position at the Six-Party Talks. A semblance of solidarity between Washington and Seoul was renewed, at least for a while.

Efforts for the amelioration of U.S.–South Korean relations were followed by a summit meeting between Kim Jong Il and Hu Jintao at Beijing on April 19, 2004.[109] They acknowledged the positive results of the Three-Party Talks and the Six-Party Talks and promised to push forward the process of the six-party formula so that the nuclear issue could be solved through dialogue and in a peaceful way. Soon thereafter, the six parties held an inaugural working group meeting in Beijing from May 12 to 14 to discuss a number of specific issues and to prepare for the third round of the Six-Party Talks. No concrete agreement was reached, however. After the meeting, the Chinese admitted that there still existed some major differences but that "frank and candid" consultations had taken place.[110] Ri Gun, head of the North Korean delegation, asserted that there was a shared view that North Korea should receive compensation for agreeing to freeze its nuclear weapons program and added that North Korea would continue to participate in the talks "with patience." Joseph DeTrani, who led the U.S. delegation, put a positive spin on the talks, saying that it had been a "good meeting." When asked if progress had been made, he responded, "Yes, definitely."[111] On the sidelines of the working group meeting, when Ri Gun had asked DeTrani what the United States would do about the LWR project if North Korea addressed the HEU program, DeTrani apparently said that the resumption of the LWR project could be "one element" of the U.S. response. Assuming it is accurate, this exchange raised questions as to whether DeTrani had exceeded his instructions not to discuss the LWR program or whether he was indicating a change in the U.S. position. This episode put both DeTrani and the Department of State in an awkward situation. Hence Adam Erili, deputy spokesman for the Department of State, clarified the U.S. position in a press conference on May 19 when he announced that the United States intended to seek the complete, verifiable, and irreversible dismantlement of North Korean nuclear programs and was not prepared to provide "inducements" to North Korea for compliance with its international obligations.[112] Kelly added that the working group session in Beijing had explored the structure of resolution—"a structure that would involve concrete actions by North Korea with corresponding measures taken by other parties in a coordinated fashion."[113] He was guardedly optimistic about a possible solution of the North Korean nuclear issue via the Six-Party Talks.

In a letter to National Security Adviser Rice, three Republican members of the U.S. Congress—Christopher Cox, Henry J. Hyde, and Jon Kyl—wanted to make sure that the Bush administration would not offer a nuclear reactor to North Korea at all.[114] They argued that since North Korea had a long and dangerous history of violating international nonproliferation agreements, the United States should take an unambiguous stand and ensure that "Kim Jong Il's negotiators fully comprehend that this aspect of the Agreed Framework will not be resurrected." This congressional pressure was designed to dampen any signs of "appeasement" of North Korea and to bolster the neoconservatives' position within the Bush administration. For all practical purposes, the Bush administration regarded the LWR project as no longer viable. On May 28, 2004, Richard Boucher, spokesman for the Department of State, categorically stated that the United States saw absolutely no future for this project but explained that the KEDO Executive Board would decide its ultimate disposition.[115]

At the third round of the Six-Party Talks held in Beijing from June 23 to 25, 2004, James Kelly indeed accommodated what China and South Korea had urged the Bush administration to do. In a seven-page document, Kelly proposed that North Korea would, as a first step, commit to dismantle all of its nuclear programs and that the parties would then reach agreement on a detailed implementation plan requiring the supervised elimination of all nuclear-related facilities and materials and a long-term monitoring program. In exchange, he offered to deliver heavy fuel oil to North Korea by South Korea and Japan and to provide "provisional multilateral security assurances" to North Korea.[116] During an initial preparatory period of about three months, North Korea would be expected to: (1) provide a complete listing of all its nuclear activities and cease all their operations; (2) permit the securing of all fissile material and the monitoring of all fuel rods; and (3) permit the observable disablement of all nuclear weapons, weapons components, and key centrifuge parts. If North Korea moved to dismantle its plutonium- and uranium-based nuclear weapons programs and facilities, the United States would give a more permanent security assurance and pay for the costs of nuclear dismantlement. This idea was an extension of the Nunn-Lugar Cooperative Threat Reduction (CTR) Program, in which the United States had assumed all the expenses for nuclear dismantlement, storage, and transfer in Ukraine and Kazakhstan.[117] In addition, the United States would begin a discussion of the steps necessary to lift economic sanctions on North Korea and to remove North Korea from the State Department's list of state sponsors of terrorism. Kelly and other U.S. delegates refrained from using the CVID formula so as not to inflame North Korean sensibilities. The U.S. government wanted to make it clear that Kelly's proposal was first presented by South Korea and had been further refined in Washington.

In return, Kim Gye Gwan reiterated North Korea's "reward for freeze" proposal as had been articulated by the North Korean Ministry of Foreign Affairs back in December 2003. He indicated that North Korea was prepared to freeze all plutonium-related facilities, including the five-megawatt nuclear reactor as well as the nuclear reprocessing plant in Yongbyon.[118] This initial freeze would lead to the ultimate dismantling of the North Korean nuclear program. He also requested that the United States would lift economic sanctions, remove North Korea from the list of state sponsors of terrorism, and provide energy equal to 2,000 kilowatts—the same amount that the light-water reactors in Kumho could have generated. The North Koreans wanted to exclude the IAEA from the verification process, preferring to create a new verification regime restricted to the countries participating in the Six-Party Talks. In an informal bilateral meeting lasting two and a half hours, Kelly and Kim elaborated further on their respective proposals. Once again Kelly urged Kim to follow the Libyan example to find an open path to better relations with the United States and other relevant nations. Kim responded that there were some people in North Korea who wanted to test a nuclear weapon and might presumably do so if no progress was made in the talks. This comment, Kelly said, "did not contribute to the comity of the meeting or to any atmosphere of trust."[119]

The Bush administration took a more flexible and concrete position at the third round of the Six-Party Talks than at the earlier rounds for several reasons. First, it accepted the wishes and recommendations of South Korea and Japan that its allies maintain a united front. The United States recognized that its rigid posture toward North Korea had created a growing cleavage with President Roh's desire for reconciliation with North Korea and with Japanese Prime Minister Koizumi's conciliatory approach toward Pyongyang as demonstrated in his second summit meeting with Kim Jong Il in Pyongyang on May 23, 2004. In testimony before the Senate Committee on Foreign Relations in July 2004, James Kelly gave credit to South Korea and Japan for presenting concrete and constructive proposals at the Six-Party Talks. Second, it was important for the United States not to alienate China and Russia in dealing with the North Korean nuclear issue. The maintenance of a broad international consensus was essential to persuading or coercing North Korea to give up its nuclear ambitions peacefully. Third, the deterioration of the U.S. position in Iraq appreciably weakened the influence of hardliners such as Cheney, Rumsfeld, Wolfowitz, and Bolton in the Bush administration and enhanced the voice of pragmatic leaders such as Powell and Kelly in interagency discussions. Most importantly, humbled by the Iraq experience, the Bush administration took the initiative in Beijing to keep a lid on the potentially explosive situation in Korea at least until the presidential election in November 2004. If the Six-Party Talks broke down beyond repair, or if North Korea declared itself as a nuclear power or tested its nuclear devices, the Democratic Party, led by its presidential candidate, Senator John F. Kerry, would have a potent issue with which it could attack Bush's incompetence and failure in foreign affairs.

The Chinese, together with the United States and South Korea, were very pleased with the modest progress made at the third round of the Six-Party Talks. On June 26, 2004, Wang Yi said that all of the parties put forward proposals and plans for the peaceful solution to the North Korean nuclear issue and characterized the meetings as "constructive, pragmatic, and substantive."[120] He announced that North Korea had expressed its willingness to give up all nuclear weapons–related programs in a "transparent way" and had offered specific plans on freezing its nuclear programs for the first time. According to Wang's statement, the working group meetings would be held to "define the scope, duration and verification as well as corresponding measures for first steps for denuclearization." The fourth round of the Six-Party Talks would take place by the end of September 2004. In spite of Wang's positive projection, the Six-Party Talks turned out to be a prolonged, difficult, and complicated way to resolve the North Korean nuclear issues. The revelation in September 2004 that South Korea had itself secretly conducted small-scale experiments in plutonium extraction in 1982 and uranium enrichment in 2000 enhanced North Korea's negotiating leverage and further complicated the prospects for the negotiations.[121] Subsequently, the South Korean government announced four principles for its nuclear policy: (1) not to develop or possess nuclear weapons; (2) to uphold the principles of nuclear transparency; (3) to comply with all international agreements and regulations on nuclear nonproliferation; and (4) to expand the scope of peaceful use of nuclear power under international supervision.[122] The United States was satisfied with South Korea's clarification, but the IAEA conducted several inspections in South Korea. At a meeting toward the end of November 2004, the IAEA Board of Governors recognized South Korea's "active cooperation" in addressing the serious concern about the secret nuclear experiments and decided not to refer the matter to the U.N. Security Council.[123]

While the Bush administration continued to express an optimistic outlook on the future of the six-party negotiations, especially after Powell's meeting with North Korean Foreign Minister Paek Nam Sun in Jakarta, Indonesia, on July 2, 2004, the Democratic Party launched a concerted criticism of Bush's policy on North Korean nuclear proliferation. As a key foreign policy adviser to Kerry, Samuel R. Berger, former national security adviser to President Clinton, accused the Bush administration of reacting "with inexplicable complacency as North Korea has crossed line after line on its way to becoming the world's first nuclear Wal-Mart."[124] Advocating a combination of a "forward-looking realism" with "moral authority," Berger proposed that if North Korea refused to accept a verifiable nationwide dismantlement of its nuclear programs in exchange for economic and political integration, the United States should join South Korea, Japan, and China in taking coercive action against North Korea. He feared that the cash-starved North Koreans might sell nuclear weapons to Al Qaeda or Hamas or radical Chechens, who would then deliver them to Washington, London, or Moscow. To be sure, Berger prescribed bitter medicine in an attempt to solve the North Korean nuclear issues.

Another outspoken critic of Bush's Korea policy, William Perry, secretary of defense in the Clinton administration, argued that the Bush administration was in a state of "paralysis" because it was "badly split" on North Korea. He expressed his confidence in the abilities of Powell, Armitage, and Kelly but criticized the hardliners, led by Cheney and Rumsfeld. He publicly declared the need for "regime change" in Washington.[125] According to Perry's estimates, North Korea produced enough plutonium to make six nuclear devices, but it had not yet perfected its highly enriched uranium project to manufacture nuclear weapons. The Democratic Party platform, adopted at its national convention in July 2004, echoed Berger's argument that "while this [Bush] Administration has been fixated on Iraq, the nuclear dangers from North Korea have multiplied." It stated: "We should maintain the Six-Party Talks, but we must also be prepared to talk directly with North Korea to negotiate a comprehensive agreement that addresses the full range of issues for ourselves and our allies. But we should have no illusions about Kim Jong Il. Any agreement must have rigorous verification and lead to complete and irreversible elimination of North Korea's nuclear weapons program." As he fell behind President Bush in public opinion polls in September 2004, Senator Kerry took the unusual step of calling a *New York Times* reporter on a Sunday to accuse the Bush administration of letting "a nuclear nightmare" develop by refusing to deal with North Korea upon entering office in 2001.[126] He also pledged to stop a further reduction of U.S. troops stationed in South Korea. As Samuel Berger and William Perry had argued, Kerry said that Bush's North Korea policy was "one of the most serious failures and challenges to the security of the United States." This theme was repeated in his debates with President Bush on September 30 and October 8, 2004. It is important to note, however, that as far as public pronouncements were concerned, the Bush administration and the Democratic Party shared the views that North Korea's nuclear armament was not acceptable, that the issue should be resolved by diplomatic means, that Kim Jong Il was not reliable, and that an effective verification regime was required to ensure the complete and irreversible dismantlement of North Korean nuclear weapons programs and facilities. The only major difference was whether the United States should exclusively rely upon the Six-Party Talks or combine multilateral and bilateral approaches toward North Korea. In the end, however, the North Korean nuclear issue had no apparent effect on the presidential election.

A STRAINED ALLIANCE

The Six-Party Talks took place in the larger context of the significant changes that the Bush administration had undertaken in its global strategy, including the restructuring of the U.S.–South Korean alliance. At the 34th Security Consultative Meeting held on December 5, 2002, in Washington, Secretary of Defense Rumsfeld and South Korean Minister of National Defense Lee Jun reaffirmed the importance of a strong U.S.–South Korean military alliance, a nuclear umbrella for South Korea, and the continuing presence of U.S. troops on the Korean Peninsula, but he agreed to adapt the alliance to changes in the global security environment. The number of U.S. troops stationed in South Korea remained at about 37,200—the third-largest deployment of American forces abroad, trailing Germany with 68,950 and Japan with 38,450 but well above Italy with 10,790 and the United Kingdom with 9,400.[127] More specifically, Rumsfeld expressed his intention to consolidate and realign U.S. troops in South Korea for the purpose of enhancing force protection, improving military readiness, and increasing efficient use of South Korean land. In effect, he explained that mutual security interests could be served best not by placing large numbers of U.S. soldiers directly in the line of fire so as to guarantee that the United States would intervene but by refining and specializing troops, weapons, and communication systems. This explanation represented the main thrust of the Rumsfeld Doctrine, which considered mobility and accuracy as key attributes of modern warfare and emphasized "new technologies" and "more lethality with fewer people."[128] He planned to make U.S. troops leaner, lighter, and faster so that they would be able to render rapid response to new global challenges, especially after the stunning terrorist attacks on September 11, 2001. The Rumsfeld plan sharply contrasted with the existing U.S. troop disposition in a "static defense" with a worldwide chain of huge bases with heavily armed ground forces pinned down in countries such as Germany, Japan, and South Korea. Adapting the alliance to Rumsfeld's goals would allow South Korea to serve as a staging area for U.S. involvement in armed conflicts elsewhere—for example, a potential military crisis over the Taiwan Straits. In a press conference on November 17, 2003, in Seoul, Rumsfeld bluntly stated: "It is capability to impose lethal power, where needed, when needed, with the greatest flexibility and with the greatest agility."[129]

In view of the heavy concentration of North Korean troops and artillery along the DMZ, the United States repudiated the old concept that U.S. troops should be deployed between the DMZ and the Han River to achieve a "tripwire effect"—the idea that in the event of North Korean armed attacks, U.S. forces would be directly targeted and hence would be automatically entangled in the military confrontations. General Leon J. LaPorte, CINCUNC and commander of USFK, deprecated the "tripwire" theory as a negative and bankrupt notion that was humiliating to soldiers of the Second Infantry Division.[130] Calling the concept of tripwire inappropriate, U.S. Ambassador to South Korea Thomas Hubbard hoped that it would not be used again. The Bush administration also reasoned that the presence of U.S. troops near the DMZ would limit the flexibility of any future American coercive military initiatives toward North Korea—such as surgical or preemptive strikes on North Korean nuclear facilities or other military installations.

It was significant that the discussions between Rumsfeld and Lee were conducted amid growing anti-American sentiments following the death of two South Korean schoolgirls struck by a U.S. military vehicle in June 2002 and the acquittals of the two U.S. soldiers responsible for their death in a military court in November. As a result, U.S. military personnel and facilities were the targets of angry protests and physical harassment. The viability of the U.S.–South Korean military alliance was threatened. In this context, Rumsfeld and Lee promised to do a better job of communicating the value of their alliance to the people of both countries. For the sake of diplomatic nicety, "both countries" were mentioned, but the main emphasis was on the people of one country, namely South Korea, where the vital importance of the bilateral alliance was under increasing scrutiny.

The two sides agreed to establish a "Future of the ROK-US Alliance Policy Initiative" (FOTA) to develop options for "modernizing and strengthening the alliance" and to find "a mutually acceptable way to relocate U.S. forces outside the city of Seoul." Included in the agenda for this initiative were the realignment of U.S. military bases to the south of the Han River, the relocation of the Yongsan Garrison from the capital, the transfer of military mission areas, including responsibility over the

Joint Security Area (JSA) within the DMZ, from the United States to South Korea, and the enhancement of U.S. military capabilities by $11 billion over three years.

On March 6, 2003, in an attempt to persuade the United States not to move its troops away from the DMZ area, South Korean Prime Minister Goh Kun raised three points to U.S. Ambassador Thomas Hubbard.[131] First, he opposed any action that would decrease the effectiveness of U.S. deterrence against North Korea. Second, he advocated to sustain the tripwire function of U.S. troops near the DMZ. Third, he preferred that the realignment of U.S. forces to the south of the Han River be delayed until the North Korean nuclear issue was satisfactorily resolved. Soon thereafter, the South Korean prime minister made an unprecedented visit to the headquarters of the U.S. Second Infantry Division in Uijongbu to show his appreciation of America's defense commitment to South Korea. He promised to provide whatever assistance the Second Division needed from the South Korean government. The main message he wanted to convey to U.S. troops was that a silent majority of South Koreans welcomed and appreciated the U.S. military presence in South Korea and hoped to make them feel comfortable.

When President Roh Moo Hyun repeated Goh's main points at the summit meeting with President Bush on May 14, 2003, the U.S. president refused to promise that the United States would not start to relocate its military bases to the south of the Han River until the North Korean nuclear issue was settled, but he confirmed America's broad commitment to "a robust forward presence" of U.S. forces on the Korean Peninsula and in the Asia-Pacific region. Flush with the initial success of the Bush Doctrine of preemptive attack in Iraq, the U.S. president was confident that this success would generate momentum for applying effective coercive diplomacy to North Korea. The two leaders agreed to consolidate U.S. forces around two key hubs and to relocate the Yongsan Garrison away from Seoul at an early date. Bush assured Roh that the realignment of U.S. bases to the south of the Han River should be pursued by "taking careful account of the political, economic and security situation on the peninsula and in Northeast Asia." They also agreed that South Korea should increase its military expenditures and expand the role of its armed forces in defending the Korean Peninsula.

At the second FOTA meeting on June 4 and 5, 2003, Richard P. Lawless (deputy assistant secretary of defense for Asia-Pacific affairs) informed Cha Young Koo (deputy minister of national defense for policy) that the United States planned to reduce about a third (12,500) of its troops stationed on the Korean Peninsula in two phases.[132] The first phase was to move U.S. forces, primarily the Second Infantry Division, from about fifteen bases near the DMZ to the Camp Casey (Tongduchon) and Camp Red Cloud (Uijongbu) areas north of the Han River during the construction of new military bases; in the second phase, the newly consolidated U.S. troops would be relocated to the two key hubs—Osan (where the 7th Air Force was stationed) and Pyongtaek (Camp Humphreys)—south of the Han River. This plan was reminiscent of the old scenario, "A Strategic Framework for the Asian Pacific Rim: Looking Toward the 21st Century" (also known as the "East Asia Strategic Initiative"), which the U.S. Department of Defense under Secretary Dick Cheney had issued on April 18, 1990. It envisaged that after a gradual reduction of U.S. troops over ten years, the South Koreans would take the lead role in their own defense. The United States had withdrawn about 7,000 Army and Air Force personnel from South Korea in 1992, but the plan's further implementation had been suspended in 1993, mainly because of the first North Korean nuclear crisis. In February 1995, the "United States Security for the East Asia Pacific Region" (also known as the "East Asia Strategic Report") announced that the United States would maintain about 100,000 forces in the Asia-Pacific region at least until the end of the twentieth century.

The George W. Bush administration's decision to move its troops to the south of the Han River was a double-edged sword for the Korean Peninsula. For South Korea, it was a wake-up call demonstrating how important the U.S. military presence near the DMZ had been to the security interests of South Korea. It challenged the Roh government to figure out not only how many additional South Korean forces and what kinds of advanced military equipment and intelligence-gathering devices would be required to fill the gap left by the departing U.S. forces from the north of the Han River, but also how to generate the enormous amount of funds for this purpose. The South Koreans also feared the possibility that the realignment or reduction of U.S. troops might have an adverse effect on foreign investments in South Korea. A group of conservative national assemblymen, mostly from the opposition Grand National Party, began a drive to collect ten million signatures to oppose the planned relocation of U.S. troops away from the DMZ.[133] For North Korea, the U.S. decision served notice that U.S. troops would no longer be "hostages" subject to manipulation by Pyongyang for its own purposes. Once removed from striking distance of North Korean artillery, the United States would gain a wider range of policy options toward North Korea. As a result, the North Koreans were concerned about the increased possibility of preemptive strikes by the United States. They assailed the planned relocation of U.S. troops as a step toward a preemptive attack against them.[134]

Following a discussion between the U.S. secretary of defense and the South Korean minister of national defense in Washington in June 2003, the third FOTA meeting on July 22 and 23 led to an agreement: even after the second phase of the U.S. military relocation was completed, the United States would still sustain a "military rotational training presence north of the Han River."[135] Learning valuable lessons from South Korea's earlier experiences with the military policies of Nixon and Carter, the confident Roh Moo Hyun, who had once advocated the withdrawal of U.S. forces from South Korea, now calmly accepted the inevitability of the U.S. decision and took a number of steps. First, he articulated a ten-year plan for self-defense capabilities in his address of August 15, 2003, the 58th anniversary of Korean liberation from Japan. He stated that the proposed realignment of the Second Infantry Division should be made in light of the North Korean nuclear issue and other circumstances on the Korean Peninsula but declared that "it is not right to leave our national security to the U.S. troops in [South] Korea for an indefinite time." He intended to help lay a firm foundation for South Korean armed forces to be fully equipped with self-reliant national defense capabilities within ten years. He reiterated his commitment to this plan on October 1, 2003, the 55th South Korean Armed Forces Day.

Second, Roh set up a committee under Prime Minister Goh Kun to develop specific measures in response to the U.S. decision. Third, he planned to increase South Korea's defense budget from 2.8% (18 trillion won, or $14.8 billion) of GDP in 2003 to about 3% in 2005 and beyond, so that South Korea would be able to modernize its armed forces and to purchase advanced military hardware (such as AWACS) from abroad. For this purpose, the South Korean government sought and obtained a U.S. commitment for more Foreign Military Sales (FMS) credits. Fourth, despite the stalemate in the Six-Party Talks and the displeasure expressed by the United States, Roh advocated a policy of peace and prosperity (his version of the sunshine policy) toward North Korea to mitigate the military tensions on the Korean Peninsula. He hoped that by sending additional troops to Iraq, he could thereby retain at least a reduced level of U.S. military presence in South Korea. Seen from Roh's perspective, there was a linkage between his commitment for South Korean troops in Iraq and the continuation of the U.S. military presence in South Korea. This view was similar to President Park's misperception in the late 1960s and early 1970s that so long as South Korean troops remained in Vietnam, the United States would not reduce or withdraw its forces from South Korea.

Armed with the Global Posture Review, which spelled out a plan to restructure the existing U.S. military bases in South Korea, Japan, and Germany and to open new bases in East European countries such as Poland, Romania, and Hungary, Rumsfeld came to Seoul in November 2003 for the first time as secretary of defense in the Bush administration.[136] On November 17, 2003, Rumsfeld and his South Korean counterpart, Cho Young Kil, expressed satisfaction with the progress made by the FOTA meetings but candidly admitted with regret that the two sides had been unable to conclude the agreements on the relocation of the Yongsan Garrison from Seoul. Viewing the huge Yongsan Garrison area from a helicopter, Rumsfeld rhetorically asked how the Americans would feel if foreign troops were occupying Central Park in New York City. He believed that the sooner the Yongsan Garrison was relocated, the easier it would be to decrease anti-American sentiment among South Koreans. In order to calm jittery feelings in South Korea, however, Rumsfeld reconfirmed the U.S. nuclear umbrella over South Korea and declared that "nothing we do will diminish our commitment to [South] Korea's security or our ability to fulfill our obligations under the Mutual Defense Treaty." Although the United States was eager to transfer ten military mission areas north of the Han River to the South Korean armed forces over three years, South Korean Minister of National Defense Cho explained that South Korea was not yet ready to assume such important responsibilities, especially that of the Joint Security Area (JSA) mission within the DMZ and the counter-fire headquarters mission. He was also concerned about the substantial amount of funds needed for military preparedness in those ten mission areas. As far as the Iraqi situation was concerned, Rumsfeld expressed his appreciation to President Roh for his decision to send additional forces to Iraq.

In his testimony before the House Committee on Armed Services on March 31, 2004, General LaPorte, CINCUNC and commander of USFK, reported that South Korea had deployed a 675-person contingent for stability operations in Iraq during 2003 and that the National Assembly had voted in February 2004 to approve the dispatch of up to 3,000 additional troops to Iraq. As mandated by the Global Posture Review, he emphasized the continuing importance of the U.S. military presence in South Korea for both "peninsula security and regional stability." More specifically, he stated that the United States and South Korea were working to enhance the combined military capabilities, to bring state-of-the-art military technologies and operational concepts to the Korean theater, strengthening the combined peninsula and regional deterrents and readiness, and that the enhancements included improved armed vehicles, air defense systems, chemical and biological defense, and advanced precision munitions. He added that North Korea must understand how serious the United States was about augmenting its military and technological capabilities to defeat any southward armed provocations.[137] The U.S. commitment to spend $11 billion (about 80% of South Korea's annual defense budget) over three years was expected to increase the lethality of U.S. military equipment, which would include advanced Patriot missiles (PAC-3), AH-64D Apache Longbow helicopters, the C-17 aircraft deploying army units equipped with Strykers (a medium-weight armored vehicle), high-speed vessels for transporting the Marine Expeditionary Forces to the Korean Peninsula, and "bunker busters" able to hit targets deep underground, which were included because of North Korea's massive underground bases, facilities, and tunnels (see table 8).

For the first five months of 2004, President Roh's political leadership remained in such disarray that he was unable to give his sustained attention to the evolving relationship between the United States and South Korea. The drama of his impeachment proceedings, instigated by a coalition of three opposition parties—the Grand National Party, the Millennium Democratic Party, and the Liberal Democratic League—and set into motion on March 12 with a National Assembly vote of 193 to 2, provided him with the fortuitous opportunity to transform the power structure in South Korea. He was accused of having violated the Election Laws. In the parliamentary elections on April 15, the new Uri Party, consisting of Roh loyalists, capitalized on the overwhelming public rejection of his impeachment and captured a majority of seats (152) in the 299-member National Assembly (see table 9). Before the elections, it had held only 47 seats in the National Assembly, which had had 273 members. The opposition Grand National Party struggled to have 121 of its members elected, largely thanks to the relentless last-ditch campaign by its new chairwoman, Representative Park Keun Hye, the eldest daughter of the late President Park Chung Hee. This number barely exceeded a third of the total members of the National Assembly, but it was enough for veto power over constitutional amendments. The other two opposition parties, the Millennium Democratic Party and the Liberal Democratic League, suffered devastating defeats by having only nine and four of their members elected, respectively. On the other hand, the Democratic Labor Party, representing a radical labor movement and espousing anti-American view, entered the National Assembly for the first time with ten members elected.[138]

The victorious members of the governing Uri Party in the National Assembly shared several distinguishing characteristics. They were for the most part young, liberal, and populist. They captured a whopping 81% (25 out of 31) of seats from the southwestern region (Kwangju and Cholla Provinces) but only 6% (4 out of 68) of seats from the southeastern region (Pusan, Taegu, Ulsan, and Kyongsang Provinces). This regional imbalance had not changed much from the time of President Kim Dae Jung. As to their political orientations, 63% of Uri Party National Assemblymen identified themselves as "progressive," but only 10% said that they were moderately conservative; 28% held middle-of-road positions.[139] When asked about the most important countries for South Korea in terms of diplomatic and trade policies, 63% named China, 26% the United States, and 2% Japan.[140] No one mentioned Russia. The Uri Party's tendency to deemphasize the United States as an ally and to recognize the growing relevance of China to South Korea's national interests was patently evident. Asked about the future status of U.S. troops stationed in South Korea, 62.1% favored an early or gradual withdrawal and 35.3% supported the status quo. The Grand National Party showed the exact opposite: 39.5% for gradual withdrawal and

60.5% for the status quo. The Democratic Labor Party demanded either early (62.5%) or gradual (37.5%) withdrawal of U.S. troops.

On the heels of the Uri Party's electoral victory, the Constitutional Court ruled on May 14 that even though President Roh had violated the Election Laws, the violation was not significant enough to warrant removing him from the presidency. Bolstered by this decision and his party's new majority in the National Assembly, the reinvigorated president intended to carry out his ambitious reform programs. In spite of his exuberant and self-confident return to the center stage of South Korean politics, he did face some potential political land mines ahead. Above all, he faced an emotionally charged, bitterly contentious, and deeply polarized populace. This polarization—by generation, region, class, ideology, and policy—pervaded all levels of political and social life in South Korea. It was particularly pronounced in South Koreans' perceptions and attitudes toward the United States and North Korea. The Roh government was criticized for its inability to resolve the controversies with China over the historical and political status of Koguryo (37 B.C.–668), one of the Three Kingdoms of Korea. The Chinese claim that Koguryo was not a Korean kingdom but rather a Chinese local government angered many South Koreans and dampened the pro-Chinese feelings among them.

The Roh government was caught up in trying to bridge the gap between the "alliance faction" (tongmaengp'a), which favored a close military and diplomatic relationship with the United States, and the "independence faction" (chajup'a), which sought to transcend South Korea's traditional dependency on the United States, to pursue a new course of independent foreign policy, and to improve inter-Korean relations. Whereas the "alliance faction" was mainly entrenched in the Ministry of Foreign Affairs and Trade as well as the Ministry of National Defense, the "independence faction" contained many of Roh's loyal aides and personal followers in the Blue House, the National Security Council, and the Uri Party. A victim of intense bureaucratic infighting, Foreign Minister Yoon Young Kwan was held responsible for the confusion and disarray among his subordinates and was forced to resign on January 15, 2004. He was replaced by Ban Ki Moon, a top-level career diplomat with extensive experience in U.S.–South Korean relations. A few diplomats identified by the National Security Council as pro-American (ch'inmi) were either reprimanded or removed from their positions. The opposition Grand National Party criticized President Roh's distinctly anti-American (panmi) orientation, and the influential conservative daily Choson Ilbo accused President Roh of conducting a "cultural revolution" to purge diplomats who had worked closely with the United States. The cleavages between the "alliance faction" and the "independence faction" in the Roh government and between the Uri Party and the Grand National Party constituted a microcosm reflecting the bipolar tendencies in society over a number of international issues, including the United States and North Korea.

Although about 5,700 U.S. troops originally designated as replacements for the Second Infantry Division in South Korea had already been diverted to Mosul, Iraq, toward the end of 2003, the Bush administration made a further decision to "rotate" the Second Brigade (about 3,600 persons) of the Second Infantry Division from South Korea to Iraq for up to one year.[141] In their telephone conversation on May 17, 2004, President Bush first congratulated President Roh on resuming his position after the two-month impeachment ordeal and then informed him that the Second Brigade was needed in Iraq to ensure a successful transfer of sovereignty from the Coalition Provisional Authority to a new interim Iraqi government on June 30, 2004. The U.S. president assured Roh that this decision in no way diminished the U.S. commitment to South Korea's defense. Roh expressed understanding and support. Bush also called Japanese Prime Minister Koizumi to inform him of the Second Brigade's deployment to Iraq.[142] A senior official of the Department of Defense made it clear on May 17 that the U.S. decision about the Second Brigade's "rotation" to Iraq was made in the larger context of the Global Posture Review and "in concert with and in coordination with our allies." Just as Bush had told Roh, this unnamed official was emphatic that this decision would result in "absolutely no diminution of our capabilities in the region and on the Korean Peninsula."[143]

Yet the news quickly generated anxiety and debate in South Korea because many South Koreans did not take the repeated American assurances at face value. The opposition Grand National Party criticized the Roh government's handling of the U.S. decision as incompetent, and other critics raised questions over the absence of prior consultations between the two governments.[144] Still others indicated that the Bush administration had displayed arrogance and unilateralism in presenting South Korea with a fait accompli, just as Nixon and Carter had done with respect to the withdrawal of U.S. troops from South Korea. The Roh government insisted that there had been sufficient prior consultations between Seoul and Washington and that no gap in South Korea's security preparedness was anticipated.[145] In response to the U.S. decision, President Roh articulated the new concept of "cooperative self-defense," which placed primary emphasis on South Korea's self-defense capabilities, while also recognizing that military cooperation with the United States played a secondary role. He developed a long-term vision to decrease South Korea's traditional dependency on U.S. defense commitments and to seek a regional collective security system, which he regarded as a universal trend.[146] He was also tempted to explore a balance of power policy toward all four major powers and to relax military tensions with North Korea. This was another manifestation of Roh's nationalistic orientation.

In a press conference on May 25, 2004, General Charles Campbell, commander of the U.S. Eighth Army and chief of staff of the CFC, indicated that the United States and South Korea would be able to undertake joint military actions not only for peacekeeping purposes in Northeast Asia but also for rapid response to worldwide armed conflicts.[147] He added that U.S. forces stationed in South Korea would function as expeditionary units to be dispatched to meet international crises. This statement was not particularly appropriate, coming as it did at a very sensitive time for U.S.–South Korean relations. The South Korean Ministry of Foreign Affairs and Trade immediately expressed its displeasure over General Campbell's unnecessary remarks and suggested that the two countries develop a written framework for prior consultations.[148] The Campbell statement, coupled with the U.S. decision to transfer a brigade of the Second Infantry Division from South Korea to Iraq, raised a discussion about revising the U.S.–South Korean Mutual Defense Treaty to make the alliance more equal and reciprocal and to specify the requirement of prior consultations in regard to any major changes in the deployment and functions of U.S. forces in South Korea. Another major agenda item for further discussion between Washington and Seoul was the question of how to transfer the CFC's wartime operational control over South Korean armed forces to the South Korean government. As the legitimate and proud leader of a sovereign state, President Roh indicated his willingness to assume this responsibility as soon as South Korea's self-defense capabilities were substantially augmented.

When the U.S. decision to withdraw a third of its troops from South Korea by the end of 2005 was publicly disclosed toward the end of May 2004, South Koreans were generally ambivalent toward the United States, but an increasing number seemed to accept the inevitability of America's diminishing role in South Korean security and diplomacy.[149] According to a nationwide opinion survey conducted in early June 2004, 52.6% of South Korean respondents said that they did not feel particularly worried about the forthcoming reduction of U.S. troops, but 47.2% said that they did.[150] The response stood in sharp contrast to the anger and apprehension of South Koreans back in the 1970s when they learned of Nixon's and Carter's decisions to reduce or withdraw U.S. troops. At least three factors accounted for this contrast. First, South Koreans had gained greater self-confidence in their ability to take care of their own national security. Second, they accepted what President Kim Dae Jung had declared after the summit meeting in June 2000—namely, there would be no more war in Korea. In the southwestern region, a traditional bastion of Kim's supporters, only 28.5% said they were worried, a figure that reached 62.4% among those in Taegu and Northern Kyongsang Province, areas that strongly opposed Kim and his protégé, President Roh Moo Hyun. As a whole, South Koreans tended to downplay the security threat from North Korea. Third, public sentiment had shifted decisively against the United States in recent years: 40.5% of South Koreans favored the proposition to abandon U.S.-centered diplomacy, only 23.9% preferred to strengthen the alliance between the United States and South Korea, and others (32.2%) wanted to maintain the status quo. As to the future of the U.S. military presence in South Korea, the responses were almost evenly divided: 50.9% supported the status quo and 48.5% favored either reduction (38.5%) or withdrawal (9.5%). In the end, however, the Bush administration accommodated the South Korean request that the United States would complete a gradual phased reduction of its troops stationed in South Korea by September 2008 and would leave a substantial portion of its military hardware behind.[151]

THE YONGSAN GARRISON

It was rather difficult for the United States and South Korea to implement the agreement between Presidents Bush and Roh Moo Hyun to move the Yongsan Garrison out of Seoul at an early date. The long history of Yongsan ("Dragon Hill") as a foreign garrison stretched back for centuries. Yongsan, a strategically important area adjacent to the Han River in Seoul, had traditionally provided a military base for occupying foreign powers, including the Mongolians in the thirteenth century and the Japanese in the sixteenth century. It served a similar purpose when the Chinese forces set up their headquarters in the area in 1882. From 1904 to 1945, the Japanese Army had a sprawling military base there.[152] During the 1945–1948 period, the U.S. military government used Yongsan as a primary center for its military and political operations. After the Korean War, the United States Forces Korea (USFK) continued to use the vast area of Yongsan, making it a virtual state within a state with all attendant facilities and privileges.

As promised during his presidential campaign in 1987, President Roh Tae Woo in early 1988 initiated an effort to move major elements of the huge U.S. military base in Yongsan away from Seoul prior to the Seoul Olympic Games, presumably because he wanted to demonstrate his nationalism and to assert independence. He met with resistance from top South Korean military leaders, however, who did not want to upset the U.S. armed forces. Moreover, the leaders of U.S. Forces Korea made extraordinary efforts to remove Kim Chong Whi, senior secretary to the president for foreign affairs and national security, from his Blue House position because he was regarded as the principal architect of Roh's initiative and because they wanted to maintain their privileges in the Yongsan Garrison.[153] After the Olympic Games, however, the United States returned part of the garrison—the Yongsan Golf

Course—to the South Korean government, and it was converted into a large city park. This was followed by a Memorandum of Agreement (MOA) and a Memorandum of Understanding (MOU), which the United States and South Korea signed in 1990 to relocate the Yongsan Garrison out of Seoul. President Roh Tae Woo agreed to assume the entire costs for this move because he did not want U.S. forces withdrawn from South Korea.

However, the negotiations for implementing the agreement stopped in mid-1993 when President Kim Young Sam determined that it would be too expensive.[154] A more important reason for this decision was to avoid disrupting the status quo of the U.S. military presence in South Korea at a time when both South Korea and the United States were preoccupied with the North Korean nuclear issue. Later on, the issue resurfaced. Aside from the Rumsfeld Doctrine for strategic flexibility, George W. Bush decided to remove the Yongsan Garrison (about 7,000 military personnel) from the capital because it had become a visible symbol and easy target for anti-American agitation in South Korea. Moreover, this highly congested and densely populated nerve center of the U.S. command and communications was vulnerable to possible attacks by North Korean artillery and missiles deployed along the DMZ. Construction of adequate anti-missile batteries in Yongsan and its vicinity was not feasible.

At the FOTA meetings, the South Koreans attempted to renegotiate the memoranda of 1990 to reduce the estimated costs (at $3 to $4 billion), to keep the headquarters of the United Nations Command (UNC) and the Combined Forces Command (CFC) in Yongsan as a symbol of the U.S. security commitment for South Korea, and to amalgamate the new accords in the Umbrella Agreement (UA) and the Implementation Agreement (IA). The UA would be subject to ratification by the South Korean National Assembly and the U.S. Senate, but the IA would be placed under the jurisdiction of the SOFA Joint Committee, cochaired by the deputy commander-in-chief of the Combined Forces Command and the director-general of the Bureau of North American Affairs in the South Korean Ministry of Foreign Affairs and Trade. While the "alliance faction" preferred to maintain the UNC and CFC headquarters in Yongsan, the young and liberal staff of the National Security Council led by Deputy Secretary General Lee Jong Suk argued for a more autonomous posture from the U.S. military presence. On January 15, 2004, President Roh made it clear that keeping the UNC headquarters in Yongsan was an "old idea."[155] His position was supported by a multitude of civic organizations in South Korea, which advocated the reduction or withdrawal of U.S. troops from South Korea.

At the Sixth FOTA meeting in Honolulu on January 17, 2004, both sides agreed to relocate the Yongsan Garrison to the Osan-Pyongtaek area (36 miles south of Seoul) by 2007, to move the UNC and CFC headquarters away from Yongsan, to leave a token contingent (less than 100 persons) for liaison and other responsibilities in Yongsan, and to maintain the Dragon Hill Hotel for use by U.S. military personnel. Satisfied with this agreement, a spokesman for the U.S. Pacific Command in Honolulu said that "the move from Yongsan will reduce our intrusive presence in the capital while enhancing our capabilities." And Lieutenant General Cha, who headed the South Korean delegation, explained: "It meets the expectations of the South Korean people. It contributes to the development of Seoul and reduces the inconvenience to Seoul residents and will help reduce anti-American sentiments."[156] The United States and South Korea at last reached a compromise on Yongsan at the Tenth FOTA meeting in Washington on July 22 and 23, 2004.[157] In the Umbrella Agreement and the Implementation Agreement, designed to supersede the 1990 MOA and MOU and the revised Land Partnership Plan (LPP), both sides agreed to complete the relocation of the U.S. military headquarters, the United Nations Command, and the Combined Forces Command (about 7,000 persons altogether) at Yongsan out of Seoul by December 2008.

SOUTH KOREAN TROOPS IN IRAQ

Another major issue that severely tested the viability of the U.S.–South Korean alliance was the war in Iraq. The Bush administration's decision in March 2003 to launch an all-out preemptive strike against Saddam Hussein's Iraq, a primary member of the "axis of evil," without the U.N. Security Council's explicit authorization, increased the burden on the already strained alliance between the United States and South Korea. The vast majority of South Koreans (about 80%), let alone their northern brethren, were opposed to the Iraq War and were afraid that it might be a prelude to an equally devastating American attack against North Korea, igniting another Korean War. An immediate challenge for President Roh Moo Hyun was finding an appropriate response to the U.S. request for South Korean troops in Iraq. It was a Catch-22 situation. If he complied with this request, he would alienate those South Koreans who had supported him in the presidential election. If, however, he honored their antiwar sentiments, he would damage the cohesion of the alliance with the United States.

After agonizing deliberations, Roh argued in his maiden speech at the National Assembly on April 2, 2003, that even if the Iraq War was without justification, it was nonetheless necessary for South Korea to dispatch noncombatant troops to Iraq for the sake of fighting against international terrorism and of upholding solidarity with the United States.[158] He added that alliance cohesion between the United States and

South Korea was important for resolving the North Korean nuclear issue peacefully and for allaying concerns among foreign investors. It was also reported that as a result of South Korea's token military participation in the Iraq War, Roh expected to obtain sizable contracts for postwar reconstruction projects. On the same day as Roh's speech, the National Assembly approved his decision by a vote of 179 to 68. Among the naysayers was a significant segment of the governing Millennium Democratic Party. Just as President Roh Tae Woo had committed a contingent of 314 noncombatant troops to the Gulf War in 1991 for medical service and air transportation, President Roh Moo Hyun sent 675 noncombatant troops (575 engineers and 100 medical personnel) to the southern Shiite city of Nasiriya. At their summit meeting on May 14, 2003, President Bush specifically thanked President Roh for his support on Iraq and welcomed South Korea's decision to deploy medical and construction units and to assist with the post-conflict humanitarian assistance and reconstruction.

As the Bush administration unexpectedly met with a fierce and dogged insurgency in Iraq during the fall of 2003, it required even further troop commitments from South Korea, Japan, and other friendly countries in support of the U.S.-led coalition's military efforts. At the 4th FOTA session in Seoul on September 3 and 4 and in a meeting between Deputy Secretary of Defense Paul Wolfowitz and Foreign Minister Yoon in Washington on September 5, the United States requested that South Korea send a light infantry unit (up to 5,000 troops) to Iraq. At this time about 60% of South Koreans opposed the dispatch of additional South Korean troops to Iraq, but 51% expressed their willingness to support it only if the U.N. Security Council passed a resolution in favor of the coalition. A number of pro-Roh members of the National Assembly and various civic organizations vehemently campaigned against the additional troop commitment to Iraq. Representative Song Yong Kil, one of Roh's loyal supporters, argued in the National Assembly on September 18 that since the Bush administration was morally bankrupt and was about to fall apart, South Korea should not commit any more soldiers in support of his unpopular Iraq policy.[159] On the other hand, Foreign Minister Yoon, along with South Korean Ambassador to the United States Han Sung Joo and other adherents of the "alliance faction," argued in favor of accommodating the U.S. request on the basis of South Korea's strategic and diplomatic considerations.[160] The National Security Council, influenced by the "independence faction," did not oppose additional troop commitment to Iraq but preferred to limit the number and functions of South Korean troops in Iraq.

On October 17 the U.N. Security Council unanimously passed Resolution 1511, which supported the timetable for cooperation between the Coalition Provisional Authority and the Governing Council of Iraq, recognized the "vital role" of the

United Nations in Iraq, authorized the formation of a "multinational force under unified command," and urged U.N. member states to assist the Iraqi reconstruction effort. The Roh government quickly took advantage of this event to announce that South Korea would send additional troops to Iraq.[161] The new Security Council resolution generated an appreciable upsurge (73.9%) in South Korean support for this announcement. After all, this had not been an easy decision for Roh because he would have to find ways to bear the new expenditures and because of the risk of losing soldiers, the accusations from North Korea, and the burden of public outcry. A spokesman for the South Korean president attempted to defuse critics when he said that "the [South] Korea-U.S. relationship, the national interest, and the recent passage of U.N. resolutions were all considered in making the decision."[162] Just as he had done in April 2003, President Roh took other important factors into consideration, such as the necessity for U.S.–South Korean cohesion to resolve the North Korea nuclear issue, the universal imperative to fight against international terrorism and weapons of mass destruction, and the need to forestall any precipitous reduction or withdrawal of U.S. forces deployed in South Korea. It was helpful to Roh that Japanese Prime Minister Koizumi decided to send Japanese troops to Iraq despite strong popular resistance. The Japanese decision prompted a feeling that "if the Japanese can do it, then we should do it as well" for many South Koreans. If, however, Japan had turned down the U.S. request, it would have given added ammunition to the opponents of Roh's decision.

At a meeting in Bangkok on October 20, 2003, President Roh told President Bush that in response to the U.S. request, he had decided to send additional South Korean troops to Iraq after considering the importance of the U.S.–South Korean alliance and South Korea's national interest. He added that "the size, type and form of the troops as well as the timing of the dispatch will be decided by taking into account public opinion, the result of the survey team and the characteristics and capability of the [South] Korean military forces." After a series of discussions at the National Security Council, the South Korean cabinet formally approved a plan to send 3,000 additional troops (1,600 engineers and medical personnel and 1,400 security forces ready for combat only in self-defense) to Iraq as early as April 2004. The plan made it clear that the South Korean troops would not be directly engaged in military operations but would assume the primary responsibility of assisting efforts for reconstruction and peace in Iraq.[163] On February 13, 2004, the National Assembly approved the plan to send additional troops to Iraq by a vote of 155 to 50 with 7 abstentions.[164] A majority of members of the governing Uri Party (consisting of pro-Roh loyalists who had left the Millennium Democratic Party) and the opposition Grand National

Party supported it, but most members of the opposition Millennium Democratic Party voted against it. About 52,000 South Korean soldiers volunteered to serve in Iraq, in part because of the substantial financial benefits and opportunities for military promotion.[165] The Roh government sent the first contingent of 3,000 military personnel to the northern city of Irbil in August 2004. The Bush administration greatly appreciated President Roh's difficult decision.

Now that the hotly contested presidential election in the United States is behind us, it remains to be seen whether President Bush can take bold and imaginative steps to restore a mutually beneficial and trustworthy framework of military alliance, economic cooperation, and diplomatic support with South Korea and to improve its relations with North Korea during his second term of office in any significant way. Reelected by a significant number of popular votes (51% vs. 48% for Senator Kerry) and bolstered by the enhanced Republican majorities in the U.S. Congress, he may be tempted to pursue a more confident, assertive, and tough-minded approach toward the North Korean nuclear issue than before. The continuing presence of Dick Cheney and Donald Rumsfeld, the replacement of Colin Powell by Condoleezza Rice as secretary of state, and the promotion of neoconservative and hardline officials in the National Security Council are expected to maintain a strong voice in the Bush administration advocating regime change in North Korea despite the departure of Paul Wolfowitz. This development in President Bush's foreign policy and national security advisers stood in sharp contrast with President Roh Moo Hyun's determination to avoid military confrontation on the Korean Peninsula and to seek a role of leadership in resolving the North Korean nuclear issue. In a speech before the World Affairs Council of Los Angeles on November 12, 2004, for example, President Roh served notice to the Bush administration that use of military means against North Korea was not acceptable under any circumstances. Since North Korea's pursuit of nuclear weapons was not an instrument to attack others or assist terrorist groups but merely an attempt to maintain self-defense, he argued, the issue could be settled peacefully by providing security assurances to North Korea.[166] On the sidelines of the APEC conference on November 20, 2004, in Santiago, Chile, Bush and Roh cobbled together a semblance of agreement on a peaceful resolution of the North Korean nuclear issue via the Six-Party Talks, but it is possible that the United States and South Korea will encounter a further policy cleavage with respect to North Korea in the years to come. After having separate meetings with Roh, Koizumi, Putin, and Hu Jintao, President Bush stated: "Five APEC members are working to convince North Korea to abandon its pursuit of nuclear weapons, and

I can report to you today, having visited with the other nations involved in that collaborative effort, that the will is strong, that the effort is united and the message is clear to Mr. Kim Jong Il: Get rid of your nuclear weapons programs."[167] He was eager to demonstrate a broad coalition of diplomatic forces on North Korea, but how strong that coalition would be or how long it would hold remained uncertain.

If the United States, South Korea, North Korea, and the other participants in the Six-Party Talks, are serious about reaching a realistic and comprehensive compromise over the major issues in the region, it appears that a certain set of reciprocal conditions and obligations should ultimately be satisfied. Chief among them are North Korea's agreement to dismantle all nuclear weapons programs and facilities in a complete and verifiable way, to join the NPT and the Missile Technology Control Regime (MTCR), and to sign and implement the international conventions on chemical and biological weapons and on international terrorism. In return, the United States should offer a legally binding commitment for negative security assurance in the form of a peace treaty, nonaggression pact, or multilateral agreement; lift economic sanctions (with exceptions for strategically sensitive items); exchange liaison offices and take steps for diplomatic normalization; consider steps to resume the LWR construction project, to deliver heavy fuel oil, or to provide alternate energy; and remove North Korea from the U.S. Department of State's list of state sponsors of terrorism. For this purpose the precedents set by Libya, Ukraine, and South Africa will be useful.[168] The other members of the Six-Party Talks—South Korea, China, Japan, and Russia—may join in efforts to address North Korea's security concerns, economic needs, and diplomatic interests. In particular, South Korea can play a pivotal role in improving relations between the United States and North Korea and organize a massive aid package similar to the Marshall Plan for North Korea.[169] Japan may eventually agree to normalize diplomatic relations with North Korea and to render important economic assistance. In addition, regional and international organizations, including the Asian Development Bank, the ASEAN Regional Forum, the European Union, the International Atomic Energy Agency, the International Monetary Fund, the World Bank, and the United Nations, will be helpful to the promotion of peace and prosperity on the Korean Peninsula.

The resumption of the Six-Party Talks toward the end of July 2005 after a thirteen-month hiatus improved the prospects for resolving the North Korean nuclear issue by diplomatic means. After a series of bilateral and multilateral negotiations, including U.S.-North Korean contacts, the delegations of the Six-Party Talks were able to issue a six-point joint statement in Beijing on September 19, 2005.[170] While North Korea committed to abandoning "all nuclear weapons and existing nuclear programs" and returning "at an early date" to the Nuclear Nonproliferation Treaty and to IAEA safeguards, the United States affirmed that it had no intention to attack or invade North Korea with nuclear or conventional weapons. The United States and North Korea agreed to respect each other's sovereignty, to exist peacefully together, and to take steps for normalizing their relations. Since North Korea insisted on its right to a peaceful nuclear energy program, the other five parties expressed their respect to this right, agreed to discuss "at an appropriate time" the subject of providing light-water nuclear reactor to North Korea, and stated their willingness to provide energy assistance to North Korea. In particular, South Korea reaffirmed its proposal to offer two million kilowatts of electric power to North Korea. The joint statement also addressed other issues—such as normalizing relations between Japan and North Korea, promoting economic cooperation in the fields of energy, trade, and investment, negotiating a permanent peace mechanism on the Korean Peninsula, and advancing security cooperation in Northeast Asia. Even though the joint statement, as a compromise of diverse interests and positions, contained a number of ambiguous elements susceptible to conflicting interpretations, it was an important document that established a set of principles for dealing with the North Korean nuclear questions and other related matters. Yet a long and tortuous road for implementing these principles seemed to lie ahead.

If the joint statement is not faithfully carried out in a timely and satisfactory manner, the United States, South Korea, and other concerned countries are likely to face an extremely grave dilemma. As far as the U.S. government is concerned, there will be definite pressure to punish North Korea economically and diplomatically, as it did toward India and Pakistan following their respective nuclear explosions. It will be difficult, although not impossible, for the United States to muster enough support at the U.N. Security Council, especially from the veto-equipped Chinese and Russian delegations, for passing the comprehensive sanctions resolution against North Korea, which would resemble the draft resolution formulated by the Clinton administration in June 1994. The United States will not completely rule out the option of preemption as the last resort but will be constrained by a combination of factors, including the Iraqi experience, South Korea's likely reservations, and the devastating consequences of North Korea's retaliation. Another option available to the United States (and Japan) is to refine, expand, and strengthen the Proliferation Security Initiative (PSI), a multinational strategy to interdict shipments of WMD materiel and contraband that originate from, or are destined for, nations of "proliferation concern," notably North Korea, but its scope, legality, and effectiveness have not yet been tested. The South Korean government supports the PSI's objectives but is reluctant to join it because North Korea would view the PSI operations as a threat to its national security, which might hinder the goal of nuclear disarmament on the

Korean Peninsula.[171] China and Russia may undermine the PSI with respect to the Korean Peninsula. Moreover, there is no assurance that a nuclear-armed North Korea would behave like China and Russia do—i.e., that it would not use its nuclear weapons (and ballistic missiles) as an instrument to threaten or blackmail South Korea, Japan, or the United States.[172] It is likely that the United States will continue to face a difficult and complex challenge from North Korea's persistent defiance and South Korea's nationalistic assertiveness.

CHAPTER SEVEN

Prospects

Once, in a discussion of the complexities of international relations, George F. Kennan suggested that there was not only "nothing final in point of time, nothing not vulnerable to the law of change," but also "nothing absolute in itself."[1] He added: "There is no friendship without some element of antagonism; no enmity without some rudimentary community of interests; no benevolent intervention which is not also in part an injury; no act of recalcitrance, no seeming evil, from which—as Shakespeare put it—some 'soul of goodness' may not be distilled." This astute observation is, mutatis mutandis, just as applicable to the sixty-year record of U.S. relations with the Korean Peninsula. Indeed, nothing in this relationship has been absolute, final, or static. It has continued, but it has also been subject to the "law of change" and the vagaries of fluidity. Friendship, enmity, antagonism, injury, intervention, recalcitrance, evil, common interest, and even the "soul of goodness" have all been part of America's complicated interactions with South Korea and North Korea.

CONTINUITY AND CHANGE

As far as the goals of U.S. policy toward Korea are concerned, I am impressed by the remarkable degree of continuity since the end of the Korean War. In NSC 170/1 ("U.S. Objectives and Courses of Action in Korea," November 1953), the Mutual Defense Treaty with South Korea, and a number of bilateral joint statements, the United States consistently upheld its primary interest in maintaining an effective containment system against North Korea and also articulated its secondary interests—to cultivate cooperative relations between Washington and Seoul, to assist economic development and commercial activities in South Korea, to support relaxation of tensions between both Koreas, and to bring about the unification of Korea with a free, independent, and representative government friendly toward the United States. Although the United States did not regard promoting human rights and liberal democracy as a central goal of its policy toward South Korea, it nonetheless encouraged the process of political liberalization as much as it could, both for its intrinsic merits and for the sake of enhancing the legitimacy, stability, and acceptability of the South Korean government, especially in the eyes of the U.S. Congress and attentive American groups. Yet whenever there was an actual or imagined conflict between protecting South Korea against possible North Korean aggression and promoting human rights and democratic principles, the United States by and large chose its commitment to protect South Korean national security.

What is especially notable, however, is the extent to which the United States has adapted the relative priorities and nuances of its goals to the changing conditions in America, in the Korean Peninsula, and in the global and regional systems. While the paramount importance of containment and deterrence has been a largely constant factor in their alliance system, the United States and South Korea at times diverged in their perceptions of threats and military preparedness. For instance, their disagreement over the appropriate number and locations of U.S. troops stationed in South Korea manifested itself during several administrations. Guided by the Guam Doctrine, President Nixon unilaterally decided to withdraw one of the two U.S. army divisions from South Korea. Later on, in the context of the "Vietnam Syndrome" and President Park's violations of human rights, President Carter announced a plan to withdraw the remaining U.S. ground forces from South Korea, but he was eventually persuaded not to carry out his plan. The George W. Bush administration, too, modified its intention to lower the U.S. military profile in South Korea mainly because of the threat of North Korean nuclear armament. Most recently, the two allies became engaged in difficult negotiations to reduce the number of U.S. troops by a third, to relocate the Second Infantry Division south of the Han River, and to move the Yongsan Garrison away from Seoul by 2008. The structure of the bilateral alliance is headed toward a sweeping change in the next few years.

In order to achieve its goals in Korea, the United States used several methods and tactics to exert its influence over South Korea's domestic and foreign policies. Most prevalent among them was a system of economic reward and punishment. So long as South Korea substantially depended on America's economic assistance and commercial cooperation throughout the 1950s and the early part of the 1960s, it was difficult for Presidents Rhee and Park to ignore Washington's preferences and recommendations. The United States was indeed indispensable in rehabilitating South

Korea's devastated economic system after the Korean War. The United States was more than generous in opening its domestic markets to further South Korea's export-led economic development strategy. Once South Korea achieved its phenomenal rate of economic growth, graduated from U.S. aid programs, and began to compete against U.S. industries in the late 1960s and 1970s, however, a series of trade disputes erupted between the two allies. For a while, economic issues threatened to overwhelm security concerns as the central issue for bilateral relations, especially during the 1980s and early 1990s. To be sure, the U.S. ability to use economic means as leverage over South Korea declined in proportion to the latter's rapid advancement in economic, technological, and commercial capabilities. The Clinton administration's success in rejuvenating the U.S. economy and in regaining its global dominance in the second half of the 1990s considerably decreased the saliency of the trade disputes between the United States and South Korea. Hence the overall state of bilateral economic relations came to be "normalized," albeit with a mixture of cooperation and conflict coming into play. The United States also needed South Korea's cooperation in promoting the APEC and the WTO and in discouraging a movement to form a regional trading bloc in Asia, such as an East Asian Economic Group, that would exclude the United States.

The more authoritarian the South Korean leaders were, the more support they attempted to obtain from the United States so that they could enhance their legitimacy both domestically and internationally. This political requirement, combined with military and economic dependencies, provided the United States with still more leverage, which it could then use to influence domestic issues in South Korea. Yet the U.S. attempts to improve human rights and to encourage democratic processes in South Korea met with mixed results. On the positive side, the United States was instrumental in urging President Rhee to step down in 1960, in forcing General Park to hold a popular presidential election in 1963, in saving Kim Dae Jung's life in 1980 and 1981, and in ensuring that President Chun fulfilled his commitment for a peaceful transfer of power in 1987 and 1988. Yet the United States also met resistance: it was unsuccessful in undoing the coups d'état in 1961 and 1979 and the harsh repressive measures imposed by President Park in 1973 and 1979. The United States gradually came to realize the diminishing effectiveness of intervening in South Korea's domestic affairs. Critics both in the United States and South Korea, however, continued to accuse American leaders of condoning or supporting South Korea's authoritarian governments. Ever since the inauguration of President Roh Tae Woo in 1988, the topic of human rights in South Korea has no longer been high on the agenda for high-level bilateral discussions. On the other hand, Republicans in the U.S. Congress have in recent years led a legislative maneuver to raise the topic of human rights in dealing with North Korea.[2] This confrontational approach sharply contrasted with that of Presidents Kim Dae Jung and Roh Moo Hyun, who have been reluctant to criticize the flagrant violations of human rights in North Korea lest they antagonize Kim Jong Il and in doing so jeopardize efforts for inter-Korean reconciliation.

As discussed in chapter 1, the competing theoretical or philosophical paradigms such as realism and liberalism serve to characterize general tendencies, but they do not fully describe the varying nuances in the multifaceted U.S. policy toward Korea. No American administration always and consistently applied a straightforward one-sided paradigm to the multitude of foreign policy issues. Every president drew on a combination of different paradigms to address specific issues and presided over the shifting balance between and among different bureaucracies. As John J. Mearsheimer suggests in *The Tragedy of Great Power Politics*, the United States often articulated its policies in liberal rhetoric but acted in accordance with realist logic. "The United States," he concludes, "speaks one way and acts another."[3] Nonetheless, it is possible to discern realist or liberal tendencies in the manner in which the United States dealt with Korean issues. One can recognize a change in the general theoretical orientations from the Clinton administration to the George W. Bush administration. However, both administrations actually shared a fair area of commonality or continuity in the distribution of bureaucratic views and positions. In fact, coming from the two divergent schools of thought and politics, Henry A. Kissinger and Joseph S. Nye Jr. share a principal prescription for U.S. foreign policy in the twenty-first century. In *Does America Need a Foreign Policy?* Kissinger, the architect of Nixon's foreign policy, states that "America's ultimate challenge is to transform its power into moral consensus, promoting its values not by imposition but by their willing acceptance in a world, that, for all its seeming resistance, desperately needs enlightened leadership."[4] In *The Paradox of American Power*, Nye, a leading foreign policy theorist in the Clinton administration, proposes that if the United States wants to remain strong, Americans, in addition to military and economic power, should pay attention to their "soft power." He explains: "A country may obtain the outcomes it wants in world politics because other countries want to follow it, admiring its values, emulating its example, aspiring to its level of prosperity and openness. In this sense, it is just as important to set the agenda in world politics and attract others as it is to force them to change through the threat or use of military or economic weapons. This aspect of power—getting others to want what you want—I call soft power."[5] In the aftermath of the Iraq War, however, it will be a daunting task for the United States to claim moral consensus, to exercise its enlightened leadership, to exert its soft power in world affairs, and to spread the imperative of procedural democracy in the world.

A major change in U.S. policy toward Korea took place in the early 1990s when the United States faced the new responsibility of managing the intricate triangular relations among the United States, South Korea, and North Korea. During the cold war, the United States and South Korea had been united in a structure of "marriage," in which North Korea was the "odd man out," without any cooperative relations with the other two players.[6] The Clinton administration, however, embarked on a period of "partial engagement" (1993–97), in which the United States carried out a constructive dialogue with North Korea about its nuclear programs, but South Korea under President Kim Young Sam was unable to make a breakthrough in its hostile relationship with North Korea. The Four-Party Talks were instituted to stimulate direct contact between the two Korean governments and to provide a forum where they could discuss a new mechanism for permanent peace on the Korean Peninsula. Neither objective was realized in the end, however. The United States attempted to mediate the differences between Seoul and Pyongyang, but its efforts produced little in the way of tangible consequences.

The development of President Kim Dae Jung's "sunshine policy" toward North Korea led to a period of "full engagement" (1998–2000), in which both South Korea and the United States, while maintaining the excellent relationship between them, were involved in a wide range of discussions and exchanges with North Korea. The inter-Korean summit meeting in June 2000 ushered in a new era for peaceful coexistence and mutual support. As discussed in chapter 6, the advent of the Bush administration's hardline policy toward North Korea to some extent dampened the euphoria for inter-Korean cooperation and reconciliation, but it has not completely impeded the nationalistic fervor, joint economic projects, and cultural exchange programs between Seoul and Pyongyang introduced under Presidents Kim Dae Jung and Roh Moo Hyun. A significant role reversal became apparent during the Six-Party Talks: it was now the South Korean government that tried to narrow the policy gap between the United States and North Korea. The compelling internal logic of the growing rapport within the Korean Peninsula is expected to continue to manifest itself, even if it comes at the expense of U.S. interests and preferences.

Viewed from the perspective of Washington's current national interests, it would be a worst-case scenario if South Korea and North Korea were to improve their relations to the extent that they would form a "marriage" and compel the United States to disengage itself from the Korean Peninsula as the "odd man out." Another undesirable scenario would be a "unit veto" system, where all three players—the United States and both Koreas—refuse to cooperate with each other. The best scenario, however, would be a very cordial and positive "ménage à trois," in which all three countries cooperate with each other. So long as the United States and North

Korea fail to come to a fundamental resolution of several pending issues, including disputes over weapons of mass destruction, the trilateral relationship will hover between the best and worst scenarios, at least for a while. If the United States and North Korea remain antagonistic to each other, South Korea may then become a pivotal player in a "romantic triangle," in which it can enjoy good relations with both the United States and North Korea and can assume the crucial role of reducing the hostilities between the two protagonists.

Over the past six decades, South Korea has been able to manage the unmistakable changes in its patron-client relationship with the United States. After having had no choice but to endure its status as a hapless, weak, poor, vulnerable, and burdensome client of its dominant and intrusive U.S. patron through the end of the 1960s, South Korea began to take a more independent, confident, and resourceful role in foreign affairs during the 1970s and 1980s. As South Korea continued to expand its economic and technological capabilities, to consolidate its liberal democratic foundations, and to assume an active and versatile diplomatic position at the end of the twentieth century and the beginning of the twenty-first, it transformed its "special" relationship with the United States into a "normal" interdependent partnership. Gone are the days when South Korea's domestic politics and foreign policy were merely a dependent variable of U.S. policy preferences and demands. The tensions, disputes, and misperceptions that South Korea has experienced with the United States in recent years can be viewed as a function of their extraordinary intimacy as well as transitional by-products of the structural transformation in their relationship. Yet both South Korea and the United States would be well advised to make a more serious effort to understand each other than they have yet done. Most important, they must recognize that domestic factors in each country will loom larger as a determinant of their military, diplomatic, and economic relations.

In general, South Korean policymakers have been highly intelligent and technically competent in dealing with their American counterparts. It is notable that a large number of top-level South Korean officers, including ministers of foreign affairs and ambassadors to Washington, who were directly involved in the management of U.S.-Korean relations, were educated in American institutions of higher learning. They had more experience and knowledge of the United States than their American counterparts did of Korea. In a few specific instances, however, South Korean leaders have tended to underestimate or misread important warning signals of forthcoming conflicts with the United States, to interject their own parochial or emotional reactions, to hazard risky approaches, and to emphasize the importance of feelings and appearance rather than focusing on substantive policy issues.[7] These tendencies threaten to put South Korea at a disadvantage when balancing domestic issues with more global concerns. For instance, containing the rise of anti-American senti-ments, particularly among young South Koreans, will be a delicate undertaking in which South Korean leaders must accommodate and represent legitimate popular concerns in a democratic system while at the same time guarding against upsetting the cooperative framework of the U.S.–South Korean friendship. As South Korea continues to develop as a mature and confident state and to solidify its international status as a rising "middle power," it is expected that its nationalistic aspirations will grow and that it will gain more policy autonomy in charting a new course for mili-tary and political relations with the United States and in dealing with the processes of reconciliation and cooperation with North Korea.

It is also possible that U.S. relations with North Korea could remain locked in a state of rhetorical hostility and diplomatic stalemate for some time despite an initial agreement at the Six-Party Talks. If North Korea is persuaded or coerced into dis-mantling its nuclear programs altogether as the Union of South Africa and Libya did or exchanging nuclear disarmament for security assurances and economic promises as Ukraine and Kazakhstan did, it is distinctly possible that the United States, in co-operation with South Korea and other interested countries, would indeed agree to consider a "bold approach" for a peaceful and comprehensive settlement of all major issues with North Korea. As a result, normalization of diplomatic and economic re-lations between the United States and North Korea might ensue, after which Amer-ica's two-Korea policy could be instituted.

If, however, North Korea, despite its isolated and impoverished conditions, refuses to dismantle its nuclear weapons programs in a verifiable and irreversible way and de-cides to test its nuclear devices, to lift a moratorium on ballistic missile tests, or to ex-port nuclear technology and ballistic missiles to other countries, the United States will seriously consider seeking a punitive economic and diplomatic sanctions resolu-tion against North Korea at the U.N. Security Council and resorting to coercive diplo-macy with credible military maneuvers. If conflicts further escalate (especially after a resolution of the Iraqi question), the United States may even be tempted to invoke the doctrine of preemptive attack against North Korea, despite President Bush's repeated promises not to invade North Korea. In this unlikely sequence of events, the Korean Peninsula would be engulfed in another tragic and devastating armed conflict.

INTER-KOREAN RELATIONS

It is most likely that future U.S. policy toward Korea will depend more upon the status of inter-Korean relations than upon other factors, such as internal conditions in the United States and both Koreas or the shifting global and regional balance of power. I assume that in the foreseeable future, the relationship between Seoul and Pyongyang will follow one of four contrasting scenarios—status quo, absorption, conflict escalation (war), or peaceful cooperation.[8] Each scenario is expected to present both a challenge and an opportunity for the United States and the other major powers interested in the Korean Peninsula.

Status Quo

In spite of the historic summit meeting between Kim Dae Jung and Kim Jong Il in June 2000 and the subsequent unfolding of closer relations between South Korea and North Korea, it is possible that no substantive or irreversible change in the status quo will be achieved in inter-Korean relations for some time. This scenario envisages a number of distinctive developments. First, both Korean governments would hesitate to implement in full, both in letter and in spirit, the Basic Agreement, the Joint Declaration on the Denuclearization of the Korean Peninsula, the Joint Statement issued by both Kims in June 2000, and other intergovernmental agreements. Second, the two sides would be either unwilling or unable to allow the free exchange of persons, goods, and ideas across the border and to take decisive steps for removing the DMZ. Third, no tangible progress would be made in improving Korea's security environment; the Six-Party Talks on North Korean nuclear issues have yet to bear fruit.

There is no doubt that the zero-sum mentality, a legacy of the Korean War as well as the cold war confrontation in general, still lingers among the influential political forces in Seoul and Pyongyang. Moreover, neither side is completely free from the logic of realist or neorealist orientations. Even though both sides can expect to receive absolute gains from cooperation, they are nonetheless reluctant to engage in a wide range of mutually beneficial cooperative activities because of their concern about relative gains in an essentially anarchic situation that lacks central authority or an enforcement mechanism. Kenneth Waltz states: "When faced with the possibility of cooperating for mutual gain, states that feel insecure must ask how the gain will be divided. They are compelled to ask not 'Will both of us gain?' but 'Who will gain more?' If an expected gain is to be divided, say, in the ratio of two to one, one state may use its disproportionate gain to implement a policy intended to damage or destroy the other. Even the prospect of large absolute gains for both parties does not elicit their cooperation so long as each fears how the other will use its increased capabilities."[9] So long as North Korea and South Korea cannot overcome the dilemma of relative gains, especially in regard to national security issues, it will be hard for both partners to pursue a genuine policy of mutual cooperation.

In particular, the North Koreans seem to fear that even if cooperation with South Korea were to give them absolute gains, it might tilt the inter-Korean balance in favor of South Korea, increase North Korea's economic dependency on South Korea, reveal to North Koreans that South Korea in fact is enjoying economic prosperity and is a vibrant democracy, and force North Korea to accept an open-door policy and economic reforms more rapidly than it would like. As far as security issues are concerned, the North Koreans prefer to deal primarily with the United States, bypassing South Korea altogether, and in the process they hope to disrupt the sense of cohesion in the U.S.–South Korean military alliance and to undermine South Korea's economic and diplomatic advantages. The Roh Moo Hyun government, however, is committed to transcend the disputes over military matters and to improve functional relations with North Korea. Roh's critics in the United States and South Korea contend that the South Korean government is vulnerable to shrewd tactical manipulation by North Korea and that North Korea's fundamental hostility toward South Korea has not changed.[10] Lee Hong Koo, who had served as South Korea's prime minister, minister of national unification, and ambassador to the United States, asserted that the North Koreans exercise complete control over the timing, scope, and speed of inter-Korean relations and implied that they could reverse the course of inter-Korean cooperation at will.[11] The status quo scenario in inter-Korean relations is not necessarily adverse to the national interests of the United States and other major powers. Even though the United States has committed itself to a policy of peaceful Korean unification, there is no compelling reason for it to take any serious initiative in breaking up the status quo or replacing it with another formulation except for the nuclear threat.

Absorption

The dire food and energy shortages that North Korea suffered in the late 1990s and early 2000s gave rise to the possibility of Korean unification occurring as a result of the presumed disintegration of North Korea—in a process resembling German unification, South Korea would absorb a crumbling North Korea. This scenario would most likely appeal to hardline realists in South Korea and the United States, as it would change the North Korean regime and thus remove the vexing problems of nuclear proliferation and conflict escalation on the Korean Peninsula once and for all. The "moderate" or pragmatic forces in South Korea and in the United States argue, however, that this scenario may not be the best long-term solution with regard to the balance of power in Northeast Asia and a unified Korea.

A number of U.S. government officials, military leaders, and policy analysts have openly questioned the viability of the Kim Jong Il regime.[12] Aside from the structural deficiencies of its centrally planned economic system, North Korea suffered from the constraints of the *chuche* (self-reliance) ideology and the heavy burden of defense expenditures. The collapse of the Soviet Union and the East European socialist regimes removed an important source of aid for and trade with North Korea. Natural calamities added a strain on the already depleted economic conditions of North Korea. As discussed in chapter 5, CIA Director John Deutch asserted that North Korea would find it harder to insulate its armed forces from worsening economic problems and that food shortages spreading to front-line military units could undermine regime stability. For the same reason General Gary E. Luck, commander of USFK, stated that North Korea would either collapse or take aggressive actions against South Korea in a desperate attempt to divert attention from its predicament. In an article in *Foreign Affairs*, Nicholas Eberstadt also argued that North Korea was more likely to implode as it slid down the path of greater poverty and increased military threat.[13] He predicted that the early absorption of North Korea by South Korea would be beneficial in the economic and military fields and that a free, democratic, and unified Korea would become a "force for stability and prosperity" in the region. Another analyst, Edward A. Olsen, wrote that it was only a matter of time before North Korea would cease to exist because of the incremental erosion of its economy, the enervation of its polity, and the obsolescence of its military.[14] Moreover, Kim Kyung Won, formerly South Korean ambassador to the United Nations and the United States, suggested that North Korean reformers or military hardliners might force Kim Jong Il out of office or that a coalition of other elements might do so because of their judgment that Kim was incompetent.[15]

Contrary to the collapsists' predictions are those who give more credit to the resilience and resourcefulness of the Kim Jong Il regime and believe that North Korea would not fall apart so easily. Selig Harrison maintained that because of a number of factors, North Korea was not likely to implode or explode anytime soon.[16] Chief among these factors were the presence of a quasi-religious nationalist mystique, a repressive totalitarian discipline, the Confucian ethos, a tradition of political centralization and obedience to authority, memories of a fratricidal war, a permanent siege mentality, and tight insularity. He favored a "soft-landing" scenario — a gradual process of Korea's peaceful unification in which neither side would be swallowed up by the other. While Han S. Park singled out the *chuche* ideology as a source of North Korea's system maintenance, Bruce Cumings added the pragmatic shrewdness of North Korea's foreign policy after the cold war, the desperate survival strategies Pyongyang undertook, and the anticolonial and revolutionary origins of this regime.[17] And Marcus Noland, a noted specialist of North Korean economy, suggested that North Korea would neither reform nor collapse but would manage to muddle through.[18]

The debate over the collapse of North Korea has been spurred in large part by its economic crises. Historically, however, economic difficulties alone have rarely been the direct cause of political instability in Leninist states. The massive famines that struck the Soviet Union and China in the 1930s and 1950s, respectively, did not endanger the regimes of Joseph Stalin and Mao Zedong. It is instructive to remember that by choosing isolation and autonomy, Sparta kept its citizens poor and powerless and stimulated few appetites, whether material or political, domestic or foreign, but still posed a formidable threat to the democratic and prosperous Athens and its allies. History has shown that popular unrest or political opposition is not always generated by poverty. In his 1856 book *The Old Regime and the Revolution*, Alexis de Tocqueville observed:

> Revolutions are not always brought about by a gradual decline from bad to worse. Nations that have endured patiently and almost unconsciously the most overwhelming oppression, often burst into rebellion against the yoke the moment it begins to grow lighter. The regime, which is destroyed by a revolution, is almost always an improvement on its immediate predecessor, and experience teaches that the most critical moment for bad governments is the one which witnesses their first steps toward reform. A sovereign who seeks to relieve his subjects after a long period of oppression is lost, unless he be a man of great genius. Evils, which are patiently endured when they seem inevitable, become intolerant when once the idea of escape from them is suggested. The very redress of grievances throws new light on those which are left untouched, and adds fresh poignancy to their smart: if the pain be less the patient's sensibility is greater.[19]

According to Tocqueville, the years prior to the French Revolution (1789) had not seen a declining standard of living but rather increasing prosperity. This prosperity, however, did not lead to greater happiness and tranquility. He wrote: "Measured with the increase of prosperity in France, men's minds grow more restless and uneasy; public discontent is embittered; the hatred of the old institutions increases. The nation visibly tends toward revolution." He found that "those districts where progress makes the greatest strides are precisely those which are to be the chief theatre of the Revolution." Tocqueville's thoughts are worth considering in the case of North Korea because they contradict the hypothesis that poverty would hasten its collapse. His modern-day disciples argue that "relative deprivation" amid prosperity may become the culprit behind popular unrest, as demonstrated in the Tiananmen Square incident of 1989.

Even though the neoconservative leaders in the United States prefer to see regime change in North Korea, it is conceivable that the U.S. government will encounter several serious problems in the event of absorption of North Korea by South Korea. Extrapolating from the experience of German unification, the United States fears that keeping a viable Korean economic system afloat after unification will be too expensive and that its economic interests in a unified Korea could suffer as a result. Another serious concern is that a precipitous unification of Korea may have a destabilizing effect on the balance of power in the Asia-Pacific region. A RAND Corporation study concluded that the unification process in Korea would prove far more tumultuous in the region than German unification did in Europe: "The emergence of a unified, economically strong Korea could lead to a new era of competition . . . centered on the possible advent of intense economic and diplomatic rivalry with Japan and the revival of historical suspicions toward China and Russia. Instability would become all the more likely if a unified Korea saw the need to obtain a nuclear weapons capability."[20] Whereas Germany after unification was firmly anchored in and integrated with the European Union and NATO, a unified Korea is likely to be a freestanding entity with no effective structure of regional economic integration or collective security. It is also possible that a unified Korea even under Seoul's leadership might adopt an excessively nationalistic international outlook, an unstable foreign and military policy, a protectionist economic posture, or an authoritarian political system, all of which would counter the traditional goals of U.S. policy in Korea. If, however, North Korea succeeds in dividing, weakening, and absorbing South Korea by means of a shrewd and effective united front strategy, it would, of course, present a grave challenge to U.S. interests not only in Korea but also in the region as a whole.[21]

Conflict Escalation

If the hardline North Korean forces assume the upper hand in making policy decisions and fail to prevent further deterioration of their economic performance and international status, one cannot completely rule out the possibility of their attempting to unify Korea by military means. In this connection it is useful to note that North Korea invaded South Korea, unilaterally nullified the Korean Armistice Agreement, deactivated the Military Armistice Commission and the Neutral Nations Supervisory Commission, neglected the Joint Declaration on the Denuclearization of the Korean Peninsula, and warned Seoul that it would be engulfed in a "sea of fire" should a new war erupt. North Korea is capable of taking up a radical position and carrying out submarine intrusions, low-intensity conflicts, commando attacks, and limited or even total armed invasion against South Korea. North Korea's top defector to South Korea, Hwang Chang Yop, declared that Kim Jong Il, armed with nuclear weapons, was determined to launch an armed attack against South Korea.[22]

The analysts who suggest that a North Korean armed provocation against the South is a possibility point to declining economic conditions in North Korea as the impetus. General Gary Luck termed this "a cornered rat syndrome," while Edward Olsen referred to the "Masada Complex" of the North Korean leadership.[23] Furthermore, Michael Green suggested that a decision in Pyongyang to unleash all of the North Korean military's destructive power on South Korea remained a dangerous possibility in the event of a regime crisis in North Korea and that there were no clear organizational "circuit breakers" that would interrupt a sudden decision at the top to wage war.[24] In the event of war, the United States is prepared to invoke its contingency plan (Operation Plan 5027), which would authorize a massive American and South Korean counterattack that would entail crossing the DMZ, taking Pyongyang, proceeding toward the Yalu and Tumen Rivers, and reunifying the peninsula.[25]

It is most unlikely, however, that North Korea will use an all-out offensive against South Korea in the next few years. South Korea not only maintains economic and financial superiority over North Korea, but it also enjoys a security guarantee from the United States as demonstrated by the Mutual Defense Treaty, the Combined Forces Command, the U.S. nuclear umbrella, and U.S. troops stationed in South Korea—irrespective of the troops' dwindling numbers and shifts in their locations. Moreover, North Korea can no longer rely upon Chinese or Russian military aid as in the past, and its own armed forces have suffered from shortages of food, fuel, and supplies; outdated military technology; and limited opportunities for training and exercises. The major credible sources that present a direct threat to South Korea and U.S. forces in South Korea are the weapons of mass destruction, missiles, and artillery. However, it is widely assumed that the top North Korean priority is survival, not suicidal military action.

Peaceful Cooperation

If rational calculations prevail in Seoul and Pyongyang, it is most likely that the two Koreas will accelerate their common efforts for peaceful coexistence and constructive engagement. Neoliberal institutionalists regard this scenario as a distinct possibility, disputing the neorealist assumptions of relative gains. Instead they assert that the uncooperative constraint of relative gains mostly applies to a two-person game and to a finite number of interactions. Robert Axelrod concludes that cooperation can emerge in a situation with an infinite number of interactions.[26] According to Robert Keohane, given the "shadow of the future," a tit-for-tat strategy of reciprocity for mutually reinforcing interactions can supercede a strategy for mutual defection, even in an anarchic situation, because "defection is in the long run unrewarding."[27] Other scholars propose that states typically focus primarily on their absolute gains and are not constrained by the gains of others and that there is a possibility of decentralized enforcement of cooperation, particularly with the assistance of international institutions.

As applied to the Korean situation, neoliberal institutionalists support the proposition that since both Korean governments can conduct an infinite number of interactions, they may be able to surmount the fear of relative gains and mutual defection and engage in mutually beneficial cooperative activities. Even if North Korea expects to gain less than South Korea does in a two-party game, it might still be persuaded to cooperate with South Korea so that improvement in inter-Korean relations can lead to North Korea's absolute gains in multinational settings—such as the Six-Party Talks, the United Nations, the ASEAN Regional Forum, the International Atomic Energy Agency, the Korean Peninsula Energy Development Organization (if it is ever reactivated), the Asian Development Bank, and other regional and international financial institutions.

Moreover, an increased level of inter-Korean functional transactions and communications in nonpolitical fields can help emphasize the underlying similarity and shared cultural beliefs, motives, and worldview of all Koreans and may serve to facilitate the formation of a unitary community in the long run. The growing linkages and parallel interests of particular groups—such as moderate or pragmatic forces and economic bureaucracies in both states—are anticipated to have positive spillover effects on other aspects of inter-Korean relations. Hence the ascendancy of moderate or pragmatic leaders in both Koreas can increase the likelihood of a scenario of peaceful cooperation and a process of gradual, cumulative, and functional Korean national integration. In the end, this neofunctionalist process may lead to the formation of a loose confederation, as implied in the Joint Statement issued by Kim Dae Jung and Kim Jong Il in June 2000 (see tables 10 and 11).

The scenario for inter-Korean peaceful cooperation would present challenges and opportunities for the United States. If both Koreas are able to expand their cooperation from economic and cultural fields into political and military realms and to adopt confidence-building measures, the importance of the U.S.–South Korean military alliance would decrease and the United States might become the "odd man out" in the changing triangular relationship, unless it manages its policy wisely and realistically. It will be most unfortunate if the United States is viewed as a major stumbling block to achieving cooperative relations, functional integration, and peaceful unification between Seoul and Pyongyang. As tension is reduced on the Korean Peninsula and conflict escalation is averted, however, the United States can enjoy a greater degree of policy flexibility, to the extent that if it so wishes, it can take further steps to disengage itself from the Korean Peninsula without upsetting the regional balance of power in Northeast Asia. For all practical purposes, it appears that the scenarios for status quo and peaceful cooperation are more desirable and feasible than those for absorption and conflict escalation in the next few years.

THE UNITED STATES AND KOREA AFTER UNIFICATION

If the Korean Peninsula were ever to be unified by absorption, confederation, or war under Seoul's dominance, it is conceivable that the government of a unified Korea would face a choice between policies of alignment and nonalignment. This choice would likely be influenced by a combination of several factors, notably Korea's domestic situation, the changing status of the United States, and the new regional environment, particularly the relationship between the United States and China.[28]

Alignment

At first glance, it would seem advantageous for Korea to continue to align itself with the United States, especially if the following three conditions are true: the reunification process is difficult, the United States remains the only strategic superpower, and the regional environment is relatively stable. By aligning itself with the United States, a unified Korean government could avail itself of significant American support and cooperation, which would help legitimize and stabilize the new government. A major component of such support would be in the form of American military power, which would help counterbalance the actual or imagined ambitions of the other major powers. The Korean government could also use a stable alliance with the United States to secure international economic cooperation and manipulate the alliance as leverage in settling international disputes. Moreover, a policy alignment with the United States would provide an effective nuclear umbrella over Korea and reduce the need for independent nuclear programs in Japan.

On the other hand, alignment with the United States could cause several problems to materialize. The United States would have the opportunity to interfere in Korea's internal affairs, leading to anti-U.S. sentiment and agitation. Korea might also be drawn into disagreements between the United States and the rest of the Pacific powers. This would complicate Korea's relations with China, Russia, and Japan and perhaps foster a strategic partnership between Beijing and Moscow against American hegemony in Asia, a tendency that has already become apparent in a series of summit meetings between China and Russia. From the U.S. perspective, a continued alignment with Korea would be important in stabilizing the region, guarding Japan's security interests, enhancing American economic benefits, and helping to smooth the process of Korean integration as much as possible. Alignment with Korea could also be held up as an example of American global leadership and commitment.

It is most likely that China and Russia would respond to a U.S.-Korean alignment with apprehension. To allay the suspicions and concerns of the other powers, it would be prudent for Korea and the United States to take a number of constructive measures. One extremely sensitive issue, the U.S. military presence, could be addressed if, for example, the United States pledges not to deploy troops in Northern Korea. If U.S. troops happened to be there for peacekeeping operations, military exercises, or a humanitarian intervention, they should be pulled out quickly. The U.S.– South Korean Mutual Defense Treaty, the Combined Forces Command, and the United Nations Command should also be modified in a way that lowers the military profile of the United States in Korea. With respect to economic issues, a regional or global consortium to aid Korean economic reconstruction could be formed, similar to the Korean Peninsula Energy Development Organization (KEDO) and the IMF-led rescue program.

Additional security concerns could be addressed by institutionalizing a new regional security forum (perhaps a Northeast Asia Security Dialogue, which has already been proposed by Canada and Australia) or by amplifying the ASEAN Regional Forum (ARF) so that all four Pacific powers can enjoy a sense of responsibility and participation in coordinating policies and guarding Korea's security interests. The United States and Korea should also apply the international arms control and disarmament regimes (the Missile Technology Control Regime and the Nuclear Nonproliferation Treaty) to Korea, expand confidence-building measures on the peninsula, and establish a nuclear weapon free zone modeled on the Treaty for the Prohibition of Nuclear Weapons in Latin America (Treaty of Tlatelolco).[29] Finally, encouraging Korea to accept a "one-plus-four" treaty with the Pacific powers similar to the "Treaty on the Final Settlement with Respect to Germany" and to sign bilateral treaties of friendship and cooperation with China, Russia, and Japan would go a long way toward ensuring a good start for a U.S.-Korean alignment.

Nonalignment

If Korea and the United States were to mismanage their political and military alignment and to alienate Korea's important internal forces or its major external players to the extent that tension, conflict, and instability dramatically escalate in and around the peninsula, it is likely that there would emerge a powerful movement to swing the pendulum of Korea's foreign policy from alignment to nonalignment (neutralization). This movement would be especially strong at a time when the international system dominated by the United States falters. As Cyril Black and other scholars suggest, neutralization becomes attractive to relatively minor states that, "by reason of strategic position or symbolic political value, have become or threaten to become the focal point of contests for control or dominant influence between principal regional or global rivals."[30] It is regarded as a method of conflict management and diplomatic compromise in a situation where the struggle for control of minor states is dangerous and destructive.

In fact, the United States applied this very concept to NSC 170/1 ("US Objectives and Courses of Action in Korea") approved by President Dwight Eisenhower on November 20, 1953.[31] The document specified that the United States should seek a "unified and neutral Korea" under a "free, independent and representative government" and with a "self-supporting economy." To this end the United States was prepared to accept: (1) a unified Korea friendly to the United States, without U.S. or other foreign forces or bases in Korea; (2) U.S. and Communist assurances of the territorial and political integrity of Korea under the ROK but foregoing all assistance pacts; and (3) a level of Korean armed forces sufficient for internal security and capable of defending Korean territory short of an attack by a major power. Whereas the Joint Chiefs of Staff opposed Korea's neutralization at the NSC meetings because the Communists would not abide by a neutralization agreement, the Department of State argued that the neutralization of Korea would remove Korea as a political and military problem, favor the security of Japan, reduce the U.S. military and economic burden, and strengthen the military position of the free world in other areas.

Even though the United States has had no real opportunity to implement this policy directive, a number of American leaders and scholars, including Senators William F. Knowland and Mike Mansfield and Professors Robert A. Scalapino, Gregory Henderson, Edwin Reischauer, Doak Barnett, Oran Young, and James Morely, have resurrected the proposal for Korea's neutralization over the years. Reischauer, for example, has advocated "a four-power agreement on the neutralization of Korea," and Morely has argued that a neutral Korea "could be offered no alliances, extended no military aid, and subjected to no subversion" and "could take no part in the power balance of the world."[32]

If its initial policy of alignment with the United States or any other Pacific power(s) were about to fall apart, a unified Korean government might see neutralization as an attractive and realistic alternative. Moreover, geostrategic reasons might cause many to see that "the Korean Peninsula fits the numerous profiles of a political candidate for neutralization."[33] Similar to Switzerland and Belgium, Korea has been a focal point of conflict for its powerful neighbor states and, in effect, a casus belli for three major wars from the 1890s to the 1950s. The advantages of neutralization would be attractive to Korean leaders. It would help protect Korea's political independence, territorial integrity, and diplomatic flexibility in large part by establishing equidistant relations with all four Pacific powers without prejudice and by assuming a role of "balancer" in the evolving balance of power system in Northeast Asia. This in turn would reduce conflict among the Pacific powers over Korea and promote peace and stability in the region. Domestically, potential division among Korean leaders over foreign policy orientations might also be averted. Above all, Korean leaders might see neutralization as an expression of national self-reliance. As Bruce Cumings states, "Ethnocentric and obnoxious to foreigners, a self-contained, autonomous Korea not besmirched by things foreign remains an ideal for many Koreans. . . . [C]alls for self-reliance and the expelling of foreign influence will always get a hearing in Korea; this is one of its most persistent foreign policy traits."[34] Moreover, Selig Harrison argues that the United States should encourage a confederation between both Koreas, pursue a phased and gradual military disengagement from South Korea, and initiate a discussion with China, Japan, and Russia for the purpose of reaching a regional neutralization agreement for Korea.[35]

In general, China and Russia would be likely to welcome and endorse neutralization because it would limit the preeminent influence of the United States, provide an "equal" opportunity for their activities, establish a buffer zone for their respective security concerns, and remove Korea from the list of flashpoints of international confrontation. The Japanese would prefer to see a continuing U.S.-Korean alignment, but they may have no serious objections to a neutralized Korea so long as it prevents the ascendancy of Chinese or Russian influence and maintains a peaceful and friendly Korean policy towards Japan.

The United States would likely be caught between its desire to maintain an alignment policy with a unified Korea as long as possible and the necessity of not vetoing Korea's neutralization once it becomes unavoidable. It would be painful for the United States to shift its traditional position toward Korea, but neutralization would still prove better than other alternatives, such as an alignment with China, a regionwide counter-alliance against the United States, and a rapid escalation of international conflicts over Korea. As NSC 170/1 suggests, the United States can live with a unified, neutral, and friendly Korea able to protect American interests in the region.

If the movement for Korean neutralization were to be judged irreversible, the United States should assume an active and constructive role to make the best of the situation. The United States could try to minimize international disputes and influence-mongering over Korea by formulating an international agreement on the neutralization of Korea that would help Korea enjoy sovereign independence, territorial integrity, a prosperous market economy, and democratic practices. The United States should also support an effective international mechanism for guaranteeing Korea's neutral status and for enforcing and supervising the agreement. The American government could also institute a regular framework for close consultation and coordination among the relevant parties, including all four Pacific powers, arrange a practical procedure to deal with violations of the agreement, and strengthen existing regional agreements and institutions regarding Korea.

At the same time, a unified Korea neutralized by international agreements (as was the case with Switzerland or Laos) or by self-neutralization (Austria) is likely to encounter a number of potential disadvantages. It might experience limited flexibility and dynamism in foreign affairs, lack an effective system of checks and balances among the major powers, bring about a "power vacuum" that would leave Korea vulnerable to outside interference, or lose the rationale for substantial foreign economic assistance. Ultimately, however, the realization of a unified, neutral, democratic, prosperous, and peaceful Korea will depend upon strong, independent, and wise political leadership in Korea and a substantial congruence of interests and capabilities among the Pacific powers.

In the next decade or so, it is expected that compared with other major powers—China, Japan, and Russia—the United States will continue to possess the most military, economic, and diplomatic ability to influence the processes and consequences of Korean reunification. In the long run, however, the crucial questions in this regard will be whether China emerges as a regional hegemon at the expense of the U.S. interests and whether the United States and China become strategic partners or competitors over Korea.[36] As the country responsible for dividing Korea along the 38th Parallel six decades ago, the United States should make every possible effort to be viewed not as an obstructionist or spoiler of the genuine Korean desire for national integration but as a supporter, honest broker, and peacemaker who can assist them in realizing their legitimate nationalistic aspirations. It will be in the best interests of the United States and Korea that the United States, a distant power with no territorial ambitions, support Korea's sovereign independence, free market economy, and good-neighbor policy and promote a regional balance of power favorable to Korea. It is expected that the United States will continue to regard Korea as a shield for protecting its more vital interests in Japan and as a buffer for countering its more serious challenges from China and to ensure that no other country establish a hegemonic status in Korea. In order to play its role wisely and constructively in the future of Korea, however, the United States would do well to transcend the historical tendency to view Korea as an extension of its interests and concerns over Japan and China and to recognize the intrinsic significance of its enduring and mutually beneficial relationship with Korea. In this context, the United States is required to formulate answers to a number of important questions: What type of leadership does the United States intend to seek in the post-Iraq world order? Can the United States deal with the serious divisiveness within its own domestic politics and foreign policy? Is the United States prepared to recognize the wisdom of emphasizing its soft power along with its military and economic power? How can it achieve moral consensus and assert enlightened leadership in foreign affairs? Can it continue to uphold its traditional values and democratic principles and overcome the vagaries of its hegemonic arrogance and unrealistic unilateralism? In this context, the Korean Peninsula can serve as a prominent case to test America's political resolve and leadership qualities in managing both domestic debates and global and regional disputes.

When U.S. troops landed at Inchon in September 1945 to occupy and govern the southern half of the Korean Peninsula temporarily, no one could have foreseen that six decades later the United States would still remain deeply entangled in the vortex of Korean affairs. In retrospect, the United States can take pride in its overall record of achieving its professed goals in spite of the tremendous sacrifices, mistakes, and frustrations along the way. Even though South Koreans deserve primary credit for all their hard-won accomplishments—their military preparedness, economic prosperity, democratic consolidation, and diplomatic versatility—the United States has played no small part in encouraging and nurturing such development in South Korea. In particular, the steadfast U.S. policy of containment and deterrence toward North Korea has made it possible for South Korea to enjoy a prolonged period of peace, to concentrate its resources on economic development, to build up its self-defense capabilities, and to pursue comparative advantages over North Korea. And as their nation matured, South Korean citizens came to enjoy democratic freedoms, among them the willingness to allow a diversity of opinions to be heard. As a result, an increasing number of South Koreans can now afford to espouse strong nationalistic aspirations, pro- and anti-American sentiments, and sympathetic attitudes toward North Koreans, with whom they share so much in common. While sustaining the basic structure of containment against North Korea, the United States has been

willing and able to engage North Korea both in bilateral negotiations, as exemplified in the Beijing Talks and the Geneva Agreed Framework, and in multilateral
diplomacy ranging from the Four-Party Talks (1997–99) to the Three-Party Talks
(2003) and the Six-Party Talks (2003–5). Yet the United States, along with South
Korea, has been unsuccessful in solving the intricate North Korean conundrum.
No matter what happens in the disputes over North Korean nuclear and missile
issues, the direction of inter-Korean relations, and the processes of Korean reunification, it is most likely that the United States will continue to assume a significant
role in the Korean Peninsula for many years to come.

APPENDIX

Tables

TABLE 1
U.S. Assistance to South Korea, in 1946–1999
(in $ millions)

	Economic Assistance			Military Assistance			Total Assistance		
	Total	Loans	Grants	Total	Loans	Grants	Total	Loans	Grants
1946–48	181.2	24.9	156.3	—	—	—	181.2	24.9	156.3
1949–52	485.6	—	485.6	12.5	—	12.5	498.1	—	498.1
1953–59	1,857.7	19.5	1,838.2	1,215.3	—	1,215.3	3,073.0	19.5	3,053.5
1960–69	2,047.4	431.2	1,616.3	2,492.0	—	2,492	4,603.8	431.5	4,172.2
1970–79	1,126.8	932.4	194.4	3,331.6	950.3	2,381.3	4,458.4	1,882.7	2,579.7
1980–89	58.4	54.1	4.3	1,280.7	1,264.2	16.5	1,339.1	1,318.3	20.8
1990–99	58.8	1.5	57.3	3.3	—	3.3	62.1	1.5	60.6

Source: U.S. Agency for International Development

TABLE 2
U.S.–South Korean Trade, 1961–2003
(in $ millions)

	U.S. Imports from South Korea	U.S. Exports to South Korea	Total
1961	7	143	150
1962	12	220	232
1963	24	184	208
1964	36	202	238
1965	62	182	244
1966	96	254	350
1967	137	305	442
1968	235	452	687
1969	312	530	842
1970	390	584	974
1971	531	678	1,209
1972	759	647	1,406
1973	1,020	1,202	2,222
1974	1,493	1,701	3,194
1975	1,539	1,880	3,419
1976	2,494	1,960	4,454
1977	3,122	2,444	5,566
1978	4,068	3,039	7,107
1979	4,340	4,594	8,934
1980	4,620	4,875	9,495
1981	5,683	6,028	11,711
1982	6,253	5,945	12,198
1983	8,272	6,262	14,534
1984	10,528	6,861	17,389
1985	10,793	6,480	17,273
1986	13,919	6,533	20,452
1987	18,363	8,746	27,109
1988	21,478	12,759	34,237
1989	20,695	15,916	36,611
1990	19,420	16,946	36,366
1991	18,608	18,904	37,512
1992	18,153	18,319	36,472
1993	18,219	17,952	36,171
1994	20,703	21,599	42,302
1995	24,344	30,418	54,762
1996	21,926	33,319	55,245
1997	21,850	30,134	51,984
1998	22,987	20,273	43,260
1999	29,601	24,942	54,543
2000	37,806	29,286	67,092
2001	31,357	22,430	53,878
2002	32,778	22,885	55,663
2003	36,963	24,098	61,061

Source: United Nations

TABLE 3

Four-Party Talks: Delegations, 1997–1999

	South Korea	North Korea	China	United States
First Session: December 9–10, 1997	Lee Si Young Moon Mu Hung	Kim Gye Gwan Ri Gun	Tang Jiaxuan Sa Zukang	Stanley Roth Charles Kartman
Second Session: March 16–21, 1998	Song Yong Sik Moon Mu Hung	Kim Gye Gwan Ri Gun	Chen Jian Wang Yi	Stanley Roth Charles Kartman
Third Session: October 21–24, 1998	Park Keun Woo Kwon Chong Rak	Kim Gye Gwan Ri Gun	Qian Yongnian Chang Jiuhuan	Stanley Roth Charles Kartman
Fourth Session: January 18–22, 1999	Park Keun Woo Kwon Chong Rak	Kim Gye Gwan Ri Gun	Qian Yongnian Chang Jiuhuan	Stanley Roth Charles Kartman
Fifth Session: April 24–27, 1999	Park Keun Woo Kwon Chong Rak	Kim Gye Gwan Chang Chang Chon	Qian Yongnian Ning Pukui	Stanley Roth Charles Kartman
Sixth Session: August 5–9, 1999	Park Keun Woo Song Min Soon	Kim Gye Gwan Chang Chang Chon	Qian Yongnian Ning Pukui	Stanley Roth Charles Kartman

Note: Head and deputy head of each delegation are listed.

TABLE 4

South Korea and North Korea: A Comparison, 2000

	South Korea	North Korea
Territory (km)	99,022	122,098
Population (1,000)	47,008	22,175
Gross National Product ($ million)	457,000	16,400
Per capita gross national product ($)	9,722	739
Rice production (1,000 tons)	5,291	1,424
Automobile production (1,000)	3,115	6.6
Exports ($ million)	172,270	560
Imports ($ million)	160,480	1,410
Defense expenditure ($ million)	12,749	2,091
Armed forces	686,000	1,082,000

Source: The South Korean National Statistical Office, The Military Balance 2002–2003, and The Bank of Korea.

TABLE 5

Six-Party Talks: Delegations, 2003–2005

	South Korea	North Korea	China	United States	Japan	Russia
First Round: August 26–29, 2003	Lee Soo Hyuck	Kim Yong Il	Wang Yi	James Kelly	Yabunaka Mitoji	Alexander Losyukov
Second Round: February 25–28, 2004	Lee Soo Hyuck	Kim Gye Gwan	Wang Yi	James Kelly	Yabunaka Mitoji	Alexander Losyukov
Third Round: June 23–26, 2004	Lee Soo Hyuck	Kim Gye Gwan	Wang Yi	James Kelly	Yabunaka Mitoji	Alexander Alekseyev
Fourth Round: July 26–August 7 and September 13–19, 2005	Song Min Soon	Kim Gye Gwan	Wu Dawei	Christopher Hill	Sasae Kenichiro	Alexander Alekseyev

Note: Head of each delegation is listed.

TABLE 6
Financial Support to KEDO, March 1995–December 2003

Country/Organization	Amount ($)
United States	40,510,600
South Korea	1,227,332,425
Japan	446,936,136
EAEC	120,287,723
Other countries	32,905,901
Grand total	2,232,568,185

Note: EAEC is European Atomic Energy Community (Euratom).

TABLE 7
Threat Perceptions in South Korea, January 5, 2004

Question: "Which country presents the most serious threat to South Korea's national security?"

Age Groups	United States	North Korea	China	Japan	Do Not Know / No Answer
Twenties	58%	20%	9%	9%	4%
Thirties	47	22	16	8	7
Forties	36	34	14	7	9
Fifties and over	18	52	8	6	16
Total	39	33	12	8	8

Source: Chosun.com (January 11, 2004)

TABLE 8
U.S. Military Forces in South Korea, May 2004

Number of U.S. forces	
Army	28,300
Air Force	8,706
Navy	400
Marines	83
Total	37,489
Army	
M-I tanks	140
Bradley armored vehicles	230
155-mm	30
227-mm	30
Missiles	300
Patriot missiles	48
Apache helicopters (AH-64D)	70
Other helicopters	120
Air Force	
F-16 fighter aircraft	70
A-10 bombers	20
Other	
LL-2 reconnaissance planes	2
RF-4C reconnaissance planes	1

Source: *Hanguk Ilbo* (May 17, 2004).

TABLE 9
South Korean National Assembly: Election Results, April 2004

	Local Districts	Proportional Representation	Total Seats	Pre-election Seats	Change
Uri Party	129	23	152	49	+103
GNP	100	21	121	137	−16
DLP	2	8	10	0	10
MDP	5	4	9	61	−52
LDL	4	0	4	10	−6
Independents / Others	3	0	3	14	−11
Total	243	56	299	271	

Note: GNP, Grand National Party; DLP, Democratic Labor Party; MDP, Millennium Democratic Party; LDL, Liberal Democratic League.

TABLE 10
Inter-Korean Trade, 1989–2004
(in $1,000)

	South Korean Exports	South Korean Imports	Total
1989	69	18,655	18,724
1990	1,188	12,278	13,446
1991	5,547	105,719	111,266
1992	10,563	162,863	173,426
1993	8,425	178,167	186,592
1994	18,249	176,298	194,547
1995	64,436	222,855	287,291
1996	69,639	182,400	252,039
1997	115,270	193,069	308,339
1998	129,679	92,264	221,943
1999	211,832	121,604	333,437
2000	272,775	152,373	425,148
2001	226,787	176,170	402,957
2002	370,155	271,575	641,730
2003	434,965	289,252	724,217
2004	438,995	258,019	697,014

Source: South Korean Ministry of Unification.

TABLE 11
South Korean Assistance to North Korea, 1995–2004
(in $1,000)

	Governmental Assistance	Nongovernmental Assistance	Total
1995	232,000	250	232,250
1996	3,050	1,550	4,600
1997	26,670	20,560	47,230
1998	11,000	20,850	31,850
1999	28,250	18,630	46,880
2000	78,630	35,130	113,760
2001	70,450	64,940	135,390
2002	83,750	51,170	134,920
2003	87,020	70,610	157,630
2004	111,512	122,670	234,182
Total	732,332	406,360	1,138,692

Source: South Korean Ministry of Unification.

Notes

CHAPTER 1. INTRODUCTION

1. Richard E. Neustadt, *Alliance Politics* (New York: Columbia University Press, 1970), 72–73.

2. I. William Zartman, *The Politics of Trade Negotiation between Africa and the European Economic Community* (Princeton, NJ: Princeton University Press, 1971), 5.

3. Robert O. Keohane, *After Hegemony: Cooperation and Discord in the World Political Economy* (Princeton, NJ: Princeton University Press, 1984), 54.

4. Joseph S. Nye Jr., *The Paradox of American Power: Why the World's Only Superpower Can't Go It Alone* (New York: Oxford University Press, 2002), 140.

5. Jean-Jacques Rousseau, *The Social Contract and Discourses*, translated by G. D. H. Cole (New York: E. P. Dutton and Company, n.d.), 6–7.

6. Leo Strauss, *What Is Political Philosophy?* (Glencoe, IL: Free Press, 1959), 10.

7. Henry Kissinger, *Does America Need a Foreign Policy? Toward a Diplomacy for the 21st Century* (New York: Simon and Schuster, 2001), 286.

8. Harold J. Laski, *The State in Theory and Practice* (London: George Allen and Unwin, 1935), 37–38.

CHAPTER 2. THE UNITED STATES FACES KOREA

1. For early Korean perceptions of the United States, see Song Byong Kie, "Swaeguk ki ui taemi insik" [Korean Perception of the United States during the Period of Seclusion], 11–53, and Lew Young Ick, "Kaehwa ki ui taemi insik" [Korean Perception of the United States during the Enlightenment Period], 55–141, in Lew Young Ick, ed., *Hangukin ui taemi insik* [Korean Perception of the United States] (Seoul: Minumsa, 1994). The Europeans—Portuguese, Spaniards, Dutchmen, Englishmen—began their direct contacts with China and Japan in the sixteenth century for commercial and missionary purposes, but Korea was ignored until the nineteenth century.

2. Pyong Choon Hahm, "The Korean Perception of the United States," in Youngnok Koo and Dae-Sook Suh, eds., *Korea and the United States: A Century of Cooperation* (Honolulu: University of Hawaii Press, 1984), 24–25. Hahm, a Harvard-educated legal scholar, served as South Korean ambassador to the United States (1973–77).

3. For the *General Sherman* incident, see Key-Hiuk Kim, *The Last Phase of the East Asian World Order: Korea, Japan, and the Chinese Empire, 1860–1882* (Berkeley: University of California Press, 1980), 51–55. For the Taewongun's rule, see Chin Young Choe, *The Rule of the Taewongun, 1864–1873: Restoration in Yi Korea* (Cambridge, MA: Harvard University Press, 1972), and James B. Palais, *Politics and Policy in Traditional Korea* (Cambridge, MA: Harvard University Press, 1975).

4. Donald N. Clark, *Living Dangerously in Korea: The Western Experience, 1900–1950* (Norwalk, CT: EastBridge, 2003), 122, 141.

5. Key-Hiuk Kim, *The Last Phase*, 56–60.

6. Ibid., 60–61.

7. For Huang's recommendation and consequences, see Lew Young Ick, [Korean Perception], 58–62.

8. For the English and Chinese texts of the treaty, see Ku Yong Nok, ed., *Hanguk kwa miguk* [Korea and the United States] (Seoul: Pakyong sa, 1983), 559–570. For the treaty negotiations, see Martina Deuchler, *Confucian Gentlemen and Barbarian Envoys: The Opening of Korea, 1875–1885* (Seattle: University of Washington Press, 1977), 113–122.

9. For the dynamics of imperialist conflicts over Korea, see C. I. Eugene Kim and Han-Kyo Kim, *Korea and the Politics of Imperialism, 1876–1910* (Berkeley: University of California Press, 1967).

10. For Min's activities in the United States, see John Kie-chiang Oh and Bonnie Bong-wan Cho Oh, *The Korean Embassy in America* (Elizabeth, NJ: Hollym International Corporation, 2003), 14–15.

11. As quoted in Hahm, "The Korean Perception," 35.

12. For the text, see U.S. Department of State, *United States Policy regarding Korea*, Part I: 1834–1941 (Research Project No. 29, Foreign Policy Studies Branch, Office of Public Affairs, May 1947), 6. (Hereafter cited as *United States Policy*, Part I.)

13. Ibid., 11–12. For the Korean origin of the Sino-Japanese War, see Chong-Sik Lee, *The Politics of Korean Nationalism* (Berkeley: University of California Press, 1965), 34–41.

14. John Chay, "The American Images of Korea to 1945," in Koo and Suh, eds., *Korea and the United States*, 53–76.

15. For the negotiations on the Sino-Japanese Treaty of Peace, see Morinosuke Kajima, ed., *The Diplomacy of Japan, 1894–1922*, vol. 1 (Tokyo: Kajima Institute of International Peace, 1976), 234–271.

16. Isabella Bird Bishop, *Korea and Her Neighbours* (1898; repr. Seoul: Yonsei University Press, 1970), 22. She visited Korea four times between 1894 and 1897.

17. *United States Policy*, Part I, 14.

18. Peter Duus, *The Abacus and the Sword: The Japanese Penetration of Korea, 1895–1910* (Berkeley: University of California Press, 1995), 103–104.

19. As quoted in *United States Policy*, Part I, 25.

20. On the Boxer indemnity funds, see Jonathan D. Spence, *The Search for Modern China* (New York: W. W. Norton, 1990), 235.

21. As cited in Duus, *The Abacus and the Sword*, 189.

22. Fareed Zakaria, *From Wealth to Power: The Unusual Origins of America's World Role* (Princeton, NJ: Princeton University Press, 1998), 172.

23. Ibid., 188, and *United States Policy*, Part I, 25–26.

24. For the Taft-Katsura memorandum, see Ku, [Korea and the United States], 571–572. This memorandum was not made public until 1924.

25. On Theodore Roosevelt's international outlook, see Henry Kissinger, *Diplomacy* (New York: Simon and Schuster, 1994), 29–55. According to Edwin O. Reischauer, "Japan had no more sympathetic friend than Theodore Roosevelt." See Reischauer, *The United States and Japan* (New York: Viking, 1957), 19–20.

26. On the negotiations on the Russo-Japanese Treaty of Peace, see Morinosuke Kajima, ed., *The Diplomacy of Japan, 1894–1922*, vol. 2 (Tokyo: Kajima Institute of International Peace, 1978), 389–399.

27. See *United States Policy*, Part I, 35–36.

28. Syngman Rhee studied at George Washington University, received an M.A. from Harvard University, and, in 1910, received a Ph.D. in politics from Princeton University. On his early life, see Lew Young Ick, *Yi Sungman ui sam kwa kkum* [The Life and Dream of Syngman Rhee] (Seoul: Chungang ilbo sa, 1996); Lew Young Ick, ed., *Yi Sungman yongu* [Studies on Syngman Rhee] (Seoul: Yonsei University Press, 2000); Chong-Sik Lee, *Syngman Rhee: The Prison Years of a Young Radical* (Seoul: Yonsei University Press, 2001); and Syngman Rhee, *The Spirit of Independence: A Primer of Korean Modernization and Reform*, translated by Han-Kyo Kim (Honolulu: University of Hawaii Press, 2001).

29. For example, see Syngman Rhee, *Japan Inside Out: The Challenge of Today* (New York: Fleming H. Revell Company, 1941), published on the eve of Pearl Harbor.

30. In 1939, Japan and Manchuria shared 73.2% of Korean exports and 88.6% of Korean imports. See Andrew J. Grajdanzev, *Modern Korea: A Study of Social and Economic Changes under Japanese Rule* (New York: The John Day Company, 1944), 226–227.

31. For the attitudes of American missionaries and educators in Korea, especially during the Samil (March 1st) independence movement, see Clark, *Living Dangerously in Korea*, 42–64.

32. As cited in *United States Policy*, Part I, 41.

33. Horace G. Underwood, *Korea in War, Revolution, and Peace* (Seoul: Yonsei University Press, 2001), 80–87, and Clark, *Living Dangerously in Korea*, 262–272.

34. On the Cairo Declaration, see U.S. Department of State, *Occupation of Japan: Policy and Progress* (Washington, DC: U.S. Government Printing Office, n.d.), 51–52, and Se-Jin Kim, ed., *Documents on Korean-American Relations, 1943–1976* (Seoul: Research Center for Peace and Unification, 1976), 27.

35. U.S. Department of State, *United States Policy regarding Korea*, Part II: 1941–1945 (Research Project No. 158, Division of Historical Policy Research, Office of Public Affairs, May 1950), 32. (Hereafter cited as *United States Policy*, Part II.)

36. Ibid., 54–55.

37. For the text of the Potsdam Proclamation, see *Occupation of Japan: Policy and Progress* (Washington, DC: U.S. Government Printing Office, n.d.), 53–55.

38. For the OSS-KPG agreement on the "Eagle Project," see *Hanmi kunsa kwanggye sa: 1871–2002* [A History of Korean-American Military Relations, 1871–2002] (Seoul: Ministry of National Defense, 2002), 136–151.

39. For Rhee's letters written to Roosevelt on May 15, 1943, August 21, 1944, and September 11, 1944, and to Hull on February 16, 1943, see *United States Policy*, Part II, 25–34.

40. As quoted in Won Sul Lee, "American Decisions on the Korean Provisional Government, 1945," *Korean Journal of International Relations* (1982), 214. On Rhee's meeting with Alger Hiss (special assistant to Secretary of State Hull) and Stanley Hornback (director of the division of Far Eastern Affairs, Department of State) at the Department of State on January 2, 1942, see Robert T. Oliver, *Syngman Rhee and American Involvement in Korea, 1942–1960: A Personal Narrative* (Seoul: Panmun Book Company, 1978), 7–8.

41. For Dean Rusk's recollection, see *Foreign Relations of the United States*, 1945, vol. 6 (Washington, DC: U.S. Government Printing Office, 1969), 1039. In his private letter to General James K. Terry on February 12, 1972, Bonesteel stated that he had known in 1945 that Kaesong was an ancient dynastic capital. He also indicated that in 1945 he had a higher position than Rusk. A copy of this unpublished letter is in the author's possession.

42. As cited in *United States Policy*, Part II, 59. U.S. Ambassador to Russia Averell Harriman also recommended to Truman that in order to counter Russian intransigence, U.S. forces should land in Korea and Dairen to accept surrender of Japanese troops. See Harry S. Truman, *Memoirs: Year of Decisions* (Garden City, NY: Doubleday, 1955), 433–434.

43. For the exchange of messages between Truman and Stalin from August 16 to 30, 1945, see Truman, *Memoirs: Year of Decisions*, 440–443. For the text of General Order No. 1 issued on September 2, 1945, see Kim, *Documents*, 28.

44. Professor Wada Haruki of Tokyo University was certain of Stalin's awareness of the Czarist proposal in 1945. Author discussion with Wada, March 5, 2004.

45. For a comprehensive and definitive assessment of the U.S. military government in South Korea, see Bruce Cumings, *The Origins of the Korean War: Liberation and Emergence of Separate Regimes, 1945–1947* (Princeton: Princeton University Press, 1981), 135–264. Also see E. Grant Meade, *American Military Government in Korea* (New York: King's Crown Press, Columbia University, 1951).

46. MacArthur had been exposed to the Korean issue early in his military career when he accompanied his father, General Arthur MacArthur, to Japan to observe the Russo-Japanese War in 1904 and served as President Theodore Roosevelt's aide-de-camp in the White House from 1906 to 1908. See Douglas MacArthur, *Reminiscences* (New York: McGraw-Hill, 1964), 30–34.

47. For the proclamation issued by General MacArthur on September 7, 1945, and the statement released by President Truman on September 18, 1945, see Kim, *Documents*, 28–29.

48. For the thesis on America's "counter-revolutionary policy," see Bruce Cumings, "American Policy and Korean Liberation," in Frank Baldwin, ed., *Without Parallel: The American-Korean Relationship since 1945* (New York: Pantheon, 1973), 39–108.

49. For the Korean People's Republic and the People's Committees, see Cumings, *The Origins of the Korean War*, 81–91, 267–350; and Dae-Sook Suh, *The Korean Communist Movement, 1918–1948* (Princeton, NJ: Princeton University Press, 1967), 297–299. In order to put forward a genuine coalition including left, center, and right, the KPR cabinet initially included Syngman Rhee (chairman), Lyuh Woon Hyung (vice chairman), Ho Hon (prime minister), Kim Ku (minister of the interior), and Kim Song Su (minister of education).

50. For economic statistics, see U.S. Department of State, *United States Policy regarding Korea*, Part III: December 1945–June 1950 (Research Project No. 252, Division of Historical Policy Research, Office of Public Affairs, December 1951), 41–46. (Hereafter cited as *United States Policy*, Part III.)

51. For the Moscow agreement, see *United States Policy*, Part II, 70–76, and Kim, *Documents*, 30.

52. On the establishment, structures, and functions of the DPRK, see Robert A. Scalapino and Chong-Sik Lee, *Communism in Korea: The Movement* (Berkeley: University of California Press, 1972); 365–376, Dae-Sook Suh, *Kim Il Sung: The North Korean Leader* (New York: Columbia University Press, 1988), 95–105; and Charles K. Armstrong, *The North Korean Revolution, 1945–1950* (Ithaca, NY: Cornell University Press, 2003).

53. For a comparison of conditions in North and South Korea during the late 1940s, see George M. McCune, *Korea Today* (Cambridge, MA: Harvard University Press, 1950).

54. As quoted in Chae-Jin Lee and Hideo Sato, *U.S. Policy toward Japan and Korea: A Changing Influence Relationship* (New York: Praeger Publications, 1982), 10. See also Kim, *Documents*, 70–71.

55. On Chang's background and the establishment of the Korean embassy, see Oh and Oh, *The Korean Embassy*, 38–53.

56. For the views of the Joint Chiefs of Staff, see *United States Policy*, Part III, 22.

57. For NSC 8, see Donald Stone Macdonald, *U.S.-Korean Relations from Liberation to Self-Reliance: The Twenty-Year Record* (Boulder, CO: Westview Press, 1992), 5–6.

58. For Rhee's letter, see *United States Policy*, Part III, 25–26.

59. For the text of Rhee's letter to Truman on August 20, 1949, see ibid., 34.

60. For the text of Acheson's speech, see Kim, *Documents*, 83–89. For a similar position expressed by General MacArthur in March 1949, see Kissinger, *Diplomacy*, 474.

61. For a discussion of Kim's meetings with Stalin and Mao, see Chae-Jin Lee, *China and Korea: Dynamic Relations* (Stanford, CA: Hoover Institution Press, 1996), 8–11.

62. Dean Acheson, *The Korean War* (New York: W. W. Norton, 1971), 20.

63. As quoted in Truman, *Memoirs: Years of Trial and Hope* (Garden City, NY: Doubleday, 1956), 336.

64. Ibid. See also "Memorandum of Conversation," June 26, 1950, in *Foreign Relations of the United States*, 1950, vol. 5 (Washington, DC: U.S. Government Printing Office, 1976), 172–173.

65. For the letter from Rhee to MacArthur on July 14 and the response from MacArthur to Rhee on July 18, see Kim, *Documents*, 117–119.

66. See *Oral History Interview with John J. Muccio*, December 27, 1973, transcript, Harry S. Truman Library, Independence, Missouri, May 1976.

67. For this debate, see Dean Rusk with Richard Rusk and Daniel S. Rapp, *As I Saw It* (New York: Penguin Books, 1991), 166–167. In a memorandum on August 21, 1950, Kennan told Secretary of State Acheson that it was beyond U.S. capabilities to keep Korea permanently out of the Soviet orbit and that "a period of Russian domination, while undesirable, is preferable to continued U.S. involvement in that unhappy area." He envisioned that Japanese influence would gradually replace Russian influence over Korea. See *Foreign Relations of the United States*, 1950, vol. 5, 623–628.

68. For Kim's appeal to Stalin and Mao, see Lee, *China and Korea*, 16–17.

69. For the complete English translation of this message, see ibid., 17.

70. For a detailed chronological description of the Korean War, see Ohn Chang Il, *Hanminjok chonjaeng sa* [War History of Korea] (Seoul: Chimmundang, 2001), 453–1031;

and Clay Blair, *The Forgotten War: America in Korea, 1950–1953* (New York: Times Books, 1987).

71. See Lee, *China and Korea*, 18. Also see K. M. Panikkar, *In Two Chinas: Memoirs of a Diplomat* (London: George Allen and Unwin, 1955). On China's decision to participate in the Korean War and its consequences, see Allen S. Whiting, *China Crosses the Yalu: The Decision to Enter the Korean War* (Stanford, CA: Stanford University Press, 1960); Sergei N. Goncharov, John W. Lewis, and Xue Litai, *Uncertain Partners: Stalin, Mao, and the Korean War* (Stanford, CA: Stanford University Press, 1993); Jian Chen, *China's Road to the Korean War: The Making of the Sino-American Confrontation* (New York: Columbia University Press, 1994); Rosemary Foot, *The Wrong War: American Policy and the Dimensions of the Korean Conflict, 1950–1953* (Ithaca, NY: Cornell University Press, 1985), 88–130; and Thomas J. Christensen, *Useful Adversaries: Grand Strategy, Mobilization, and Sino-American Conflict, 1947–1958* (Princeton, NJ: Princeton University Press, 1996), 138–193.

72. For the minutes of the Truman-MacArthur meeting, see *Foreign Relations of the United States, 1950*, vol. 5, 948–960. For MacArthur's explanations, see Douglas MacArthur, *Reminiscences*, 360–364.

73. As quoted in Roy E. Appleman, *South to the Naktong, North to the Yalu: United States Army in the Korean War* (Washington, DC: U.S. Government Printing Office, 1961), 765.

74. *Foreign Relations of the United States, 1950*, vol. 5, 1237.

75. For the pessimistic views expressed by U.S. leaders, see Lee, *China and Korea*, 27–28.

76. For the text of NSC 48/5, see *Foreign Relations of the United States, 1951*, vol. 7, pt. 1 (Washington, DC: U.S. Government Printing Office, 1983), 439–442.

77. For the discussions between Kennan and Malik, see ibid., 460–462, 483–486, 493–494, 507–511. On the ceasefire negotiations, see Rosemary Foot, *A Substitute for Victory: The Politics of Peacemaking at the Korean Armistice Talks* (Ithaca, NY: Cornell University Press, 1990); William H. Vatcher Jr., *Panmunjom: The Story of the Korean Military Armistice Negotiations* (New York: Frederick A. Praeger, 1958); Sydney D. Bailey, *The Korean Armistice* (New York: St. Martin's Press, 1992); and William Stueck, *Rethinking the Korean War: A New Diplomatic and Strategic History* (Princeton, NJ: Princeton University Press, 2002), 143–181.

78. See *Oral History Interview with John J. Muccio*, February 10 and 18, 1971, transcript, Harry S. Truman Library, Independence, Missouri, January 1972. In a meeting with South Korean Ambassador Yang Yu Chan on June 9, Assistant Secretary of State Rusk denied the rumor that the United States had a proposal for peace negotiations. For Muccio's subsequent meeting with President Rhee on June 30, see *Foreign Relations of the United States, 1951*, vol. 7, pt. 1, 604–605.

79. "Memorandum of Discussion at the 150th Meeting of the National Security Council, Thursday, June 18, 1953," in *Foreign Relations of the United States, 1952–1954*, vol. 15, pt. 2 (Washington, DC: U.S. Government Printing Office, 1984), 1200–1205.

80. For the text of Eisenhower's letter, see Dwight D. Eisenhower, *Mandate for Change, 1953–1956* (Garden City, NY: Doubleday, 1963), 185–186.

81. For the telegram from General Mark Clark (CINCUNC) to the JCS on July 5, 1952, the telegram from Clark to General J. Lawton Collins (Army chief of staff) on April 26, 1953, Eighth Army Commander General Maxwell Taylor's paper of May 4, 1953, and a memoran-

dum on a Department of State–JCS meeting on May 29, 1953, see *Foreign Relations of the United States, 1952–1954*, vol. 15, pt. 1 (Washington, DC: U.S. Government Printing Office, 1984), 377–379, 940–943, 965–968, 1114–1119.

82. *Oral History Interview with John J. Muccio*, 1973.

83. For such suspicions as early as July 1951, see Oliver, *Syngman Rhee and American Involvement in Korea*, 375.

84. For the letter from Dulles to Rhee delivered by Assistant Secretary of State for Far Eastern Affairs Walter S. Robertson on June 26, 1953, see *Foreign Relations of the United States, 1952–1954*, vol. 15, pt. 2, 1238–1240.

85. Ibid., 1291–1292.

86. For contrasting views of Rhee's personality, see Stephen Jin-Woo Kim, *Master of Manipulation: Syngman Rhee and the Seoul-Washington Alliance, 1953–1960* (Seoul: Yonsei University Press, 2001), 13–23. For Muccio's recollections, see *Oral History Interview with John J. Muccio*, 1971.

87. For the Korean Armistice Agreement, see Kim, *Documents*, 157–179.

88. W. D. Reeve, *The Republic of Korea: A Political and Economic Study* (New York: Oxford University Press, 1963), 103.

89. As cited in David Rees, *Korea: The Limited War* (Baltimore: Penguin, 1970), 460–461.

90. *Foreign Relations of the United States, 1952–1954*, vol. 15, pt. 1, 1122–1123.

91. As cited in *Foreign Relations of the United States, 1952–1954*, vol. 15, pt. 2, 1190.

92. For NSC 154, see ibid., 1170–1176.

93. For the U.S. draft treaty of July 6, 1953, and the South Korean draft treaty of July 9, 1953, see ibid., 1339–1340, 1359–1361.

94. For the "Memorandum of Conversation" between Rhee and Dulles on August 5, 1953, see ibid., 1466–1473.

95. For the text of the treaty, see Kim, *Documents*, 185–186.

96. For the letter from Dulles to Rhee on July 24, 1953, see *Foreign Relations of the United States, 1952–1954*, vol. 15, pt. 1, 1430–1432.

97. Ibid., 1569–1570.

98. For a report on the Rhee-Nixon meeting and President Eisenhower's letters to Rhee dated November 4, 1953, and January 2, 1954, see *Foreign Relations of the United States, 1952–1954*, vol. 15, pt. 2, 1609–1610, 1685–1686. The text of President Rhee's letter to Eisenhower is not available. Rhee insisted that his promise to Nixon and the contents of his letter be kept absolutely confidential.

99. Ibid., 1620–1624.

100. "Statement by the Sixteen Allied Nations," Geneva Conference, June 15, 1954, in *Department of State Bulletin*, June 28, 1954, 973–974. For an excellent discussion of the Geneva Conference, see Kim, *Master of Manipulation*, 160–175.

101. For the record of the summit meeting, see "Hagerty Diary, July 27, 1954," in *Foreign Relations of the United States, 1952–1954*, vol. 15, pt. 2, 1839–1847. James C. Hagerty was press secretary to and a confidant of President Eisenhower.

102. For the "Agreed Minute" of the summit conference dated July 31, 1954, and the joint statement issued on July 30, see ibid., 1859–1862.

103. Macdonald, *U.S.-Korean Relations*, 201.

104. For the "Memorandum of Conversation" between Herter and Yang on May 16, see *Foreign Relations of the United States*, 1958–1960, vol. 18 (Washington, DC: U.S. Government Printing Office, 1994), 606–608.

105. Ibid., 610.

106. "Telegram from the Embassy in Korea to the Department of State," April 2, 1960, in ibid., 611–613.

107. Ibid., 620. On the April Uprising, see Quee-Young Kim, *The Fall of Syngman Rhee* (Berkeley: Institute of East Asian Studies, University of California, 1983).

108. "Memorandum of Telephone Conversation with the President in Augusta," April 19, 1960, in *Foreign Relations of the United States*, 1958–1960, vol. 18, 623.

109. "Telegram from the Embassy in Korea to the Department of State," April 19, 1960, in ibid., 620–622.

110. "Telegram from the Embassy in Korea to the Department of State," April 21, 1960, in ibid., 629–633.

111. For Herter's telegram, see ibid., 634–637.

112. "Telegram from the Embassy in Korea to the Department of State," April 26, 1960, in ibid., 640–644.

113. As the Park Chung Hee government did not grant Rhee's plea to return to Seoul, he died in Honolulu in 1965 at the age of ninety. Soon thereafter, Rhee's remains were transferred from Honolulu to the National Cemetery in Seoul. On the last months of Rhee's presidency, see Oliver, *Syngman Rhee and American Involvement*, 476–491.

114. For the "Memorandum of Conversation" between Eisenhower and Huh on June 20, see *Foreign Relations of the United States*, 1958–1960, vol. 18, 668–672.

115. For a critical assessment of the Chang government, see Sungjoo Han, *The Failure of Democracy in South Korea* (Berkeley: University of California Press, 1974).

116. For the CIA's reports between April 21 and 26, 1961, see *Foreign Relations of the United States*, 1961–1963, vol. 22 (Washington, DC: U.S. Government Printing Office, 1996), 456–457.

117. Ibid., 449. One of the unintended casualties of the coup was future president Kim Dae Jung. In early May he was elected to the National Assembly from Kangwon Province in a by-election, but the National Assembly was dissolved before he could be sworn in.

118. For the Chang-Green discussion, see Macdonald, *U.S.-Korean Relations*, 209–210.

119. For "Telegram from the Department of State to Secretary of State Rusk at Geneva," May 16, 1961, see *Foreign Relations of the United States*, 1961–63, vol. 22, 452–454.

120. For the Korean version of Yun's meeting with Green and Magruder, see *Hanguk hyondae sa charyo* [Documents on Modern Korean History] (Seoul: Choson ilbo sa, 1996), 204–206.

121. "Telegram from the Department of State to the Embassy in Korea," May 16, 1961, in *Foreign Relations of the United States*, 1961–1963, vol. 22, 455–456.

122. As reported in Macdonald, *U.S.-Korean Relations*, 211.

123. "Telegram from the Department of State to the Embassy in Korea," May 17, 1961, in *Foreign Relations of the United States*, 1961–1963, vol. 22, 461–462.

124. As quoted in Macdonald, *U.S.-Korean Relations*, 213.

125. See "Special National Intelligence Estimate," May 31, 1961, and "Memorandum by Robert H. Johnson of the National Security Council Staff," June 6, 1961, in *Foreign Relations of the United States*, 1961–1963, vol. 22, 468–473.

126. See Macdonald, *U.S.-Korean Relations*, 216.

127. For the "Memorandum of Conversation" between Kennedy and Park on November 14 and the record of their brief meeting on November 15, 1961, see *Foreign Relations of the United States, 1961–1963*, vol. 22, 535–539. For a positive assessment of the summit meeting made by the South Korean Ministry of Foreign Affairs, see *Yuksip nyondae ui hanguk oegyo* [Korean Diplomacy during the 1960s] (Seoul: Ministry of Foreign Affairs, 1971), 40–41.

128. For U.S. concerns about Park's pro-Communist activities, for example, see *Foreign Relations of the United States, 1961–1963*, vol. 22, 468–469. After the fall of Dien Bien Phu in 1954, President Rhee had offered to send two or three South Korean divisions to Indochina, but the offer was not accepted.

129. On the economic issues, see the "Memorandum of Conversation" between Park and Rusk on November 14, 1961, see ibid., 529–534.

130. For the letter from Ambassador Berger to Secretary of State Rusk on December 15, 1961, see ibid., 542–548.

131. For a dicussion of both treaties, see Lee, *China and Korea*, 59–61.

132. For the "Memorandum of Conversation" between Rhee and Dulles on August 5, 1953, see *Foreign Relations of the United States, 1952–1954*, vol. 15, pt. 2, 1466–1473.

133. On the Rhee-Yoshida meeting, see Robert D. Murphy, *Diplomat among Warriors* (Garden City, NY: Doubleday, 1964), 351, and Kim Yong Shik, *Saebyok ui yaksok* [Promise at the Morning] (Seoul: Kimyong sa, 1993), 159–163. As the American and South Korean ambassadors, respectively, Murphy and Kim were both present at the Rhee-Yoshida meeting.

134. The full text of the "Memorandum of Conversation" between Rhee and Dulles on August 6, 1953, was declassified in 1974.

135. For the "Memorandum of Conversation" between Kennedy and Ikeda on June 20, 1961, see *Foreign Relations of the United States, 1961–1963*, vol. 22, 489–490.

136. On Yasuoka's role in drafting the Japanese emperor's "Imperial Rescript Ending the War" in 1945, see Herbert P. Bix, *Hirohito and the Making of Modern Japan* (New York: HarperCollins, 2000), 525. On Yasuoka's active support for Japan–South Korean diplomatic normalization, see Yagi Nobuo's memoir *Fusei aika* [Worldly Elegy] (n.p., 1971).

137. *Foreign Relations of the United States, 1961–1963*, vol. 22, 556–557.

138. Ibid., 567–571.

139. Ibid., 565–566.

140. For a photocopy of the Kim-Ohira memorandum written in Japanese, see Lee Do Sung, *Pak Chonghui wa hanil hoedam* [Park Chung Hee and Korean-Japanese Negotiations] (Seoul: Hansong, 1995).

141. For the "Memorandum of Conversation" between Rusk and Kim on October 29, 1962, see *Foreign Relations of the United States, 1961–1963*, vol. 22, 610–612.

142. Lee and Sato, *U.S. Policy toward Japan and Korea*, 30. For the text of the joint communiqué between President Park and Secretary of State Rusk on January 29, 1964, see Kim, *Documents*, 283–284.

143. Unpublished letter from Bundy to the author, February 6, 1980.

144. For the Treaty of Basic Relations and other agreements, see Lee Do Sung, [Park Chung Hee and Korean-Japanese Negotiations], 391–407. For the English versions, see *Contemporary Japan* 28, no. 3 (May 1966), 678–686.

145. For an excellent discussion of the U.S. role in Japan–South Korea relations, see Victor D. Cha, *Alignment despite Antagonism: The U.S.-Korea-Japan Security Triangle* (Stanford, CA: Stanford University Press, 1999).

146. Min Yong Lee, "The Vietnam War: A Machiavellian Adventure toward a Security State," unpublished paper, July 2000.

147. As quoted in U.S. Senate, *United States Security Agreements and Commitments Abroad, Republic of Korea: Hearings before the Subcommittee on United States Security Agreements and Commitments Abroad of the Committee on Foreign Relations,* pt. 6 (Washington, DC: U.S. Government Printing Office, 1970), 1543.

148. Ibid., 1524.

149. Ibid., 1720–1722. For the "Memorandum of Conversation" between Park and Johnson on November 1, 1966, see *Foreign Relations of the United States, 1964–1968,* vol. 29, pt. 1 (Washington, DC: U.S. Government Printing Office, 2000), 205–207.

150. "Notes on Conversation" between Johnson and Park, in ibid., 302–304.

151. Rostow's memorandum to President Johnson, December 29, 1967, in ibid., 305–306.

152. See *United States Security Agreements and Commitments Abroad,* 1552.

153. See *Foreign Relations of the United States, 1964–1968,* vol. 29, pt. 1, 311. Ambassador Porter conveyed this message to South Korean Prime Minister Chung Il Kwon on January 24, 1968.

154. For the Park-Porter meeting, see "Telegram from the Embassy in Korea to the Department of State," January 24, 1968, in ibid., 311–313.

155. For the telegram from General Charles H. Bonesteel III (CINCUNC and commander, USFK) to the Joint Chiefs of Staff on January 24, 1968, see ibid., 313–315.

156. For the "Memorandum of Record" on the telephone conversation with Eisenhower, January 29, 1968, see ibid., 550–552.

157. For the *Pueblo* incident, see Rusk, *As I Saw It,* 391–397.

158. *Foreign Relations of the United States, 1964–1968,* vol. 29, pt. 1, 537–538.

159. For Goldberg's statement of January 26, 1968, see Kim, *Documents,* 344–348.

160. For Rusk's address on February 10, 1968, see ibid., 348–349.

161. For the text of Johnson's letter to Park on February 3, 1968, see *Foreign Relations of the United States, 1964–1968,* vol. 29, pt. 1, 322–323.

162. For the text of Park's letter to Johnson on February 5, 1968, see ibid., 329–330.

163. For the "Telegram from the Department of State to the Embassy in Korea," February 6, 1968, see ibid., 335–336.

164. For the report on the Park-Vance meeting on February 12, see ibid., 369–371.

165. On the meeting between Chung and Vance on February 14, see ibid., 375–376.

166. For the "Memorandum from Cyrus R. Vance to President Johnson," February 20, 1968, see ibid., 384–391. For the candid and revealing discussions between Johnson and Vance on February 15, see ibid., 376–383.

167. For the "Summary of Conversations Between President Johnson and President Pak," April 17, 1968, see ibid., 419–421. For a South Korean view, see [Korean Diplomacy during the 1960s], 42–43.

168. See *Foreign Relations of the United States, 1964–1968,* vol. 29, pt. 1, 376–391 and 411–414.

169. For the North Korean document and the statements issued by General Woodward, President Johnson, and Secretary of State Rusk, see *Department of State Bulletin*, January 6, 1969, 1–3. The North Koreans displayed the *Pueblo* at Wonsan Harbor and then moved it to the Taedong River near the area where the *General Sherman* had been destroyed.

170. For the "Memorandum from the Under Secretary of State (Katzenbach) to President Johnson," December 23, 1968, see *Foreign Relations of the United States, 1964–1968*, vol. 29, pt. 1, 455–458. This group included the deputy secretary of defense and the deputy director of the CIA.

171. See "National Security Action Memorandum No. 298," ibid., 21–22.

CHAPTER 3. THE DYNAMICS OF STRUCTURAL ADJUSTMENT

1. See Henry Kissinger, *Diplomacy* (New York: Simon and Schuster, 1994), 704–712.

2. For his inaugural address, see *Public Papers of the Presidents of the United States, Richard Nixon, 1969* (Washington, DC: U.S. Government Printing Office, 1971).

3. For the text of the U.S. statement, see Se-Jin Kim, ed., *Documents on Korean-American Relations*, 356–357.

4. Henry Kissinger, *White House Years* (Boston: Little, Brown, 1979), 312–321. For Nixon's view, see Richard M. Nixon, *RN: The Memoirs of Richard Nixon* (New York: Grosset and Dunlap, 1978), 382–385.

5. U.S. National Security Council, "Korean Contingency Planning," National Security Study Memorandum 53, April 26, 1969. This "top secret/sensitive" document was declassified in 1993.

6. For the text, see *Public Papers, Richard Nixon, 1969*, 544–556.

7. For the exchange of statements by Nixon and Park, see ibid., 676–681.

8. For the recollection of the South Korean Ambassador to the United States during the summit meeting, see Kim Yong Shik, *Huimang kwa tojon* [Hope and Challenge] (Seoul: Tonga ilbo sa, 1987), 184.

9. Lee Dong Won, minister of foreign affairs from 1964 to 1966 under President Park, claimed that the mistreatment of Nixon in 1966 led to his decision to withdraw U.S. troops from South Korea. See Lee Dong Won, *Taet'ongnyong ul kurimyo* [Missing the President] (Seoul: Koryowon, 1992).

10. For the joint statement, see *Public Papers, Richard Nixon, 1969*, 681–682.

11. Kim, [Hope and Challenge], 186–187. The referendum passed on October 17, 1969.

12. For a very positive seven-point assessment of the summit meeting, see *Yuksip nyondae ui hanguk oegyo* [Korean Diplomacy during the 1960s] (Seoul: Ministry of Foreign Affairs, 1971), 44–45.

13. See Wookhee Shin and Youngho Kim, "Alliance in Transition: South Korean–U.S. Security Relations, 1968–72," unpublished paper, July 2000. Prior to the Nixon-Park summit meeting in August 1969, Nixon had told U.S. Ambassador to South Korea William Porter that he should remove U.S. troops from South Korea because he was under great pressure from Wilbur Mills, chairman of the House Ways and Means Committee. See Porter's testimony before the House Committee on International Relations, *Investigation of Korean-American*

Relations: Hearings before the Subcommittee on International Organizations, pt. 4 (Washington, DC: U.S. Government Printing Office, 1978), 38.

14. U.S. National Security Council, "U.S. Programs in Korea," National Security Decision Memorandum 48, March 20, 1970. This "top secret" document was declassified in 1993.

15. *Investigation of Korean-American Relations,* pt. 4, 41.

16. Shin and Kim, "Alliance in Transition."

17. House Committee on International Relations, *Human Rights in Korea and the Philippines: Implications for U.S. Policy: Hearings* (Washington, DC: U.S. Government Printing Office, 1975), 41.

18. For Laird's plan, see House Committee on Armed Services, *Hearings on Review of the Policy Decision to Withdraw United States Ground Forces from Korea* (Washington, DC: U.S. Government Printing Office, 1978), 89.

19. On South Korean participation in the Vietnam War, see Min Yong Lee, "The Vietnam War," unpublished paper, July 2000.

20. *Public Papers of the Presidents of the United States, Richard Nixon, 1973* (Washington, DC: U.S. Government Printing Office, 1975), 358.

21. On Zhou's July 15 visit to North Korea, see *Zhou Enlai waijiao huadong dashiji* [A Chronicle of Zhou Enlai's Major Diplomatic Activities] (Beijing: Shijie zhishi chubanshe, 1993), 597.

22. For reactions in South Korea, see Chae-Jin Lee, "South Korea: Political Competition and Government Adaptation," *Asian Survey,* January 1972, 43–45.

23. See Kim, [Hope and Challenge], 235–237.

24. Nixon's letter to President Park on November 29, 1971. This "secret" document was declassified in 1997.

25. U.S. Department of State, "Letter to President Park from President Nixon" (telegram to the U.S. embassy in Seoul), December 6, 1971. This document was declassified in 1997.

26. For the text of the joint communiqué, see Richard H. Solomon, ed., *The China Factor: Sino-American Relations and the Global Scene* (Englewood Cliffs, NJ: Prentice-Hall, 1981), 296–300.

27. Henry Kissinger, *White House Years,* 1061.

28. Kissinger, *Diplomacy,* 728–729.

29. For Zhou's visit to North Korea, March 7–9, 1972, see *Zhou Enlai waijiao huadong dashiji,* 624.

30. Kim, [Hope and Challenge], 258–260.

31. For the development of inter-Korean relations, see Chae-Jin Lee, "South Korea: The Politics of Domestic-Foreign Linkage," *Asian Survey,* January 1973, 94–101, and Don Oberdorfer, *The Two Koreas: A Contemporary History,* rev. ed. (New York: Basic Books, 2001), 23–26.

32. For the "top secret/sensitive/exclusively eyes only" record of the conversation between Kissinger and Deng Xiaoping at the Waldorf Astoria Hotel, see William Burr, ed., *The Kissinger Transcripts* (New York: New Press, 1999), 283–284.

33. As cited in Chae-Jin Lee, *China and Korea: Dynamic Relations* (Stanford, CA: Hoover Institution Press, 1996), 67.

34. U.S. Department of State, "Martial Law and Government Changes" (telegram from the Department of State), October 17, 1972. This "limited official use" document was declassified in 1997. For the U.S. views, see Oberdorfer, *The Two Koreas,* 37–41.

35. For the Ford-Park joint communiqué, see *Department of State Bulletin*, December 23, 1974, 877–878.

36. U.S. National Security Council, "Minutes," December 1, 1974. This declassified document is available at the Ford Library, Ann Arbor, Michigan.

37. *Department of State Bulletin*, May 26, 1975, 669.

38. Ibid., June 2, 1975, 734.

39. *New York Times*, June 21, 1975.

40. *Department of State Bulletin*, December 29, 1975, 913–916.

41. U.S. Department of State, "Development of U.S. Policy toward South Korean Development of Nuclear Weapons" (telegram from the Department of State), February 28, 1975. This "secret/sensitive" document was partially declassified in 1996. See also "ROK Plans to Develop Nuclear Weapons and Missiles" (telegram from the Department of State), March 4, 1975.

42. "U.S. Policy towards Korea" (telegram to the Department of State), June 24, 1975. This document was declassified in 1997.

43. Lee, *China and Korea*, 68.

44. "Memorandum of Conversation" between Ford and Teng Hsiao-p'ing (Deng Xiaoping), December 4, 1975. This document was declassified in 1997.

45. For the divergent views, see *Axe-Murders at Panmunjom* (Seoul: Korea Herald, 1976), and *The Truth of the Panmunjom Incident* (Pyongyang: Foreign Languages Publishing House, 1976).

46. House Committee on International Relations, *Deaths of American Military Personnel in the Korean Demilitarized Zone* (Washington, DC: U.S. Government Printing Office, 1976), 6.

47. Kissinger is conspicuously silent on this issue in his massive two-volume memoirs covering his tenure as secretary of state, *Years of Upheaval* (Boston: Little, Brown, 1982) and *Years of Renewal* (New York: Simon and Schuster, 1999).

48. U.S. Department of State, "FORMIN Pak's Requests Call on Secretary prior UNGA" (telegram to the Department of State), August 20, 1976. This "confidential" document was declassified in 1995.

49. U.S. Department of State, "President Park Speaks out on Panmunjom Incident" (telegram to the Department of State), August 20, 1976. This "limited official use" document was declassified in 1995.

50. The White House, "August 18 Incident at Panmunjom: U.S.-Korean Relations (Memorandum of Conversation)," September 15, 1976. This "secret/sensitive" document was declassified in 1995.

51. As quoted in Frank Gibney, "The Ripple Effect in Korea," *Foreign Affairs*, October 1977, 160. For an extensive discussion of Carter's military policy toward Korea, see Lee and Sato, *U.S. Policy toward Japan and Korea*, 104–127.

52. *Washington Post*, January 9, 1977.

53. *Korea Herald*, October 19, 1976.

54. Ibid., November 5, 1976.

55. For President Park's New Year's press conference on January 12, see *New York Times*, January 13, 1977.

56. U.S. National Security Council, "Korea" (Presidential Review Memorandum/NSC 13), January 26, 1977. This "secret" document was partially declassified in 1991.

57. *Department of State Bulletin*, May 7, 1977, 190–191.

58. As explained in Cyrus Vance, *Hard Choices: Critical Years in America's Foreign Policy* (New York: Simon and Schuster, 1983), 128.

59. Quoted in *Korea Herald*, February 3, 1977.

60. The main contents of Carter's letter were mentioned in Park's letter written to Carter on February 26, 1977.

61. The South Korean Ministry of Foreign Affairs published the English text of President Park's letter of February 26, 1977.

62. Zbigniew Brzezinski, *Power and Principle: Memoirs of the National Security Adviser, 1977–1981* (New York: Farrar Straus Giroux, 1983), 127.

63. Vance, *Hard Choices*, 129.

64. William H. Gleysteen Jr., *Massive Entanglement, Marginal Influence: Carter and Korea in Crisis* (Washington, DC: Brookings Institution Press, 1999), 24, and author discussion with Michael Armacost, October 1, 2003.

65. As cited in Lee and Sato, *U.S. Policy toward Japan and Korea*, 108–109.

66. *Hearings on Review of the Policy Decision*, 79.

67. *Korea Herald*, March 9, 1977.

68. For Carter's meeting with Park, see Park Tong Jin, *Kirun morodo ttusun hana* [Long Road, but One Goal] (Seoul: Tonga ch'ulp'an sa, 1992), 102–110. Park remembers the meeting as being positive and constructive.

69. Author Interview, June 11, 1979.

70. Author Interview, June 27, 1979.

71. Author Interview, June 21, 1979.

72. *Korea Herald*, April 16, 1977.

73. Ibid., April 29, 1977.

74. As described in Gleysteen, *Massive Entanglement*, 24.

75. U.S. National Security Council, "U.S. Policy in Korea" (Presidential Directive/ NSC 12), May 5, 1977. This "top secret/sensitive/eyes only" document was partially declassified in 1984.

76. *Washington Post*, May 19, 1977.

77. U.S. Department of Defense, "U.S. Policy in Korea" (Memorandum for the President), May 16, 1977. This "top secret" document was partially declassified in 1997.

78. Lee and Sato, *U.S. Policy toward Japan and Korea*, 111–112.

79. The White House released Carter's letter of July 21, 1977.

80. See the memorandum to Brzezinski by Vance's secretary Peter Tarnoff on September 2, 1977.

81. As reported in Gleysteen, *Massive Entanglement*, 18.

82. For Carter's message, see *Department of State Bulletin*, December 12, 1977, 852–854.

83. Author interviews with North Korean diplomats, June 30, 1977. See also Gleysteen, *Massive Entanglement*, 42.

84. For a discussion of the positions held by U.S. senators, see Vance, *Hard Choices*, 128–129.

85. For Senator Culver's view, see *U.S. News and World Report*, June 20, 1977.

86. *Public Papers of the Presidents of the United States, Jimmy Carter*, 1978 (Washington, DC: U.S. Government Printing Office, 1979), 122.

87. *New York Times*, March 21, 1978.

88. *Hearings on Review of the Policy Decision*, 1–7.

89. *Department of State Bulletin*, June 1978.

90. As reported in *Korea Herald*, April 26, 1978.

91. Jimmy Carter, *Keeping Faith: Memoirs of a President* (New York: Bantam Books, 1982), 205–206.

92. As discussed in Gleysteen, *Massive Entanglement*, 28.

93. *Public Papers of the Presidents of the United States, Jimmy Carter, 1979* (Washington, DC: U.S. Government Printing Office, 1980), 247–248.

94. Kim, [Hope and Challenge], 443.

95. Vance, *Hard Choices*, 129.

96. Gleysteen, *Massive Entanglement*, 45–47, and Park, [Long Road, but One Goal], 111.

97. "Memorandum of Conversation," June 30, 1979. This "secret" document was declassified in 1997.

98. Vance, *Hard Choices*, 130.

99. As discussed in Kim, [Hope and Challenge], 449–455.

100. For the text, see *Department of State Bulletin*, August 1979, 16–17.

101. Kim, [Hope and Challenge], 456.

102. Gleysteen, *Massive Entanglement*, 42–45.

103. Park, [Long Road, but One Goal], 117–118. For a concise comparison of Seoul's and Pyongyang's views on the proposed tripartite talk, see Byung Chul Koh, *The Foreign Policy Systems of North and South Korea* (Berkeley: University of California Press, 1984), 182–186.

104. Park, [Long Road, but One Goal], 120.

105. In a letter to President Park in August 1979, Carter expressed his satisfaction with the release of eighty-six persons on July 17, 1979. This "confidential" letter was declassified in 1996; it is available at the Carter Library, Atlanta, Georgia.

106. *Department of State Bulletin*, September 1979, 37.

107. The South Korean Ministry of Foreign Affairs issued a statement to welcome Carter's announcement on July 21, 1979.

108. The sentence was removed in order not to complicate the hope that Park would release more persons from prisons.

109. Gleysteen, *Massive Entanglement*, 19.

110. For a detailed discussion of the Koreagate controversies, see Lee and Sato, *U.S. Policy toward Japan and Korea*, 73–90.

111. For Hanna's testimony, see House Committee on Standards of Official Conduct, *Korean Influence Investigation: Hearings* (Washington, DC: U.S. Government Printing Office, 1978), 234–235.

112. As quoted in *Korea Week*, February 10, 1977.

113. See Senate Select Committee on Ethics, *Korean Influence Inquiry: Executive Session Hearings* (Washington, DC: U.S. Government Printing Office, 1978), 1606.

114. *Korean Influence Investigation*, 394–396.

115. *Investigation of Korean-American Relations*, pt. 4, 81.

116. Ibid., 84.

117. Ibid., 60.

118. *Investigation of Korean-American Relations*, pt. 5, 157.

119. *Investigation of Korean-American Relations*, pt. 4, 247.

120. *Washington Post*, October 24, 27, and 29, 1976.

121. Park, [Long Road, but One Goal], 84–85.

122. Author interview with Hahm Pyong Choon, January 1977.

123. As cited in Kim, [Hope and Challenge], 298–299.

124. Ibid., 321–322.

125. Ibid., 322.

126. Ibid., 340–341.

127. Ibid., 344–348.

128. *Korean Influence Investigation*, 10.

129. For the text of Kim's response, see ibid., 187–218.

130. Richard C. Holbrooke, "Korea and the United States: The Era Ahead," *Department of State Bulletin*, February 1979, 29–32. Author interview with a senior South Korean official, July 5, 1979.

131. Author interviews with William Clark Jr. (political counselor, U.S. embassy, Seoul), June 14 and July 3, 1979.

132. Park, [Long Road, but One Goal], 37.

133. As discussed in Gleysteen, *Massive Entanglement*, 52.

134. Park, [Long Road, but One Goal], 133.

135. For the full text of this letter, see John A. Wickham Jr., *Korea on the Brink: A Memoir of Political Intrigue and Military Crisis* (Washington, DC: Brassey's, 2000), 35.

136. Carter's and Choi's letters were dated October 27 and 28, 1979, respectively.

137. Gleysteen, *Massive Entanglement*, 203–207.

138. For Vance's press conference, see *Department of State Bulletin*, December 1979, 25–28.

139. Gleysteen, *Massive Entanglement*, 61.

140. Author interview with Gleysteen, April 2, 2001.

141. For Brewster's view, see Wickham, *Korea on the Brink*, 79.

142. As quoted in Gleysteen, *Massive Entanglement*, 82.

143. "Korea Focus: Discussion with MG Chon Tu Hwan" (telegram to the Department of State), December 15, 1979. This "secret" document was partially declassified in 1993. It is not included in Gleysteen's memoirs, perhaps because of its political sensitivity.

144. Wickham, *Korea on the Brink*, 64–65.

145. Carter's message was dated December 17, 1979, and Choi responded on December 20, 1979.

146. As recalled in Wickham, *Korea on the Brink*, 114–118.

147. On the Kwangju incident, see Donald Clark, ed., *The Kwangju Uprising* (Boulder, CO: Westview Press, 1988).

148. For a collection of U.S. statements and actions during the Kwangju incident, see U.S. Information Agency, "United States Government Statement on the Events in Kwangju, Republic of Korea, May 1980," issued on June 19, 1989.

149. In 1996 the Seoul District Criminal Court held Chun Doo Hwan and Roh Tae Woo, along with a number of other former military and government leaders, responsible for the

illegal military actions on December 12, 1979, for the Kwangju massacre in May 1980, and for extensive corruption. Chun was given a death sentence and a fine of $132 million, and Roh was sentenced with an imprisonment for twenty-two and a half years and a fine of $158 million. Others received less severe sentences. The appellate court commuted Chun's sentence to life imprisonment and Roh's sentence to seventeen years in prison and reduced their fines. In April 1997 the Supreme Court accepted the decisions made by the lower courts. It was ironic that in December 1997 President Kim Young Sam, in cooperation with President-elect Kim Dae Jung, pardoned Chun and Roh and twenty-three accomplices in the interest of national harmony and reconciliation. The fines were not forgiven, however. Chun and Roh attended the inauguration of President Kim Dae Jung on February 25, 1998.

150. Gleysteen, *Massive Entanglement*, 194.

151. The letter was declassified in 1998.

152. Chun's letter to Carter was dated September 8, 1980.

153. See Zbigniew Brzezinski, "Memorandum: Kim Dae Jung" to President Carter, September 16, 1980. This "secret" memorandum was partially declassified in 1997. The explanation based on Confucianism was originally provided by Donald Gregg, a staff member of the National Security Council, in a "secret" memorandum to Brzezinski (dated September 16, 1980).

154. For the text of this resolution, see *Korea and the United States Congress: 1945–2000* (Washington, DC: The South Korean Embassy in the United States, 2001), 544–545.

155. In a memorandum to Brzezinski on October 16, 1980, Donald Gregg suggested that President Carter did not need to see the letter from Lee Hee Ho, but Brzezinski decided to pass it on to the president. The letter is available in the Carter Library, Atlanta, Georgia.

156. Author discussion with Allen, July 25, 2003. He was unhappy that Kim Dae Jung had publicly criticized the Reagan administration for embracing President Chun. See Richard V. Allen, "On the Korea Tightrope, 1980," *New York Times*, January 21, 1998, and Richard Holbrooke and Michael Armacost, "A Future Leader's Moment of Truth," ibid., December 24, 1997.

157. Carter, *Keeping Faith*, 578. Upset by student demonstrations at the University of California (Berkeley), Governor Reagan was instrumental in encouraging the Board of Regents to dismiss Chancellor Clark Kerr in 1967.

158. For Carter's letter, see "Presidential Letter" (telegram from the White House), December 1, 1980. This "secret" document was declassified in 1998. For Gleysteen's confidential reports on Kim Dae Jung, see "Delivery of Presidential Letter" (telegram to the Department of State), December 6, 1980, and "Korea Focus: Prospects on Kim Dae Jung" (telegram to the Department of State), December 30, 1980, both declassified in 1996. Neither of the two documents is included in Gleysteen's memoirs.

159. "Confidential Attachment" from "D.A." to Brzezinski on November 26, 1980. The attachment is available in the Carter Library, Atlanta, Georgia.

160. Allen, "On the Korea Tightrope."

161. For Sohn's confidential report dated December 9, 1980, see *Hanguk hyondae sa charyo* [Documents on Modern Korean History] (Seoul: Choson ilbo sa, 1996), 377.

162. Author discussion with Kim Kyung Won, October 17, 2002.

163. For Roh's version, see *Wolgan Choson* [Monthly Choson], May 1999, 77–78.

CHAPTER 4. THE PASSING OF THE COLD WAR

1. For the text of the joint communiqué issued by Presidents Reagan and Chun, see *Department of State Bulletin*, March 1981, 14–15.

2. George Bush, "Continuity and Change in U.S.-Korean Relations," *Current Policy*, no. 1155 (1989).

3. Henry Kissinger, *Diplomacy* (New York: Simon and Schuster, 1994), 765.

4. George P. Shultz, *Turmoil and Triumph: My Years as Secretary of State* (New York: Charles Scribner's Sons, 1993), 975.

5. William Gleysteen, "Agenda Suggestions for Reagan-Chun Meeting" (telegram to the Department of State), January 22, 1981. This "secret" document was declassified in 1996.

6. See Alexander Haig's memorandum for the president, "Your Meeting with Chun Doo-Hwan, President of the Republic of Korea," January 29, 1981. This "secret" document was declassified in 1993.

7. For the exchange of remarks, see *Public Papers of the Presidents of the United States, Administration of Ronald Reagan, 1981* (Washington, DC: U.S. Government Printing Office, 1982), 66–67.

8. Author discussion with Kim Kyung Won, October 17, 2002. As secretary general to the president, Kim took part in the Reagan-Chun summit meeting.

9. For the text of the joint communiqué, see *Department of State Bulletin*, March 1981, 14–15. The South Koreans included a reference to the tripartite proposal in the draft communiqué, but Haig rejected it. See also William H. Gleysteen Jr., *Massive Entanglement, Marginal Influence: Carter and Korea in Crisis* (Washington, DC: Brookings Institution Press, 1999), 45.

10. Alexander M. Haig Jr., *Caveat: Realism, Reagan, and Foreign Policy* (New York: Macmillan, 1984), 57, 90.

11. "ROK President Chun's Meeting with the Secretary at the State Department," February 6, 1981. This "secret" document was declassified in 1996.

12. Report prepared by Robert G. Rich (director, Office of Korean Affairs, Department of State), February 13, 1981. This "confidential" document was declassified in 1996.

13. "Talking Points" prepared for Secretary of State Haig, June 3, 1981. This "confidential" and "secret" document was partially declassified in 1996.

14. For Kennedy's speech of January 25, 1982, and the international appeal signed by about one hundred leaders all over the world, see *Korea and the United States Congress: 1945–2000* (Washington, DC: The Korean Embassy, 2001), 1144–1149.

15. Paul Wolfowitz, "Briefing Memorandum: Your January-February Trip to East Asia" for Secretary of State Shultz on January 26, 1983. This "secret" document was declassified in 1995.

16. For a detailed discussion of the incident, see Alexander Dallin, *Black Box: KAL 007 and the Superpowers* (Berkeley: University of California Press, 1985).

17. For Reagan's statements on September 2, 4, 5, 7, 8, and 10, see *Department of State Bulletin*, October 1983, 3–14.

18. U.S. National Security Council, "U.S. Response to Soviet Destruction of KAL Airliner" (NSDD 102), September 5, 1983. This "confidential" and "secret" document was partially declassified in 1986.

19. Anatoly Dobrynin, *In Confidence: Moscow's Ambassador to America's Six Cold War Presidents* (New York: Times Books, 1995), 539. For a U.S. version of the Shultz-Gromyko meeting, see Jack F. Matlock Jr., *Reagan and Gorbachev* (New York: Random House, 2004), 66–69.

20. The text of Kim's statement appears in *Massacre in the Sky* (Seoul: Korea Overseas Information Service, 1983), 25–30.

21. For the text of the diplomatic note, see *Department of State Bulletin*, October 1983, 15.

22. Ibid., 15.

23. Dobrynin, *In Confidence*, 536.

24. For biographical information about the deceased, see *New York Times*, October 10, 1983. In addition to Burma, President Chun planned to visit India, Sri Lanka, Brunei, Australia, and New Zealand.

25. C. Kenneth Quinones and Joseph Tragert, *The Complete Idiot's Guide to Understanding North Korea* (New York: Alpha Books, 2003), 311.

26. Shultz, *Turmoil and Triumph*, 976.

27. George Shultz, "Korea: Your Meetings with President Chun" (memorandum for the president), November 1, 1983.

28. U.S. Department of State, "Talking Points for First Meeting with President Chun," a secret memorandum prepared for President Reagan, November 1983.

29. For the text of Reagan's speech, see *Department of State Bulletin*, January 1984, 18–22. The South Korean government initially resisted Reagan's plan to speak before the National Assembly because his expected emphasis on democracy and human rights might be viewed as an indirect criticism of Chun's rule, but it eventually relented. Author discussion with C. Kenneth Quinones, May 25, 2004.

30. For the joint statement, see *Department of State Bulletin*, January 1984, 27–29.

31. Author discussion with David Lambertson, October 2002.

32. For the joint press conference by Presidents Reagan and Chun on April 26, 1985, see *Department of State Bulletin*, August 1985, 44–45.

33. Shultz, *Turmoil and Triumph*, 976.

34. Ibid., 979.

35. For the process of political democratization in South Korea, see Chae-Jin Lee, "Challenge of Democratization," in G. Cameron Hurst III, ed., *Korea 1988: A Nation at the Crossroads* (Lawrence: Center for East Asian Studies, University of Kansas, 1988), 11–34, and John Kie-chiang Oh, *Korean Politics* (Ithaca, NY: Cornell University Press, 1999), 89–97.

36. As reported in *Hanguk Ilbo*, June 9, 1987.

37. Author discussion with Kim Kyung Won, October 17, 2002.

38. For the contents of Reagan's letter, see James Lilley with Jeffrey Lilley, *China Hands: Nine Decades of Adventure, Espionage, and Diplomacy in Asia* (New York: Public Affairs, 2004), 277.

39. As cited in Don Oberdorfer, *The Two Koreas: A Contemporary History*, rev. ed. (New York: Basic Books, 2001), 168–169.

40. Author discussion with James Lilley, May 24, 2004.

41. For the text of a confidential report on the Chun-Sigur conversation, see "Assistant Secretary Sigur's Meeting with President Chun Do Hwan" (telegram to the Department of State), June 24, 1987. This "secret" document was declassified in 1996.

42. For a discussion on Sigur's visit with Kim Dae Jung, see "ASEC Sigur's Meeting with KDJ: Current Status" (telegram to the Department of State), June 24, 1987. This "secret" document was declassified in 1996.

43. Lilley and Lilley, *China Hands*, 280.

44. For the text of Sigur's statement on June 26, see "Statement by A/S Sigur at White House" (telegram to the U.S. embassy in Seoul), June 26, 1987. It was declassified in 1996.

45. *Tonga Ilbo*, June 30, 1987.

46. James Lilley, "Meeting with Roh Tae-Woo, April 4," April 5, 1988. This "confidential" document was released in March 2004 in response to the author's Freedom of Information Act (FOIA) request.

47. James Lilley, "Assistant Secretary Sigur's Meeting with President Chun," September 19, 1987. This "secret" document was released in March 2004 in response to the author's FOIA request.

48. James Lilley, "ASEC Sigur's Call on ROK DEFMIN Chung: Don't Worry; the Military Will Not Intervene," September 17, 1987. This "confidential" document was released in March 2004 in response to the author's FOIA request. Chung was a high school classmate of Roh Tae Woo; Chung, Roh, and Chun Doo Hwan came from Taegu, attended the Korean Military Academy together, and organized *Hanahoe* (One Association), a tightly-knit unofficial group in the South Korean military.

49. James Lilley, "ASEC Sigur Meets the Two Kims," September 18, 1987. This "confidential" document was released in March 2004 in response to the author's FOIA request.

50. Author discussion with James Lilley, December 1995.

51. As recorded in Shultz, *Turmoil and Triumph*, 981.

52. James Lilley, "Meeting with Roh Tae-Woo, April 4."

53. "Luncheon for Secretary Shultz by President Roh, Tae Woo, July 18, 1988," July 19, 1988. This "confidential" document was released in March 2004 in response to the author's FOIA request.

54. "Secretary Shultz's Departure Statement from Korea, July 18," July 20, 1988. This document was unclassified.

55. For the text, see *Department of State Bulletin*, January 1989, 17.

56. For U.S. consultations with South Korea and other countries prior to October 31, 1988, see "ROK President Roh's Visit: US Policy re N. Korea" (telegram from the Department of State), October 25, 1988. This "secret" document was declassified in 1995.

57. "Policy/Regulation Changes Regarding North Korea: Informing Seoul, Tokyo, Moscou [sic] and Beijing" (telegram from the Department of State), October 28, 1988. This "confidential" document was declassified in 1995.

58. See Anderson's statement before the Subcommittee on Asian and Pacific Affairs, House Committee on International Relations, July 25, 1990.

59. George Bush, "Continuity and Change in U.S.-Korean Relations."

60. James Baker, "U.S. Foreign Policy Priorities and FY 1991 Budget Request," *Current Policy*, no. 1254 (1990).

61. For a discussion of the Beijing Talks, see Chae-Jin Lee, "U.S. Policy toward North Korea in the 1990s," *Korean Studies* 16 (1992), 13–28.

62. Author interview with Raymond Burghardt in Beijing, August 1989.

63. Author interview with a senior North Korean diplomat in Beijing, August 1989.

64. Richard H. Solomon, "The Last Glacier: The Korean Peninsula and the Post–Cold War Era," *U.S. Department of State Dispatch*, February 11, 1991, 105–108.

65. For an explanation of the bill (S. 1439), see Senator Nunn's speech in *Congressional Record: Senate*, July 31, 1989.

66. U.S. Department of Defense, "A Strategic Framework for the Asian Pacific Rim: Looking toward the 21st Century," April 18, 1990. This is commonly referred to as the East Asia Strategic Initiative (EASI).

67. Richard H. Solomon, "The Last Glacier."

68. See Roh Tae Woo's interview in *Wolgan Choson* [Monthly Choson], May 1999, 135.

69. For the recollection by the South Korean minister of foreign affairs at the time, see Lee Sang Ock, *Chonhwanki ui hanguk oegyo* [Korean Diplomacy at the Time of Transformation] (Seoul: Sam kwa kkum, 2002), 499–503.

70. *Korea Herald*, January 24, 1992. This meeting had been arranged by Desaix Anderson (deputy assistant secretary of state for East Asian and Pacific affairs) and Ho Jong (North Korean deputy ambassador to the United Nations). It took place after the North Koreans had signed the nuclear safeguards agreement with the International Atomic Energy Agency on December 26, 1991.

71. Arnold Kanter, "North Korea, Nuclear Proliferation, and U.S. Policy: Collective Engagement in a New Era" (statement before the Subcommittee on East Asian and Pacific Affairs, Senate Committee on Foreign Relations), February 6, 1992.

72. Author discussion with Arnold Kanter, May 1998.

73. As cited in Lee Sang Ock, [Korean Diplomacy], 503. Author discussion with Robert Carlin (participant in the Kanter-Kim meeting), April 19, 2004.

74. *Asahi Shimbun*, March 3, 1992.

75. *Washington Times*, April 15, 1992.

76. For his inaugural address, see Roh Tae Woo, *Korea: A Nation Transformed* (Oxford: Pergamon Press, 1990), 53–58.

77. Ibid., 59–61.

78. Ibid., 4–10.

79. Ibid., 49.

80. Lilley and Lilley, *China Hands*, 290–291.

81. Author interview with Choi Ho Jung, October 23, 2002. See also Choi Ho Jung, *Pitparaen yonggwang sogae huhoenun optta* [No Regrets in the Faded Glory] (Seoul: Samhwa ch'ulp'an sa, 1999). In August 1988, U.S. Ambassador to South Korea James Lilley cooperated with U.S. Ambassador to China Winston Lord in obtaining the Chinese government's permission to allow South Korean Foreign Minister Choi Kwang Soo's stopover at the Beijing Airport on his way to Pakistan. Lord met with Choi at the airport. See Lilley and Lilley, *China Hands*, 291.

82. On the evolution of Gorbachev's policy toward the Korean Peninsula, see Oberdorfer, *The Two Koreas*, 197–204.

83. For Roh Tae Woo's recollection of his meeting with Dobrynin, see *Wolgan Choson*, May 1999, 96–98. The Inter-Action Council was an international meeting of former heads of

state and other high-level government leaders organized by former West German chancellor Helmut Schmidt.

84. Author discussion with Ro Jai Bong, September 25, 2002. There are conflicting views on whether Roh mentioned $3 billion in his meeting with Dobrynin or not.

85. George Bush and Brent Scowcroft, *A World Transformed* (New York: Alfred A. Knopf, 1998), 290.

86. See "Roh Tae Woo's Meeting with Gorbachev, Visit to Washington" (telegram to the Department of State), May 31, 1990. This "confidential" document was declassified in 1995.

87. On the Bush-Gorbachev meetings, see Bush and Scowcroft, *A World Transformed*, 279–290.

88. Author discussions with Choi Ho Jung, October 23, 2002, and with Ro Jai Bong, September 25, 2002.

89. For his press conference, see Roh Tae Woo, *Korea*, 47–49.

90. The exchange of remarks between Roh and Gorbachev is based on "MOFA Readout on Roh-Gorbachev Meeting" (telegram to the Department of State), June 12, 1990. This "secret" document was declassified in 1995.

91. See *Wolgan Choson*, 99, and Roh Chang Hee, *Oegyogwan samsip saminui hoesang* [Recollections by Thirty Three Diplomats] (Seoul: Yogang ch'ulpa'n sa, 2002), 75–82. At the summit meeting Roh Chang Hee served as presidential chief of protocol and interpreter.

92. *Wolgan Choson*, 104.

93. Mikhail Gorbachev, *Memoirs* (New York: Doubleday, 1995), 544.

94. Author interview with Alexander Panov (he accompanied Shevardnadze to Pyongyang and later became Moscow's ambassador to Seoul and then to Tokyo), April 1992.

95. *Minju Choson*, September 19, 1990.

96. Author interview with Choi Ho Jung, October 23, 2002.

97. *Rodong Sinmun*, October 5, 1990.

98. For the text, see *Korea Herald*, December 15, 1990.

99. Author discussion with Kuriyama Takakazu, February 22, 2004.

100. Okonogi Masao, *Nihon to kitachosen* [Japan and North Korea] (Tokyo: PHP Kenkyusho, 1991), 12–21.

101. Michael H. Armacost, *Friends or Rivals? The Insider's Account of U.S.-Japan Relations* (New York: Columbia University Press, 1996), 146. Armacost used the term "jolted."

102. For the Roh-Kanemaru meeting, see *Wolgan Choson*, 124–125.

103. Michael H. Armacost, *Friends or Rivals?* 147.

104. Okonogi Masao, ed., *Kitachosen handobuku* [North Korea Handbook] (Tokyo: Kodansha, 1997), 430–438.

105. For Baker's statement, see *U.S. Department of State Dispatch*, July 8, 1991, 486.

106. For Lee's meeting with Liu, see Lee Sang Ock, [Korean Diplomacy], 128–130.

107. For a discussion of Li Peng's visit to Pyongyang, see Chae-Jin Lee, *China and Korea: Dynamic Relations* (Stanford, CA: Hoover Institution Press, 1996), 120–122.

108. *China Daily*, May 10, 1991.

109. As cited in Lee Sang Ock, [Korean Diplomacy], 120–122.

110. Bush and Scowcroft, *A World Transformed*, 545.

111. For the development of Roh Tae Woo's nonnuclear policy, see *Wolgan Choson*, 130–139, and Lee Sang Ock, [Korean Diplomacy], 456–471.

112. As cited in Quinones and Tragert, *The Complete Idiot's Guide*, 362–363.

113. Author interview with Lee Sang Ock, September 17, 2002. See also Lee Sang Ock, [Korean Diplomacy], 465.

114. Author discussion with Ronald Lehman, February 26, 2004.

115. On economic relations between China and South Korea, see Chae-Jin Lee, *China and Korea*, 133–168. On the status of the Korean minority in China, see Chae-Jin Lee, *China's Korean Minority: The Politics of Ethnic Education* (Boulder, CO: Westview Press, 1986).

116. As reported in Lee Sang Ock, [Korean Diplomacy], 148–149.

117. *Korea Herald*, August 25, 1992, and *Los Angeles Times*, August 24, 1992.

118. For the Korean-language text of the Joint Declaration, see Lee Sang Ock, [Korean Diplomacy], 272–274.

119. Joint news conference held by Presidents Bush and Roh in Seoul on January 6, 1992.

120. *Korea Newsreview*, June 27, 1987.

121. Il SaKong, *Korea in the World Economy* (Washington, DC: Institute for International Economics, 1993), 133.

122. See Chae-Jin Lee, "U.S. Policy toward South Korea," in Donald N. Clark, ed., *Korea Briefing, 1993* (Boulder, CO: Westview Press, 1993), 70.

123. *1990 Trade Policy Agenda and 1989 Annual Report of the President of the United States on the Trade Agreements Program* (Washington, DC: U.S. Government Printing Office, 1990), 41.

124. George Bush, "Continuity and Change in US-Korean Relations."

125. For the text of his speech, see Roh Tae Woo, *Korea*, 11–17.

126. As quoted in *Los Angeles Times*, October 18, 1989.

127. *1990 Trade Policy Agenda*, 33.

128. Richard H. Solomon, "The Last Glacier."

129. For the text of Bush's speech on January 6, 1992, see George Bush, "The U.S. and Korea: Entering a New World," *U.S. Department of State Dispatch*, January 13, 1992.

130. Ibid.

CHAPTER 5. FROM CONTAINMENT TO ENGAGEMENT

1. For Clinton's inaugural address, see *Los Angeles Times*, January 21, 1993.

2. For Aspin's views, see *Hearings before the Committee on Armed Services, United States Senate*, 103rd Congress, 1st sess. (Washington, DC: U.S. Government Printing Office, 1994).

3. For his statement before the Senate Committee on Foreign Relations on January 13, 1993, see *U.S. Department of State Dispatch*, January 25, 1993, 47.

4. Ibid.

5. As reported in *Newsreview*, April 10, 1993.

6. For a detailed and authoritative reconstruction of U.S. policy on the North Korean nuclear question, see Joel S. Wit, Daniel B. Poneman, and Robert L. Gallucci, *Growing Critical: The First North Korean Nuclear Crisis* (Washington, DC: Brookings Institution Press, 2004), 41.

7. *U.S. Department of State Dispatch*, May 24, 1993, 383.

8. C. Kenneth Quinones, *Kitachosen: beikokumusho tantokan no koshohiroku* [North Korea: A Memoir of Negotiations by a U.S. Department of State Official] (Tokyo: Chuoko-ron shinsha, 2000), 143–144.

9. The U.S. delegation included Charles Kartman, C. Kenneth Quinones, and Robert Carlin, and the North Korean delegation included Kim Gye Gwan, Ho Jong, and Ri Gun. They all played an important role in the subsequent development of U.S.–North Korean negotiations.

10. *U.S. Department of State Dispatch*, June 14, 1993. For a detailed history of U.S.–North Korean negotiations, see Leon D. Sigal, *Disarming Strangers: Nuclear Diplomacy with North Korea* (Princeton, NJ: Princeton University Press, 1998), and Don Oberdorfer, *The Two Koreas: A Contemporary History*, rev. ed. (New York: Basic Books, 2001), 251–368.

11. Quinones, [North Korea], 182–183.

12. The statement was issued on June 12, 1993.

13. The South Koreans complained about using the term "joint statement" in the announcement and the official name "Democratic People's Republic of Korea." Author interviews with C. Kenneth Quinones, March 2, 1998, and October 4, 2002.

14. Author interview with a top-level South Korean official, May 2003.

15. Ibid.

16. For the text of their joint news conference, see *U.S. Department of State Dispatch*, July 19, 1993, 512–513. In his memoir, former president Clinton did not say much about this meeting but noted South Korea's "famous hospitality." Bill Clinton, *My Life* (New York: Alfred A. Knopf, 2004), 529.

17. Ibid., 509–512.

18. *New York Times*, July 12, 1993. For Kang Sok Ju's threat, see Quinones, [North Korea], 196–197.

19. For President Kim's recollection, see Kim Young Sam, *Kim Yongsam taet'ongnyong hoego rok* [President Kim Young Sam's Memoirs], vol. 1 (Seoul: Choson ilbo sa, 2000), 145–153.

20. Author discussions with Gallucci, November 22–23, 1996, and February 20–21, 1998.

21. *U.S. Department of State Dispatch*, July 26, 1993, 535. This statement was issued by each side separately in part because the South Koreans were concerned about more joint documents between the United States and North Korea.

22. Ibid., 535–536.

23. *Los Angeles Times*, November 8, 1993.

24. See the text of the November 23 joint press conference in *U.S. Department of State Dispatch*, December 6, 1993, 847.

25. The Principals Committee meeting included Warren Christopher (secretary of state), Les Aspin (secretary of defense), Anthony Lake (assistant to the president for national security affairs), Samuel Berger (deputy assistant to the president for national security affairs), John Shalikashvili (chairman of the Joint Chiefs of Staff), R. James Woolsey (director of the Central Intelligence Agency), and Leon Fuerth (national security adviser to the vice president). On this meeting, see Wit, Poneman, and Gallucci, *Growing Critical*, 106–107.

26. Author interviews with Anthony Lake, November 15, 2001, and Chung Chong Wook, April 10, 2003.

27. Joint press conference, November 23, 1993.

28. Kim Young Sam, [Memoirs], 218.

29. Wit, Poneman, and Gallucci, *Growing Critical*, 139. In his memoir, Clinton did not mention the substance of his difficult discussions with Kim Young Sam. Clinton, *My Life*, 561.

30. Libya voted against the resolution, and China, Brazil, India, Indonesia, and Lebanon abstained. Four other countries did not participate in the vote.

31. For the text, see *Korea Herald*, April 2, 1994. On the multilateral diplomatic maneuvers at the U.N. Security Council, see Wit, Poneman, and Gallucci, *Growing Critical*, 155–161.

32. On the interbureaucratic dynamics between the two positions, see ibid., 140–141.

33. As quoted in *Los Angeles Times*, March 18, 1994.

34. For the text of Perry's speech, see *U.S. Department of State Dispatch*, May 9, 1994, 275–279.

35. On U.S. military plans and estimates, see Oberdorfer, *The Two Koreas*, 315–324.

36. Author interviews with William Perry, September 13, 1999, and Anthony Lake, November 15, 2001. See also Ashton B. Carter and William J. Perry, *Preventive Defense: A New Security Strategy for America* (Washington, DC: Brookings Institution Press, 1999), 123–133.

37. U.N. Security Council, "Draft Resolution," June 1994.

38. As reported in *Newsweek*, June 27, 1994.

39. On China's changing positions, see Chae-Jin Lee, *China and Korea*, 95–96.

40. Ambassador Han Seung Soo invited Carter to his home and briefed him on the history of relations and agreements between North Korea and South Korea. Han had been a professor at Seoul National University, a member of the National Assembly, and minister of trade and industry. Author interview with Han, October 31, 2002. At a luncheon in Atlanta hosted by Georgia Governor Zell Miller in June 1994, the Japanese emperor wished Carter well in his forthcoming visit to North Korea. Author discussion with Kuriyama Takakazu (he accompanied the emperor to Georgia as Japanese ambassador to the United States), February 22, 2004.

41. Jimmy Carter, "Report of Our Trip to Korea, June 1994." Cited with permission from the Carter Library, Atlanta, Georgia. For an excellent discussion of the Carter visit, see Wit, Poneman, and Gallucci, *Growing Critical*, 206–246. For a positive assessment of Carter's contribution as having saved Clinton from "a near disaster," see Selig S. Harrison, *Korean Endgame: A Strategy for Reunification and U.S. Disengagement* (Princeton, NJ: Princeton University Press, 2002), 215–220.

42. Author interview with Lee Hong Koo, October 18, 2002.

43. For President Kim's discussions with Ambassador Laney and President Clinton, see Kim Young Sam, [Memoirs], 312–320. Kim claimed that he stopped the U.S. plans to evacuate American citizens from South Korea and to attack North Korea.

44. For Kim's letter, see Clinton, *My Life*, 603.

45. For the text of Clinton's statement, Gallucci's condolences, and South Korea's objections, see Quinones, [North Korea], 301–305.

46. Ibid., 330–335. Thomas Hubbard and Kim Gye Gwan were entrusted with the task of finalizing the Agreed Statement in Geneva.

47. Ibid., 327–330.

48. Author interview with Thomas Hubbard, December 9, 2002.

49. Author discussion with Kuriyama Takakazu (Japanese ambassador to the United States, 1992–95), February 22, 2004.

50. As candidly admitted by Gallucci in *Newsreview*, June 1, 1996.

51. Author interview with Han Seung Soo, October 31, 2002.

52. Author interview with Han Sung Joo, November 26, 2002.

53. For a discussion of the Geneva Agreed Framework and U.S.–North Korean relations under President Clinton, see Chae-Jin Lee, "U.S. Policy toward North Korea: The Dilemma of Containment and Engagement," *Korea and World Affairs* 20, no. 3 (Fall 1996), 357–379; and Chae-Jin Lee, "U.S. Policy toward North Korea: Engagement and Deterrence," in *The Challenges of Reconciliation and Reform in Korea* (Washington, DC: The Korean Economic Institute of America, 2002), 167–194.

54. Author interview with Thomas Hubbard, December 9, 2002.

55. Wit, Poneman, and Gallucci, *Growing Critical*, 142.

56. For the Confidential Minute, see Quinones and Tragert, *The Complete Idiot's Guide*, 369–371.

57. *U.S. Department of State Dispatch*, October 31, 1994, 721.

58. Warren Christopher, *In the Stream of History: Shaping Foreign Policy for a New Era* (Stanford, CA: Stanford University Press, 1998), 218.

59. Selig S. Harrison, *Korean Endgame*, 3–5.

60. The South Korean statement was issued on October 18, 1994—three days before the Agreed Framework was signed.

61. *Newsreview*, October 22, 1994.

62. While the United States initially proposed to establish the "Korean Energy Development Organization" (KEDO), North Korea insisted on calling it the "Korean Peninsula Energy Development Organization." As a compromise, the United States accepted the "Korean Peninsula Energy Development Organization" but kept the original acronym, KEDO, by arguing that the letter *p* is often silent in English pronunciation. Author discussions with Gallucci, February 20–21, 1998.

63. Author interview with Han Sung Joo, November 26, 2002.

64. *U.S. Department of State Dispatch*, June 19, 1995, 511.

65. For the text of their joint press conference, see *U.S. Department of State Dispatch*, August 7, 1995, 607.

66. James A. Baker III, *The Politics of Diplomacy: Revolution, War, and Peace, 1989–1992* (New York: G. P. Putnam's Sons, 1995), 598. Another former secretary of state, Henry Kissinger, argued later that the Agreed Framework probably had the exact opposite effect on nuclear nonproliferation efforts because it could encourage other rogue states to initiate nuclear weapons programs so that they could receive a comparable buyout. See *Does America Need a Foreign Policy?* 129.

67. Author interview with a U.S. diplomat, October 1995. On U.S.–North Korean negotiations over setting up a liaison office, see Quinones, [North Korea], 412–421.

68. Author discussion with Han Song Ryol (member of the North Korean Mission to the United Nations), May 1995.

69. See the text of Lord's "Address to the Korea-United States 21st Century Council," February 8, 1996.

70. *U.S. Department of State Dispatch*, February 6, 1995, 84, and *Federal Register*, February 16, 1995.

71. As quoted in *Los Angeles Times*, March 3, 1996.

72. Winston Lord, "Address," February 8, 1996.

73. *Los Angeles Times*, June 13, 1996.

74. Deutch testified on February 22, 1996.

75. As quoted in *Los Angeles Times*, March 30, 1966.

76. See the text of Dole's speech, "America and Asia: Restoring U.S. Leadership in the Pacific," May 9, 1966.

77. As quoted in *Los Angeles Times*, September 18, 1994.

78. *U.S. Department of State Dispatch*, March 13, 1995, 205.

79. FBIS-EAS, February 22, 1996, 22–23.

80. Ibid., April 5, 1996, 19.

81. Ibid., April 12, 1996, 32–33.

82. *New York Times*, April 9, 1996.

83. Author interview with Lake, November 15, 2001, and author discussions with Yoo, January 31, 2001, and April 19, 2004. Yoo served as director of the Bureau of American Affairs, minister of political affairs at the South Korean embassy in Washington, vice minister of foreign affairs, and ambassador to the United Nations. In 1978 and 1979, Lake, as director of the policy planning staff in the Department of State, and Yoo, as director of the Bureau of American Affairs, had participated in the planning sessions for the Carter-Park summit meeting.

84. For the text of their joint statement, see *Korea Herald*, April 17, 1996.

85. For Kim's further elaboration, see Kim Young Sam, [Memoirs], 214.

86. For the exchange of letters between Kim and Jiang, see ibid., 216.

87. FBIS-EAS, April 18, 1996, 27–28.

88. Ibid., May 7, 1996, 14–15.

89. United Nations Security Council, S/PRST/1996/42, October 15, 1996.

90. *New York Times*, December 30, 1996.

91. His statement was issued by the White House Office of the Press Secretary on December 29, 1996.

92. For China's approach to the case, see Chae-Jin Lee and Stephanie Hsieh, "China's Two-Korea Policy at Trial: The Hwang Chang Yop Crisis," *Pacific Affairs* (Fall 2001), 321–341.

93. For the preparatory meetings, see *T'ongil Paekso* [Unification White Paper] (Seoul: Ministry of Unification, 1999), 156–165.

94. *People's Korea*, October 11, 1997.

95. Ibid., December 27, 1997.

96. Chae-Jin Lee, "South Korean Foreign Relations Face the Globalization Challenges," in Samuel S. Kim, ed., *Korea's Globalization* (New York: Cambridge University Press, 2000), 170–195.

97. As quoted in *Fortune*, February 16, 1998, 86.

98. *Los Angeles Times*, January 17, 1998.

99. As cited in ibid., January 4, 1998.

100. For his inaugural address, see *Korea Herald*, January 26, 1998.

101. Author interview with Lim Dong Won, April 1998.

102. Author interview with a high-level South Korean official, October 2002.

103. See Clinton's "Remarks" welcoming Kim to the White House on June 9, 1998, in *Public Papers of the Presidents of the United States: Administration of William J. Clinton, 1998*, Book I (Washington, DC: U.S. Government Printing Office, 1999), 916–922.

104. For the joint press conference, see ibid.

105. For the English text of this memorandum, see *Hanbando munjae chuyo hyonan charyo chip* [Documents on the Major Current Problems of the Korean Peninsula] (Seoul: Ministry of Foreign Affairs and Trade, 2004), 228.

106. For the view of the South Korean Ministry of Foreign Affairs, see *Oegyo Paekso* [Diplomatic White Paper] (Seoul: Ministry of Foreign Affairs, 2000), 164–166.

107. *T'ongil Paekso* (2000), 176.

108. Public Law 105–277, October 21, 1998.

109. See "U.S. Policy Toward North Korea," in a hearing before the Committee on International Relations, House of Representatives, September 24, 1998.

110. Ibid.

111. Richard L. Armitage, "A Comprehensive Approach to North Korea," *National Defense University Strategic Forum*, no. 159, March 1999. The group included Paul D. Wolfowitz (Paul H. Nitze School of Advanced International Studies, Johns Hopkins University), General Robert W. RisCassi (former commander, USFK), and Robert A. Manning (Council on Foreign Relations).

112. Author interview with William Perry, September 13, 1999. Perry held meetings with his South Korean and Japanese counterparts from April 23 to 26, 1999, in Honolulu; on May 24 in Tokyo; on May 29 in Seoul; and on June 25 and 26 in Washington.

113. As revealed in Perry's speech at the Asia Society, San Francisco, June 16, 2004.

114. For a report on his role and assessments, see Philip W. Yun, "Facing the Boogeyman: A Korean American Diplomat Recounts His Trips to North Korea," *Korea Society Quarterly* 4, no. 1 (2003), 6–14.

115. For their press conference on July 2, 1999, see *Public Papers of the Presidents: Administration of William J. Clinton, 1999*, Book II (Washington, DC: U.S. Government Printing Office, 2001), 1126–1127.

116. They met on the sidelines of an ASEAN Regional Forum (ARF) meeting in Singapore on July 27, 1999.

117. See *Review of United States Policy toward North Korea: Findings and Recommendations*, October 12, 1999.

118. See Wendy Sherman's press conference, October 5, 2000. For South Korea's positive assessment of TCOG meetings in 1999, see *Oegyo Paekso* [Diplomatic White Paper] (Seoul: Ministry of Foreign Affairs, 2000), 150–163.

119. Author discussion with a South Korean official, September 5, 1999. Asked who proposed that he visit Pyongyang, Perry emphatically responded, "Of course, I did." Interview with Perry, September 13, 1999. For Japanese views on the Perry process, see Michael J. Green, *Japan's Reluctant Realism* (New York: Palgrave, 2001), 128–130.

120. The group consisted of Gilman, Doug Bereuter (chairman, Subcommittee on Asia and the Pacific), Sonny Callahan (chairman, Subcommittee on Foreign Operations), Christopher Cox (chairman, Republican Policy Committee), Tillie Fowler (vice chair, Republican Conference), Porter Goss (chairman, Permanent Select Committee on Intelligence),

Joe Knollenberg (Subcommittee on Foreign Operations), Floyd Spence (chairman, Committee on Armed Forces), and Curt Weldon (chairman, Subcommittee on Military Research and Development).

121. Selig S. Harrison, *Korean Endgame*, 113–116.

122. Madeleine A. Albright, "The Testing of American Foreign Policy," *Foreign Affairs* 77, no. 6 (November-December 1998), 60.

123. U.S. Department of State, Office of the Spokesman, Press Statement, May 27, 1999.

124. The White House, Office of the Press Secretary, Fact Sheet, September 17, 1999.

125. Park, Lim, Chung, and other principal persons who had been involved in the pre-summit negotiations with North Korea were indicted for illegal financial transactions in 2003; after interrogations by South Korean prosecutors, Chung committed suicide in August 2003.

126. For the text, see *New York Times*, June 15, 2000.

127. Author discussion with Park Jae Kyu, September 23, 2002.

128. Author interview with Lee Hong Koo (South Korean ambassador to the United States, 1998–2000), October 18, 2002. He served as deputy prime minister of national unification (1993–94) and prime minister (1994–95).

129. U.S. Department of State, Office of the Spokesman, Press Release, June 15, 2000.

130. *Rodong Sinmun*, July 2, 2000.

131. U.S. Department of State, Office of the Spokesman, Press Stakeout of Secretary Albright, July 28, 2000. For North Korea's positive report, see *Rodong Sinmun*, July 30, 2000.

132. The report was issued on July 27, 2000.

133. U.S. Department of State, Office of the Spokesman, October 6, 2000.

134. Author discussion with Charles Kartman, January 28, 2003. On the Clinton-Jo meeting, see *New York Times*, October 11, 2000. *Rodong Sinmun* had a front-page report on the meeting (October 12, 2000) but without a photograph.

135. U.S. Department of State, remarks released on October 10 and 11, 2000.

136. *Los Angeles Times*, October 13, 2000. The joint communiqué was drafted by Charles Kartman and Robert Carlin, and an early version was given to North Korean Vice Minister of Foreign Affairs Kim Gye Gwan in Berlin in January 2000. Author discussion with Robert Carlin, April 19, 2004.

137. *Rodong Sinmun*, October 13, 2000.

138. For her activities in Pyongyang, see *People's Korea*, October 28, 2000.

139. See ibid., October 24, 2000, and *Los Angeles Times*, October 24, 2000.

140. As reported by Robin Wright (*Los Angeles Times* diplomatic correspondent who accompanied Secretary Albright to Pyongyang) on *CNBC Interview*, March 15, 2003.

141. For her visit to Pyongyang and Seoul, see Madeleine K. Albright, *Madam Secretary: A Memoir* (New York: Miramax Books, 2003), 455–472.

142. Author discussion with Koh, November 8, 2001. See also Harold H. Koh, "A Breakthrough in North Korea," *Washington Post*, November 2, 2000.

143. *New York Times*, March 6 and 7, 2001.

144. *Hanguk Ilbo*, October 25, 2000. On Albright's meeting with Kim Dae Jung, see her "Press Briefing" on the plane en route to Washington from Seoul, October 26, 2000.

145. *New York Times*, March 6, 2001.

146. Author discussion with Robert J. Einhorn, September 10, 2002.

147. Author discussion with Samuel Berger, May 9, 2002.

148. *New York Times*, December 21, 2000.

149. Albright, *Madam Secretary*, 470.

150. The White House, Office of the Press Secretary, Statement by the President, December 28, 2000.

151. Clinton, *My Life*, 938.

152. William Perry's speech at the Asia Society, San Francisco, June 16, 2004.

153. *New York Times*, March 6, 2001.

154. In September 1999 North Korea asked KEDO to increase the average monthly wage for North Korean workers at Kumho from $110 to $600. After the negotiations failed to resolve the issue, North Korea withdrew 100 workers from Kumho in April 2000. KEDO brought Uzbekistani workers to Kumho in 2001. See *T'ongil Paekso* (2002), 250–251.

155. Author discussion with Minister of Unification Lim Dong Won, September 1999.

CHAPTER 6. IN SEARCH OF HEGEMONIC DIPLOMACY

1. For an earlier discussion of this question, see Chae-Jin Lee, "U.S. Policy Toward North Korea: Engagement and Deterrence," in *The Challenges of Reconciliation and Reform in Korea* (Washington, DC: Korea Economic Institute of America, 2002), 167–194.

2. Condoleezza Rice, "Promoting the National Interest," *Foreign Affairs* 79, no. 1 (January/February 2000), 45–62.

3. *Los Angeles Times*, January 27, 2001.

4. As cited in *Korea Herald*, January 31, 2001.

5. Author interview with Thomas Hubbard, December 9, 2002.

6. *Korea Herald*, February 9, 2001. It was reported that when Lee read a lengthy prepared text for about forty minutes at the Department of State, the busy Powell became visibly irritated. No substantive discussion took place between them.

7. For the text of the joint statement, see *Korea Update*, March 2001.

8. As recalled by Kim Dae Jung in *Hanguk Ilbo*, June 16, 2003.

9. *Los Angeles Times*, March 8, 2001.

10. Author discussion with a senior member of the South Korean delegation, December 2001.

11. *New York Times*, March 7, 2001.

12. *Los Angeles Times*, March 9, 2001.

13. Ibid., March 3, 2001.

14. Statement of General Thomas A. Schwartz before the Senate Armed Services Committee, March 27, 2001.

15. *New York Times*, May 2, 2001.

16. The White House, Office of the Press Secretary, June 6, 2001.

17. For this interpretation, see *New York Times*, June 7, 2001. It is possible that former president George H. W. Bush, along with other individuals such as William Perry, played a role in influencing his son's decision on North Korea. *New York Times*, June 10, 2001.

18. For the European Union's active involvement in Korean affairs, including the visit made by Goran Persson (Sweden's prime minister and president of the European Union) to Pyongyang and Seoul, see *New York Times*, May 1, 4, and 15, 2001.

19. As quoted in *Japan Times*, June 8, 2001.

20. For the Pritchard-Ri meeting, see *New York Times*, June 14, 2001. Even before the Bush announcement, however, Pritchard had informally met with Han Song Ryol, a North Korean diplomat, in New York in an attempt to "lower the temperature" between the United States and North Korea. This information was included in Pritchard's remarks at the World Korean Forum in Washington, September 27, 2004.

21. *People's Korea*, May 26, 2001.

22. *Hanguk Ilbo*, June 22, 2001.

23. *Los Angeles Times*, July 28, 2001.

24. For the Moscow Declaration issued by Kim and Putin on August 4, 2001, see *Rodong Sinmun*, August 5, 2001. On the Kim-Jiang summit meeting of September 3, 2001, see ibid., September 4, 2001.

25. *People's Korea*, October 13, 2001.

26. For the text of his address, see *New York Times*, January 30, 2002.

27. Interview with Robin Wright, CNBC, March 15, 2003.

28. David Frum, *The Right Man: The Surprise Presidency of George W. Bush* (New York: Random House, 2003), 17–18.

29. Bob Woodward, *Bush at War* (New York: Simon and Schuster, 2002), 340.

30. As quoted in *Newsweek*, May 27, 2002.

31. *People's Korea*, February 9, 2002.

32. *Korea Herald*, February 19 and 20, 2002.

33. On the Bush-Kim summit meeting, see *Los Angeles Times*, February 20, 2002.

34. Ibid., February 21, 2002.

35. Author discussion with Yang Sung Chul (South Korean ambassador to the United States, 2000–2003), November 14, 2002.

36. As quoted in *New York Times*, February 20, 2002.

37. *Rodong Sinmun*, February 23, 2002; *People's Korea*, February 23, 2002; and *Los Angeles Times*, February 24, 2002.

38. The Nuclear Posture Review was submitted by the Department of Defense to Congress on December 31, 2001. For the leaked document, see *Los Angeles Times*, March 9, 2002. Excerpts are available at globalsecurity.org.

39. *New York Times*, March 14, 2002.

40. The White House, *The National Security Strategy of the United States of America*, September 17, 2002.

41. Statement issued by Richard Boucher (spokesman for the Department of State) on October 16, 2002; see *New York Times*, October 16, 2002. According to Pritchard, the U.S. government used an elaborate procedure to reconfirm Kang's admission that North Korea indeed had the HEU program. He explained this procedure at the World Korean Forum, Washington, D.C., September 27, 2004.

42. For the South Korean text, see *Chungang Ilbo*, October 18, 2002.

43. Jeong Se Hyun claimed that his press conference statement was quoted out of context and that he did not question the veracity of Kelly's report. Author conversation with Jeong, August 28, 2004.

44. For the statement issued by the North Korean Ministry of Foreign Affairs on October 25, 2002, see *People's Korea*, October 26, 2002.

45. As quoted in *Korea Herald*, October 31, 2002.

46. James A. Baker III, "No More Caving on North Korea," *Washington Post*, October 23, 2002.

47. Anthony Lake and Robert Gallucci, "Negotiating With Nuclear North Korea," *Washington Post*, November 6, 2002. They argued that if the Agreed Framework had not been concluded, North Korea would by now have enough plutonium for thirty nuclear weapons per year—more than India, Pakistan, and Israel combined.

48. See the text in *Korea Times*, October 28, 2002. The Bush administration refused to accept the South Korean proposal to insert the term "through dialogue" in the joint statement.

49. Discussion with Wi Sung Lak (director-general, Bureau of North American Affairs, South Korean Ministry of Foreign Affairs and Trade), August 2, 2003.

50. Author interview with Thomas Hubbard, December 9, 2002.

51. For U.S. reactions to Roh's election, see Ari Fleischer's Daily Press Briefing on December 20, 2002; *New York Times*, December 20, 2002; and *Los Angeles Times*, December 20, 2002.

52. *Los Angeles Times*, February 8, 2003.

53. As reported in *New York Times*, February 11, 2003. The South Korean visitor cited in this report denied that he had made such a statement.

54. For Roh's address, see *Korea Herald*, February 26, 2003.

55. Ibid., January 25, 2003.

56. *New York Times*, March 4, 2003.

57. As quoted in *Los Angeles Times*, March 4, 2003.

58. Ibid., March 6, 2003.

59. Ibid., March 3, 2003.

60. Other cosponsors were Evan Bayh (D-IN), Wayne A. Allard (R-CO), Jim Bunning (R-KY), John Ensign (R-NV), and Jeff Sessions (R-AL).

61. Nicholas D. Kristof, "Secret, Scary Plans," *New York Times*, February 28, 2003.

62. As cited in *Far Eastern Economic Review*, March 6, 2003, 13. Shi's article, "*Ruhe renshi he duidai chaoxian heweiqi*" [How to Recognize and Manage the Korean Nuclear Crisis], was first published on the Chinese-language website takungpao.com on January 15, 2003. A senior official of the South Korean Embassy in Beijing believed that Shi made the statement with the Chinese government's blessing. Author interview with this official, June 9, 2005.

63. For a useful discussion on China's "proactive and engaging" stance toward the North Korean nuclear issue, see Jae Ho Chung, "China's Korea Policy under the New Leadership: Stealth Changes in the Making?" *Journal of East Asian Affairs* 18, no. 1 (Spring/Summer 2004), 1–18.

64. *Los Angeles Times*, April 10, 2003.

65. On the Yoon-Li meeting, see *China Daily*, April 11, 2003.

66. *Rodong Sinmun*, April 13, 2003.

67. Ibid., April 19, 2003.

68. As cited in *Korea Herald*, April 17, 2003.

69. For this exchange between Kelly and Ri, see James A. Kelly, "Dealing With North Korea's Nuclear Programs," statement before the Senate Committee on Foreign Relations, July 15, 2004.

70. For Bush's interview, see *New York Times*, April 25, 2003.

71. For example, see statements issued by the North Korean Ministry of Foreign Affairs on April 6 and 18, 2003, in *Rodong Sinmun*, April 7 and 19, 2003.

72. As reported later on washingtonpost.com, December 6, 2003.

73. As cited by Nicholas D. Kristof, "Empire of a Devil," *New York Times*, April 29, 2003.

74. *China Daily*, April 26 and 27, 2003.

75. For the text, see *Korea Update*, website of the South Korean embassy in Washington (www.koreaemb.org), May 2003.

76. See the lengthy interview with Lee Soo Hyuck in *Wolgan Chungang* [Monthly Chungang], September 2004, 166.

77. *Los Angeles Times*, July 19, 2003.

78. Ibid., August 5, 2003.

79. Ibid., September 10, 2003.

80. *New York Times*, August 26, 2003.

81. For the outlines of South Korea's proposals made at the Six-Party Talks, see *Hanbando munjae chuyo hyonan charyo chip* [Documents on the Major Current Problems of the Korean Peninsula] (Seoul: Ministry of Foreign Affairs and Trade, 2004), 39–51.

82. As quoted in *Far Eastern Economic Review*, September 11, 2003, 15.

83. *China Daily*, August 30–31, 2003. At this time Secretary Powell was able to accept the term "through dialogue."

84. *Los Angeles Times*, September 10, 2003.

85. *New York Times*, September 3, 2003.

86. As quoted in ibid., October 14, 2003.

87. *Hanguk Ilbo*, October 7, 2003.

88. As quoted in *New York Times*, October 22, 2003.

89. For Wu's activities in Pyongyang, see *Rodong Sinmun*, October 31, 2003.

90. Author discussion with Robert Carlin, April 19, 2004.

91. This bill (S. 1903), which was cosponsored by Senator Evan Bayh (D-IN), was introduced on November 20, 2003, and was referred to the Senate Committee on the Judiciary. For a critical assessment of this bill, see Hazel Smith, "Brownback Will Not Solve North Korea's Problems," in *Jane's Intelligence Review*, February 2004, 42–45.

92. *New York Times*, December 8, 2003.

93. For Lee's explanation, see *Korea Herald*, December 4 and 6, 2003.

94. *Los Angeles Times*, December 9, 2003.

95. For the Bush-Wen meeting, see *New York Times*, December 10, 2003.

96. On December 19, 2003, the United States, Britain, and Libya announced that Libya would voluntarily abandon its nuclear, chemical, and biological weapons and allow international inspectors to dismantle its WMD programs and facilities. Libya also promised to destroy

all ballistic missiles (developed with North Korea's assistance) with a range beyond 200 miles, as prescribed by the Missile Technology Control Regime. Subsequently, Libya agreed to pay $2.7 billion to the families of victims of the Pan Am jet destroyed over Lockerbie, Scotland, in 1988, $170 million to the families of the victims of a French UTA passenger jet blown up over West Africa in 1989, and $35 million to some of the victims of a bombing at a Berlin disco in 1986. In response, the United States and other countries agreed to lift economic and diplomatic sanctions on Libya and to normalize diplomatic relations with it.

97. See his commentary in *New York Times*, January 21, 2004.

98. See Barbara Demick's well-written report in *Los Angeles Times*, October 10, 2003.

99. As reported on the Korean-language website chosun.com, January 11, 2004.

100. James A. Kelly, "Opening Remarks," Senate Committee on Foreign Relations, March 2, 2004.

101. For the contents of his proposal, see *Korea Herald*, February 25, 2004, and [Documents on the Major Current Problems of the Korean Peninsula], 39–51.

102. For a North Korean version of the Kelly-Kang meeting in October 2002, see *Rodong Sinmun*, October 19, 2003.

103. For more specific reports on Khan's activities, see *New York Times*, February 2, February 27, March 14, and March 16, 2004. Evidently Khan earned $100 million by selling the HEU technology to Libya in the mid-1990s.

104. Author interviews with senior South Korean diplomats, August 27, 2004.

105. For the English text of Wang's statement, see [Documents on the Major Current Problems], 48. See also *Japan Times*, February 29, 2004.

106. *Hanguk Ilbo*, March 1, 2004.

107. Kelly testified at the Senate Committee on Foreign Relations on March 2, 2004.

108. The joint press conference by Powell and Ban took place on March 4, 2004, at the Department of State.

109. For details on Kim's unofficial visit to China from April 19 to 21, 2004, and the texts of Kim's and Hu Jintao's speeches, see *People's Korea*, April 24, 2004. See also *China Daily*, April 22, 2004, and *Beijing Review*, April 29, 2004. As usual, China offered free aid to North Korea in connection with Kim's visit.

110. *China Daily*, May 15–16, 2004.

111. *Washington Times*, May 19, 2004.

112. Adam Ereli, Daily Press Briefing, May 19, 2004.

113. James A. Kelly, "An Overview of U.S. East Asia Policy," testimony to the House Committee on International Relations, June 2, 2004.

114. As reported in *Washington Times*, May 20, 2004.

115. See Boucher's Daily Press Briefing, May 28, 2004.

116. For Kelly's proposal, see *New York Times* and *Los Angeles Times*, June 24, 2004. James A. Kelly presented a detailed report to the Senate Committee on Foreign Relations on July 15, 2004. For a concise and balanced assessment of the third round of the Six-Party Talks, see B. C. Koh, "Six-Party Talks: Round 3," in IFES Forum, Institute for Far Eastern Studies, Kyungnam University, Seoul, July 1, 2004.

117. In January 1994, President Clinton joined Russian President Boris Yeltsin and Ukraine President Leonid Kravchuk in signing the Trilateral Agreement in Moscow, which

specified the negative security assurance, the application of the Nunn-Lugar Cooperative Threat Reduction Program, and a package of economic and energy assistance for Ukraine. A similar arrangement was made for Kazakhstan. Russia concluded a bilateral agreement for nuclear disarmament of Beralus.

118. For the statement issued by the North Korean Ministry of Foreign Affairs on June 28, 2004, see *Rodong Sinmun*, June 29, 2004.

119. See Kelly's statement before the Senate Committee on Foreign Relations, July 15, 2004.

120. For the English text of Wang's statement, see [Documents on the Major Current Problems], 52. See also *China Daily*, June 28, 2004.

121. For South Korea's admission of nuclear experiments, the investigations by the International Atomic Energy Agency, and North Korea's reactions, see *Los Angeles Times*, September 3 and 5, 2004, and *New York Times*, September 7 and 9, 2004. For the statement issued by the North Korean Ministry of Foreign Affairs on September 11, 2004, accusing the United States of applying "double standards" to the South Korean nuclear issue, see *People's Korea*, September 11, 2004.

122. *Hanguk Ilbo*, September 20, 2004.

123. As reported in *Los Angeles Times*, November 27, 2004.

124. Samuel R. Berger, "Foreign Policy for a Democratic President," *Foreign Affairs* 83, no. 3 (May/June 2004), 47–63. After the FBI investigated Berger's removal of classified documents from the National Archives, he stepped down as an advisor to Kerry in July 2004.

125. William Perry spoke at the Asia Society in San Francisco on June 16, 2004.

126. See David E. Sanger's report in *New York Times*, September 13, 2004.

127. This information is from *The Military Balance (2002–2003)* (London: International Institute for Strategic Studies, 2002).

128. As quoted in *Los Angeles Times*, December 21, 2003.

129. *New York Times*, November 18, 2003.

130. See the Korean-language website donga.com, April 21, 2003. A month earlier, another high-ranking U.S. official had called the term "tripwire" unfair and expressed his hope that it would not be used in the future. See www.donga.com, March 19, 2003.

131. See www.donga.com, March 6, 2003.

132. This information was not immediately publicized. See *Hanguk Ilbo*, May 28, 2004.

133. As reported in *New York Times*, June 16, 2003.

134. *Minju Choson* (North Korean government newspaper), June 1, 2004, as reported on donga.com, June 4, 2004.

135. See the text of the joint statement issued on July 23, 2003.

136. On the plans for Eastern Europe, see *Los Angeles Times*, November 12, 2003.

137. Leon J. LaPorte, statement before the House Committee on Armed Services, March 31, 2004.

138. For the election results, see *Hanguk Ilbo*, April 16, 2004, and www.donga.com, April 16, 2004. The Grand National Party had 137 seats before the elections; the Millennium Democratic Party had 61 seats; the Liberal Democratic League had 10 seats.

139. *Hanguk Ilbo*, April 28, 2004. This survey was conducted for 130 of the 152 Uri Party members elected to the National Assembly.

140. After the historical controversies over the Kingdom of Koguryo demonstrated China's arrogant and hegemonic tendencies in the summer of 2004, there was a reversal in the views of the Uri Party National Assemblymen. Now 72% of them cited the importance of the United States, and only 9% mentioned China.

141. *Chosun Ilbo*, May 17, 2004. On May 18, 2004, the U.S. Department of Defense issued a news release concerning the deployment of about 3,600 service members from South Korea to Iraq.

142. See Press Gaggle with Scott McCellan, Presidential Press Secretary, May 17, 2004, and *Los Angeles Times*, May 18, 2004.

143. Background Roundtable by senior defense and military officials, May 17, 2004.

144. For example, see www.donga.com, May 18, 2004, and *Hanguk Ilbo*, May 20, 2004.

145. Ibid., May 18 and 28, 2004.

146. For Roh's views, see *Hanguk Ilbo*, June 7, 2004.

147. For General Campbell's comment and its consequences, see chosun.com, May 27, 2004, and donga.com, May 28, 2004.

148. www.chosun.com, May 27, 2004.

149. For the evolution of U.S. decisions, see *Hanguk Ilbo*, May 28, 2004.

150. This survey was conducted by Media Research, a leading survey organization, and was reported in *Hanguk Ilbo*, June 8, 2004.

151. On October 6, 2004, the United States and South Korea announced their agreement to reduce the number of U.S. troops (12,500) in South Korea as follows—5,000 in 2004, 3,000 in 2005, 2,000 in 2006, and 2,500 in 2007 and 2008. After this reduction is completed, the United States will have about 25,000 troops in South Korea. For a discussion of this agreement, see *Hanguk Ilbo*, October 7, 2004.

152. For a useful review of Yongsan as a foreign military base, see *Hanmi kunsa kwangye sa: 1871–2002* [A History of Korean-American Military Relations: 1871–2002] (Seoul: Ministry of National Defense, 2002), 667–673.

153. Author discussion with James Lilley (U.S. ambassador to South Korea, 1986–89), May 24, 2004. See also James Lilley with Jeffrey Lilley, *China Hands: Nine Decades of Adventure, Espionage, and Diplomacy in Asia* (New York: Public Affairs, 2004), 294–295.

154. Author discussion with Chung Chong Wook (senior secretary to the president for foreign affairs and national security, 1993–95), April 2003.

155. For Roh's comment on January 15, see www.chosun.com, January 16, 2004. He criticized some politicians and bureaucrats who attempted to prevent the United States from moving its headquarters to Pyongtaek.

156. As quoted in *Los Angeles Times*, January 18, 2004.

157. The South Korean Ministry of National Defense released the joint statement of the Tenth FOTA meeting on July 26, 2004. For further information, see *Korea Update* (issued by the South Korean embassy in Washington), August 9, 2004, and *Korea Herald*, July 24, 2004.

158. For his speech, see ibid., April 3, 2003.

159. See www.donga.com, September 18, 2003.

160. For Yoon's position, see *Korea Herald*, September 26, 2003.

161. For the excerpts of the U.N. Security Council resolution, see *New York Times*, October 17, 2003.

162. As quoted in *Los Angeles Times*, October 18, 2003.

163. Ibid., December 24, 2003.

164. For the National Assembly decision, see *Korea Herald*, February 14, 2004.

165. On the financial benefits, see *Los Angeles Times*, February 14, 2004.

166. For President Roh's speech, see *Los Angeles Times*, November 13, 2004, and *Hanguk Ilbo*, November 15, 2004.

167. See the text of Bush's speech at the CEO summit, closing session, Santiago, Chile, November 20, 2004. The Bush statement was reminiscent of President Reagan's earlier declaration made in Berlin, "Mr. Gorbachev, tear down this wall."

168. The South Koreans were skeptical that North Korea would follow the Libyan model without security assurances and economic assistance. Author interview with senior South Korean diplomats, August 27, 2004. In 1989, South African President F. W. de Klerk announced his decision to destroy its nuclear devices and to dismantle all nuclear weapons programs and facilities. It joined the NPT regime and signed the full-scope nuclear safeguards agreement with the IAEA in 1991. The following year the IAEA verified the destruction and dismantlement of South African nuclear devices and facilities. No other security assurance was provided, but economic sanctions on South Africa were removed.

169. It was revealed that at his meeting with Kim Jong Il on June 17, 2005, in Pyongyang, South Korean Minister of Unification Chung Dong Yong offered a bold package of economic benefits, including electricity, food, and chemical fertilizer, for North Korea in return for a peaceful resolution of the nuclear and other related issues. See *Los Angeles Times*, July 13, 2005, and *Hanguk Ilbo*, July 14, 2005.

170. For the fourth round of the Six-Party Talks and the joint statement, see *Los Angeles Times*, September 19 and 20, 2005.

171. For South Korean views on the PSI, see [Documents on the Major Current Problems], 127. The PSI was first proposed by President Bush in his speech in Krakow, Poland, on June 1, 2003.

172. Selig S. Harrison is confident that the United States can live with a nuclear-armed North Korea, just as it does with a nuclear-armed China, given its strategic nuclear capabilities in the Pacific region. See Harrison, *Korean Endgame*, xxxii.

CHAPTER 7. PROSPECTS

1. George F. Kennan, *Russia and the West under Lenin and Stalin* (Boston: Little, Brown, 1960), 398.

2. For example, the U.S. House of Representatives in July 2004 unanimously passed the North Korean Human Rights Act of 2004 (H.R. 4011). After the U.S. Senate unanimously adopted a modified version of the House bill, the House of Representatives unanimously passed the Senate-approved bill in October 2004. President Bush signed this bill into law on October 18, 2004.

3. John J. Mearsheimer, *The Tragedy of Great Power Politics* (New York: W. W. Norton, 2001), 26.

4. Henry Kissinger, *Does America Need a Foreign Policy? Toward a Diplomacy for the 21st Century* (New York: Simon and Schuster, 2001), 288.

5. Joseph S. Nye Jr., *The Paradox of American Power: Why the World's Only Superpower Can't Go It Alone* (New York: Oxford University Press, 2002), 8–9.

6. For the models of triangular relationship, see Lowell Dittmer, "The Strategic Triangle: A Critical Review," in Ilpyong Kim, ed., *The Strategic Triangle* (New York: McGraw-Hill, 1987), 17–33.

7. Dr. Paul S. Crane, an American surgeon who had practiced medicine in South Korea for decades, observed that for Koreans "appearance is of more importance than substance" and that "it is more important to have things appear well than they actually be well." See Paul S. Crane, *Korean Patterns* (Seoul: The Royal Asiatic Society, Korea Branch, 1967), 25–26.

8. For a discussion of the four scenarios and the positions of the four major powers, see Chae-Jin Lee, "Conflict and Cooperation: The Pacific Powers and Korea," in Nicholas Eberstadt and Richard J. Ellings, eds., *Korea's Future and the Great Powers* (Seattle: University of Washington Press, 2001), 51–87.

9. Kenneth Waltz, *Theory of International Politics* (New York: McGraw-Hill, 1979), 105.

10. For an argument made by a conservative critic of President Roh's policy toward North Korea, see *Los Angeles Times*, July 16, 2004.

11. Lee Hong Koo spoke at the Asia Society in San Francisco on June 16, 2004.

12. Chae-Jin Lee, "Diplomacy after Unification: A Framework for Policy Choices in Korea," in Byung Chul Koh, ed., *Korea: Dynamics of Diplomacy and Unification* (Claremont, CA: Keck Center, Claremont McKenna College, 2001), 161–178.

13. Nicholas Eberstadt, "Hastening Korean Reunification," *Foreign Affairs* 76, no. 2 (March/April 1997), 77–92. For a further elaboration of his thesis, see Nicholas Eberstadt, *The End of North Korea* (Washington, DC: American Enterprise Institute Press, 1999).

14. Edward A. Olsen, "Coping with the Korean Peace Process: An American View," *Korean Journal of Defense Analysis* 9, no. 1 (Summer 1997), 161, and *Toward Normalizing U.S.-Korea Relations: In Due Course?* (Boulder, CO: Lynne Rienner, 2002).

15. Kyung Won Kim, "No Way Out: North Korea's Impending Collpase," *Harvard International Review* (Spring 1996), 22–71. If North Korea faced a complete international embargo, Marcus Noland has predicted, it might collapse in two years. Noland, *Korea after Kim Jong-il* (Washington, DC: Institute for International Economics, 2004), 41.

16. Selig S. Harrison, "Promoting a Soft Landing in Korea," *Foreign Policy* (Spring 1997), 57–75, and *Korean Endgame: A Strategy for Reunification and U.S. Disengagement* (Princeton, NJ: Princeton University Press, 2002), 5–11.

17. Han S. Park, *North Korea: The Politics of Unconventional Wisdom* (Boulder, CO: Lynne Rienner, 2002), and Bruce Cumings, *North Korea: Another Country* (New York: New Press, 2004), 198–199.

18. Marcus Noland, "Why North Korea Will Muddle Through," *Foreign Affairs* 76, no. 4 (July/August 1997), 105–118, and *Avoiding the Apocalypse: The Future of the Two Koreas* (Washington, DC: Institute for International Economics, 2000).

19. Alexis de Tocqueville, *The Old Regime and the Revolution*, translated by John Bonner (New York: Harper and Brothers Publishers, 1856), 214.

20. James A. Winnefeld and others, *A New Strategy and Fewer Forces: The Pacific Dimension* (Santa Monica, CA: RAND, 1991), 42.

21. President Roh Moo Hyun's intention to abolish the National Security Law in 2004 further intensified a process of ideological and political polarization in South Korea. His conservative critics argued that the intention amounted to a unilateral concession to North Korea's united front strategy.

22. Author interviews with Hwang Chang Yop, November 1997 and August 1999. Hwang, a former secretary of the Korean Workers' Party, claimed that it was "a matter of common knowledge" among his colleagues that North Korea had nuclear weapons and that there was no division between hardliners and pragmatists in North Korea because of Kim Jong Il's monolithic rule.

23. Olsen, "Coping with the Korean Peace Process," 167.

24. Michael Green, "North Korean Regime Crisis: U.S. Perspectives and Responses," *Korean Journal of Defense Analysis* 9, no. 2 (Winter 1997), 16. Green joined the National Security Council under President George W. Bush and participated in the Six-Party Talks in Beijing.

25. For Operation Plan 5027, see Oberdorfer, *The Two Koreas*, 314.

26. Robert Axelrod, *The Evolution of Cooperation* (New York: Basic Books, 1984).

27. Robert O. Keohane, *After Hegemony: Cooperation and Discord in the World Political Economy* (Princeton, NJ: Princeton University Press, 1984), 75.

28. For a discussion of Korea's policy choices, see Lee, "Diplomacy after Unification."

29. For the treaty, see *Arms Control and Disarmament Agreements* (Washington, DC: U.S. Arms Control and Disarmament Agency, 1990), 68–80.

30. Cyril E. Black, Richard A. Falk, Klaus Knorr, and Oran R. Young, *Neutralization and World Politics* (Princeton, NJ: Princeton University Press, 1969), v–vi.

31. *Foreign Relations of the United States 1952–1954*, vol. 15, pt. 2 (Washington, DC: U.S. Government Printing Office, 1984), 1620–1624.

32. As quoted in In K. Hwang, *One Korea via Permanent Neutrality: Peaceful Management of Korean Unification* (Cambridge: MA: Schenkman Books, 1987), 67–68.

33. Ibid., 45.

34. Bruce Cumings, *Korea's Place in the Sun: A Modern History* (New York: W. W. Norton, 1997), 137–138.

35. Harrison, *Korean Endgame*, xxiii, 347–356.

36. For the inevitability of a hegemonic contest between the United States and China in Asia, see Mearsheimer, *The Tragedy of Great Power Politics*, 396–402, and Richard Bernstein and Ross H. Munro, "The Coming Conflict with America," *Foreign Affairs* 76, no. 2 (March/April 1997), 18–32. On the other hand, a number of scholars and commentators argue that, as a "second-rank middle power," China does not matter much in world affairs and therefore does not pose a threat to the United States. See Gerald Segal, "Does China Matter?" *Foreign Affairs* 78, no. 5 (September/October 1999), 24–36. Still others propose that the United States should pursue "strategic engagement" with China in economic, diplomatic, and military areas. For example, see George J. Gilboy, "The Myth Behind China's Miracle," *Foreign Affairs* 83, no. 4 (July/August 2004), 33–48.

Index

absorption option for unification, 283–86

Acheson, Dean, 25, 27, 29, 31

Agreed Framework (Geneva): G. W. Bush and, 216; R. Dole on, 185; highly enriched uranium program of NK and, 223; Kelly and, 249; overview of, 177–80; U.S. Congress and, 181–82, 214–15

Agreed Statement, 175–76

Agreement on the Establishment of the Korean Peninsula Energy Development Organization (KEDO): W. Clinton and, 185; delays and, 208; establishment of, 180–81; financial support to, 300; heavy fuel oil and, 225; suspension of, 244–45

Albert, Carl, 96, 98

Albright, Madeleine K.: G. W. Bush policy and, 219; W. Clinton visit to NK and, 207; HEU program and, 224; Jo and, 204; NK and, 199; Paek Nam Sun and, 202–3; W. Perry and, 197–98; visit to NK by, 5, 205–6

Allen, Horace N., 14, 15–16

Allen, Richard V., 110, 111

alliance between U.S. and South Korea: Agreed Statement and, 175–77; changes in, 280–81; deterioration of, 242; economic relations and, 153–57; fragility of, 237–38; history of, 294–95; inter-Korean relations and, 202; military exercises, joint, and, 165, 170, 265; NK and, 218; renewal of, 251; restructuring of during G. W. Bush administration, 256–66; trade and, 3, 121, 298; troops in Iraq and, 268–71; U.S. assistance to SK, 261, 297; U.S. view of, 276. See also military troops (U.S.) in South Korea

"alliance faction" in South Korea, 263–64, 267

Anderson, Desaix, 131

Anglo-French War with China, 9

Annan, Kofi, 235

anti-American rhetoric: after Six-Party Talks, 242; in NK, 136, 217, 222; Roh Moo Hyun and, 247; in SK, 193, 226–27; Yongsan Garrison and, 267

APEC framework, 157

APEC summit meeting, 225

Armacost, Michael, 110, 124, 145

Armitage, Richard L., 196, 231, 245

Arnold, Archibald V., 21, 22

Arthur, Chester A., 12

ASEAN Regional Forum (ARF), 6, 202, 218, 288, 290

Asian Games, 151

Aspin, Les, 159

Axelrod, Robert, 288

axe-murder incident, 79–80

"axis of evil" reference, 219–23

Baker, James A., III, 131, 146, 147, 151, 182, 224

ballistic missiles of North Korea, 196, 197, 205–7

Ban Ki Moon, 250–51, 263

Basic Agreement, 147–48

Bayard, Thomas F., 12

beef exports from U.S., 155

Beijing Talks, 131–36

Berger, Samuel (ambassador), 50

Berger, Samuel (National Security Adviser), 206, 255

Biden, Joseph R., Jr., 217, 230

bilateral talks (North Korea and U.S.): about nuclear weapons, 161–62; Agreed Framework and, 177–80; between Albright and Paek Nam Sun, 202–3; during Six-Party Talks, 239–40, 248–49, 253

Nixon, Richard M.: China policy of, 70–75; EC-121 incident and, 65–66; Guam Doctrine and, 2, 64–65, 67–68; military presence in SK and, 68–70; Park Chung Hee and, 2, 68, 75; philosophy of, 64; S. Rhee and, 39; SK and, 66–67; 38th Parallel and, 33
Noland, Marcus, 284–85
North-South Declaration, 178
"North-South Joint Declaration on the Denuclearization of the Korean Peninsula," 149–50
Nuclear Nonproliferation Treaty (NPT), 160, 272
"Nuclear Posture Review," 222
nuclear reactors. *See* light-water moderated reactors
nuclear weapons programs: Beijing Talks and, 132–33; highly enriched uranium, 149, 223–29, 249–50; IAEA inspection of, 160–61; Japan, NK, and, 144, 145–46; Kim Young Sam view of, 168; at Kumchangri, 200; of NK, as threat to SK, 162–63, 247–48, 300; north-south joint declaration on, 149–50; of Park Chung Hee, 77–78; Proliferation Security Initiative and, 273–74; in SK, 140, 254; U.S. and, 133, 148–49
Nunn, Sam, 133–34
Nunn-Lugar Cooperative Threat Reduction Program, 252–53
Nunn-Warner Amendment, 133–35
Nye, Joseph S., Jr., 5, 278

Obuchi Keizo, 197
Ohira Masayoshi, 54
Olney, Richard, 13
Olympic Games in Seoul, 121, 126, 129
O'Neill, Thomas P., Jr., 96, 98, 100
Operation Everready, 34, 39, 40, 44
Operation Plan 5027, 170, 287
Opium War, 9

Paek Nam Sun, 202–3, 205, 255
Paek Sun Yop, 34
Pak Chong-yang, 12
Pak Hon Yong, 21, 26
Panikkar, K. M., 29
Park Chul Un, 137
Park Chung Hee: assassination of, 102–4; Carter and, 83, 84, 85–86, 91–93, 94; coup d'état by, 46; Guam Doctrine and, 67–68; Japan and, 52; Johnson and, 59, 61; J. F. Kennedy and, 49–50; Kim Il Sung and, 73–75; Koreagate

and, 97–98, 99, 101; martial law, constitution, and, 75, 102; Nixon and, 2, 68, 69, 70; nuclear weapons program of, 77–78; U.S. opening of China and, 71, 72; Vance and, 60–61; Vietnam War and, 55–56
Park Chung Soo, 180
Park Jae Kyu, 202
Park Keun Hye, 262
Park Tong Jin: axe-murder incident and, 80; Carter and, 82; cigarette trade and, 155; Koreagate and, 100, 102; Ranard and, 98; troop reduction and, 85; Vance and, 93
Park Tong Son, 95, 96, 97, 99, 100–101
Passman, Otto, 100, 101
Peng Dehuai, 36
Percy, Charles H., 116
Perry, Matthew C., 9
Perry, William, 170, 171, 196–99, 204, 255
Poneman, Daniel B., 168
Porter, William, 57, 69, 96, 97
Potsdam Conference, 18
Powell, Colin: conventional forces and, 218; Dai and, 238–39; on HEU program, 224; as moderate, 212, 216–17; NK and, 214; Paek Nam Sun and, 255; Roh Moo Hyun and, 228; Six-Party Talks and, 250–51; Yoon and, 233, 242
preemption, Bush doctrine of, 222–23
Primakov, Yevgeni, 138
Pritchard, Charles "Jack," 217, 239, 247
Proliferation Security Initiative, 6, 273–74
public opinion: in SK, about Agreed Framework, 180; in SK, about military troops, 262–63, 265–66; in U.S., about Korea, 166
Putin, Vladimir, 218, 238
Pyun Yong Tae, 38

Qian Qichen, 146–47, 151, 152, 172, 228, 232
Qi Haotian, 205
Quinones, C. Kenneth, 119, 161, 174

Ra Jong Il, 228
Ranard, Donald, 98
Rangoon, Burma, 119–20
Reagan, Ronald: Chun and, 112, 113–15, 121; Kim Dae Jung and, 110; Korean Air Lines Flight 007 and, 117–19; NK attacks on, 116; philosophy of, 113; SK policy under, 3; visit to Seoul by, 120–21